CONVERSATIONAL
KOREAN

CONVERSATIONAL
KOREAN

Everyday Phrases and Vocabulary
Ideal for K-Pop and K-Drama Fans!

The Calling

TUTTLE Publishing

Tokyo | Rutland, Vermont | Singapore

"Books to Span the East and West"

Tuttle Publishing was founded in 1832 in the small New England town of Rutland, Vermont [USA]. Our core values remain as strong today as they were then—to publish best-in-class books which bring people together one page at a time. In 1948, we established a publishing outpost in Japan—and Tuttle is now a leader in publishing English-language books about the arts, languages and cultures of Asia. The world has become a much smaller place today and Asia's economic and cultural influence has grown. Yet the need for meaningful dialogue and information about this diverse region has never been greater. Over the past seven decades, Tuttle has published thousands of books on subjects ranging from martial arts and paper crafts to language learning and literature—and our talented authors, illustrators, designers and photographers have won many prestigious awards. We welcome you to explore the wealth of information available on Asia at **www.tuttlepublishing.com**.

Published by Tuttle Publishing, an imprint of Periplus Editions (HK) Ltd.

www.tuttlepublishing.com

레전드 한국어 회화사전
Copyright © Language Books, 2019
All rights reserved.
Originally published in Korea by Language Books
English translation rights arranged with Language Books in care of Danny Hong Agency, Seoul.

ISBN: 978-0-8048-5607-2

Distributed by

North America, Latin America & Europe
Tuttle Publishing
364 Innovation Drive, North Clarendon
VT 05759-9436 U.S.A.
Tel: 1 (802) 773-8930
Fax: 1 (802) 773-6993
info@tuttlepublishing.com
www.tuttlepublishing.com

Asia Pacific
Berkeley Books Pte Ltd
3 Kallang Sector #04-01
Singapore 349278
Tel: (65) 6741 2178
Fax: (65) 6741 2179
inquiries@periplus.com.sg
www.tuttlepublishing.com

26 25 24 23   10 9 8 7 6 5 4 3 2 1   2301TP
Printed in Singapore

TUTTLE PUBLISHING® is a registered trademark of Tuttle Publishing, a division of Periplus Editions (HK) Ltd.

Contents

The Smaller Chili Pepper Is Hotter!

This traditional proverb means "good things come in small packages," and seems to fit Korea perfectly. As a small East-Asian nation with growing status in the world, Korea has much to offer. We are proud of the many Koreans who are doing their best in their chosen field. Their hard work is paying off. It is perhaps thanks to them that you have become interested in Korea and in learning the Korean language. Although it may be a challenging tongue for some, your passion for Korean culture and language too will pay off.

As with all foreign language learning, it is important to speak with a certain cultural awareness, not just to swap words or sentences in one language for another. I have written this book with this point in mind, and have presented Korean sentences using polite language forms as much as possible, and making sure each sentence is the proper way to express yourself in a particular situation.

You can't learn everything about Korea overnight, but we have included a lot of tips throughout the book about aspects of the country's culture, which will help you feel more confident and knowledgeable when talking with Korean people. You'll also find online audio files at the link on page 9 with recordings of all key language in the book to help you achieve correct pronunciation. I hope these will be helpful to you.

Which brings me to another Korean saying, "Even a one-thousand-li road begins with a single step," the equivalent of "A journey of a thousand miles begins with a single step" in English. Whatever you do, start with a small step. And keep learning!

Special thanks to my friend Colin who always helps actively regardless of the time difference! Your help is always appreciated. And to my daughter Christine who grew up as my English helper, thank you. She was proud to help with this work. Also,I would like to thank my publisher for their efforts in getting this book published. Finally, I give all my glory to God, who is always the reason for my life.

Joenghee Kim, The Calling

About This Book

In this book you'll find some of the most commonly used Korean expressions, to help you with daily communication and to lay the foundation for your Korean language learning.

1. Nearly 3,000 expressions for practical daily situations!

This book contains expressions for beginner to intermediate Korean learners, with 12 chapters of 76 must-have units covering some 500 topics and almost 3,000 expressions. The main focus is on informal Korean spoken by young people, but many expressions can be made more formal by adding the "-yo" that you will see in brackets at the end of certain phrases throughout the book.

2. Romanized Korean lets you speak Korean immediately!

Korean pronunciation by way of the Roman alphabet is not a perfect match but is helpful nonetheless. The contents of this book are romanized to mirror standard Korean pronunciation as closely as possible, to help beginners speak confidently.

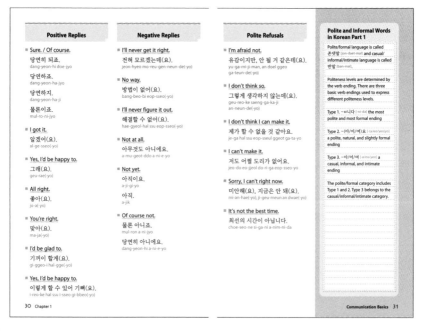

Positive Replies

- Sure. / Of course.
  당연히 되죠.
  dang-yeon-hi doe-jyo
  당연하죠.
  dang-yeon-ha-jyo
  당연하지.
  dang-yeon-ha-ji
  물론이죠.
  mul-ro-ni-jyo
- I got it.
  알겠어(요).
  al-ge-sseo(-yo)
- Yes, I'd be happy to.
  그래(요).
  geu-rae(-yo)
- All right.
  좋아(요).
  jo-a(-yo)
- You're right.
  맞아(요).
  ma-ja(-yo)
- I'd be glad to.
  기꺼이 할게(요).
  gi-ggeo-i hal-gge(-yo)
- Yes, I'd be happy to.
  이렇게 할 수 있어 기뻐(요).
  i-reo-ke hal ssu i-sseo gi-bbeo(-yo)

30 Chapter 1

Negative Replies

- I'll never get it right.
  전혀 모르겠는데(요).
  jeon-hyeo mo-reu-gen-neun-de(-yo)
- No way.
  방법이 없어(요).
  bang-beo-bi eop-sseo(-yo)
- I'll never figure it out.
  해결할 수 없어(요).
  hae-gyeol-hal ssu eop-sseo(-yo)
- Not at all.
  아무것도 아니에요.
  a-mu-geot-ddo a-ni-e-yo
- Not yet.
  아직이요.
  a-ji-gi-yo
  아직.
  a-jik
- Of course not.
  물론 아니죠.
  mul-ron a-ni-jyo
  당연히 아니에요.
  dang-yeon-hi a-ni-e-yo

Polite Refusals

- I'm afraid not.
  유감이지만, 안 될 거 같은데(요).
  yu-ga-mi-ji-man, an doel ggeo ga-teun-de(-yo)
- I don't think so.
  그렇게 생각하지 않는데(요).
  geu-reo-ke saeng-ga-ka-ji an-neun-de(-yo)
- I don't think I can make it.
  제가 할 수 없을 것 같아요.
  je-ga hal ssu eop-sseul ggeot ga-ta-yo
- I can't make it.
  저도 어쩔 도리가 없어요.
  jeo-do eo-jjeol do-ri-ga eop-sseo-yo
- Sorry, I can't right now.
  미안해(요), 지금은 안 돼(요).
  mi-an-hae(-yo), ji-geu-meun an dwae(-yo)
- It's not the best time.
  최선의 시간이 아닙니다.
  choe-seo-ne si-ga-ni a-nim-ni-da

Polite and Informal Words in Korean Part 1

Polite/formal language is called 존댓말 (jon-daet-mal) and casual/informal/intimate language is called 반말 (ban-mal).

Politeness levels are determined by the verb ending. There are three basic verb endings used to express different politeness levels.

Type 1. ~ㅂ니다 (-ni-da) the most polite and most formal ending

Type 2. ~(아/어/여)요 (-(a/eo/yeo)yo) a polite, natural, and slightly formal ending

Type 3. ~아/어/여 (-a/eo/yeo) a casual, informal, and intimate ending

The polite/formal category includes Type 1 and 2. Type 3 belongs to the casual/informal/intimate category.

Communication Basics 31

3. Background information!

Information panels are inserted regularly throughout the book to help you gain an understanding of Korea's culture and history. From basic tips to current trends, not only will this information expand your knowledge base but it will also provide context to the Korean language.

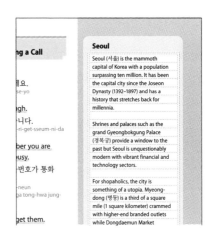

4. Strengthen your basic vocabulary with easy-to-understand pictures!

More than 500 illustrations are included in the book, to help you remember key vocabulary words. Topics range from daily routines to social life and more. New words are introduced with romanized pronunciation (in blue) and Hangul alphabet pronunciation (in square brackets).

5. Online audio recordings for intensive speaking practice!

Wherever a section of the book has a headphones logo, this means we have provided online audio recordings for the words and phrases in that section, recorded by a Korean voice actress. Listen regularly and repeat loudly to strengthen your Korean language skills. You can access the online audio files via this link: tuttlepublishing.com/conversational-korean

The Basics

About the **Republic of Korea**

The Flag of the Republic of Korea
(태극기 [태극끼] tae-geuk-ggi)

✓ **Name of Country**   Republic of Korea
(대한민국 [대:한민국] dae-han-min-guk)

✓ **Location**   Northeast Asia (동북아시아 [동북:아시아] dong-bug-a-si-a)

✓ **Capital**   Seoul (서울 [서울] seo-ul)

✓ **Official Language**   Korean (한국어 [한:구거] han-gu-geo)

✓ **Population**   51.78 million

✓ **Area**   38,700 square miles (100,364 km²)

✓ **GDP** $1631 billion

✓ **Currency**   South Korean Won (KRW) (원 [원] won)

The Korean Language and Alphabet
한국어와 한글 han-gu-geo-wa han-geul

Hangul 한글 han-geul

Hangul is the name of the Korean alphabet. This written form of the Korean language was commissioned by King Sejong (1397–1450) at the beginning of the Joseon Dynasty and was made the nation's official script in 1446.

Hangul today is composed of nineteen consonants and twenty-one vowels.

1. Consonants 자음 ja-eum 🎧

Tip: Consonants in the Korean alphabet may vary in sound depending on whether they are the initial or final letter in a syllable. Some consonants only appear in either the initial or final position in a syllable.

- ### 9 plain consonants

letter	name of the letter	sample word	meaning
ㄱ	기역 gi-yeok	가구 [가구] ga-gu	furniture
ㄴ	니은 ni-eun	나비 [나비] na-bi	butterfly
ㄷ	디귿 di-geut	다리미 [다리미] da-ri-mi	(clothing) iron
ㄹ	리을 ri-eul	라디오 [라디오] ra-di-o	radio
ㅁ	미음 mi-eum	마차 [마:차] ma-cha	carriage, wagon
ㅂ	비읍 bi-eup	바지 [바지] ba-ji	trousers, pants
ㅅ	시옷 si-ot	사탕 [사탕] sa-tang	candy
ㅇ	이응 i-eung	아기 [아기] a-gi	baby
ㅈ	지읒 ji-eut	자유 [자유] ja-yu	freedom

• 5 aspirated consonants

letter	name of the letter	sample word	meaning
ㅊ	치읓 chi-eut	차표 [차표] cha-pyo	ticket
ㅋ	키윽 ki-euk	카메라 [카메라] ka-me-ra	camera
ㅌ	티읕 ti-eut	타조 [타:조] ta-jo	ostrich
ㅍ	피읖 pi-eup	파도 [파도] pa-do	wave
ㅎ	히읗 hi-eut	하마 [하마] ha-ma	hippopotamus

• 5 tense consonants

letter	name of the letter	sample word	meaning
ㄲ	쌍기역 ssang-gi-yeok	까치 [까:치] gga-chi	magpie
ㄸ	쌍디귿 ssang-di-geut	딸기 [딸:기] ddal-gi	strawberry
ㅃ	쌍비읍 ssang-bi-eup	빨래 [빨래] bbal-rae	laundry
ㅆ	쌍시옷 ssang-si-ot	쌍둥이 [쌍둥이] ssang-dung-i	twins
ㅉ	쌍지읒 ssang-ji-eut	짜장면 [짜장면] jja-jang-myeon	black bean sauce noodles

Tip: Consonants in the Korean alphabet can be combined into 11 consonant clusters, which always appear in the final position in a syllable.
They are: ㄳ, ㄵ, ㄶ, ㄺ, ㄻ, ㄼ, ㄽ, ㄾ, ㄿ, ㅀ, and ㅄ.

2. Vowels 모음 mo-eum

Tip: The vowel ㅇ [이응 i-eung] is silent.

- **6 simple vowels**

letter	name of the letter	sample word	meaning
ㅏ	아 a	바나나 [바나나] ba-na-na	banana
ㅓ	어 eo	어머니 [어머니] eo-meo-ni	mother
ㅗ	오 o	도로 [도:로] do-ro	road
ㅜ	우 u	구두 [구두] gu-du	shoes
ㅡ	으 eu	드레스 [드레스] deu-re-seu	dress
ㅣ	이 i	기린 [기린] gi-rin	giraffe

- **9 compound vowels**

letter	name of the letter	sample word	meaning
ㅐ	애 ae	냄새 [냄:새] naem-sae	smell
ㅔ	에 e	세제 [세:제] se-je	detergent
ㅘ	와 wa	과일 [과:일] gwa-il	fruit
ㅙ	왜 wae	돼지 [돼:지] dwae-ji	pig
ㅚ	외 oe	외국 [외:국/웨:국] oe-guk/we-guk	foreign country
ㅝ	워 wo	권투 [권:투] gwon-tu	boxing
ㅞ	웨 we	웨이터 [웨이터] we-i-teo	waiter
ㅟ	위 wi	취미 [취:미] chwi-mi	hobby
ㅢ	의 ui	의자 [의자] ui-ja	chair

6 vowels with the Y sound

letter	name of the letter	sample word	meaning
ㅑ	야 ya	야구 [야:구] ya-gu	baseball
ㅓ	여 yeo	여자 [여자] yeo-ja	woman
ㅛ	요 yo	교수 [교:수] gyo-su	professor
ㅠ	유 yu	유리 [유리] yu-ri	glass
ㅒ	얘 yae	얘기 [얘:기] yae-gi	story
ㅖ	예 ye	예약 [예:약] ye-yak	reservation

Parts of Speech

The following abbreviations are used in the book.

n.	noun	명사
v.	verb	동사
adj.	adjective	형용사
adv.	adverb	부사
d.n.	dependent noun	의존명사

Chapter 1

Communication Basics

Hello! 안녕하세요!
an-nyeong-ha-se-yo!
Hi! 안녕!
an-nyeong!

How are you? 어떻게 지내(요)?
eo-ddeo-ke ji-nae(-yo)?

Pretty good. / I'm doing well. 잘 지내(요).
jal ji-nae(-yo)

Nice to meet you. 만나서 반가워(요).
man-na-seo ban-ga-wo(-yo)

Long time no see. 오랜만입니다.
o-raen-ma-nim-ni-da

Goodbye. 안녕(히 가세요).
 an-nyeong(-hi ga-se-yo)
= 잘 가(요). jal ga(-yo)

See you again. 또 만나(요).
ddo man-na(-yo)

Thank you. / Thanks. 감사합니다.
gam-sa-ham-ni-da
= 고마워(요).
go-ma-wo(-yo)

You're welcome. 천만에(요).
cheon-ma-ne(-yo)

Excuse me. 실례합니다.
sil-rye-ham-ni-da.

I'm sorry. 미안해(요). mi-an-hae(-yo)
= 죄송해요.
joe-song-hae-yo/
jwe-song-hae-yo

It's okay. 괜찮아(요).
gwaen-cha-na(-yo)

First Meetings 1

- Hello. / Hi. 안녕(하세요).
  an-nyeoung(-ha-se-yo)

- How do you do?
  처음 뵙겠습니다.
  cheo-eum boep-gget-sseum-ni-da

- Good morning.
  좋은 아침이에요.
  jo-eun a-chi-mi-e-yo

  잘 잤어(요)? jal ja-sseo(-yo)?
  안녕히 주무셨어요?
  an-nyeong-hi ju-mu-syeo-sseo-yo?

- I don't think we've met.
  I'm Ji-na Kim.
  초면인 것 같네요.
  저는 김지나입니다.
  cho-myeo-nin geot gat-ne-yo.
  jeo-neun gim-ji-na-im-ni-da

  Tip: Give your family name first in Korean.

- Nice to meet you.
  만나서 반가워(요).
  man-na-seo ban-ga-wo(-yo)

- Nice to meet you too.
  저도 반갑습니다.
  jeo-do ban-gap-sseum-ni-da

- I'm honored to meet you.
  만나 뵙게 되어 영광입니다.
  man-na boep-gge doe-eo yeong-
  gwang-im-ni-da

First Meetings 2

- I've heard so much about you.
  말씀 많이 들었어요.
  mal-sseum ma-ni deu-reo-sseo-yo

- Seong-hee, have you met
  Jun-ho Kim?
  성희 씨, 김준호 씨 아세요?
  seong-hi ssi, gim-jun-ho ssi a-se-yo?

- My name is Jin-su Park.
  I'm a friend of Jun-ho Kim.
  박진수라고 합니다.
  김준호의 친구입니다.
  bak-jjin-su-ra-go ham-ni-da.
  gim-jun-ho-e chin-gu-im-ni-da

- Have we ever met before?
  전에 우리 만난 적 있나요?
  jeo-ne u-ri man-nan jeok in-na-yo?

- May I have your business card?
  명함 있으세요?
  myeong-ham i-sseu-se-yo?

- Here's my card.
  제 명함입니다.
  je myeong-ha-mim-ni-da

Small Talk 1

- Long time no see.
  오랜만입니다.
  o-raen-ma-nim-ni-da

- I haven't seen you for a long
  time.
  오랫동안 뵙지 못했네요.
  o-raet-ddong-an boep-jji mo-taet-ne-yo

- I'm sorry I haven't called for a
  long time.
  오랫동안 연락하지 못해
  죄송합니다.
  o-raet-ddong-an yeol-ra-ka-ji mo-tae
  joe-song-ham-ni-da

- Did you have a meal?
  식사했어(요)?
  sik-ssa-hae-sseo(-yo)?

  Tip: This is a typical standard greeting and
  shouldn't be taken literally.

- How are you? /
  How are you doing?
  어떻게 지내(요)?
  eo-ddeo-ke ji-nae(-yo)?

  잘 지내(요)?
  jal ji-nae(-yo)?

- How have you been doing?
  어떻게 지내셨어요?
  eo-ddeo-ke ji-nae-syeo-sseo-yo?

Small Talk 2

- How are your parents doing?
  부모님은 모두 잘 계세요?
  bu-mo-ni-meun mo-du jal gye-se-yo?

- How's your family doing?
  가족들은 모두 잘 지내(요)?
  ga-jok-ddeu-reun mo-du jal ji-nae(-yo)?

- How's it going?
  별일 없어(요)?
  byeol-ril eop-sseo(-yo)?

- How was your weekend?
  주말 어땠어(요)?
  ju-mal eo-ddae-sseo(-yo)?

- You haven't changed a bit.
  하나도 안 변했네(요).
  ha-na-do an byeon-haen-ne(-yo)

- I haven't seen much of you
  lately.
  요즘 보기 힘드네(요).
  yo-jeum bo-gi him-deu-ne(-yo)

- What's the matter?
  어디 안 좋아(요)?
  eo-di an jo-a(-yo)?

  무슨 일이에요?
  mu-seun i-ri-e-yo?

Small Talk 3

■ Pretty good. / I'm doing well.
잘 지내(요).
jal ji-nae(-yo)

■ Not too bad. / So so.
그럭저럭(요).
geu-reok-jjeo-reok(-yo)

그럭저럭 지내(요).
geu-reok-jjeo-reok ji-nae(-yo)

■ Same as usual.
여전해(요).
yeo-jeon-hae(-yo)

■ Nothing special.
별일 없어(요).
byeol-ril eop-sseo(-yo)

특별한 일 없어(요).
teuk-bbyeol-han il eop-sseo(-yo)

■ I'm just in a bad mood.
그냥 기분이 안 좋아(요).
geu-nyang gi-bu-ni an jo-a(-yo)

■ Say hello to your parents for me.
제 대신 부모님께 안부 전해
주세요.
je dae-sin bu-mo-nim-gge an-bu jeon-
hae ju-se-yo

Saying Goodbye 1

■ Goodbye.
잘 가(요). / 안녕(히 가세요).
jal ga(-yo) / an-nyeong(-hi ga-se-yo)

■ See you tomorrow.
내일 만나(요). / 내일 봬요.
nae-il man-na(-yo) / nae-il bwae-yo

■ Good night.
잘 자(요).
jal ja(-yo)

안녕히 주무세요.
an-nyeong-hi ju-mu-se-yo

■ See you again.
또 만나(요).
ddo man-na(-yo)

■ See you later.
이따가 만나(요).
i-dda-ga man-na(-yo)

■ See you there, then.
그럼, 거기에서 만나(요).
geu-reom, geo-gi-e-seo man-na(-yo)

■ Let's get together soon.
조만간에 만나(요).
jo-man-ga-ne man-na(-yo)

■ Have a nice day.
좋은 날 되세요.
jo-eun nal doe-se-yo

Saying Goodbye 2

- Have a nice weekend.
  주말 잘 보내(요).
  ju-mal jal bo-nae(-yo)

- Take care.
  조심히 가세요.
  jo-sim-hi ga-se-yo

  살펴 가세요.
  sal-pyeo ga-se-yo

- I'll see myself out.
  나오지 마(세요).
  na-o-ji ma(-se-yo)

  Tip: When a visitor is leaving, they can say this to the host.

- Keep in touch.
  연락하고 지내자.
  yeol-ra-ka-go-ji-nae-ja

- Enjoy your trip!
  즐거운 여행 되세요!
  jeul-geo-un yeo-haeng doe-se-yo!

- Have fun. / Have a good day.
  다녀오세요.
  da-nyeo-o-se-yo

  Tip: The Korean here does not translate well into English. This is used in Korea to send off someone who is leaving home for the day.

Welcoming & Homecoming

- Welcome to Seoul.
  서울에 오신 것을 환영합니다.
  seo-u-re o-sin geo-seul
  hwa-nyeong-ham-ni-da

- Welcome to my home.
  저희 집에 오신 것을
  환영합니다.
  jeo-hi ji-be o-sin geo-seul
  hwa-nyeong-ham-ni-da

- I hope you'll like it here.
  이곳이 마음에 들었으면
  좋겠어(요).
  i-go-si ma-eu-me deu-reo-sseu-myeon
  jo-ke-sseo(-yo)

- Welcome. / Come on in.
  어서 오세요.
  eo-seo o-se-yo

- Come in.
  들어오세요.
  deu-reo-o-se-yo

- I'm home. / I'm back.
  다녀왔습니다.
  da-nyeo-wat-sseum-ni-da

  Tip: Children say this to a parent when they come home from school.

Getting Someone's Attention

■ Excuse me.

실례합니다.

sil-rye-ham-ni-da

■ Can I get past, please?

좀 비켜 주시겠어요?

jom bi-kyeo ju-si-ge-sseo-yo?

■ Hello!

여보세요!

yeo-bo-se-yo!

Tip: This is also used when saying hello on the phone.

■ Ma'am!

아주머니!

a-ju-meo-ni!

■ Sir!

아저씨!

a-jeo-ssi!

■ Hey! / Excuse me!

여기요!

yeo-gi-yo!

저기요!

jeo-gi-yo!

Tip: When you want someone's attention, use these phrases.

Wanting to Talk

■ I have something to tell you.

할 말이 있는데(요).

hal ma-ri in-neun-de(-yo)

■ Can I talk to you for a minute?

이야기 좀 해도 될까(요)?

i-ya-gi jom hae-do doel-gga(-yo)?

얘기 좀 해도 될까(요)?

yae-gi jom hae-do doel-gga(-yo)?

Tip: 얘기 [yae-gi] is short for 이야기 [i-ya-gi].

■ May I interrupt you?

말씀 중에 죄송합니다.

mal-sseum jung-e joe-song-ham-ni-da

끼어들어서 미안합니다.

ggi-eo-deu-reo-seo mi-an-ham-ni-da

■ Let me tell you something.

제 말 좀 들어 봐요.

je mal jom deu-reo bwa-yo

내 말 좀 들어 봐(요).

nae mal jom deu-reo bwa(-yo)

■ Guess what? / You know what?

있잖아(요).

it-jja-na(-yo)

Introductions 소개 so-gae

n. name, first name 이름 [이름] i-reum 	n. name 성명 [성:명] seong-myeong = 성함 [성:함] seong-ham	n. business card 명함 [명함] myeong-ham
	n. introduction 소개 [소개] so-gae	v. to introduce 소개하다 [소개하다] so-gae-ha-da
n. gender 성별 [성:별] seong-byeol	n. man 남자 [남자] nam-ja	n. woman 여자 [여자] yeo-ja
	n. male 남성 [남성] nam-seong	n. female 여성 [여성] yeo-seong
	n. sir 아저씨 [아저씨] a-jeo-ssi = 아재 [아재] a-jae	n. ma'am 아주머니 [아주머니] a-ju-meo-ni = 아줌마 [아줌마] a-jum-ma
n. age 나이 [나이] na-i = 연세 [연세] yeon-se	n. senior, elder 노인 [노:인] no-in = 늙은이 [늘그니] neul-geu-ni	n. adult 어른 [어:른] eo-reun = 성인 [성인] seong-in
	n. youth 청년 [청년] cheong-nyeon = 젊은이 [절므니] jeol-meu-ni	n. youth, teenager 청소년 [청소년] cheong-so-nyeon
	n. kid, child 어린이 [어리니] eo-ri-ni = 아이 [아이] a-i	n. baby 아기 [아기] a-gi

Asking for Information

■ May I have your name? /
What's your name?

성함이 어떻게 되세요?

seong-ha-mi eo-ddeo-ke doe-se-yo?

이름이 뭐예요?

i-reu-mi mwo-ye-yo?

Tip: 성함 [seong-ham] **is the polite way of
saying** 이름 [i-reum], **both meaning "name."**

■ What do you do for a living?

무슨 일 하세요?

mu-seun il ha-se-yo?

직업이 뭐예요?

ji-geo-bi mwo-ye-yo?

■ What's your nationality?

어느 나라 사람이에요?

eo-neu na-ra sa-ra-mi-e-yo?

Tip: **Adding** 사람 [sa-ram] **to "country" means
the people of that country.**

■ Where are you from?

어디에서 왔어(요)?

eo-di-e-seo wa-sseo(-yo)?

Tip: **This question means one's country or
region of birth.**

■ How many languages do you
speak?

몇 개 국어를 하세요?

meot gae gu-geo-reul ha-se-yo?

The Korean Wave

The Korean Wave (Hallyu 한류) is a cultural export with economic benefits in the billions.

In the 1990s, South Korean film, TV dramas and K-pop began attracting attention throughout Southeast Asia. The success of boy band H.O.T. in China and of the TV series *Winter Sonata* in Japan were early examples of a growing interest in Korean popular culture overseas. More recent examples are the global TV hits *Squid Game* and *Crash Landing On You*.

Parasite (2019) directed by Bong Joon-ho became the first Korean film to win the Palme d'Or at the Cannes Film Festival and won a Golden Globe for best foreign-language film.

Perhaps most successful of all are the boy band BTS who have achieved worldwide popularity, and were the most listened-to group on Spotify in 2021, with 16.3 million streams. In the same year they were appointed Special Presidential Envoys and performed at the United Nations.

The Ministry of Culture earmarks millions each year in subsidies and promotion to sustain this new branding of Korea. What began as a regional success story is now international.

Introducing Oneself

■ Let me introduce myself.

제 소개를 할게요.

je so-gae-reul hal-gge-yo

내 소개를 할게(요).

nae so-gae-reul hal-gge(-yo)

■ May I introduce myself?

저를 소개해도 될까요?

jeo-reul so-gae-hae-do doel-gga-yo?

■ Hello, I'm Ji-na Kim.

안녕하세요, 김지나라고 합니다.

an-nyeong-ha-se-yo, gim-ji-na-ra-go ham-ni-da

■ Just call me Ji-na.

그냥 지나라고 불러 주세요.

geu-nyang ji-na-ra-go bul-reo ju-se-yo

■ Hello, I'm Ji-na Kim, a friend of Ji-mi's.

안녕하세요, 저는 지미의 친구 김지나입니다.

an-nyeong-ha-se-yo, jeo-neun ji-mi-e chin-gu gim-ji-na-im-ni-da

Giving Information

■ I'm from Korea.

한국에서 왔어(요).

han-gu-ge-seo wa-sseo(-yo)

■ I'm Korean.

한국 사람입니다.

han-guk sa-ra-mim-ni-da

■ I work for AB company.

저는 AB회사에 다닙니다.

jeo-neun e-i-bi-hoe-sa-e da-nim-ni-da

■ I work at a bank.

저는 은행에서 일합니다.

jeo-neun eun-haeng-e-seo il-ham-ni-da

■ I am a senior at Hankuk University.

저는 한국대학 4학년입니다.

jeo-neun han-guk-ddae-hak sa-hang-nyeo-nim-ni-da

■ I'm single.

미혼이에요.

mi-ho-ni-e-yo

■ I'm married.

결혼했어요.

gyeol-hon-hae-sseo-yo

Gratitude 1

- Thank you. / Thanks.
  고맙습니다. go-map-sseum-ni-da
  고마워(요). go-ma-wo(-yo)

- Thank you very much.
  매우 감사합니다.
  mae-u gam-sa-ham-ni-da
  매우 고마워(요).
  mae-u go-ma-wo(-yo)

  Tip: Some Koreans will say 너무 고마워(요)
  [neo-mu go-ma-wo(-yo)], **literally "thank you too much."**

- I don't know how to thank you enough.
  뭐라고 감사해야 할지 모르겠네(요).
  mwo-ra-go gam-sa-hae-ya hal-jji mo-reu-gen-ne(-yo)

- Thank you anyway.
  어찌됐든 고맙습니다.
  eo-jji-dwaet-ddeun go-map-sseum-ni-da
  아무튼 고마워(요).
  a-mu-teun go-ma-wo(-yo)

- Thank you for everything.
  여러 가지로 감사합니다.
  yeo-reo ga-ji-ro gam-sa-ham-ni-da
  여러 가지로 고마워(요).
  yeo-reo ga-ji-ro go-ma-wo(-yo)

Gratitude 2

- I'd like to express my thanks.
  감사의 뜻을 전합니다.
  gam-sa-e ddeu-seul jeon-ham-ni-da

- You're a lifesaver.
  당신은 제 생명의 은인이에요.
  dang-si-neun je saeng-myeong-e eu-ni-ni-e-yo

- I'll never forget what you have done for me.
  제 평생 당신의 은혜를 잊지 못할 거예요.
  je pyeong-saeng dang-si-ne eun-hye-reul it-jji mo-tal ggeo-ye-yo

- Thank you for all the trouble you've gone to.
  마음 써 주셔서 감사드립니다.
  ma-eum sseo ju-syeo-seo gam-sa-deu-rim-ni-da

- Thank you very much for your help.
  도와주셔서 대단히 감사드립니다.
  do-wa-ju-syeo-seo dae-dan-hi gam-sa-deu-rim-ni-da

- I appreciate the invitation.
  초대에 감사드립니다.
  cho-dae-e gam-sa-deu-rim-ni-da

Gratitude 3

■ I appreciate your concern.

당신의 관심에 감사합니다.

dang-si-ne gwan-si-me gam-sa-ham-ni-da

■ Thank you for your kindness.

당신의 친절에 감사합니다.

dang-si-ne chin-jeo-re gam-sa-ham-ni-da

■ Thank you for giving me a chance.

제게 기회를 주셔서 감사합니다.

je-ge gi-hoe-reul ju-syeo-seo gam-sa-ham-ni-da

■ Thank you for giving me directions.

길을 안내해 주셔서 감사합니다.

gi-reul an-nae-hae ju-syeo-seo gam-sa-ham-ni-da

■ Thank you for waiting.

기다려 주셔서 감사합니다.

gi-da-ryeo ju-syeo-seo gam-sa-ham-ni-da

■ I appreciate your consideration.

배려해 주셔서 감사합니다.

bae-ryeo-hae ju-syeo-seo gam-sa-ham-ni-da

Responding to Gratitude

■ You're welcome.

천만에(요).

cheon-ma-ne(-yo)

■ Don't mention it.

별말씀을(요).

byeol-mal-sseu-meul(-yo)

■ My pleasure.

뭘(요).

mwol(-yo)

■ I'm honored by your words.

과찬의 말씀이십니다.

gwa-cha-ne mal-sseu-mi-sim-ni-da

■ I should be the one to thank you.

오히려 제가 감사해야죠.

o-hi-ryeo je-ga gam-sa-hae-ya-jyo

■ No big deal.

뭐 대단한 일도 아닌데(요).

mwo dae-dan-han il-do a-nin-de(-yo)

■ I'm honored to help you.

당신을 도울 수 있어서 제가 영광입니다.

dang-si-neul do-ul ssu i-sseo-seo je-ga yeong-gwang-im-ni-da

Apologies 1

- I'm sorry.

  미안합니다.

  mi-an-ham-ni-da

  미안해(요).

  mi-an-hae(-yo)

  죄송합니다.

  joe-song-ham-ni-da

- I apologize to you.

  사과드립니다.

  sa-gwa-deu-rim-ni-da

- I'm sorry about that.

  그것에 대해 미안합니다.

  geu-geo-se dae-hae mi-an-ham-ni-da

- I'm sorry to disturb you.

  폐를 끼쳐서 죄송합니다.

  pye-reul ggi-cheo-seo joe-song-ham-
  ni-da

- Excuse me for being late.

  늦어서 죄송합니다.

  neu-jeo-seo joe-song-ham-ni-da

- I'm sorry to have kept you
  waiting so long.

  오래 기다리게 해서 미안합니다.

  o-rae gi-da-ri-ge hae-seo mi-an-ham-
  ni-da

Apologies 2

- It won't happen again.

  다시는 이런 일이 일어나지 않을
  것입니다.

  da-si-neun i-reon i-ri i-reo-na-ji a-neul
  ggeo-sim-ni-da

- I'm sorry if it offended you.

  기분 나빴다면 미안해(요).

  gi-bun na-bbat-dda-myeon
  mi-an-hae(-yo)

- I'd like to say I'm sorry.

  미안하다는 말을 하고 싶어(요).

  mi-an-ha-da-neun ma-reul ha-go si-
  peo(-yo)

- I don't know how to apologize.

  뭐라고 사과해야 할지
  모르겠어(요).

  mwo-ra-go sa-gwa-hae-ya hal-jji
  mo-reu-ge-sseo(-yo)

  Tip: 사과 also means "apple." A friend might
  toss you an apple as a joke if they want to make
  up with you in a funny or casual way!

- Please accept my apology.

  부디 제 사과를 받아 주세요.

  bu-di je sa-gwa-reul ba-da ju-se-yo

- I owe you an apology for my
  mistake.

  제 실수에 대해 사과드립니다.

  je sil-ssu-e dae-hae sa-gwa-deu-rim-
  ni-da

Making a Mistake

■ I'm sorry, I couldn't help it.
미안해요, 저도 어쩔 수 없어요.
mi-an-hae-yo, jeo-do eo-jjeol ssu
eop-sseo-yo

■ I'm sorry, I forgot.
미안해(요), 깜박 잊었어(요).
mi-an-hae(-yo), ggam-bak i-jeo-sseo(-yo)

■ I'm sorry, I didn't do it on purpose.
미안해(요), 고의가 아니었어(요).
mi-an-hae(-yo), go-i-ga a-ni-eo-sseo(-yo)

■ Give me a chance to make it up to you.
만회할 기회를 주세요.
man-hoe-hal gi-hoe-reul ju-se-yo

■ I can only blame myself.
그저 제 탓입니다.
geu-jeo je ta-sim-ni-da

■ Sorry I blew it.
제가 망쳐서 죄송합니다.
je-ga mang-cheo-seo joe-song-ham-ni-da

Answering Apologies

■ That's okay. / It's okay.
괜찮아(요).
gwaen-cha-na(-yo)

■ I'm the one who must apologize.
저야말로 사과를 드려야죠.
jeo-ya-mal-ro sa-gwa-reul
deu-ryeo-ya-jyo

■ You're forgiven.
용서할게(요).
yong-seo-hal-gge(-yo)

■ Let's forgive and forget.
서로 용서하고 잊어버리자.
seo-ro yong-seo-ha-go i-jeo-beo-ri-ja

■ Don't worry about that.
걱정하지 마(세요).
geok-jjeong-ha-ji ma(-se-yo)

■ There's nothing to forgive.
미안해할 거 없어(요).
mi-an-hae-hal ggeo eop-sseo(-yo)

Poor Understanding

- Sorry, but I can't hear you.
  미안해(요), 못 들었어(요).
  mi-an-hae(-yo), mot deu-reo-sseo(-yo)

  Tip: "I misheard you" has a one-syllable difference from "I can't hear you" : 잘못 들었어요 [jal-mot deu-reo-sseo(-yo)]

- You're speaking too quickly for me.
  말이 너무 빨라(요).
  ma-ri neo-mu bbal-ra(-yo)

- I didn't quite get that.
  잘 모르겠어(요).
  jal mo-reu-ge-sseo(-yo)

- I didn't catch what you said.
  당신의 말을 이해할 수 없어요.
  dang-si-ne ma-reul i-hae-hal ssu eop-sseo-yo

- What does that mean?
  무슨 뜻이죠?
  mu-seun ddeu-si-jyo?

- What did you say?
  뭐라고(요)?
  mwo-ra-go(-yo)?

Asking to Be Excused

- Excuse me, may I get through?
  실례지만, 좀 비켜 주세요.
  sil-rye-ji-man, jom bi-kyeo ju-se-yo

- Excuse me for just a moment, I'll be back soon.
  잠시 실례해요, 곧 돌아올게요.
  jam-si sil-rye-hae-yo, got do-ra-ol-gge-yo

- Something happened, I've got to go.
  일이 있어서, 가야겠어(요).
  i-ri i-sseo-seo, ga-ya-ge-sseo(-yo)

- Can you keep an eye on my bag? Nature's calling.
  화장실에 가려는데, 제 가방 좀 봐 줄 수 있어요?
  hwa-jang-si-re ga-ryeo-neun-de, je ga-bang jom bwa jul ssu i-sseo-yo?

- Excuse me, but I think you're sitting in my seat.
  실례지만, 제 자리에 앉아 계신 것 같은데요.
  sil-rye-ji-man, je ja-ri-e an-ja gye-sin geot ga-teun-de-yo

Positive Replies

- Sure. / Of course.

  당연히 되죠.
  dang-yeon-hi doe-jyo

  당연하죠.
  dang-yeon-ha-jyo

  당연하지.
  dang-yeon-ha-ji

  물론이죠.
  mul-ro-ni-jyo

- I got it.

  알겠어(요).
  al-ge-sseo(-yo)

- Yes, I'd be happy to.

  그래(요).
  geu-rae(-yo)

- All right.

  좋아(요).
  jo-a(-yo)

- You're right.

  맞아(요).
  ma-ja(-yo)

- I'd be glad to.

  기꺼이 할게(요).
  gi-ggeo-i hal-gge(-yo)

- Yes, I'd be happy to.

  이렇게 할 수 있어 기뻐(요).
  i-reo-ke hal ssu i-sseo gi-bbeo(-yo)

Negative Replies

- I'll never get it right.

  전혀 모르겠는데(요).
  jeon-hyeo mo-reu-gen-neun-de(-yo)

- No way.

  방법이 없어(요).
  bang-beo-bi eop-sseo(-yo)

- I'll never figure it out.

  해결할 수 없어(요).
  hae-gyeol-hal ssu eop-sseo(-yo)

- Not at all.

  아무것도 아니에요.
  a-mu-geot-ddo a-ni-e-yo

- Not yet.

  아직이요.
  a-ji-gi-yo

  아직.
  a-jik

- Of course not.

  물론 아니죠.
  mul-ron a-ni-jyo

  당연히 아니에요.
  dang-yeon-hi a-ni-e-yo

Polite Refusals

▪ I'm afraid not.

유감이지만, 안 될 거 같은데(요).

yu-ga-mi-ji-man, an doel ggeo
ga-teun-de(-yo)

▪ I don't think so.

그렇게 생각하지 않는데(요).

geu-reo-ke saeng-ga-ka-ji
an-neun-de(-yo)

▪ I don't think I can make it.

제가 할 수 없을 것 같아요.

je-ga hal ssu eop-sseul ggeot ga-ta-yo

▪ I can't make it.

저도 어쩔 도리가 없어요.

jeo-do eo-jjeol do-ri-ga eop-sseo-yo

▪ Sorry, I can't right now.

미안해(요), 지금은 안 돼(요).

mi-an-hae(-yo), ji-geu-meun an dwae(-yo)

▪ It's not the best time.

최선의 시간이 아닙니다.

choe-seo-ne si-ga-ni a-nim-ni-da

Polite and Informal Words in Korean Part 1

Polite/formal language is called 존댓말 [jon-daet-mal] and casual/informal/intimate language is called 반말 [ban-mal].

Politeness levels are determined by the verb ending. There are three basic verb endings used to express different politeness levels.

Type 1. −ㅂ니다 [-ni-da] the most polite and most formal ending

Type 2. −(아/어/여)요 [-(a/eo/yeo)yo] a polite, natural, and slightly formal ending

Type 3. −아/어/여 [-a/eo/yeo] a casual, informal, and intimate ending

The polite/formal category includes Type 1 and 2. Type 3 belongs to the casual/informal/intimate category.

Other Replies 1

■ It's possible.
이것은 가능해(요).
i-geo-seun ga-neung-hae(-yo)

■ Maybe. / Perhaps.
아마도(요).
a-ma-do(-yo)

■ Well . . .
글쎄(요).
geul-sse(-yo)

■ It depends.
경우에 따라 달라(요).
gyeong-u-e dda-ra dal-ra(-yo)

그것에 달려 있어(요).
geu-geo-se dal-ryeo i-sseo(-yo)

■ I'll give it some thought.
좀 고려해 볼게(요).
jom go-ryeo-hae bol-gge(-yo)

■ It's hard to believe.
믿기 어려운데(요).
mit-ggi eo-ryeo-un-de(-yo)

■ I can't believe it.
믿을 수 없어(요).
mi-deul ssu eop-sseo(-yo)

Other Replies 2

■ Stop joking around.
농담하지 마(세요).
nong-dam-ha-ji ma(-se-yo)

장난치지 마(세요).
jang-nan-chi-ji ma(-se-yo)

■ That's a lame joke.
썰렁해(요).
sseol-reong-hae(-yo)

■ I don't feel like it.
그럴 기분이 아니에요.
geu-reol gi-bu-ni a-ni-e-yo

■ Can you understand what I said?
내 말 이해했어(요)?
nae mal i-hae-hae-sseo(-yo)?

■ No comment.
드릴 말씀이 없습니다.
deu-ril mal-sseu-mi eop-sseum-ni-da

Agreeing 1

- Right.
  맞아(요).
  ma-ja(-yo)

- That's it.
  바로 그거예요.
  ba-ro geu-geo-ye-yo

- So do I.
  저도요.
  jeo-do-yo

- I think so.
  저도 이렇게 생각해요.
  jeo-do i-reo-ke saeng-ga-kae-yo
  저도 그렇게 생각해요.
  jeo-do geu-reo-ke saeng-ga-kae-yo

- That's a good idea.
  좋은 생각이에요.
  jo-eun saeng-ga-gi-e-yo

- There is no objection on my part.
  이견이 없는데(요).
  i-gyeo-ni eom-neun-de(-yo)

Agreeing 2

- I agree.
  동의합니다.
  dong-i-ham-ni-da
  찬성합니다.
  chan-seong-ham-ni-da
  찬성해(요).
  chan-seong-hae(-yo)

- Yes, indeed.
  그렇고말고(요).
  geu-reo-ko-mal-go(-yo)

- Absolutely.
  두말하면 잔소리(죠).
  du-mal-ha-myeon jan-so-ri(-jyo)

- You're right on the money.
  옳으신 말씀입니다.
  o-reu-sin mal-sseu-mim-ni-da

- I totally agree with you.
  무조건 찬성합니다.
  mu-jo-ggeon chan-seong-ham-ni-da
  전부 찬성해(요).
  jeon-bu chan-seong-hae(-yo)

- It's unanimous then.
  만장일치입니다.
  man-jang-il-chi-im-ni-da

Disagreeing 1

■ Is that so?
그래(요)?
geu-rae(-yo)?

■ I'm not sure.
잘 모르겠어(요).
jal mo-reu-ge-sseo(-yo)

■ You don't say.
그럴리가(요).
geu-reol-ri-ga(-yo)

■ That might be right.
그럴지도 모르죠.
geu-reol-jji-do mo-reu-jyo

■ That's not always the case.
꼭 그런 건 아니에요.
ggok geu-reon geon a-ni-e-yo

■ That's not always true.
꼭 옳은 건 아니에요.
ggok o-reun geon a-ni-e-yo

Disagreeing 2

■ I disagree.
전 반대예요.
jeon ban-dae-ye-yo

■ I can't support your opinion.
당신의 의견을 지지하지 않아요.
dang-si-ne ui-gyeo-neul ji-ji-ha-ji a-na-yo

■ I disagree with you.
당신의 생각에 동의하지 않아요.
dang-si-ne saeng-ga-ge dong-i-ha-ji a-na-yo

■ I'm opposed to that idea.
그 계획에 반대해(요).
geu gye-hoe-ge ban-dae-hae(-yo)

■ Are you sure about that?
그것에 대해 확신해(요)?
geu-geo-se dae-hae hwak-ssin-hae(-yo)?

Warnings 1

- Watch out.

조심해(요).

jo-sim-hae(-yo)

- Watch out for the cars.

차 조심해(요).

cha jo-sim-hae(-yo)

- Watch your tongue.

말할 때 좀 주의해(요).

mal-hal ddae jom ju-i-hae(-yo)

- Be quiet.

좀 조용히 해(요).

jom jo-yong-hi hae(-yo)

- Don't ask for trouble.

쓸데없는 짓 하지 마(세요).

sseul-dde-eom-neun jit ha-ji ma(-se-yo)

- Don't do that.

그렇게 하지 마(세요).

geu-reo-ke ha-ji ma(-se-yo)

- Don't tell anyone.

아무한테도 말하면 안 돼(요).

a-mu-han-te-do mal-ha-myeon
an dwae(-yo)

- Don't try to flatter me.

비행기 태우지 마(세요).

bi-haeng-gi tae-u-ji ma(-se-yo)

Warnings 2

- Don't be rude.

무례하게 굴지 마(세요).

mu-rye-ha-ge gul-ji ma(-se-yo)

- Don't touch me.

날 건들지 마(세요).

nal geon-deul-ji ma(-se-yo)

- Stop bugging me.

날 귀찮게 하지 마(세요).

nal gwi-chan-ke ha-ji ma(-se-yo)

- Don't get on my nerve.

내 성질 건드리지 마(세요).

nae seong-jil geon-deu-ri-ji ma(-se-yo)

- Don't mind me.

상관하지 마(세요).

sang-gwan-ha-ji ma(-se-yo)

- Don't try to get out of it.

오리발 내밀지 마(세요).

o-ri-bal nae-mil-ji ma(-se-yo)

- Stop badgering them.

그를 괴롭히지 마(세요).

geu-reul goe-ro-pi-ji ma(-se-yo)

- Consider your surroundings.

분위기 파악 좀 해(요).

bun-wi-gi pa-ak jom hae(-yo)

Advising 1

■ Remember this.

기억해(요).

gi-eo-kae(-yo)

명심해(요).

myeong-sim-hae(-yo)

■ Do your best.

최선을 다해라.

choe-seo-neul da-hae-ra

■ Shame on you.

부끄러운 줄 알아라.

bu-ggeu-reo-un jul a-ra-ra

■ Pay no attention.

마음에 담아두지 마(세요).

ma-eu-me da-ma-du-ji ma(-se-yo)

■ You shouldn't act on impulse.

충동적으로 하지 마(세요).

chung-dong-jeo-geu-ro ha-ji ma(-se-yo)

■ You can say what you want to say.

하고 싶은 말 있으면 다 해라.

ha-go si-peun mal i-sseu-myeon da hae-ra

Advising 2

■ Get real.

꿈꾸지 마(세요).

ggum-ggu-ji ma(-se-yo)

꿈 깨(요).

ggum ggae(-yo)

■ You should face the problem.

문제에 맞서라.

mun-je-e mat-sseo-ra

■ Keep up the good work.

계속 노력해라.

gye-sok no-ryeo-kae-ra

■ Don't get your hopes up.

너무 기대하지 마(세요).

neo-mu gi-dae-ha-ji ma(-se-yo)

■ Would you behave yourself?

좀 얌전히 있을래(요)?

jom yam-jeon-hi i-sseul-rae(-yo)?

■ Brace yourself.

마음의 준비를 잘해라.

ma-eu-me jun-bi-reul jal-hae-ra

Paying Compliments

■ Great!

대단해(요)!
dae-dan-hae(-yo)!

훌륭해(요)!
hul-ryung-hae(-yo)!

끝내주네(요)!
ggeun-nae-ju-ne(-yo)!

■ That's terrific! / That's awesome!

정말 멋져(요)!
jeong-mal meot-jjeo(-yo)!

정말 굉장해(요)!
jeong-mal goeng-jang-hae(-yo)!

■ Good job!

잘했어(요)!
jal-hae-sseo(-yo)!

■ You're ahead of your time!

넌 시대를 앞선 사람이야!
neon si-dae-reul ap-sseon sa-ra-mi-ya!

■ There's really nothing you can't do!

정말 못하는 게 없구나!
jeong-mal mo-ta-neun ge eop-ggu-na!

Encouraging Someone

■ Come on!

힘내(요)!
him-nae(-yo)!

■ Cheer up!

기운 내(요)!
gi-un nae(-yo)!

■ Go for it!

파이팅!
pa-i-ting!

Tip: People often say 화이팅 [hwa-i-ting] to mean the same as 파이팅 [pa-i-ting]

■ You can do it!

넌 할 수 있어(요)!
neon hal ssu i-sseo(-yo)!

■ Good luck!

행운을 빌어(요)!
haeng-u-neul bi-reo(-yo)!

■ Don't give up.

포기하지 마(세요).
po-gi-ha-ji ma(-se-yo)

■ I'm on your side.

난 네 편이야.
nan ne pyeo-ni-ya

Asking a Favor

■ Can I ask you a favor?
일 좀 부탁해도 될까(요)?
il jom bu-ta-kae-do doel-gga(-yo)?

■ Could you help me?
도와줄 수 있어(요)?
do-wa-jul ssu i-sseo(-yo)?

■ Would you mind opening the window?
창문 좀 열어 줄래(요)?
chang-mun jom yeo-reo jul-rae(-yo)?

■ Would you like to join me?
함께 갈래(요)?
ham-gge gal-rae(-yo)?

■ Would you mind bringing me a drink?
마실 것 좀 주실래요?
ma-sil ggeot jom ju-sil-rae-yo?

Hurrying Someone

■ Hurry up.
어서.
eo-seo

서둘러(요).
seo-dul-reo(-yo)

■ We have to hurry.
우리는 서둘러야 해(요).
u-ri-neun seo-dul-reo-ya hae(-yo)

■ Let's rush.
서두르자.
seo-du-reu-ja

■ I'm in a hurry.
제가 좀 급해서요.
je-ga jom geu-pae-seo-yo

■ Please step on it.
좀 더 서둘러 주세요.
jom deo seo-dul-reo ju-se-yo

■ Quickly, quickly!
빨리, 빨리!
bbal-ri, bbal-ri!

■ There's no time to lose.
지체할 시간이 없어(요).
ji-che-hal si-ga-ni eop-sseo(-yo)

Guessing

■ It figures.
그럴 줄 알았어(요).
geu-reol jjul a-ra-sseo(-yo)

■ You guessed right.
네가 맞았어(요).
ne-ga ma-ja-sseo(-yo)

■ The results met our expectations.
결과는 우리가 예상한 것과
같아(요).
gyeol-gwa-neun u-ri-ga ye-sang-han
geot-ggwa ga-ta(-yo)

■ Just a wild guess.
그냥 내 멋대로 추측했어(요).
geu-nyang nae meot-ddae-ro
chu-cheu-kae-sseo(-yo)

■ The chances are slim.
가능성은 적어(요).
ga-neung-sseong-eun jeo-geo(-yo)

■ I had no idea you were coming.
네가 올 줄 생각도 못했어(요).
ne-ga ol jjul saeng-gak-ddo mo-tae-
sseo(-yo)

■ That was unexpected.
그 일은 의외예요.
geu i-reun ui-oe-ye-yo

Polite and Informal Words in Korean Part 2

Generally, 반말 [ban-mal] (informal speech) is considered to be the most intimate and casual way of speaking with others in Korean. Therefore, you should only use 반말 to speak to someone who is the same age or younger than you. If you don't know the other person's age or social status, you should not use 반말 under any circumstances.

Many words have a polite form that you can use in formal situations:

word	basic	polite
rice, meal	밥 bap	진지 jin-ji
age	나이 na-i	연세 yeon-se
home, house	집 jip	댁 daek
saying	말 mal	말씀 mal-sseum
exist	있다 it-dda	계시다 gye-si-da
eat	먹다 meok-dda	드시다 deu-si-da

Sympathizing

■ I'm very sorry.
너무 아쉬워(요).
neo-mu a-swi-wo(-yo)

■ I'm really sorry to hear that.
유감이네(요).
yu-ga-mi-ne(-yo)

■ Don't lose heart.
너무 실망하지 마(세요).
neo-mu sil-mang-ha-ji ma(-se-yo)

■ What bad luck!
운이 안 좋았어(요)!
u-ni an jo-a-sseo(-yo)!

■ That's too bad!
그거 너무 안됐군(요)!
geu-geo neo-mu an-dwaet-ggun(-yo)!

■ What a pity!
어머, 가엾어라!
eo-meo, ga-yeop-sseo-ra!

Blaming Someone 1

■ Silly!
바보!
ba-bo!

■ You're so stupid!
넌 정말 어리석어!
neon jeong-mal eo-ri-seo-geo!

■ You're insane.
미쳤구나.
mi-cheot-ggu-na

■ Have you lost your mind?
생각이 없어(요)?
saeng-ga-gi eop-sseo(-yo)?

정신 나갔어(요)?
jeong-sin na-ga-sseo(-yo)?

■ What impudence!
뻔뻔하구나!
bbeon-bbeon-ha-gu-na!

철면피구나!
cheol-myeon-pi-gu-na!

염치가 없구나!
yeom-chi-ga eop-ggu-na!

■ What a shame!
부끄러운 줄 모르는구나!
bu-ggeu-reo-un jul mo-reu-neun-gu-na!

Blaming Someone 2

■ You're disgusting.
정말 구역질 나(요).
jeong-mal gu-yeok-jjil na(-yo)

■ You're so childish.
정말 유치해(요).
jeong-mal yu-chi-hae(-yo)

■ Grow up.
철 좀 들어라.
cheol jom deu-reo-ra

■ You're really something.
정말 너란 건.
jeong-mal neo-ran geon

■ How could you do this?
어떻게 이럴 수 있어(요)?
eo-ddeo-ke i-reol ssu i-sseo(-yo)?

■ How dare you talk to me like that!
어찌 감히 나한테 그렇게 말할 수 있어(요)!
eo-jji gam-hi na-han-te geu-reo-ke mal-hal ssu i-sseo(-yo)!

Making a Call

■ Is Se-jin there?
세진이 있어(요)?
se-ji-ni i-sseo(-yo)?

■ Hello, this is Seung-jun.
Is Hyun-su there?
여보세요, 승준인데(요).
현수 있어(요)?
yeo-bo-se-yo, seung-ju-nin-de(-yo).
hyeon-su i-sseo(-yo)?

■ Could I speak to Ji-yun?
지윤이하고 통화하고 싶은데(요).
ji-yu-ni-ha-go tong-hwa-ha-go
si-peun-de(-yo)

■ Can you talk right now?
지금 통화하기 괜찮아(요)?
ji-geum tong-hwa-ha-gi gwaen-cha-na(-yo)?

■ I'm sorry for calling so late.
이렇게 늦었는데 전화드려서 정말 죄송합니다.
i-reo-ke neu-jeot-neun-de
jeon-hwa-deu-ryeo-seo jeong-mal
joe-song-ham-ni-da

■ I'm just returning your call.
전화하셨다고 해서 전화드렸습니다.
jeon-hwa-ha-syeot-dda-go hae-seo
jeon-hwa-deu-ryeot-sseum-ni-da

Receiving a Call 1

■ Excuse me, who's calling please?

실례지만, 누구세요?

sil-rye-ji-man, nu-gu-se-yo?

■ May I ask what this is about?

무슨 일이세요?

mu-seun i-ri-se-yo?

■ Is this an emergency?

급한 용무 있어(요)?

geu-pan yong-mu i-sseo(-yo)?

■ Who would you like to speak to?

어느 분 찾으세요?

eo-neu bun cha-jeu-se-yo?

■ Is he expecting your call?

그를 바꿔 드릴까요?

geu-reul ba-ggwo deu-ril-gga-yo?

■ She's on the phone. Could you call back later?

그녀는 통화 중인데요.
이따가 다시 전화하시겠어요?

geu-nyeo-neun tong-hwa jung-in-de-yo. i-dda-ga da-si jeon-hwa-ha-si-ge-sseo-yo?

Receiving a Call 2

■ It's me.

바로 전데요.

ba-ro jeon-de-yo

■ Are you the one I spoke with a short time ago?

조금 전에 저와 통화하셨던 분인가요?

jo-geum jeo-ne jeo-wa tong-hwa-ha-syeot-ddeon bu-nin-ga-yo?

■ Could you speak a little bit louder?

좀 크게 말해 줄래(요)?

jom keu-ge mal-hae jul-rae(-yo)?

■ Coud you lower your voice a little bit?

좀 작게 말해 줄래(요)?

jom jak-gge mal-hae jul-rae(-yo)?

■ Could you speak more slowly?

좀 천천히 말해 줄래(요)?

jom cheon-cheon-hi mal-hae jul-rae(-yo)?

■ Could you repeat that?

다시 한 번 말해 줄래(요)?

da-si han beon mal-hae jul-rae(-yo)?

■ I can't hear you very well.

잘 안 들려(요).

jal an deul-ryeo(-yo)

Transferring a Call

■ Hold on, please.
잠시 기다려 주세요.
jam-si gi-da-ryeo ju-se-yo

■ I'll put you through.
연결해 드리겠습니다.
yeon-gyeol-hae deu-ri-get-sseum-ni-da

■ The phone number you are trying to call is busy.
연결하려는 전화번호가 통화 중이에요.
yeon-gyeol-ha-ryeo-neun
jeon-hwa-beon-ho-ga tong-hwa jung-
i-e-yo

■ Hold on and I'll get them.
기다리세요, 바꿔 드릴게요.
gi-da-ri-se-yo, ba-ggwo deu-ril-gge-yo

■ Hold on and I'll put you through to an English speaker.
끊지 마세요, 영어 할 수 있는 분을 바꿔 드릴게요.
ggeun-chi ma-se-yo, yeong-eo hal ssu
in-neun bu-neul ba-ggwo deu-ril-gge-yo

■ It's for you.
네 전화야.
ne jeon-hwa-ya

당신 전화예요.
dang-sin jeon-hwa-ye-yo

Seoul

Seoul (서울) is the mammoth capital of Korea with a population surpassing ten million. It has been the capital city since the Joseon Dynasty (1392–1897) and has a history that stretches back for millennia.

Shrines and palaces such as the grand Gyeongbokgung Palace (경복궁) provide a window to the past but Seoul is unquestionably modern with vibrant financial and technology sectors.

For shopaholics, the city is something of a utopia. Myeong-dong (명동) is a third of a square mile (1 square kilometer) crammed with higher-end branded outlets while Dongdaemun Market (동대문 시장 [dong-dae-mun si-jang]) and Namdaemun Market (남대문 시장 [nam-dae-mun si-jang]) provide more traditional retail and wholesale experiences.

If you're on the lookout for international food, try the districts of Samcheong-dong (삼청동), Insa-dong (인사동) and Itaewon (이태원).

Calling Back

- **I'll get back to you later.**

  다음에 전화할게(요).

  da-eu-me jeon-hwa-hal-gge(-yo)

  다음에 전화드릴게요.

  da-eu-me jeon-hwa-deu-ril-gge-yo

- **Can I call you back?**

  제가 다시 전화드릴까요?

  je-ga da-si jeon-hwa-deu-ril-gga-yo?

- **I'll get in touch with you soon.**

  제가 잠시 후에 전화드릴게요.

  je-ga jam-si hu-e jeon-hwa-deu-ril-gge-yo

- **Please call me back in ten minutes.**

  10분 후에 제가 다시 전화드리겠습니다.

  sip-bbun hu-e je-ga da-si jeon-hwa-deu-ri-get-sseum-ni-da

- **Should I get him to call you back?**

  그에게 다시 전화하라고 할까(요)?

  geu-e-ge da-si jeon-hwa-ha-ra-go hal-gga(-yo)?

Delaying a Call

- **I'm on the phone.**

  통화 중이에요.

  tong-hwa jung-i-e-yo

- **He is not here now.**

  그는 지금 없는데(요).

  geu-neun ji-geum eom-neun-de(-yo)

- **Sorry, he's just left.**

  죄송합니다만, 그는 방금 나갔습니다.

  joe-song-ham-ni-da-man, geu-neun bang-geum na-gat-sseum-ni-da

- **I'm a bit busy right now.**

  지금 좀 바빠서(요).

  ji-geum jom ba-bba-seo(-yo)

- **I'm a little busy, I'll call you later.**

  지금 말하기 불편해서, 이따가 전화할게(요).

  ji-geum mal-ha-gi bul-pyeon-hae-seo, i-dda-ga jeon-hwa-hal-gge(-yo)

- **If anyone calls, tell them I'm not here.**

  전화 오면, 나 없다고 해(요).

  jeon-hwa o-myeon, na eop-dda-go hae(-yo)

Messages

■ Can I take a message?

메시지 남기시겠어요?

me-si-ji nam-gi-si-ge-sseo-yo?

■ I'm sorry but he's busy. Would you like to leave a message?

죄송합니다만, 그가 바빠서요.
메시지 남기시겠어요?

joe-song-ham-ni-da-man,
geu-ga ba-bba-sseo-yo.
me-si-ji nam-gi-si-ge-sseo-yo?

■ Please text me.

문자메시지 주세요.

mun-jja-me-si-ji ju-se-yo

■ Tell him to call me.

저한테 전화하라고 그에게 전해
주세요.

jeo-han-te jeon-hwa-ha-ra-go geu-e-ge
jeon-hae ju-se-yo

■ Ask him to call me at 123-4567.

그에게 123-4567로 전화하라고
전해 주세요.

geu-e-ge il-i-sa-me sa-o-ryuk-chil-ro
jeon-hwa-ha-ra-go jeon-hae ju-se-yo

■ Just tell her that I called.

제가 연락했다고 그녀에게 전해
주세요.

je-ga yeol-ra-kaet-dda-go geu-nyeo-e-
ge jeon-hae ju-se-yo

Wrong Numbers

■ You have the wrong number.

전화 잘못 거셨어요.

jeon-hwa jal-mot geo-syeo-sseo-yo

■ There's no one here by that name.

그런 사람 없어(요).

geu-reon sa-ram eop-sseo(-yo)

■ What number did you want?

어디에 전화하셨어요?

eo-di-e jeon-hwa-ha-syeo-sseo-yo?

■ You should double check the number.

전화번호를 다시 확인해 보세요.

jeon-hwa-beon-ho-reul da-si hwa-gin-
hae bo-se-yo

■ I must have the wrong number.

제가 잘못 걸었네요.

je-ga jal-mot geo-reon-ne-yo

Hanging Up

■ Call you soon.

곧 전화할게(요).

got jeon-hwa-hal-gge(-yo)

■ Thank you for calling.

전화해 주셔서 감사합니다.

jeon-hwa-hae ju-syeo-seo
gam-sa-ham-ni-da

■ Well, I have to get off the line
now.

그럼, 전화 끊어야겠어(요).

geu-reom, jeon-hwa
ggeu-neo-ya-ge-sseo(-yo)

■ Don't forget to call me.

나한테 연락하는 것
잊지 마(세요).

na-han-te yeol-ra-ka-neun geot
it-jji ma(-se-yo)

■ Contact me anytime.

언제든지 저에게 연락하세요.

eon-je-deun-ji jeo-e-ge yeol-ra-ka-se-yo

Office Calls

■ Hello, Sam-dong Company, Sales
Department, Jun Lee speaking.

안녕하세요, 삼동 회사 영업부,
이준입니다.

an-nyeong-ha-se-yo, sam-dong hoe-sa
yeong-eop-bbu, i-jun-im-ni-da

■ Thank you for calling Sam-dong
Company.

삼동 회사에 전화해 주셔서
감사합니다.

Sam-dong hoe-sa-e jeon-hwa-hae
ju-syeo-seo gam-sa-ham-ni-da

■ I'm calling about tomorrow's
meeting.

내일 회의를 확인하려고
전화했습니다.

nae-il hoe-i-reul hwa-gin-ha-ryeo-go
jeon-hwa-haet-sseum-ni-da

■ May I speak to someone in HR?

인사부로 돌려 주세요.

in-sa-bu-ro dol-ryeo ju-se-yo

Chapter 2

Making Conversation

A Day 하루 Ha-ru

day 하루 [하루] ha-ru	n. morning, breakfast 아침 [아침] a-chim	v. wake up 깨다 [깨:다] ggae-da v. get up 일어나다 [이러나다] i-reo-na-da
	n. morning, a.m. 오전 [오:전] o-jeon	n. breakfast 아침 식사 [아침 식싸] a-chim sik-ssa
	n. day time 낮 [낟] nat n. lunch time, lunch 점심 [점:심] jeom-sim	n. lunch 점심 식사 [점:심 식싸] jeom-sim sik-ssa
	n. afternoon, p.m. 오후 [오:후] o-hu	v. work, do one's job, labor 일하다 [일:하다] il-ha-da
	n. evening, dinner 저녁 [저녁] jeo-nyeok	n. dinner 저녁 식사 [저녁 식싸] jeo-nyeok sik-ssa
	n. night 밤 [밤] bam	v. sleep 자다 [자다] ja-da n. sleep 잠 [잠] jam n. dream 꿈 [꿈] ggum

Waking & Getting Up 1

■ You have to wake up.
일어나야 해(요).
i-reo-na-ya hae(-yo)

■ Rise and shine!
일어나, 아침이야!
i-reo-na, a-chi-mi-ya!

■ Are you up?
일어났어(요)?
i-reo-na-sseo(-yo)?

■ I just woke up.
막 일어났어(요).
mak i-reo-na-sseo(-yo)

■ Get up now, or you'll be late.
일어나, 아니면 늦을 거야.
i-reo-na, a-ni-myeon neu-jeul ggeo-ya

■ It's time to get up.
일어날 시간이에요.
i-reo-nal si-ga-ni-e-yo

■ Why didn't you wake me up?
왜 안 깨웠어(요)?
wae an ggae-wo-sseo(-yo)?

■ Oh no, I overslept.
이런, 늦잠을 잤어(요).
i-reon, neut-jja-meul ja-sseo(-yo)

Waking & Getting Up 2

■ Please wake me up early
tomorrow.
내일 아침에 일찍 깨워 줘(요).
nae-il a-chi-me il-jjik ggae-wo jwo(-yo)

■ I wake up early in the morning.
나는 일찍 일어나(요).
na-neun il-jjik i-reo-na(-yo)

■ I'm a morning person.
나는 아침형 인간이에요.
na-neun a-chim-hyeong in-ga-ni-e-yo

Tip: If you're a night person, you can say
저녁형 인간 [jeo-nyeo-kyeong in-gan].

■ I usually wake up at six o'clock in
the morning.
나는 보통 아침 6시에
일어나(요).
na-neun bo-tong a-chim yeo-seot-ssi-e
i-reo-na(-yo)

■ Sometimes I can't wake up in
the morning.
때때로 아침에 못 일어나(요).
ddae-ddae-ro a-chi-me mot i-reo-na(-yo)

■ I need to get a wake-up call in
the morning.
아침에 모닝콜이 필요해(요).
a-chi-me mo-ning-ko-ri pi-ryo-hae(-yo)

Washing & Brushing Teeth

■ **Wash your hands first.**
먼저 손을 씻어(요).
meon-jeo so-neul ssi-seo(-yo)

■ **I need to wash my face to wake up.**
잠을 깨려면 세수를 해야겠어(요).
ja-meul ggae-ryeo-myeon se-su-reul hae-ya-ge-sseo(-yo)

■ **Would you bring a towel for me?**
수건 좀 갖다줄래(요)?
su-geon jom gat-dda-jul-rae(-yo)?

■ **Brush your teeth three times a day.**
하루에 세 번 이를 닦아야 해(요).
ha-ru-e se beon i-reul da-gga-ya hae(-yo)

■ **Don't forget to brush your teeth after eating.**
식사 후에 양치하는 것 잊지 마(세요).
sik-ssa hu-e yang-chi-ha-neun geot it-jji ma(-se-yo)

■ **Can I use this new toothbrush?**
이 새 칫솔을 써도 될까(요)?
i sae chit-sso-reul sseo-do doel-gga(-yo)?

Shower & Bathing

■ **I take a bath every day.**
나는 매일 목욕해(요).
na-neun mae-il mo-gyo-kae(-yo)

■ **Take a bath quickly.**
어서 목욕해라.
eo-seo mo-gyo-kae-ra

■ **I need a quick shower.**
서둘러 샤워해야 해(요).
seo-dul-reo sya-wo-hae-ya hae(-yo)

■ **Taking a cold shower is good for your health.**
찬물로 샤워하는 것은 건강에 좋아(요).
chan-mul-ro sya-wo-ha-neun geo-seun geon-gang-e jo-a(-yo)

■ **Your showers are too long.**
너는 샤워를 너무 오래 해(요).
neo-neun sya-wo-reul neo-mu o-rae hae(-yo)

■ **I take a shower every morning after jogging.**
매일 아침 조깅하고 나서 샤워를 해(요).
mae-il a-chim jo-ging-ha-go na-seo sya-wo-reul hae(-yo)

Shampooing

- I had no time to shampoo this morning.

  아침에 머리 감을 시간이 없어(요).

  a-chi-me meo-ri ga-meul si-ga-ni eop-sseo(-yo)

- I make it a rule to shampoo my hair every morning.

  아침에 머리 감는 습관이 있어(요).

  a-chi-me meo-ri gam-neun seup-ggwa-ni i-sseo(-yo)

- Last night, I was shampooing my hair when the water went off.

  지난밤에, 머리를 감는데 물이 안 나왔어(요).

  ji-nan-ba-me, meo-ri-reul gam-neun-de mu-ri an na-wa-sseo(-yo)

- I usually shampoo in the eveing because there's not enough time in the morning.

  아침에 시간이 없기 때문에 보통 저녁에 머리를 감아(요).

  a-chi-me si-ga-ni eop-ggi ddae-mu-ne bo-tong jeo-nyeo-ge meo-ri-reul ga-ma(-yo)

Busan

Busan (부산) is the nation's second largest city and the main port city in Korea. It is notable for its world-class port and beautiful beaches including Haeundae (해운대), Gwangalli (광안리) and Songjeong (송정).

Other must-sees include the world's largest department store, Shinsegae in Centum City (신세계 백화점 센텀시티 [sin-se-gye bae-kwa-jeom sen-teom-si-ti]) and Jagalchi (자갈치), the seafood market, which is more than a hundred years old.

Busan has also gained international recognition thanks to its many annual festivals, such as BIFF (Busan International Film Festival 부산 국제 영화제 [bu-san guk-jje yeong-hwa-je]). Movie stars and fans flock to his event every October.

Busan is located in southeastern Korea. To get there takes about three hours from Seoul by KTX (Korean Train Express) and about four hours by express bus. Busan's subway offers convenient travel within the city.

Having a Meal 1

- Breakfast is ready!
  아침 식사 준비 다 됐어(요)!
  a-chim sik-ssa jun-bi da dwae-sseo(-yo)!

- What should I make for breakfast?
  아침 식사로 뭐 준비하지(요)?
  a-chim sik-ssa-ro mwo jun-bi-ha-ji(-yo)?

- I don't eat breakfast.
  나는 아침 식사를 안 해(요).
  na-neun a-chim sik-ssa-reul an hae(-yo)

- I don't feel like having breakfast this morning.
  오늘 아침은 식사할 기분이 아니에요.
  o-neul a-chi-meun sik-ssa-hal gi-bu-ni a-ni-e-yo

- Our meal is ready, so let's eat.
  식사 준비 다 됐어, 먹자.
  sik-ssa jun-bi da dwae-sseo, meok-jja

- My stomach is rumbling because I didn't have breakfast yet.
  아직 식사를 못 해서, 배에서 꼬르륵 소리가 나고 있어(요).
  a-jik sik-ssa-reul mot hae-seo, bae-e-seo ggo-reu-reuk so-ri-ga na-go i-sseo(-yo)

Having a Meal 2

- Would you like to have dinner together?
  우리 같이 저녁 먹을래(요)?
  u-ri ga-chi jeo-nyeok meo-geul-rae(-yo)?

- What should we do for dinner?
  저녁 식사로 우리 뭘 먹을까(요)?
  jeo-nyeok sik-ssa-ro u-ri mwol meo-geul-gga(-yo)?

- Will you come to my house for dinner?
  저녁 식사하러 우리 집에 올래(요)?
  jeo-nyeok sik-ssa-ha-reo u-ri ji-be ol-rae(-yo)?

- Don't be picky.
  편식하지 마(세요).
  pyeon-si-ka-ji ma(-se-yo)

- Finish up your plate.
  남기지 말고 다 먹어(요).
  nam-gi-ji mal-go da meo-geo(-yo)

- Have you finished?
  밥 다 먹었어(요)?
  bap da meo-geo-sseo(-yo)?

- Do you want some more rice?
  밥 더 줄까(요)?
  bap deo jul-gga(-yo)?

Getting Dressed 1

■ These pants are too tight.

이 바지 너무 끼어(요).

i ba-ji neo-mu ggi-eo(-yo)

■ I was dressed casually in jeans and T-shirt.

청바지와 티셔츠로 간편하게 입었어(요).

cheong-ba-ji-wa ti-syeo-cheu-ro gan-pyeon-ha-ge i-beo-sseo(-yo)

■ Mi-hee is wearing a white blouse and a pink skirt.

미희는 하얀 블라우스에 분홍 치마를 입고 있어(요).

mi-hi-neun ha-yan beul-ra-u-seu-e bun-hong chi-ma-reul ip-ggo i-sseo(-yo)

Tip: Koreans often say 핑크 [ping-keu] using the word derived from English for "pink" instead of the traditional Korean word 분홍 [bun-hong].

■ It's cold out so put on your coat.

밖은 추우니 코트를 입어라.

ba-ggeun chu-u-ni ko-teu-reul i-beo-ra

■ Take off your coat and relax.

외투를 벗고 쉬어(요).

oe-tu-reul beot-ggo swi-eo(-yo)

Getting Dressed 2

■ Which tie should I wear?

어떤 넥타이를 매면 좋을까(요)?

eo-ddeon nek-ta-i-reul mae-myeon jo-eul-gga(-yo)?

■ That dress suits you.

그 원피스 너한테 잘 어울리는데.

geu won-pi-seu neo-han-te jal eo-ul-ri-neun-de

■ The blue hat doesn't really work.

파란색 모자는 정말 안 어울려(요).

pa-ran-saek mo-ja-neun jeong-mal an eo-ul-ryeo(-yo)

■ What should I wear today?

오늘 뭘 입으면 좋을까(요)?

o-neul mwol i-beu-myeon jo-eul-gga(-yo)?

■ He wears the same clothes every day.

그는 항상 같은 옷이에요.

geu-neun hang-sang ga-teun o-si-e-yo

■ You're dressed up from head to toe.

머리부터 발끝까지 차려 입었구나.

meo-ri-bu-teo bal-ggeut-gga-ji cha-ryeo i-beot-ggu-na

Makeup

■ I need to put on some makeup.

화장해야 해(요).

hwa-jang-hae-ya hae(-yo)

■ I have no time to do my makeup in the morning.

아침에 화장할 시간이 없어(요).

a-chi-me hwa-jang-hal si-ga-ni eop-sseo(-yo)

■ You don't have to wear makeup.

화장 안 해도 괜찮아(요).

hwa-jang an hae-do gwaen-cha-na(-yo)

■ She usually spends an hour doing her makeup.

그녀는 보통 화장하는 데 한 시간 걸려(요).

geu-nyeo-neun bo-tong hwa-jang-ha-neun de han si-gan geol-ryeo(-yo)

■ You look good.

괜찮게 꾸몄는데(요).

gwaen-chan-ke ggu-myeon-neun-de(-yo)

■ She follows the latest trends.

그녀는 최신 유행을 따라(요).

geu-nyeo-neun choe-sin yu-haeng-eul dda-ra(-yo)

Watching TV

■ What's on TV this evening?

오늘 저녁에 텔레비전에서 뭐 해(요)?

o-neul jeo-nyeo-ge tel-re-bi-jeo-ne-seo mwo hae(-yo)?

■ What's on the KBS?

KBS에서 뭘 방송하고 있어(요)?

ke-i-bi-e-seu-e-seo mwol bang-song-ha-go i-sseo(-yo)?

Tip: KBS is short for Korean Broadcasting System.

■ What programs do you like?

어떤 프로그램을 좋아해(요)?

eo-ddeon peu-ro-geu-rae-meul jo-a-hae(-yo)?

■ Let's change the channel.

채널을 바꿔라.

chae-neo-reul ba-ggwo-ra

■ Stop flipping channels.

채널 바꾸지 마(세요).

chae-neol ba-ggu-ji ma(-se-yo)

■ Hand me the remote control, please.

리모컨 좀 줘(요).

ri-mo-keon jom jwo(-yo)

Going to Bed

■ It's time to go to bed.

잘 시간이야.

jal si-ga-ni-ya

■ I have to go to bed.

자러 가야겠어(요).

ja-reo ga-ya-ge-sseo(-yo)

■ Are you still up?

아직 안 자(요)?

a-jik an ja(-yo)?

■ It's almost midnight.

벌써 한밤중이야.

beol-sseo han-bam-jung-i-ya

■ Will you turn off the light?

불 좀 꺼 줄래(요)?

bul jom ggeo jul-rae(-yo)?

■ Do you need another blanket?

담요를 더 드릴까요?

dam-nyo-reul deo deu-ril-gga-yo?

■ Don't use your phone in bed.

잠자리에서 휴대폰 하지 마(세요).

jam-jja-ri-e-seo hyu-dae-pon ha-ji ma(-se-yo)

Tip: 잠자리 [jam-jja-ri] "the place where you sleep" also means "dragonfly" and has a slightly different pronunciation: [jam-ja-ri]

Sleeping Habits

■ My husband has bad sleeping habits.

남편의 잠버릇은 좋지 않아(요).

nam-pyeo-ne jam-bbeo-reu-seun jo-chi a-na(-yo)

■ My wife tosses and turns a lot in her sleep.

아내는 자면서 자꾸 뒤척여(요).

a-nae-neun ja-myeon-seo ja-ggu dwi-cheo-gyeo(-yo)

■ You snored like a bulldog last night.

넌 간밤에 코를 엄청 골았어(요).

neon gan-ba-me ko-reul eom-cheong go-ra-sseo(-yo)

■ He started snoring as soon as he fell asleep.

그는 잠들자마자 코를 골기 시작했어(요).

geu-neun jam-deul-ja-ma-ja ko-reul gol-gi si-ja-kae-sseo(-yo)

■ Jeong-won talks in her sleep.

정원이는 잘 때 잠꼬대를 해(요).

jeong-wo-ni-neun jal ddae jam-ggo-dae-reul hae(-yo)

■ He grinds his teeth in bed.

그는 잘 때 이를 갈아(요).

geu-neun jal ddae i-reul ga-ra(-yo)

Deep Sleep

■ I slept well last night.

어젯밤에 푹 잤어(요).

eo-jet-bba-me puk ja-sseo(-yo)

■ We all fell asleep so fast.

우리 모두 금방
곯아떨어졌어(요).

u-ri mo-du geum-bang
go-ra-ddeo-reo-jeo-sseo(-yo)

■ I didn't sleep well.

그다지 잘 자지 못했어(요).

geu-da-ji jal ja-ji mo-tae-sseo(-yo)

■ Did you not sleep well?

잘 못 잤어(요)?

jal mot ja-sseo(-yo)?

■ I haven't been getting much
sleep lately.

요즘 잠을 잘 못 자(요).

yo-jeum ja-meul jal mot ja(-yo)

■ You'll feel better after a good
sleep.

잘 자고 나면 훨씬 좋아질 거예요.

jal ja-go na-myeon hwol-ssin jo-a-jil
ggeo-ye-yo

Dreaming

■ Sweet dreams!

좋은 꿈 꿔(요)!

jo-eun ggum ggwo(-yo)!

■ I dream of him from time to time.

가끔 그의 꿈을 꿔(요).

ga-ggeum geu-e ggu-meul ggwo(-yo)

■ If you dream of pigs, you should
buy a lottery ticket!

돼지꿈을 꾸면, 복권을 사(세요)!

dwae-ji-ggu-meul ggu-myeon,
bok-ggwo-neul sa(-se-yo)!

■ I had a strange dream last night.

어제 이상한 꿈을 꿨어(요).

eo-je i-sang-han ggu-meul
ggwo-sseo(-yo)

■ I had a nightmare.

악몽을 꿨어(요).

ang-mong-eul ggwo-sseo(-yo)

■ I had a nightmare, so I couldn't
get back to sleep.

악몽을 꿔서, 다시 잠들 수
없었어(요).

ang-mong-eul ggwo-seo, da-si jam-deul
ssu eop-sseo-sseo(-yo)

The Home 집 jip

n. house, home
집 [집] jip
n. home 가정 [가정]
ga-jeong

n. room 방 [방]
bang

n. door 문 [문]
mun

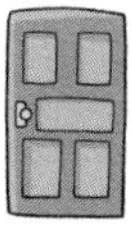

n. window 창문 [창문]
chang-mun

n. bed 침대 [침:대]
chim-dae

n. desk 책상 [책쌍]
chaek-ssang

n. chair 의자 [의자]
ui-ja

n. living room
거실 [거실]
geo-sil

n. television, TV
텔레비전 [텔레비전]
tel-re-bi-jeon

n. sofa 소파 [소파]
so-pa

n. kitchen
부엌 [부억] bu-eok
= 주방 [주방] ju-bang

n. dining table
식탁 [식탁] sik-tak

n. refrigerator
냉장고 [냉:장고]
naeng-jang-go

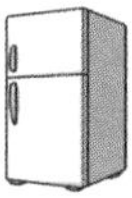

n. electric range
전기 레인지 [전기 레인지]
jeon-gi re-in-ji
= 인덕션 레인지 [인덕션 레인지]
in-deok-ssyeon re-in-ji

n. sink 싱크대 [싱크대]
sing-keu-dae

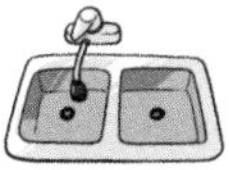

n. bathroom
욕실 [욕씰]
yok-ssil

n. toilet, restroom
화장실 [화장실]
hwa-jang-sil

n. washstand
세면대 [세:면대]
se-myeon-dae

v. wash
씻다 [씯따]
ssit-dda

n. washing one's face
세수 [세:수] se-su

v. brush one's teeth
양치하다 [양치하다]
yang-chi-ha-da

n. cleaning 청소 [청소] cheong-so 	n. cleaner 청소기 [청소기] cheong-so-gi 	n. wastebasket, trash can 쓰레기통 [쓰레기통] sseu-re-gi-tong = 휴지통 [휴지통] hyu-ji-tong
	n. washing machine 세탁기 [세:탁끼] se-tak-ggi 	n. laundry, doing the laundry 빨래 [빨래] bbal-rae = 세탁 [세:탁] se-tak
v. wear, put on 입다 [입따] ip-dda n. clothes 옷 [옫] ot 	n. T-shirt 티셔츠 [티셔츠] ti-syeo-cheu 	n. jacket 재킷 [재킫] jae-kit
	n. pants, trousers 바지 [바지] ba-ji 	n. jeans 청바지 [청바지] cheong-ba-ji
	n. skirt 치마 [치마] chi-ma 	n. underwear 속옷 [소:곧] so-got 
	n. socks 양말 [양말] yang-mal 	n. cap, hat 모자 [모자] mo-ja
n. shoes 신발 [신발] sin-bal	n. dress shoes 구두 [구두] gu-du	n. sneakers 운동화 [운:동화] un-dong-hwa
n. bag 가방 [가방] ga-bang	n. handbag 핸드백 [핸드백] haen-deu-baek	n. wallet, purse 지갑 [지갑] ji-gap

The Restroom

- Where is the restroom?
화장실이 어디 있어(요)?
hwa-jang-si-ri eo-di i-sseo(-yo)?

- Nature is calling.
화장실에 다녀올게(요).
hwa-jang-si-re da-nyeo-ol-gge(-yo)

- Someone is in the restroom.
화장실에 누가 있어(요).
hwa-jang-si-re nu-ga i-sseo(-yo)

- Can I use the toilet?
화장실 좀 써도 돼(요)?
hwa-jang-sil jom sseo-do dwae(-yo)?

- I have to go to the bathroom first.
화장실 좀 먼저 가야겠어(요).
hwa-jang-sil jom meon-jeo ga-ya-ge-sseo(-yo)

- The bathroom is right next to my room.
화장실은 내 방 바로 옆에 있어(요).
hwa-jang-si-reun nae bang ba-ro yeo-pe i-sseo(-yo)

Bathroom Manners

- You should flush the toilet.
변기 물을 꼭 내리세요.
byeon-gi mu-reul ggok nae-ri-se-yo

- Please put your toilet paper in the toilet.
화장실 휴지는 변기에 버리세요.
hwa-jang-sil hyu-ji-neun byeon-gi-e beo-ri-se-yo

- Put the sanitary napkin in the trash can.
생리대는 휴지통에 버리세요.
saeng-ri-dae-neun hyu-ji-tong-e beo-ri-se-yo

- Don't make a mess.
어지르지 마(세요).
eo-ji-reu-ji ma(-se-yo)

- Don't spit on the floor.
바닥에 침을 뱉지 마(세요).
ba-da-ge chi-meul baet-jji ma(-se-yo)

- Don't talk on the big white phone.
변기에 토하지 마(세요).
byeon-gi-e to-ha-ji ma(-se-yo)

The Call of Nature

■ I have to go and pee.

소변 보러 가야겠어(요).

so-byeon bo-reo ga-ya-ge-sseo(-yo)

오줌 누러 가야겠어(요).

o-jum nu-reo ga-ya-ge-sseo(-yo)

쉬하러 가야겠어.

swi-ha-reo ga-ya-ge-sseo

■ I have to go poop.

대변을 보고 싶어(요).

dae-byeo-neul bo-go si-peo(-yo)

대변이 마려워(요).

dae-byeo-ni ma-ryeo-wo(-yo)

똥 마려워.

ddong ma-ryeo-wo

Tip: 오줌 [o-jum] and 쉬 [swi] meaning "pee" and 똥 [ddong] "poop," are informal words.

■ I can't hold it any longer!

더 이상 참을 수 없어(요)!

deo i-sang cha-meul ssu eop-sseo(-yo)!

■ I just pooped.

화장실에서 대변을 봤어(요).

hwa-jang-si-re-seo dae-byeo-neul bwa-sseo(-yo)

■ I couldn't poop.

대변을 보지 못했어(요).

dae-byeo-neul bo-ji mo-tae-sseo(-yo)

Bathroom Issues

■ The toilet doesn't flush properly.

변기가 제대로 안 내려가(요).

byeon-gi-ga je-dae-ro an nae-ryeo-ga(-yo)

■ The toilet bowl is clogged.

변기가 막혔어(요).

byeon-gi-ga ma-kyeo-sseo(-yo)

■ The bathroom light doesn't work.

욕실 전등이 고장 났어(요).

yok-ssil jeon-deung-i go-jang na-sseo(-yo)

■ The bathroom light doesn't turn on.

욕실의 전등이 안 켜져(요).

yok-ssi-re jeon-deung-i an kyeo-jeo(-yo)

■ The tap is leaking.

수도꼭지가 새(요).

su-do-ggok-jji-ga sae(-yo)

■ There is no toilet paper in the bathroom.

화장실에 휴지가 없어(요).

hwa-jang-si-re hyu-ji-ga eop-sseo(-yo)

The Living Room

■ After dinner, we all have tea in the living room.

저녁 식사 후, 우리 모두
거실에서 차를 마셔(요).

jeo-nyeok sik-ssa hu, u-ri mo-du
geo-si-re-seo cha-reul ma-syeo(-yo)

■ I wish the living room was more spacious.

거실이 좀 더 넓으면 좋겠어(요).

geo-si-ri jom deo neol-beu-myeon
jo-ke-sseo(-yo)

■ There is no TV in the living room.

거실에 TV가 없어(요).

geo-si-re ti-bi-ga eop-sseo(-yo)

■ The living room is a mess.

거실이 엉망이에요.

geo-si-ri eong-mang-i-e-yo

■ We need to redo the entire living room.

거실 전체를 다시
꾸며야겠어(요).

geo-sil jeon-che-reul da-si
ggu-myeo-ya-ge-sseo(-yo)

Good Dreams & Bad Dreams in Korean Culture

These are some common beliefs about the meaning of dreams in Korean culture.

1. Pigs
Pigs symbolize wealth and good fortune. Therefore, if you dream of a pig coming toward you or of holding a pig in your arms, you may have good luck in the near future. Usually Koreans will buy lottery tickets after having pig dreams.

2. Fire
Fire in reality can be a terrible thing, but if you dream of fire, it might be auspicious. A big fire means you could have great success, like winning a jackpot. However, if you extinguish the fire, your good luck will vanish.

3. Water
Dreaming of clean and clear water is also auspicious, but dreaming about a small expanse of water would not be favorable: it means you should hope for more—an ocean is better than a small stream.

4. Teeth
Losing teeth in a dream is a bad omen, meaning someone close to you (usually a family member or relative) will get ill or die. Top teeth symbolize someone of higher status and bottom teeth symbolize someone of lower status.

The Refrigerator

■ I'll put the leftovers in the fridge.

남은 음식은 냉장고에 있어(요).

na-meun eum-si-geun naeng-jang-go-e
i-sseo(-yo)

■ The refrigerator is open.
Close the door, please.

냉장고 문이 열려 있네(요).
문 좀 닫아 줘(요).

naeng-jang-gomu-niyeol-ryeoin-ne(-yo).
mun jom da-da jwo(-yo)

■ My refrigerator is full of junk
food.

우리 집 냉장고는 가공식품으로
가득해(요).

u-ri jip naeng-jang-go-neun
ga-gong-sik-pu-meu-ro ga-deu-kae(-yo)

■ What's the volume of this
refrigerator?

이 냉장고의 용량은 얼마예요?

i naeng-jang-go-e yong-nyang-eun
eol-ma-ye-yo?

■ The fridge was unplugged so
the ice melted.

냉장고 코드가 빠져 있어서
얼음이 녹았어(요).

naeng-jang-go ko-deu-ga bba-jeo
i-sseo-seo eo-reu-mi no-ga-sseo(-yo)

Preparing Meals

■ I'm in the middle of making
dinner.

저녁 식사를 준비하고 있어(요).

jeo-nyeok sik-ssa-reul jun-bi-ha-go
i-sseo(-yo)

■ What shall we have for dinner?

오늘 저녁에 뭐 먹을까(요)?

o-neul jeo-nyeo-ge mwo
meo-geul-gga(-yo)?

■ It's almost ready. Just a minute.

거의 다 됐어요.
잠시 기다려 주세요.

geo-i da dwae-sseo-yo.
jam-si gi-da-ryeo ju-se-yo

■ Dinner will be ready in about
ten minutes.

10분쯤이면 저녁이
다 준비돼(요).

sip-bbun-jjeu-mi-myeon jeo-nyeo-gi
da jun-bi-dwae(-yo)

■ Will you help me set the table?

식탁 차리는 것을 좀
도와줄래(요)?

sik-tak cha-ri-neun geo-seul jom
do-wa-jul-rae(-yo)?

Cooking

- She cooked it until the water boiled away.

  그녀는 물이 졸아들 때까지 조리했어(요).

  geu-nyeo-neun mu-ri jo-ra-deul ddae-gga-ji jo-ri-hae-sseo(-yo)

- I made your favorite.

  네가 좋아하는 걸 만들었어(요).

  ne-ga jo-a-ha-neun geol man-deu-reo-sseo(-yo)

- I've prepared bulgogi for dinner.

  저녁 식사로 불고기를 준비했어(요).

  jeo-nyeok sik-ssa-ro bul-go-gi-reul jun-bi-hae-sseo(-yo)

- The delicous cooking smell makes my mouth water.

  음식 냄새 때문에 군침이 돌아(요).

  eum-sik naem-sae ddae-mu-ne gun-chi-mi do-ra(-yo)

- How does it taste?

  맛 어때(요)?

  mat eo-ddae(-yo)?

- Help yourself.

  맛있게 드세요.

  ma-dit-gge deu-se-yo

Recipes

- Would you mind sharing the recipe?

  이 요리 어떻게 만들었는지 알려 줄 수 있어(요)?

  i yo-ri eo-ddeo-ke man-deu-reon-neun-ji al-ryeo jul ssu i-sseo(-yo)?

- I just use my mom's old recipe.

  엄마가 쓰던 요리법대로 했을 뿐이에요.

  eom-ma-ga sseu-deon yo-ri-bbeop-ddae-ro hae-sseul bbu-ni-e-yo

- Just follow the steps in this recipe.

  이 요리법대로 따라 하세요.

  i yo-ri-bboep-ddae-ro dda-ra ha-se-yo

- Can I borrow that japchae recipe?

  잡채 레시피 좀 알려 줄래(요)?

  jap-chae re-si-pi jom al-ryeo jul-rae(-yo)?

  Tip: 잡채 [jap-chae] is a Korean dish made by mixing sweet potato noodles with thin slices of stir-fried vegetables and meat.

- What do you think of my new recipe?

  내 새로운 레시피 어때(요)?

  nae sae-ro-un re-si-pi eo-ddae(-yo)?

Doing the Dishes

■ Put your dishes in the sink.
그릇을 개수대에 넣어 주세요.
geu-reu-seul gae-su-dae-e neo-eo ju-se-yo

■ Could you clear the table and load the dishwasher?
식탁을 다 치우고 그릇을 식기세척기에 넣어 줄래(요)?
sik-ta-geul da chi-u-go geu-reu-seul sik-ggi-se-cheok-ggi-e neo-eo jul-rae(-yo)?

■ I'll do the dishes.
내가 설거지 할게(요).
nae-ga seol-geo-ji hal-gge(-yo)

■ He said he'd help me do the dishes.
그는 설거지를 도와준다고 (말)했어(요).
geu-neun seol-geo-ji-reul do-wa-jun-da-go (mal-)hae-sseo(-yo)

■ I'll do the dishes since you cooked dinner.
당신이 저녁을 했으니, 설거지는 제가 할게요.
dang-si-ni jeo-nyeo-geul hae-sseu-ni, seol-geo-ji-neun je-ga hal-gge-yo

Kitchenware

■ The kitchen in this apartment is fully equipped.
이 아파트의 부엌은 모든 설비가 잘 갖춰져 있어(요).
i a-pa-teu-e bu-eo-keun mo-deun seol-bi-ga jal ga-chwo-jeo i-sseo(-yo)

■ The pans are arranged neatly in the cupboard.
그 냄비들은 찬장에 가지런히 있어(요).
geu naem-bi-deu-reun chan-jjang-e ga-ji-reon-hi i-sseo(-yo)

■ Your kitchen is so organized!
부엌이 잘 정리되어 있군(요)!
bu-eo-ki jal jeong-ri-doe-eo it-ggun(-yo)!

■ You should handle those bowls with care.
이 식기들을 주의해 주세요.
i sik-ggi-deu-reul ju-i-hae ju-se-yo

■ The longer you use a frying pan, the better it becomes for cooking.
프라이팬은 오래 쓸수록 길들여져서 쓰기 좋아(요).
peu-ra-i-pae-neun o-rae sseul-ssu-rok gil-deu-ryeo-jeo-seo sseu-gi jo-a(-yo)

Ranges

- A microwave is a necessity in modern life.

전자레인지는 현대 생활의
필수품이죠.

jeon-ja-re-in-ji-neun hyeon-dae
saeng-hwa-re pil-ssu-pu-mi-jyo

- A microwave can reduce cooking time.

전자레인지는 조리 시간을
줄여 줘(요).

jeon-ja-re-in-ji-neun jo-ri si-ga-neul
ju-ryeo jwo(-yo)

- You shouldn't put metal in the microwave.

전자레인지는 금속을 넣으면
안 돼요.

jeon-ja-re-in-ji-neun geum-so-geul
neo-eu-myeon an dwae-yo

- One of those burners doesn't work.

가스레인지 중 하나가 작동을
안 해(요).

ga-seu-re-in-ji jung ha-na-ga jak-ddong-
eul an hae(-yo)

- That stove has a gas leak.

가스레인지에서 가스가 새(요).

ga-seu-re-in-ji-e-seo ga-seu-ga sae(-yo)

Bulgogi Recipe

How to make **bulgogi** (불고기),
Korean beef barbecue:

- **Ingredients** (4 servings)
1 lb (450 g) flank steak
5 tablespoons soy sauce
2½ tablespoons white sugar
1 tablespoon chopped scallion
2 tablespoons minced garlic
2 tablespoons sesame seeds
2 tablespoons sesame oil
½ teaspoon ground black pepper
optional : onions, carrot or peppers

- **Directions**
① Place the beef in a shallow dish.
Combine all the other ingredients in
a small bowl. Pour over beef.

② Cover and refrigerate for at least
1 hour or overnight.

③ Preheat an outdoor grill for high
heat, and lightly oil the cooking
surface.

④ When the grill is hot, quickly
cook the beef until slightly charred
and cooked through, 1 to 2 minutes
per side.

Table Manners

■ I enjoyed the meal.
잘 먹었어(요).
jal meo-geo-sseo(-yo)
잘 먹었습니다.
jal meo-geot-sseum-ni-da

■ Wash your hands before the meal.
밥 먹기 전에 손을 씻어라.
bap meok-ggi jeo-ne so-neul ssi-seo-ra

■ Don't talk with your mouth full.
입에 밥이 있을 때 말하지
마(세요).
i-be ba-bi i-sseul ddae mal-ha-ji
ma(-se-yo)

■ You should clean your plate.
밥을 남기지 마(세요).
ba-beul nam-gi-ji ma(-se-yo)

■ Don't put your elbows on the table.
팔꿈치를 식탁 위에 올려놓지
마(세요).
pal-ggum-chi-reul sik-tak wi-e
ol-ryeo-no-chi ma(-se-yo)

■ Put the phone away at the table.
식탁에서 휴대폰을 치워라.
sik-ta-ge-seo hyu-dae-po-neul chi-wo-ra

Personal Hygiene

■ Be extra careful about personal hygiene.
특히 개인 위생에 신경 쓰세요.
teu-ki gae-in wi-saeng-e sin-gyeong
sseu-se-yo

■ She always washes her hands when she gets home.
그녀는 집에 돌아오면 항상 손을
먼저 씻어(요).
geu-nyeo-neun ji-be do-ra-o-myeon
hang-sang so-neul meon-jeo ssi-seo(-yo)

■ Wash your hands to prevent the spread of germs.
세균이 퍼지지 않도록 손을
씻어라.
se-gyu-ni peo-ji-ji an-to-rok so-neul
ssi-seo-ra

■ They have no sense of hygiene.
그들은 위생 관념이 없어(요).
geu-deu-reun wi-saeng gwan-nyeo-mi
eop-sseo(-yo)

■ She's obsessed with neatness.
그녀는 결벽증이 있어(요).
geu-nyeo-neun gyeol-byeok-jjeung-i
i-sseo(-yo)

Cleaning 1

■ I have to vacuum.

(진공)청소기로 청소해야 해(요).

(jin-gong-)cheong-so-gi-ro
cheong-so-hae-ya hae(-yo)

■ Can you dust the shelves?

선반의 먼지 좀 털어 줄래(요)?

seon-ba-ne meon-ji jom teo-reo
jul-rae(-yo)?

■ I clean my room everyday.

매일 방 청소를 해(요).

mae-il bang cheong-so-reul hae(-yo)

■ You are responsible for sweeping.

청소는 원래 네 일이잖아(요).

cheong-so-neun won-rae ne
i-ri-ja-na(-yo)

■ Your room is so messy. Tidy it up!

방이 어질러졌구나. 정리 좀 하자!

bang-i eo-jil-reo-jeot-ggu-na. jeong-ri
jom ha-ja!

■ Clean every nook and corner.

구석구석 깨끗이 청소해라.

gu-seok-ggu-seok ggae-ggeu-si
cheong-so-hae-ra

■ Start cleaning here.

여기부터 청소합시다.

yeo-gi-bu-teo cheong-so-hap-ssi-da

Cleaning 2

■ We all cleaned the house together.

우리는 함께 대청소를 했어(요).

u-ri-neun ham-gge dae-cheong-so-reul
hae-sseo(-yo)

■ I clean the house from top to bottom once a month.

매달 한 번 대청소를 해(요).

mae-dal han beon dae-cheong-so-reul
hae(-yo)

■ Please help me clean.

청소하는 걸 도와주세요.

cheong-so-ha-neun geol do-wa-ju-se-yo

■ Since I swept the floor, would you mop it?

내가 바닥을 청소했으니,
네가 걸레질 할래(요)?

nae-ga ba-da-geul cheong-so-hae-sseu-
ni, ne-ga geol-re-jil hal-rae(-yo)?

■ I want my house to be clean without cleaning it.

청소하지 않아도 집이 깨끗하면
좋겠어(요).

cheong-so-ha-ji a-na-do ji-bi
ggae-ggeu-ta-myeon jo-ke-sseo(-yo)

Trash & Recycling

■ Why didn't you put out the trash?

왜 쓰레기를 안 버렸어(요)?

wae sseu-re-gi-reul an
beo-ryeo-sseo(-yo)?

■ Would you take out the garbage?

쓰레기 좀 버려 줄래(요)?

sseu-re-gi jom beo-ryeo jul-rae(-yo)?

■ Did you put out the garbage last
night?

어젯밤에 쓰레기 내다 놨어(요)?

eo-jet-bba-me sseu-re-gi nae-da
nwa-sseo(-yo)?

■ You should separate the
garbage before disposing of it.

쓰레기는 분류해서 버려야
해(요).

sseu-re-gi-neun bul-ryu-hae-seo beo-
ryeo-ya hae(-yo)

■ When is garbage day?

쓰레기 수거일은 언제예요?

sseu-re-gi su-geo-i-reun eon-je-ye-yo?

■ Where should I put the
recyclables?

재활용 쓰레기는 어디에 버려야
해(요)?

jae-hwa-ryong sseu-re-gi-neun eo-di-e
beo-ryeo-ya hae(-yo)?

Doing the Laundry 1

■ I need to do my laundry today.

오늘 빨래해야 해(요).

o-neul bbal-rae-hae-ya hae(-yo)

■ I'll run the washing machine.

세탁기를 돌려야겠어(요).

se-tak-ggi-reul dol-ryeo-ya-ge-sseo(-yo)

■ Put the laundry into the washing
machine.

빨래를 세탁기에 넣어라.

bbal-rae-reul se-tak-ggi-e neo-eo-ra

■ How much detergent do I need?

세제를 얼마나 넣어(요)?

se-je-reul eol-ma-na neo-eo(-yo)?

■ Don't mix whites and colors.

하얀 옷하고 색깔 옷을 섞지
마(세요).

ha-yan o-ta-go saek-ggal o-seul seok-jji
ma(-se-yo)

■ This sweater can't be washed in
hot water.

이 스웨터는 뜨거운 물에 빨 수
없어(요).

i seu-we-teo-neun ddeu-geo-un mu-re
bbal ssu eop-sseo(-yo)

Doing the Laundry 2

- When it's sunny, the laundry dries in no time.

  날씨가 좋으면, 빨래가 빨리 말라(요).

  nal-ssi-ga jo-eu-myeon, bbal-rae-ga bbal-ri mal-ra(-yo)

- Did you hang the laundry out to dry?

  옷을 잘 널었어(요)?

  o-seul jal neo-reo-sseo(-yo)?

- I forgot to put the clothes out to dry.

  옷 너는 걸 잊어버렸어(요).

  ot neo-neun geol i-jeo-beo-ryeo-sseo(-yo)

- Please help me fold up the clothes.

  옷 개는 거 좀 도와줄래(요)?

  ot gae-neun geo jom do-wa-jul-rae(-yo)?

- Will you iron the shirts?

  셔츠 다려 줄래(요)?

  syeo-cheu da-ryeo jul-rae(-yo)?

Interior Design

- I like furnishing houses.

  집 꾸미는 걸 좋아해(요).

  jip ggu-mi-neun geol jo-a-hae(-yo)

- I'm interested in architecture and furniture design.

  인테리어와 가구 디자인에 관심이 많아(요).

  in-te-ri-eo-wa ga-gu-di-ja-i-ne gwan-si-mi ma-na(-yo)

- I don't like the interior design of my new house.

  새 집 인테리어가 마음에 안 들어(요).

  sae jip in-te-ri-eo-ga ma-eu-me an deu-reo(-yo)

- The new curtains don't match the color of the walls.

  새 커튼은 벽 색깔과 어울리지 않아(요).

  sae keo-teu-neun byeok saek-ggal-gwa eo-ul-ri-ji a-na(-yo)

- The living-room interior's a bit old-fashioned.

  거실의 인테리어가 좀 구식이에요.

  geo-si-re in-te-ri-eo-ga jom gu-si-gi-e-yo

Driving 1

■ I got my driver's license last week.
지난주에 운전면허를 땄어(요).
ji-nan-ju-e un-jeon-myeon-heo-reul
dda-sseo(-yo)

■ I can't drive very well.
운전을 잘 못해(요).
un-jeo-neul jal mo-tae(-yo)

■ My driver's license expires next month.
내 운전면허증은 다음 달이 만기예요.
nae un-jeon-myeon-heo-jjeung-eun
da-eum da-ri man-gi-ye-yo

■ I recently renewed my driver's license.
최근에 운전면허증을 갱신했어(요).
choe-geu-ne un-jeon-myeon-heo-jjeung-eul gaeng-sin-hae-sseo(-yo)

■ He had his license revoked for drunk driving.
그는 음주운전 사고로 운전면허가 취소됐어(요).
geu-neun eum-ju-un-jeon sa-go-ro
un-jeon-myeon-heo-ga
chwi-so-dwae-sseo(-yo)

Driving 2

■ You're driving too fast. Slow down!
너무 빨라(요). 속도를 줄여(요)!
neo-mu bbal-ra(-yo). sok-ddo-reul
ju-ryeo(-yo)!

■ Watch out! That's a red light!
조심해요! 빨간 불이에요!
jo-sim-hae-yo! bbal-gan bu-ri-e-yo!

■ Fasten your seat belt.
안전벨트를 매(세요).
an-jeon-bel-teu-reul mae(-se-yo)

■ Go straight and turn right at the lights.
직진한 다음 신호등에서 우회전해(요).
jik-jjin-han da-eum sin-ho-deung-e-seo
u-hoe-jeon-hae(-yo)

■ Do you mind if I drive?
내가 교대로 운전해 줄까(요)?
nae-ga gyo-dae-ro un-jeon-hae
jul-gga(-yo)?

■ Are you sure this is the right road?
이 길로 가는 게 맞아(요)?
i gil-ro ga-neun ge ma-ja(-yo)?

■ He knows a lot about cars.
그는 차에 대해 많이 알아(요).
geu-neun cha-e dae-hae ma-ni a-ra(-yo)

Parking

- **Where is the parking lot?**
  주차장이 어디예요?
  ju-cha-jang-i eo-di-ye-yo?

- **Can I park here?**
  여기에 주차해도 돼요?
  yeo-gi-e ju-cha-hae-do dwae-yo?

- **There is a parking lot behind the building.**
  이 건물 뒤에 주차장이 있어(요).
  i geon-mul dwi-e ju-cha-jang-i i-sseo(-yo)

- **There is no space to park here.**
  여기에 자리가 없어(요).
  yeo-gi-e ja-ri-ga eop-sseo(-yo)

- **How much is it per hour for parking?**
  시간당 주차비가 얼마예요?
  si-gan-dang ju-cha-bi-ga eol-ma-ye-yo?

- **Is parking free?**
  무료 주차예요?
  mu-ryo ju-cha-ye-yo?

- **No parking.**
  주차 금지.
  ju-cha geum-ji

Taking the Subway in Korea

Subways in Korea offer convenient transportation. They operate in five major cities: Seoul (서울), Busan (부산), Daegu (대구), Gwangju (광주) and Daejeon (대전).

Seoul's subway system covers a large area. There are nine main lines along with additional ones that service places such as Incheon Airport (인천 공항 [in-cheon gong-hang]). Each subway line has a designated color for ease of use.

To ride the subway, you should buy a transportation card or ticket. You can buy a Single Journey Ticket at the ticket vending machines and a rechargeable card at convenience stores. The subway fare varies according to the total distance.

How to buy a ticket at the ticket vending machine:

1. Select "ENG" for the English menu and choose the button "buy a Single Journey Ticket."
2. Select your destination.
3. Select the number of tickets.
4. Put in the money.

Traffic

■ I got caught in traffic.
길이 심하게 막혀(요).
gi-ri sim-ha-ge ma-kyeo(-yo)

■ The traffic is really bad today.
오늘 교통은 심하게 막혀(요).
o-neul gyo-tong-eun sim-ha-ge
ma-kyeo(-yo)

■ What's the holdup ahead?
앞에 차가 왜 막히지(요)?
a-pe cha-ga wae ma-ki-ji(-yo)?

■ There must have been an
accident up ahead.
앞에서 교통사고가 난 것
같은데(요).
a-pe-seo gyo-tong-sa-go-ga nan geot
ga-teun-de(-yo)

■ The traffic on this street is
always heavy.
이 길은 항상 막혀(요).
i gi-reun hang-sang ma-kyeo(-yo)

■ I hate rush hour.
러시아워는 너무 싫어(요).
reo-si-a-wo-neun neo-mu si-reo(-yo)

Traffic Offenses 1

■ Pull over to the right.
오른쪽으로 차를 세워 주세요.
o-reun-jjo-geu-ro cha-reul se-wo
ju-se-yo

■ May I see your driver's license?
운전면허증을 좀 보여 주세요.
un-jeon-myeon-heo-jjeung-eul jom
bo-yeo ju-se-yo

■ Step out of the car, please.
차에서 내리세요.
cha-e-seo nae-ri-se-yo

■ Please blow into this
breathalyzer.
음주측정기를 불어 주세요.
eum-ju-cheuk-jjeong-gi-reul bu-reo
ju-se-yo

■ You were driving over the
speed limit.
제한 속도를 위반하셨어요.
je-han sok-ddo-reul
wi-ban-ha-syeo-sseo-yo

■ You didn't stop for the red light.
정지 신호에서 멈추지
않았어(요).
jeong-ji sin-ho-e-seo meom-chu-ji
a-na-sseo(-yo)

Traffic Offenses 2

- Have you ever been stopped for speeding?
속도위반으로 걸린 적 있어(요)?
sok-ddo-wi-ba-neu-ro geol-rin jeok i-sseo(-yo)?

- How much is the fine?
벌금은 얼마예요?
beol-geu-meun eol-ma-ye-yo?

- I got a parking ticket.
주차위반 딱지를 받았어(요).
ju-cha-wi-ban ddak-jji-reul ba-da-sseo(-yo)

- You shouldn't jaywalk.
무단횡단을 하면 안 됩니다.
mu-dan-hoeng-da-neul ha-myeon an doem-ni-da

- This lane is for left turns only.
이 차선은 좌회전 전용입니다.
i cha-seo-neun jwa-hoe-jeon jeo-nyong-im-ni-da

- This is a one-way street.
여기는 일방통행입니다.
yeo-gi-neun il-bang-tong-haeng-im-ni-da

House Hunting 1

- I'm looking for a new house.
새 집을 찾고 있어(요).
sae ji-beul chat-ggo i-sseo(-yo)

- Could you recommend some places?
추천해 줄 곳이 있어(요)?
chu-cheon-hae jul go-si i-sseo(-yo)?

- How big a place are you looking for?
얼마나 큰 집을 찾으세요?
eol-ma-na keun ji-beul cha-jeu-se-yo?

- Do you have something close to a subway station?
지하철역에서 좀 가까운 집이 있어(요)?
ji-ha-cheol-ryeo-ge-seo jom ga-gga-un ji-bi i-sseo(-yo)?

- How many rooms does this apartment have?
이 아파트는 방이 몇 개예요?
i a-pa-teu-neun bang-i myeot gae-ye-yo?

- I'd like a two-bedroom apartment.
방 두 개짜리 아파트를 원해(요).
bang du gae-jja-ri a-pa-teu-reul won-hae(-yo)

House Hunting 2

- What's the public transportation like?

  대중교통은 어때(요)?

  dae-jung-gyo-tong-eun eo-ddae(-yo)?

- It's just ten minutes' walk from the subway.

  지하철역까지 걸어서 10분밖에 안 걸려(요).

  ji-ha-cheol-ryeok-gga-ji geo-reo-seo sip-bbun-ba-gge an geol-ryeo(-yo)

- What floor is it on?

  집이 몇 층이에요?

  ji-bi myeot cheung-i-e-yo?

- How much is the rent?

  방세가 얼마예요?

  bang-sse-ga eol-ma-ye-yo?

- The rental fee is sky-high in my area.

  우리 동네는 집세가 아주 비싸(요).

  u-ri dong-ne-neun jip-sse-ga a-ju bi-ssa(-yo)

- How long is the lease?

  임대 기간은 언제까지예요?

  im-dae gi-ga-neun eon-je-gga-ji-ye-yo?

Housing Contracts

- I want to sign the lease.

  계약하겠어요.

  gye-ya-ka-ge-sseo-yo

- When is the landlord coming?

  집주인이 언제 오세요?

  jip-jju-i-ni eon-je o-se-yo?

- Your rent is due on the 1st of each month.

  월세는 매월 1일에 냅니다.

  wol-sse-neun mae-wol i-ri-re naem-ni-da

- It's 500,000 won a month. Utilities are included.

  임대료는 한 달에 50만 원입니다. 공과금 포함입니다.

  im-dae-ryo-neun han da-re o-sim-man wo-nim-ni-da. gong-gwa-geum po-ha-mim-ni-da

- You'll have to pay six months' rent in advance.

  6개월치 집세를 선불로 내야 합니다.

  yuk-ggae-wol-chi jip-sse-reul seon-bul-ro nae-ya ham-ni-da

- When can I move in?

  제가 언제 입주할 수 있어요?

  je-ga eon-je ip-jju-hal ssu i-sseo-yo?

Packing

■ Are you all packed?
이삿짐을 다 정리했어(요)?
i-sat-jji-meul da jeong-ri-hae-sseo(-yo)?

■ I have to pack everything before moving.
이사 전에 짐을 다 싸야 해(요).
i-sa jeo-ne ji-meul da ssa-ya hae(-yo)

■ We usually rent a moving van.
우리는 보통 이삿짐차를 빌려(요).
u-ri-neun bo-tong i-sat-jjim-cha-reul bil-ryeo(-yo)

■ If you need any help moving, let me know.
이사할 때 도움이 필요하면, 언제든지 말해(요).
i-sa-hal ddae do-u-mi pi-ryo-ha-myeon, eon-je-deun-ji mal-hae(-yo)

■ We often move using full packing services.
보통 포장이사로 이사해(요).
bo-tong po-jang-i-sa-ro i-sa-hae(-yo)

■ Do you know any reliable moving companies?
믿을 만한 이삿짐센터 알고 있어(요)?
mi-deul man-han i-sat-jjim-sen-teo al-go i-sseo(-yo)?

Moving 1

■ I'm worried about the expense of moving.
이사 비용이 골치 아파(요).
i-sa bi-yong-i gol-chi a-pa(-yo)

■ I will sell some of my belongings before I move out.
이사 가기 전에 물건들을 팔아야겠어(요).
i-sa ga-gi jeo-ne mul-geon-deu-reul pa-ra-ya-ge-sseo(-yo)

■ I hear you're moving soon.
곧 이사 간다면서(요).
got i-sa gan-da-myeon-seo(-yo)

■ My family is planning to move house in a month.
우리 가족은 한 달 후 이사할 계획이에요.
u-ri ga-jo-geun han dal hu i-sa-hal gye-hoe-gi-e-yo

■ My studio is too small. I'm moving to a two-bedroom apartment.
내 원룸은 너무 작아요. 방 두 개짜리 아파트로 이사할 거예요.
nae won-ru-meun neo-mu ja-ga-yo.
bang du gae-jja-ri a-pa-teu-ro i-sa-hal ggeo-ye-yo

Moving 2

- Can you give me a hand with organizing my things?

  짐 정리하는 것을 도와줄 수 있어(요)?

  jim jeong-ri-ha-neun geo-seul do-wa-jul ssu i-sseo(-yo)?

- When will they turn on the gas?

  언제 가스가 되나요?

  eon-je ga-seu-ga doe-na-yo?

- Are pets allowed?

  반려동물 키울 수 있나요?

  bal-ryeo-dong-mul ki-ul ssu in-na-yo?

- Is Wi-Fi included?

  와이파이가 포함되어 있나요?

  wa-i-pa-i-ga po-ham-doe-eo in-na-yo?

- Can you tell me where the nearest supermarket is?

  집에서 가장 가까운 슈퍼마켓은 어디예요?

  ji-be-seo ga-jang ga-gga-un syu-peo-ma-ke-seun eo-di-ye-yo?

- Is this a safe neigborhood?

  여기는 안전한 동네인가요?

  yeo-gi-neun an-jeon-han dong-ne-in-ga-yo?

Housewarming

- Let me invite you to my new home this weekend.

  이번 주말에 우리 새 집에 초대할게(요).

  i-beon ju-ma-re u-ri sae ji-be cho-dae-hal-gge(-yo)

- When is the housewarming party?

  언제 집들이 해(요)?

  eon-je jip-ddeu-ri hae(-yo)?

- What should I bring to a housewarming party?

  집들이에 뭘 가져가야 하지(요)?

  jip-ddeu-ri-e mwol ga-jeo-ga-ya ha-ji(-yo)?

  Tip: For housewarming party presents, offer tissues or detergent. They signify good luck in a new home.

- They will have a housewarming party tomorrow.

  내일 그들은 집들이를 해(요).

  nae-il geu-deu-reun jip-ddeu-ri-reul hae(-yo)

- I was invited to their housewarming party.

  그의 집들이 초대를 받았어(요).

  geu-e jip-ddeu-ri cho-dae-reul ba-da-sseo(-yo)

Chapter 3

The Stuff of Life

Weather & Seasons 날씨 & 계절 nal-ssi & gye-jeol

n. weather 날씨 [날씨] nal-ssi 	n. sun 해 [해] hae = 태양 [태양] tae-yang	n. sky 하늘 [하늘] ha-neul
	n. cloud 구름 [구름] gu-reum	n. wind 바람 [바람] ba-ram
	n. rain 비 [비] bi	n. shower 소나기 [소나기] so-na-gi
	n. snow 눈 [눈ː] nun	n. typhoon 태풍 [태풍] tae-pung
n. temperature 온도 [온도] on-do = 기온 [기온] gi-on	adj. cool 시원하다 [시원하다] si-won-ha-da	adj. cold 춥다 [춥따] chup-dda
	adj. hot 덥다 [덥ː따] deop-dda	adj. warm 따뜻하다 [따뜨타다] dda-ddeu-ta-da
n. season 계절 [계ː절/게ː절] gye-jeol/ge-jeol	n. spring 봄 [봄] bom	n. summer 여름 [여름] yeo-reum
	n. fall, autumn 가을 [가을] ga-eul	n. winter 겨울 [겨울] gyeo-ul

Asking about the Weather

- How's the weather today?

  오늘 날씨 어때(요)?

  o-neul nal-ssi eo-ddae(-yo)?

- What's the weather like there?

  그곳 날씨 어때(요)?

  geu-got nal-ssi eo-ddae(-yo)?

- How's the weather out there?

  밖의 날씨 어때(요)?

  ba-gge nal-ssi eo-ddae(-yo)?

- What will the temperature be tomorrow?

  내일 몇 도예요?

  nae-il myeot do-ye-yo?

- Do you like this kind of weather?

  이런 날씨 좋아해(요)?

  i-reon nal-ssi jo-a-hae(-yo)?

- Do you think the weather will hold?

  이런 날씨가 계속 될까(요)?

  i-reon nal-ssi-ga gye-sok doel-gga(-yo)?

Forecasts

- What's the weather forecast for today?

  오늘 일기예보에서 뭐래(요)?

  o-neul il-gi-ye-bo-e-seo mwo-rae(-yo)?

- Do you know the weather report for tomorrow?

  내일 일기예보 알아(요)?

  nae-il il-gi-ye-bo a-ra(-yo)?

- What's the weather forecast for the weekend?

  주말 일기예보에서 뭐래(요)?

  ju-mal il-gi-ye-bo-e-seo mwo-rae(-yo)?

- Check the weather report!

  일기예보 좀 봐(요)!

  il-gi-ye-bo jom bwa(-yo)!

- The weather forecast was wrong again.

  일기예보는 또 틀렸어(요).

  il-gi-ye-bo-neun ddo teul-ryeo-sseo(-yo)

- Weather forecasts aren't reliable.

  일기예보는 믿을 수 없어(요).

  il-gi-ye-bo-neun mi-deul ssu eop-sseo(-yo)

Sunny Days

■ It's a fine day today, isn't it?
오늘 날씨가 참 좋죠?
o-neul nal-ssi-ga cham jo-chyo?

■ It's really bright today.
정말 화창한 날씨예요.
jeong-mal hwa-chang-han nal-ssi-ye-yo

■ The sky is so clear.
하늘이 참 맑아(요).
ha-neu-ri cham mal-ga(-yo)

■ We've been having lovely weather lately.
요즘 날씨가 계속 괜찮네(요).
yo-jeum nal-ssi-ga gye-sok gwaen-chan-ne(-yo)

■ I hope this weather will last.
이런 날씨가 계속되면 좋겠어(요).
i-reon nal-ssi-ga gye-sok-ddoe-myeon jo-ke-sseo(-yo)

■ I hope it will be fine tomorrow.
내일 맑아야 할 텐데(요).
nae-il mal-ga-ya hal ten-de(-yo)

Cloudy Days

■ There are lots of clouds in the sky.
하늘에 구름이 많아(요).
ha-neu-re gu-reu-mi ma-na(-yo)

■ It's cloudy.
날씨가 흐려(요).
nal-ssi-ga heu-ryeo(-yo)

■ It's dull and gloomy.
날씨가 우중충해(요).
nal-ssi-ga u-jung-chung-hae(-yo)

■ The sky has become very dark.
날이 어두워졌어(요).
na-ri eo-du-wo-jeo-sseo(-yo)

■ It became cloudy suddenly.
갑자기 날씨가 흐려졌어(요).
gap-jja-gi nal-ssi-ga heu-ryeo-jeo-sseo(-yo)

■ Where did those clouds come from?
저 구름은 어디에서 왔어(요)?
jeo gu-reu-meun eo-di-e-seo wa-sseo(-yo)?

■ It was cloudy all day.
하루 종일 흐린 날이에요.
ha-ru jong-il heu-rin na-ri-e-yo

Rainy Days

- It's raining.

  비가 와(요).

  bi-ga wa(-yo)

  비가 내려(요).

  bi-ga nae-ryeo(-yo)

- It's sprinkling.

  비가 보슬보슬 내리네(요).

  bi-ga bo-seul-bo-seul nae-ri-ne(-yo)

  비가 부슬부슬 내리네(요).

  bi-ga bu-seul-bu-seul nae-ri-ne(-yo)

- Has the rain stopped yet?

  비가 그쳤어(요)?

  bi-ga geu-cheo-sseo(-yo)?

- It looks like it's going to rain.

  곧 비가 올 것 같아(요).

  got bi-ga ol ggeot ga-ta(-yo)

- It was raining on and off.

  비가 오락가락하는데(요).

  bi-ga o-rak-gga-ra-ka-neun-de(-yo)

- Since it looks like rain, take your umbrella!

  비가 올 것 같으니까, 우산 가져가(요)!

  bi-ga ol ggeot ga-teu-ni-gga, u-san ga-jeo-ga(-yo)!

Hanok, Traditional Korean Houses

Hanok (한옥) is the word for a traditional Korean house. There are two types, one tile-roofed and luxurious for the noble class and the other thatch-roofed and simple for commoners.

One of the benefits of hanok accommodation is the unique sub-floor heating system known as ondol (온돌). Another benefit is that they are environmentally friendly. The materials needed to build a hanok house are entirely chemical-free. The pillars, rafters, doors, windows and floor are wooden while the paper used to cover the doors and window frames are made from tree pulp. As the building materials used are all natural, hanok houses have excellent breathability, perfect for escaping the summer heat.

There are several hanok villages in Korea that you can experience for yourself, including Jeonju Hanok Village (전주 한옥 마을 [jeon-ju ha-nok ma-eul]), Andong Hahoe Folk Village (안동 하회 마을 [an-dong ha-hoe ma-eul]), Bukchon Hanok Village (북촌 한옥 마을 [buk-chon ha-nok ma-eul]), Namsangol Hanok Village (남산골 한옥 마을 [nam-san-gol ha-nok ma-eul]) and Naganeupseong Folk Village (낙안읍성 민속 마을 [na-ga-neup-sseong min-sok ma-eul]).

Thunder & Lightning

■ It's thundering.
천둥이 쳐(요).
cheon-dung-i cheo(-yo)

■ I saw a flash of lightning.
번개 치는 걸 봤어(요).
beon-gae chi-neun geol bwa-sseo(-yo)

■ What a clap of thunder!
천둥이 심하게 쳐(요).
cheon-dung-i sim-ha-ge cheo(-yo)

■ Did you hear the thunder last
night?
간밤에 천둥 치는 거 들었어(요)?
gan-ba-me cheon-dung chi-neun geo
deu-reo-sseo(-yo)?

■ The sudden clap of thunder
made me jump.
갑자기 천둥이 쳐서
움칫했어(요).
gap-jja-gi cheon-dung-i cheo-seo
um-chi-tae-sseo(-yo)

■ During the night, there was a
loud thunderstorm.
밤새 요란한 천둥을 동반한
큰 비가 내렸어(요).
bam-sae yo-ran-han cheon-dung-eul
dong-ban-han keun bi-ga nae-ryeo-
sseo(-yo)

Spring

■ It's getting warmer.
날씨가 따뜻해졌어(요).
nal-ssi-ga dda-ddeu-tae-jeo-sseo(-yo)

■ Winter has changed to spring.
겨울이 가고 봄이 와(요).
gyeo-u-ri ga-go bo-mi wa(-yo)

■ I feel spring is in the air.
봄 기운이 느껴져(요).
bom gi-u-ni neu-ggyeo-jeo(-yo)

■ How long does spring usually
last?
봄은 보통 얼마나 되지(요)?
bo-meun bo-tong eol-ma-na doe-ji(-yo)?

■ The weather is very changeable
in the spring.
봄에는 날씨 변화가 많아(요).
bo-me-neun nal-ssi byeon-hwa-ga
ma-na(-yo)

■ Spring is my favorite season.
봄은 내가 좋아하는 계절이에요.
bo-meun nae-ga jo-a-ha-neun
gye-jeo-ri-e-yo

Yellow & Fine Dusts

- The dust-storm season has come back.
  황사의 계절이 돌아왔어(요).
  hwang-sa-e gye-jeo-ri do-ra-wa-sseo(-yo)

- The sky's really yellow. Let's stay inside.
  하늘이 정말 노랗구나. 안에 있자.
  ha-neu-ri jeong-mal no-ra-ku-na. a-ne it-jja

- Breathing fine dust is very harmful for your health.
  미세먼지를 마시면 건강에 매우 해로워(요).
  mi-se-meon-ji-reul ma-si-myeon geon-gang-e mae-u hae-ro-wo(-yo)

- To protect yourself from the dust, wear a mask.
  미세먼지로부터 보호하려면, 마스크를 써야 해(요).
  mi-se-meon-ji-ro-bu-teo bo-ho-ha-ryeo-myeon, ma-seu-keu-reul sseo-ya hae(-yo)

- The fine dust has been getting worse recently.
  요즘 미세먼지는 갈수록 심해져(요).
  yo-jeum mi-se-meon-ji-neun gal-ssu-rok sim-hae-jeo(-yo)

Summer

- It's terribly hot.
  날씨가 정말 더워(요).
  nal-ssi-ga jeong-mal deo-wo(-yo)

- What a scorcher!
  푹푹 찌네(요)!
  puk-puk jji-ne(-yo)!

- It's getting warmer.
  점점 더워져(요).
  jeom-jeom deo-wo-jeo(-yo)

- It is hot in here.
  여기는 너무 더워(요).
  yeo-gi-neun neo-mu deo-wo(-yo)

- It's really humid today.
  오늘 정말 후덥지근하네(요).
  o-neul jeong-mal hu-deop-jji-geun-ha-ne(-yo)

- Today is the hottest day this summer.
  오늘은 이번 여름 중 가장 더운 날이에요.
  o-neu-reun i-beon yeo-reum jung ga-jang deo-un na-ri-e-yo

The Rainy Season

■ The rainy season is here.
장마철에 들어섰어(요).
jang-ma-cheo-re deu-reo-seo-sseo(-yo)

■ How long does the rainy
season last?
장마철이 얼마나 길어(요)?
jang-ma-cheo-ri eol-ma-na gi-reo(-yo)?

■ The rainy season is over.
장마가 끝났어(요).
jang-ma-ga ggeun-na-sseo(-yo)

■ Because of the rainy season, it's
very humid.
장마철이라서, 매우 습해(요).
jang-ma-cheo-ri-ra-seo, mae-u
seu-pae(-yo)

■ An umbrella is a must in the
rainy season.
장마철에는 우산이
필수품이에요.
jang-ma-cheo-re-neun u-sa-ni
pil-ssu-pu-mi-e-yo

■ After the monsoon it will get
very hot.
장마가 끝나고 아주 더워질
거예요.
jang-ma-ga ggeun-na-go a-ju deo-wo-jil
ggeo-ye-yo

Typhoons

■ A typhoon is coming.
태풍이 오고 있어(요).
tae-pung-i o-go i-sseo(-yo)

■ A storm warning is out today.
오늘 태풍 경보가 있어(요).
o-neul tae-pung gyeong-bo-ga
i-sseo(-yo)

■ It's stormy.
폭풍우가 왔어(요).
pok-pung-u-ga wa-sseo(-yo)

■ The wind is getting stronger.
바람이 점점 세져(요).
ba-ra-mi jeom-jeom se-jeo(-yo)

■ The typhoon hit the eastern
coast.
태풍이 동해안에 상륙했습니다.
tae-pung-i dong-hae-a-ne
sang-ryu-kaet-sseum-ni-da

■ How many typhoons usually hit
in the summer?
여름에 보통 태풍이 몇 번 오는
거예요?
yeo-reu-me bo-tong tae-pung-i myeot
beon o-neun geo-ye-yo?

Autumn

▪ Autumn is the season of "high sky and plump horses."

가을은 "천고마비"의 계절입니다.

ga-eu-reun "cheon-go-ma-bi"-e gye-jeo-rim-ni-da

Tip: 천고마비 [cheon-go-ma-bi] is an idiom to describe autumn. It means "The sky is getting higher and horses are getting fatter."

▪ Autumn has stolen up on us.

어느덧 가을이 왔어(요).

eo-neu-deot ga-eu-ri wa-sseo(-yo)

▪ An autumn breeze is softly blowing.

가을 바람이 솔솔 불어(요).

ga-eul ba-ra-mi sol-sol bu-reo(-yo)

▪ Autumn is a good season for reading.

가을은 독서의 계절입니다.

ga-eu-reun dok-sseo-e gye-jeo-rim-ni-da

▪ Our appetites improve in fall.

가을이 되면 식욕이 좋아져(요).

ga-eu-ri doe-myeon si-gyo-gi jo-a-jeo(-yo)

▪ Fall has flown by.

가을은 눈 깜빡할 사이에 지나갔어(요).

ga-eu-reun nun ggam-bba-kal sa-i-e ji-na-ga-sseo(-yo)

Autumn Leaves

▪ The fall leaves are changing color.

단풍이 물들고 있어(요).

dan-pung-i mul-deul-go i-sseo(-yo)

▪ We're going to go maple-viewing next weekend.

다음 주말에 단풍 구경 가(요).

da-eum ju-ma-re dan-pung gu-gyeong ga(-yo)

▪ Look at those reds and yellows.

저 울긋불긋한 단풍을 보세요.

jeo ul-geut-bbul-geu-tan dan-pung-eul bo-se-yo

▪ The leaves of the ginkgo trees are beginning to yellow.

은행나무가 노랗게 물들기 시작했어(요).

eun-haeng-na-mu-ga no-ra-ke mul-deul-gi si-ja-kae-sseo(-yo)

▪ The hills are ablaze with autumnal tints.

산에 단풍이 들어서 불바다 같아(요).

sa-ne dan-pung-i deu-reo-seo bul-ba-da ga-ta(-yo)

Winter

■ The winter season is coming soon.
곤 겨울이 와(요).
got gyeo-u-ri wa(-yo)

■ It's getting colder and colder.
날씨가 점점 추워져(요).
nal-ssi-ga jeom-jeom chu-wo-jeo(-yo)

■ It is exceptionally cold this winter.
올겨울은 유난히 춥네(요).
ol-ggyeo-u-reun yu-nan-hi chum-ne(-yo)

■ Winter is in full swing.
동장군이 기승을 부리고 있어(요).
dong-jang-gu-ni gi-seung-eul bu-ri-go i-sseo(-yo)

Tip: 동장군 [dong-jang-gun] **means bitter, cold winter weather.**

■ I'm shivering with cold.
추워서 덜덜 떨려(요).
chu-wo-seo deol-deol ddeol-ryeo(-yo)

■ I'm chilled to the bone.
뼛속까지 추워(요).
bbyeo-ssok-gga-ji chu-wo(-yo)

Snow

■ It's snowing heavily.
함박눈이 와(요).
ham-bang-nu-ni wa(-yo)

■ We're having a snowstorm.
눈보라가 쳐(요).
nun-bo-ra-ga cheo(-yo)

■ It was the middle of a snowstorm and I could hardly see.
눈보라가 몰아쳐서 거의 볼 수 없었어(요).
nun-bo-ra-ga mo-ra-cheo-seo geo-i bol ssu eop-sseo-sseo(-yo)

■ It snowed hard yesterday.
어제 폭설이 내렸어(요).
eo-je pok-sseo-ri nae-ryeo-sseo(-yo)

■ A blanket of snow covered the ground.
땅 위에 눈이 소복히 쌓였어(요).
ddang wi-e nu-ni so-bo-ki ssa-yeo-sseo(-yo)

■ Do you think it will stick?
눈이 얼어 붙을까(요)?
nu-ni eo-reo bu-teul-gga(-yo)?

The Date 날짜 nal-jja

n. date 날짜 [날짜] nal-jja	d.n. year 년(年) [년] nyeon n. year 연 [연] yeon	n./d.n. month 월(月) [월] wol = 달 [달] dal	n./d.n. day 일(日) [일] il
	n./d.n. week 주(週) [주] ju = 주일 [주일] ju-il	n. day of the week 요일 [요일] yo-il	n. calendar 달력 [달력] dal-ryeok

n. Monday
월요일 [워료일]
wo-ryo-il

n. Tuesday
화요일 [화요일]
hwa-yo-il

n. Wednesday
수요일 [수요일]
su-yo-il

n. Thursday
목요일 [모교일]
mo-gyo-il

n. Friday
금요일 [그묘일]
geu-myo-il

n. Sunday
일요일 [이료일]
i-ryo-il

n. Saturday
토요일 [토요일]
to-yo-il

n./adv. today
오늘 [오늘]
o-neul

n./adv. yesterday
어제 [어제] eo-je

n./adv. tomorrow
내일 [내일] nae-il

the day before yesterday
그제 [그제] geu-je

the day after tomorrow
모레 [모:레] mo-re

Seollal (Lunar New Year's Day)

■ Happy New Year!
새해 복 많이 받으세요!
sae-hae bok ma-ni ba-deu-se-yo!

■ May peace and happiness be
yours in the New Year!
새해에는 평안하고 행복하세요!
sae-hae-e-neun pyeong-an-ha-go
haeng-bo-ka-se-yo!

■ Koreans feast on rice cake soup
on New Year's Day.
한국인은 설날에 떡국을
먹어(요).
han-gu-gi-neun seol-ra-re ddeok-ggu-
geul meo-geo(-yo)

■ We dressed up for New Year's.
우리는 설빔으로 차려입었어(요).
u-ri-neun seol-bi-meu-ro
cha-ryeo-i-beo-sseo(-yo)

Tip: 설빔 [seol-bim] **are new clothes worn for
Seollal.**

■ Lunar New Year's Day is the
biggest holiday in Korea.
설날은 한국에서 가장 큰
명절이에요.
seol-ra-reun han-gu-ge-seo ga-jang
keun myeong-jeo-ri-e-yo

New Year's Resolutions

■ Let's drink a toast to the New
Year!
새해를 위해 건배!
sae-hae-reul wi-hae geon-bae!

■ What resolutions did you make
for the New Year?
신년 결심으로 뭘 세웠어(요)?
sin-nyeon gyeol-ssi-meu-ro mwol
se-wo-sseo(-yo)?

■ My New Year's resolution is to
drink less alcohol.
올해 술을 줄일 거예요.
ol-hae su-reul ju-ril ggeo-ye-yo

■ I will study Korean hard in the
New Year.
새해에는 한국어 공부를 열심히
할 거예요.
sae-hae-e-neun han-gu-geo gong-bu-
reul yeol-ssim-hi hal ggeo-ye-yo

■ I've never kept my resolutions in
the past.
새해 결심을 실천한 적 한 번도
없어(요).
sae-hae gyeol-ssi-meul sil-cheon-han
jeok han beon-do eop-sseo(-yo)

Chuseok

■ Chuseok is August 15, according to the lunar calendar.
추석은 음력 8월 15일입니다.
chu-seo-geun eum-nyeok pa-rwol si-bo-il-im-ni-da

■ Chuseok is like Korean Thanksgiving.
추석은 한국의 "추수감사절" 같아(요).
chu-seo-geun han-gu-ge "chu-su-gam-sa-jeol" ga-ta(-yo)

■ Koreans visit their family graves during chuseok.
한국인은 추석에 성묘하러 가(요).
han-gu-gi-neun chu-seo-ge seong-myo-ha-reo ga(-yo)

■ Koreans eat song-pyeon during chuseok.
한국인은 추석에 송편을 먹어(요).
han-gu-gi-neun chu-seo-ge song-pyeo-neul meo-geo(-yo)

Tip: 송편 [song-pyeon] is a kind of rice cake made from rice powder and the needles of the pine tree.

■ We enjoyed the full moon during chuseok.
추석에 보름달을 즐겼어(요).
chu-seo-ge bo-reum-dda-reul

Christmas

■ Christmas is almost here.
곧 크리스마스예요.
got keu-ri-seu-ma-seu-ye-yo

■ We decorated the tree last weekend.
우리는 지난 주말에 트리를 꾸몄어(요).
u-ri-neun ji-nan ju-ma-re teu-ri-reul ggu-myeo-sseo(-yo)

■ Are you sending Christmas cards this year?
올해 크리스마스 카드 보낼 거예요?
ol-hae keu-ri-seu-ma-seu ka-deu bo-nael ggeo-ye-yo?

■ What are your plans for Christmas?
크리스마스에 뭐 할 거예요?
keu-ri-seu-ma-seu-e mwo hal ggeo-ye-yo?

■ Please tell me what I'm getting for Christmas.
크리스마스 선물이 뭔지 말해 줘(요).
keu-ri-seu-ma-seu seon-mu-ri mwon-ji mal-hae jwo(-yo)

Birthdays

■ It's my birthday today.

오늘은 바로 내 생일이에요.

o-neu-reun ba-ro nae saeng-i-ri-e-yo

■ How did you know that today
was my birthday?

오늘이 내 생일인지 어떻게
알았어(요)?

o-neu-ri nae saeng-i-rin-ji eo-ddeo-ke
a-ra-sseo(-yo)?

■ We have the same birthday!

우리 생일은 같은 날이에요!

u-ri saeng-i-reun ga-teun na-ri-e-yo!

■ My birthday is only a week away.

내 생일이 일주일밖에
안 남았어(요).

nae saeng-i-ri il-jju-il-ba-gge
an na-ma-sseo(-yo)

■ Do you know that tomorrow is
grandfather's birthday?

내일이 할아버지 생신인 거 알고
있어(요)?

nae-i-ri hal-a-beo-ji saeng-si-nin geo
al-go i-sseo(-yo)?

Tip: 생신 [saeng-sin] is a polite way of saying
생일 [saeng-il] "birthday."

Celebrations

■ Happy birthday!

생일 축하합니다!

saeng-il chu-ka-ham-ni-da!

생일 축하해(요)!

saeng-il chu-ka-hae(-yo)!

■ Congratulations on your
wedding!

결혼 축하합니다!

gyeol-hon chu-ka-ham-ni-da!

■ Great job!

잘했어(요)!

jal-hae-sseo(-yo)!

■ You did it!

해냈구나!

hae-naet-ggu-na!

■ I wish you the best of luck!

행운을 빌어(요)!

haeng-u-neul bi-reo(-yo)!

■ God bless you!

신의 축복이 있기를!

si-ne chuk-bbo-gi it-ggi-reul!

■ I'm really happy for you.

정말 잘됐어(요).

jeong-mal jal-dwae-sseo(-yo)

Hobbies 취미 chwi-mi

n. hobby 취미 [취:미] chwi-mi 	n. sport 운동 [운:동] un-dong = 스포츠 [스포츠] seu-po-cheu 	v. run, dash 달리다 [달리다] dal-ri-da = 뛰다 [뛰다] ddwi-da
n. fitness center 헬스클럽 [헬스클럽] hel-seu-keul-reop 	n. swimming 수영 [수영] su-yeong 	n. ball 공 [공:] gong
n. tennis 테니스 [테니스] te-ni-seu 	n. badminton 배드민턴 [배드민턴] bae-deu-min-teon 	n. table tennis, ping-pong 탁구 [탁꾸] tak-ggu
n. football, soccer 축구 [축꾸] chuk-ggu 	n. baseball 야구 [야:구] ya-gu 	n. basketball 농구 [농구] nong-gu
n. volleyball 배구 [배구] bae-gu 	n. skiing 스키 [스키] seu-ki 	n. skating 스케이트 [스케이트] seu-ke-i-teu
n. boxing 권투 [권:투] gwon-tu 	n. yoga 요가 [요가] yo-ga 	n. golf 골프 [골프] gol-peu

n. music 음악 [으막]
eu-mak

n. song 노래 [노래]
no-rae

n. singer 가수 [가수]
ga-su

n. musical instrument
악기 [악끼]
ak-ggi

n. piano 피아노 [피아노]
pi-a-no

n. guitar 기타 [기타]
gi-ta

n. performance
연주 [연:주]
yeon-ju

n. concert 음악회 [으마쾨/
으마퀘] eu-ma-koe/eu-ma-kwe
= 콘서트 [콘서트]
kon-seo-teu

n. musical
뮤지컬 [뮤지컬]
myu-ji-keol

n. movie, film 영화 [영화]
yeong-hwa

n. theater 극장 [극짱]
geuk-jjang

n. actor
배우 [배우] bae-u

n. book 책 [책] chaek

n. reading
독서 [독써]
dok-sseo

n. bookstore 서점 [서점]
seo-jeom

n. photograph,
photo, picture
사진 [사진]
sa-jin

n. camera 카메라 [카메라]
ka-me-ra

n. picture 그림 [그:림]
geu-rim

n. climbing 등산 [등산]
deung-san

n. fishing 낚시 [낙씨]
nak-ssi

n. camping 야영 [야:영]
ya-yeong
= 캠핑 [캠핑]
kaem-ping

Asking about Hobbies

■ What do you like to do?

뭐 하는 거 좋아해(요)?

mwo ha-neun geo jo-a-hae(-yo)?

■ Do you have any hobbies?

취미가 있어(요)?

chwi-mi-ga i-sseo(-yo)?

■ Do you have any particular
hobbies?

어떤 특별한 취미가 있어(요)?

eo-ddeon teuk-bbeol-han chwi-mi-ga
i-sseo(-yo)?

■ What do you do when you have
free time?

한가할 때 보통 뭐 해(요)?

han-ga-hal ddae bo-tong mwo hae(-yo)?

■ What do you do for recreation?

기분 전환하고 싶을 때
뭐 해(요)?

gi-bun jeon-hwan-ha-go si-peul ddae
mwo hae(-yo)?

Talking about Hobbies

■ I have a lot of hobbies.

내 취미는 다양해(요).

nae chwi-mi-neun da-yang-hae(-yo)

■ I have no particular hobby.

특별한 취미가 없어(요).

teul-bbeol-han chwi-mi-ga eop-sseo(-yo)

■ I have little interest in those
things.

그런 일에 대해서는 흥미가 별로
없어(요).

geu-reon i-re dae-hae-seo-neun
heung-mi-ga byel-ro eop-sseo(-yo)

■ I play the piano for fun.

취미로 피아노를 쳐(요).

chwi-mi-ro pi-a-no-reul cheo(-yo)

■ Her hobbies include music,
dancing, sports and cooking.

그녀의 취미는 음악, 춤, 운동과
요리예요.

geu-nyeo-e chwi-mi-neun eu-mak,
chum, un-dong-gwa yo-ri-ye-yo

Taking Pictures

▪ Taking pictures is one of my hobbies.

사진 찍기는 내 취미 중 하나예요.

sa-jin jjik-ggi-neun nae chwi-mi jung ha-na-ye-yo

▪ I like to take pictures of people.

사람 찍기를 좋아해(요).

sa-ram jjik-ggi-reul jo-a-hae(-yo)

▪ How long have you been taking pictures?

얼마나 오랫동안 사진을 찍었어(요)?

eol-ma-na o-raet-ddong-an sa-ji-neul jji-geo-sseo(-yo)?

▪ What kind of camera do you have?

어떤 카메라를 가지고 있어(요)?

eo-ddeon ka-me-ra-reul ga-ji-go i-sseo(-yo)?

▪ I just use the automatic settings.

난 그냥 자동 모드로 찍어(요).

nan geu-nyang ja-dong mo-deu-ro jji-geo(-yo)

Sports 1

▪ What sports do you like?

어떤 운동하기를 좋아해(요)?

eo-ddeon un-dong-ha-gi-reul jo-a-hae(-yo)?

▪ I like any kind of sport.

어떤 운동이든 좋아해(요).

eo-ddeon un-dong-i-deun jo-a-hae(-yo)

▪ I'm a sports nut.

나는 운동광이에요.

na-neun un-dong-gwang-i-e-yo

▪ I'm not good at sports.

운동에 소질이 없어(요).

un-dong-e so-ji-ri eop-sseo(-yo)

▪ I like watching sports more than playing them.

운동은 하는 것보다 보는 것을 좋아해(요).

un-dong-eun ha-neun geot-bbo-da bo-neun geo-seul jo-a-hae(-yo)

▪ I need to exercise.

요즘 운동 부족이에요.

yo-jeum un-dong bu-jo-gi-e-yo

Sports 2

■ I take a walk everyday.
매일 산보해(요).
mae-il san-bbo-hae(-yo)

■ I'll run from today.
오늘부터 달리기를 할 거예요.
o-neul-bu-teo dal-ri-gi-reul hal
ggeo-ye-yo

■ I'll keep on doing yoga.
계속해서 요가를 하려고(요).
gye-so-kae-seo yo-ga-reul
ha-ryeo-go(-yo)

■ I like swimming best.
수영을 가장 좋아해(요).
su-yeong-eul ga-jang jo-a-hae(-yo)

■ I'm like a stone in the water.
수영을 못해(요).
su-yeong-eul mo-tae(-yo)

맥주병이에요.
maek-jju-bbyeong-i-e-yo

■ In the winter, I'm going to go skiing.
겨울이 되면, 스키를 타러 가(요).
gyeo-u-ri doe-myeon, seu-ki-reul ta-reo
ga(-yo)

Samgye-tang

Samgye-tang (삼계탕) is ginseng chicken soup, a popular summer stamina food in Korea.

"Sam" means ginseng, "gye" means chicken and "tang" means soup. It is a hot soup but most Koreans enjoy it in the summer season, especially on the three hottest days (collectively called "sambok [삼복]" or individually as "chobok [초복]," "jungbok [중복]" and "malbok [말복]" in the lunar calendar). You can also have it during the winter season, of course. As the Korean saying goes, eating hot soup is "fighting heat with heat."

Samgye-tang is very nutritious. Its ingredients are a small young chicken, ginseng, jujubes, garlic and glutinous rice.

Ball Games 1

■ I'm into tennis these days.
요즘 테니스에 빠졌어(요).
yo-jeum te-ni-seu-e bba-jeo-sseo(-yo)

■ Let's play together sometime.
시간 내서 우리 함께 치러 가(요).
si-gan nae-seo u-ri ham-gge chi-reo
ga(-yo)

■ I often watch baseball games
on TV.
종종 TV에서 중계하는 야구
경기를 봐(요).
jong-jong ti-bi-e-seo jung-gye-ha-neun
ya-gu gyeong-gi-reul bwa(-yo)

■ Our team won the game 3–1
yesterday.
어제 우리는 3 대 1로 이겼어(요).
eo-je u-ri-neun sam dae il-ro
i-gyeo-sseo(-yo)

■ I play third base on my baseball
team.
야구팀에서 3루수를 맡고
있어(요).
ya-gu-ti-me-seo sam-ru-su-reul mat-ggo
i-sseo(-yo)

■ The game ended in a tie.
경기는 무승부였어(요).
gyeong-gi-neun mu-seung-bu-yeo-
sseo(-yo)

Ball Games 2

■ I'm just a bench warmer.
나는 후보 선수예요.
na-neun hu-bo seon-su-ye-yo

■ Who's your favorite soccer team?
어떤 축구팀을 응원해(요)?
eo-ddeon chuk-ggu-ti-meul
eung-won-hae(-yo)?

■ The soccer match was very close
yesterday.
어제 축구 경기는 상당히
접전이었어(요).
eo-je chuk-ggu gyeong-gi-neun
sang-dang-hi jeop-jjeo-ni-eo-sseo(-yo)

■ Soccer is of no interest to me at all.
축구에 흥미가 없어(요).
chuk-ggu-e heung-mi-ga eop-sseo(-yo)

■ I'm pretty passionate about golf.
요즘 골프에 빠졌어(요).
yo-jeum gol-peu-e bba-jeo-sseo(-yo)

■ How about playing a round of
golf?
우리 골프 한 게임 칠까(요)?
u-ri gol-peu han ge-im chil-gga(-yo)?

Listening to Music

- I like listening to music.

  음악 듣는 것을 좋아해(요).

  eu-mak deut-neun geo-seul jo-a-hae(-yo)

- What kind of music do you like?

  어떤 음악을 좋아해(요)?

  eo-ddeon eu-ma-geul jo-a-hae(-yo)?

- Who's your favorite singer?

  좋아하는 가수는 누구예요?

  jo-a-ha-neun ga-su-neun nu-gu-ye-yo?

- I love to listen to all kinds of music.

  음악이라면 다 듣기 좋아해(요).

  eu-ma-gi-ra-myeon da deut-ggi jo-a-hae(-yo)

- Classical music relaxes me.

  클래식 음악을 들으면 긴장이 풀려(요).

  keul-rae-sik eu-ma-geul deu-reu-myeon gin-jang-i pul-ryeo(-yo)

- I listen to pop music whenever I can.

  시간이 날 때는 팝 음악을 들어(요).

  si-ga-ni nal ddae-neun pap eu-ma-geul deu-reo(-yo)

Playing Instruments

- Do you play any musical instruments?

  어떤 악기를 연주할 수 있어(요)?

  eo-ddeon ak-ggi-reul yeon-ju-hal ssu i-sseo(-yo)?

- I can play the piano.

  피아노를 칠 수 있어(요).

  pi-a-no-reul chil ssu i-sseo(-yo)

- I have played the violin since I was ten.

  10살부터 바이올린을 켰어(요).

  yeol-ssal-bu-teo ba-i-ol-ri-neul kyeo-sseo(-yo)

- I played the guitar for ten years when I was child.

  어릴 때부터 10년 동안 기타를 쳤어(요).

  eo-ril ddae-bu-teo sim-nyeon dong-an gi-ta-reul cheo-sseo(-yo)

- She was playing the flute.

  그녀는 플루트를 연주하고 있었어(요).

  geu-nyeo-neun peul-ru-teu-reul yeon-ju-ha-go i-sseo-sseo(-yo)

- I have no talent for music.

  음악적 소질이 없어(요).

  eu-mak-jjeok so-ji-ri eop-sseo(-yo)

Watching Movies 1

■ I like to watch movies.
영화 보기를 좋아해(요).
yeong-hwa bo-gi-reul jo-a-hae(-yo)

■ I'm a movie addict.
영화광이에요.
yeong-hwa-gwang-i-e-yo

■ What kinds of movies do you like?
어떤 영화를 좋아해(요)?
eo-ddeon yeong-hwa-reul jo-a-hae(-yo)?

■ I love mysteries, especially detective movies.
미스터리 영화, 특히 탐정물을 좋아해(요).
mi-seu-teo-ri yeong-hwa, teu-ki tam-jeong-mu-reul jo-a-hae(-yo)

■ I often watch action films.
액션영화를 자주 봐(요).
aek-ssyeon-yeong-hwa-reul ja-ju bwa(-yo)

■ It was a scary movie so I couldn't sleep that night.
무서운 영화라서 그날 밤에 잠을 잘 수 없었어(요).
mu-seo-un yeong-hwa-ra-seo geu-nal ba-me ja-meul jal ssu eop-sseo-sseo(-yo)

Watching Movies 2

■ The movie I enjoyed most so far is *Mission: Impossible*.
지금까지 가장 좋았던 영화는 〈미션 임파서블〉이에요.
ji-geum-gga-ji ga-jang jo-at-ddeon yeong-hwa-neun <mi-syeon im-pa-seo-beu>-ri-e-yo

■ Who stars in the movie?
그 영화 주연은 누구예요?
geu yeong-hwa ju-yeo-neun nu-gu-ye-yo?

■ That's my favorite part in the movie.
저것이 영화에서 가장 좋아하는 부분이에요.
jeo-geo-si yeong-hwa-e-seo ga-jang jo-a-ha-neun bu-bu-ni-e-yo

■ I saw that movie more than five times.
그 영화는 다섯 번 이상 봤어(요).
geu yeong-hwa-neun da-seot beon i-sang bwa-sseo(-yo)

■ I have seen all of her films.
그녀가 주연한 영화를 다 봤어(요).
geu-nyeo-ga ju-yeon-han yeong-hwa-reul da bwa-sseo(-yo)

Reading Books 1

- My hobby is reading novels.
  내 취미는 소설 읽는 거예요.
  nae chwi-mi-neun so-seol il-neun
  geo-ye-yo

- I'm a bookworm.
  나는 책벌레예요.
  na-neun chaek-bbeol-re-ye-yo

- I devote my free time to reading.
  한가할 때 책 읽기를 좋아해(요).
  han-ga-hal ddae chaek il-ggi-reul
  jo-a-hae(-yo)

- I don't have much time to read.
  책 읽을 시간이 별로 없어(요).
  chaek il-geul si-ga-ni byeol-ro
  eop-sseo(-yo)

- Do you read a lot?
  책 많이 봐(요)?
  chaek ma-ni bwa(-yo)?

- How many books do you read a
  month?
  한 달에 몇 권 읽어(요)?
  han da-re myeot gwon il-geo(-yo)?

Reading Books 2

- I read more than fifty books a
  year.
  1년에 50권 이상 읽어(요).
  il-ryeo-ne o-sip-ggwon i-sang il-geo(-yo)

- I love science-fiction novels.
  공상과학 소설을 좋아해(요).
  gong-sang-gwa-hak so-seo-reul
  jo-a-hae(-yo)

- Who's your favorite author?
  좋아하는 작가가 누구예요?
  jo-a-ha-neun jak-gga-ga nu-gu-ye-yo?

- I like Mun-yeol Lee, I've read all
  of his books.
  이문열을 좋아해서, 그의 책은
  이미 다 봤어(요).
  i-mu-nyeo-reul jo-a-hae-seo, geu-e
  chae-geun i-mi da bwa-sseo(-yo)

  Tip: 이문열 is a famous Korean writer.

- I don't know much about comic
  books.
  만화책은 잘 몰라(요).
  man-hwa-chae-geun jal mol-ra(-yo)

Collecting

- What do you collect?

  어떤 걸 수집하기 좋아해(요)?

  eo-ddeon geol su-ji-pa-gi jo-a-hae(-yo)?

- I collect coins from all over the world.

  전 세계 동전을 모으고 있어(요).

  jeon se-gye dong-jeo-neul mo-eu-go i-sseo(-yo)

- I started to collect antiques from last year.

  작년부터 골동품을 모으기 시작했어(요).

  jang-nyeon-bu-teo gol-ddong-pu-meul mo-eu-gi si-ja-kae-sseo(-yo)

- I have been collecting Star Wars memorabilia since I was a child.

  어릴 때부터 스타워즈 수집품을 모아왔어(요).

  eo-ril ddae-bu-teo seu-ta-wo-jeu su-jip-pu-meul mo-a-wa-sseo(-yo)

- Do you want to see my grandfather's ceramics collection?

  할아버지가 수집하신 도자기 볼래(요)?

  ha-ra-beo-ji-ga su-ji-pa-sin do-ja-gi bol-rae(-yo)?

Other Hobbies

- Jin-seon hand knits sweaters for her children.

  진선이는 아이들에게 입힐 스웨터를 손수 뜨개질해(요).

  jin-seo-ni-neun a-i-deu-re-ge i-pil seu-we-teo-reul son-su ddeu-gae-jil-hae(-yo)

- In fishing, patience is the name of the game.

  낚시에서 중요한 것은 인내력이라고 생각해(요).

  nak-ssi-e-seo jung-yo-han geo-seun in-nae-ryeo-gi-ra-go saeng-ga-kae(-yo)

- We like hunting but we don't like hiking.

  우리는 사냥은 좋아하지만, 하이킹은 좋아하지 않아(요).

  u-ri-neun sa-nyang-eun jo-a-ha-ji-man, ha-i-king-eun jo-a-ha-ji a-na(-yo)

- We are pretty evenly matched at Go.

  우리는 바둑의 맞수예요.

  u-ri-neun ba-du-ge mat-ssu-ye-yo

- Jeong-tae enjoys billiards.

  정태는 당구를 즐겨(요).

  jeong-tae-neun dang-gu-reul jeul-gyeo(-yo)

Animals & Plants 동물 & 식물 dong-mul & sing-mul

n. animal 동물 [동ː물] dong-mul	n. pet 반려동물 [발ː려동물] bal-ryeo-dong-mul	n. veterinarian, vet 수의사 [수의사/수이사] su-ui-sa/su-i-sa
n. dog, canine 개 [개ː] gae	n. cat, feline 고양이 [고양이] go-yang-i	n. tropical fish 열대어 [열때어] yeol-ddae-eo
n. plant 식물 [싱물] sing-mul	n. tree 나무 [나무] na-mu	n. flower 꽃 [꼳] ggot

Pets 1

- **I like pets.**
  반려동물이 좋아(요).
  bal-ryeo-dong-mu-ri jo-a(-yo)

- **What kind of pets do you have?**
  어떤 반려동물을 키우고
  있어(요)?
  eo-ddeon bal-ryeo-dong-mu-reul ki-u-go
  i-sseo(-yo)?

- **What kind of pet do you want
  to have?**
  어떤 반려동물 키우고 싶어(요)?
  eo-ddeon bal-ryeo-dong-mul ki-u-go
  si-peo(-yo)?

- **Did you have a pet when you
  were growing up?**
  어렸을 때 반려동물을 키워
  봤어(요)?
  eo-ryeo-sseul ddae bal-ryeo-dong-mu-
  reul ki-wo bwa-sseo(-yo)?

- **Which one is better as a pet,
  a puppy or a kitten?**
  어떤 반려동물이 더 좋아(요),
  강아지? 고양이?
  eo-ddeon bal-ryeo-dong-mu-ri deo jo-
  a(-yo), gang-a-ji? go-yang-i?

  Tip: Koreans used to say 애완동물 [ae-wan-
  dong-mur] for pet, but nowadays more and
  more people say 반려동물 [bal-ryeo-dong-mur]
  instead.

Pets 2

- **Today I found a stray cat in the
  park.**
  오늘 공원에서 버려진 고양이를
  발견했어(요).
  o-neul gong-wo-ne-seo beo-ryeo-jin
  go-yang-i-reul bal-gyeon-hae-sseo(-yo)

- **My parents won't let me have a
  dog.**
  부모님이 반려동물 기르는 걸
  허락하지 않으세요.
  bu-mo-ni-mi bal-ryeo-dong-mul
  gi-reu-neun geol heo-ra-ka-ji a-neu-se-yo

- **I'm sorry. No pets allowed.**
  죄송합니다.
  반려동물은 들어올 수 없어요.
  joe-song-ham-ni-da.
  bal-ryeo-dong-mu-reun deu-reo-ol ssu
  eop-sseo-yo

- **Are pets allowed here?**
  여기에 반려동물을 데려와도
  돼(요)?
  yeo-gi-e bal-ryeo-dong-mu-reul
  de-ryeo-wa-do dwae(-yo)?

- **It's pretty hard to take care of
  animals.**
  동물 키우는 건 여간 힘든 일이
  아니에요.
  dong-mul ki-u-neun geon yeo-gan
  him-deun i-ri a-ni-e-yo

Canines 1

■ It's fun to take a stroll with a dog.

개를 데리고 산책하기를
좋아해(요).

gae-reul de-ri-go san chae-ka-gi-reul
jo-a-hae(-yo)

■ He is a five-year old mongrel.

다섯 살 난 잡종 개를 키우고
있어(요).

da-seot sal nan jap-jjong gae-reul ki-u-
go i-sseo(-yo)

■ I'm giving the puppy some food.

강아지에게 먹이를 주고
있어(요).

gang-a-ji-e-ge meo-gi-reul ju-go
i-sseo(-yo)

■ I named the puppy Ddol-ddo-ri.

강아지 이름을 똘똘이라고
했어(요).

gang-a-ji i-reu-meul ddol-ddo-ri-ra-go
hae-sseo(-yo)

■ My dog is as gentle as a lamb.

우리 강아지는 온순해(요).

u-ri gang-a-ji-neun on-sun-hae(-yo)

■ My dog is pretty tame.

우리 개는 잘 길들여져 있어(요).

u-ri gae-neun jal gil-deu-ryeo-jeo
i-sseo(-yo)

Korean Festivals

Cherry Blossom Festivals
(벚꽃 축제 [beot-ggot chuk-jje])
When spring comes, there are many spots to appreciate cherry blossoms in Korea. From the beginning of March when the weather is still cool, beautiful light pink cherry blossoms spread across the nation. The peak season is the middle of April, but this depends on weather and locations. Check the suggested viewing dates each spring season.

Two of the best cherry blossom festivals are in Yeouido (여의도, Seoul 서울) and Gunhangje (군항제, Jinhae in Gyeongsang-do 경상도 진해). Bring your selfie-stick!

Boryeong Mud Festival (보령 머드축제 [bo-ryeong meo-deu-chuk-jje])
This popular festival slides into Boryeong every July. The region, some 120 miles (200 km) outside Seoul, is known for Daecheon Beach (대천 해수욕장 [dae-cheon hae-su-yok-jjang]), natural scenery, and of course mud. Rich in minerals, the mud here used to be used in cosmetics. Today though, it's more about good, grimy fun with mud slides, mud massages, mud everything. The first Mud Festival was in 1998.

Canines 2

■ My dog pees and poos
everywhere.

우리 개는 아무데서나 대소변을
봐(요).

u-ri gae-neun a-mu-de-seo-na
dae-so-byeo-neul bwa(-yo)

■ The dog and the children were
running around.

그 개는 아이들과 이리저리
뛰어다녀(요).

geu gae-neun a-i-deul-gwa i-ri-jeo-ri
ddwi-eo-da-nyeo(-yo)

■ My dog needs a bath.

우리 개는 목욕해야 해(요).

u-ri gae-neun mo-gyo-kae-ya hae(-yo)

■ My dog died last week. She was
seventeen.

우리 개가 지난주에 죽었어요.
17살이었죠.

u-ri gae-ga ji-nan-ju-e ju-geo-sseo-yo.
yeo-ril-gop-ssa-ri-eot-jjyo

■ I have to get my dog neutered.

강아지 중성화 수술을 해야
해(요).

gang-a-ji jung-seong-hwa su-su-reul
hae-ya hae(-yo)

Felines

■ My cat clawed me on the hand.

고양이가 발톱으로 나를
할퀴었어(요).

go-yang-i-ga bal-to-beu-ro na-reul
hal-kwi-eo-sseo(-yo)

■ Don't play with the cat's tail.

고양이 꼬리로 장난치지 마라.

go-yang-i ggo-ri-ro jang-nan-chi-ji
ma-ra

■ The kitten gnawed the slippers.

새끼 고양이가 슬리퍼를
물어(요).

sae-ggi go-yang-i-ga seul-li-peo-reul
mu-reo(-yo)

■ My cat had three kittens.

우리 고양이가 새끼를 세 마리
낳았어(요).

u-ri go-yang-i-ga sae-ggi-reul se ma-ri
na-a-sseo(-yo)

■ I have to feed them now.

지금 고양이들에게 밥 줘야
해(요).

ji-geum go-yang-i-deu-re-ge bap jwo-ya
hae(-yo)

■ The cat is purring.

고양이가 목을 그르렁거려(요).

go-yang-i-ga mo-geul
geu-reu-reong-geo-ryeo(-yo)

Other Pets

■ My hamster likes to eat cabbage.

내 햄스터는 양배추를
좋아해(요).

nae haem-seu-teo-neun yang-bae-chu-reul jo-a-hae(-yo)

■ Keep hamsters in a cage.

햄스터를 우리에 넣어서
기르세요.

haem-seu-teo-reul u-ri-e neo-eo-seo gi-reu-se-yo

■ He has a pet snake.

그는 애완용 뱀을 키워(요).

geu-neun ae-wa-nyong bae-meul ki-wo(-yo)

■ Some people keep beetles as pets.

어떤 사람은 반려동물로
딱정벌레를 키워(요).

eo-ddeon sa-ra-meun bal-ryeo-dong-mul-ro ddak-jjeong-beol-re-reul ki-wo(-yo)

■ He killed his goldfish by overfeeding it.

그는 금붕어에게 먹이를 너무
많이 줘서 죽이고 말았어(요).

geu-neun geum-bung-eo-e-ge meo-gi-reul neo-mu ma-ni jwo-seo ju-gi-go ma-ra-sseo(-yo)

Makgeolli

Makgeolli (막걸리) is a traditional Korean alcoholic beverage: a milky, off-white, light and sparkling rice wine. Its ABV (alcohol by volume) is not high and a recommended side snack is pajeon (파전), scallion pancake.

The drink itself contains various nutrients, including protein, carbohydrates, fat, fiber, vitamins, lactobacillus and enzymes.

Makgeolli is made in many places across Korea, and regional variations include makgeolli made with ingredients such as corn, jujubes or even pine nuts.

Growing Plants 1

- Ji-hee is watering her plants.

  지희는 화분에 물을 주고
  있어(요).

  ji-hi-neun hwa-bu-ne mu-reul ju-go
  i-sseo(-yo)

- We planted beans in three pots.

  우리는 화분 세 개에 콩을
  심었어(요).

  u-ri-neun hwa-bun se gae-e kong-eul
  si-meo-sseo(-yo)

- You shouldn't water plants more
  than once a week.

  식물에 물 주는 건 일주일에
  한 번 이상 하면 안 돼(요).

  sing-mu-re mul ju-neun geon il-jju-i-re
  han beon i-sang ha-myeon an dwae(-yo)

- You overwatered that.

  물을 너무 많이 줬어(요).

  dang-si-neun geu-geo-se mu-reul
  neo-mu ma-ni jwo-sseo(-yo)

- I planted tulip bulbs in my
  garden.

  정원에 튤립 뿌리를 심었어(요).

  jeong-wo-ne tyul-rip bbu-ri-reul
  si-meo-sseo(-yo)

Growing Plants 2

- I bedded some houseplants in
  the garden yesterday.

  어제 실내 식물을 정원에 옮겨
  심었어(요).

  eo-je sil-rae sing-mu-reul jeong-wo-ne
  om-gyeo si-meo-sseo(-yo)

- I have been spending a lot of
  time gardening recently.

  요즘 정원 가꾸기에 시간을 많이
  들여(요).

  yo-jeum jeong-won ga-ggu-gi-e si-ga-
  neul ma-ni deu-ryeo(-yo)

- What kind of plant is that?

  저건 어떤 식물이에요?

  jeo-geon eo-ddeon sing-mu-ri-e-yo?

- I'm growing vegetables in my
  yard for my family.

  가족을 위해 마당에 채소를
  기르고 있어(요).

  ga-jo-geul wi-hae ma-dang-e chae-so-
  reul gi-reu-go i-sseo(-yo)

- I should weed the garden.

  정원의 잡초를 뽑아야 해(요).

  jeong-wo-ne jap-cho-reul bbo-ba-ya
  hae(-yo)

Drinking 음주 eum-ju

n. alcohol 술 [술] sul	n. beer 맥주 [맥쭈] maek-jju	n. champagne 샴페인 [샴페인] syam-pe-in
n. liquor, spirits 양주 [양주] yang-ju	n. whisky 위스키 [위스키] wi-seu-ki	n. ice 얼음 [어름] eo-reum
n. wine 포도주 [포도주] po-do-ju	n. soju (Korean distilled spirits) 소주 [소주] so-ju	n. white rice wine (makgeolli) 막걸리 [막껄리] mak-ggeol-ri n. sweet rice wine 동동주 [동동주] dong-dong-ju

Drinking Capacity

■ How much can you drink?

주량이 얼마나 돼(요)?

ju-ryang-i eol-ma-na dwae(-yo)?

■ Are you a heavy drinker?

주량이 세(요)?

ju-ryang-i se(-yo)?

주량이 커(요)?

ju-ryang-i keo(-yo)?

■ I am a heavy drinker.

나는 술고래예요.

na-neun sul-go-rae-ye-yo

■ I hardly get drunk on beer.

나는 맥주에 안 취해(요).

na-neun maek-jju-e an chwi-hae(-yo)

■ I can drink more than I used to.

주량이 점점 늘어(요).

ju-ryang-i jeom-jeom neu-reo(-yo)

■ I get drunk easily.

나는 술이 약해(요).

na-neun su-ri ya-kae(-yo)

Drinking Habits

■ What are you like when you're drunk?

술 취하면 어떻게 돼(요)?

sul chwi-ha-myeon eo-ddeo-ke dwae(-yo)?

■ When I'm drunk you can't tell.

정말 술버릇이 없어(요).

jeong-mal sul-beo-reu-si eop-sseo(-yo)

■ He's pretty bad when he's wasted.

그는 술을 마시면, 술주정을 해(요).

geu-neun su-reul ma-si-myeon, sul-jju-jeong-eul hae(-yo)

■ When I drink, I laugh a lot.

술을 마시면, 많이 웃어(요).

su-reul ma-si-myeon, ma-ni u-seo(-yo)

■ When I drink, I cry.

술을 마시면, 울어(요).

su-reul ma-si-myeon, u-reo(-yo)

■ You're so drunk, you're saying the same thing over and over.

넌 완전히 취했어(요), 같은 걸 자꾸 말하잖아(요).

neon wan-jeon-hi chwi-hae-sseo(-yo), ga-teun geol ja-ggu mal-ha-ja-na(-yo)

Drinking Advice

- I suggested that she shouldn't drink.

  그녀에게 술을 마시면 안 된다고 했어(요).

  geu-nyeo-e-ge su-reul ma-si-myeon an doen-da-go hae-sseo(-yo)

- Don't drink to excess.

  술 취하지 마(세요).

  sul chwi-ha-ji ma(-se-yo)

- Don't drink your life away.

  인생을 술로 허송세월하지 마(세요).

  in-saeng-eul sul-ro heo-song-se-wol-ha-ji ma(-se-yo)

- It's dangerous to drink and drive.

  음주운전은 위험합니다.

  eum-ju-un-jeo-neun wi-heom-ham-ni-da

- If you drink, drink in moderation.

  술을 마신다면, 절제해서 마셔야 합니다.

  su-reul ma-sin-da-myeon, jeol-jje-hae-seo ma-syeo-ya ham-ni-da

Soju

Soju (소주) is without question the liquor most associated with Korea and one of the top-selling drinks on the planet. It is clear and colorless with two production methods, the weaker made by diluting spirits, the other made by distilling alcohol from fermented grains.

Traditional grains used in soju production are rice, wheat, and barley although modern producers may use potatoes or tapioca in place of rice.

Soju is common throughout Korea and a particular brand may represent a given region. The brand Chamiseul (참이슬) is Seoul's representative soju.

Soju today has an ABV (alcohol by volume) in the range of 17 to 34 percent. In 1924, the Jinro (진로) brand had an ABV of 35 percent, but percentages overall have decreased. Lighter fruit-flavored soju has been marketed toward women and younger drinkers since 2015.

Quitting Drinking

■ I'm going to quit drinking.

술을 끊을 거예요.

su-reul ggeu-neul ggeo-ye-yo

■ He's taking a break from drinking.

그는 당분간 술을 마시지 않아(요).

geu-neun dang-bun-gan su-reul ma-si-ji a-na(-yo)

■ I'm on the wagon.

금주 중입니다.

geum-ju jung-im-ni-da

■ You'd better quit drinking.

술을 끊는 게 좋겠어(요).

su-reul ggeun-neun ge jo-ke-sseo(-yo)

■ I stopped drinking for my health.

건강 때문에 술을 끊었어(요).

geon-gang ddae-mu-ne su-reul ggeu-neo-sseo(-yo)

■ That he had quit drinking was a complete lie.

그가 술을 끊었다는 말은 완전 거짓말이었어(요).

geu-ga su-reul ggeu-neot-dda-neun ma-reun wan-jeon geo-jin-ma-ri-eo-sseo(-yo)

Smoking

■ Can I smoke here?

여기에서 담배 피워도 돼(요)?

yeo-gi-e-seo dam-bae pi-wo-do doae(-yo)?

■ He is a heavy smoker.

그는 골초예요.

geu-neun gol-cho-ye-yo

■ He only smokes out of habit.

그는 습관적으로 담배를 피워(요).

geu-neun seup-ggwan-jeo-geu-ro dam-bae-reul pi-wo(-yo)

■ Let's have a smoke!

담배 한 대 피우자!

dam-bae han dae pi-u-ja!

■ I don't inhale.

담배를 피울 때 연기를 마시지 않아(요).

dam-bae-reul pi-ul ddae yeon-gi-reul ma-si-ji a-na(-yo)

■ It is not polite to smoke at the table.

식사 중에 담배를 피우는 것은 실례예요.

sik-ssa jung-e dam-bae-reul pi-u-neun geo-seun sil-rye-ye-yo

Cigarettes

■ May I trouble you for a light?

담뱃불 빌려도 될까(요)?

dam-baet-bbul bil-ryeo-do doel-gga(-yo)?

■ He is offering me a cigarette.

그는 내게 담배를 권해(요).

geu-neun nae-ge dam-bae-reul gwon-hae(-yo)

■ What do you think about e-cigarettes?

전자 담배 어때(요)?

jeon-ja dam-bae eo-ddae(-yo)?

■ Each pack contains twenty cigarettes.

담배 한 갑에 20개비가 들어 있어(요).

dam-bae han ga-be i-sip-ggae-bi-ga deu-reo i-sseo(-yo)

■ Everyone knows that smoking is bad for you.

흡연이 해롭다는 건 누구나 알고 있어(요).

heu-byeo-ni hae-rop-dda-neun geon nu-gu-na al-go i-sseo(-yo)

Tip: There are many nonsmoking areas in Korea. You should check whether smoking is allowed before lighting up.

Quitting Smoking

■ I decided to stop smoking.

담배를 끊기로 결심했어(요).

dam-bae-reul ggeun-ki-ro gyeol-ssim-hae-sseo(-yo)

■ No smoking here, please.

여기는 금연입니다.

yeo-gi-neun geu-myeo-nim-ni-da

■ You are not allowed to smoke in this building.

이 빌딩은 금연 건물입니다.

i bil-ding-eun geu-myeon geon-mu-rim-ni-da

■ No smoking.

금연 구역.

geu-myeon gu-yeok

■ He is a nonsmoker.

그는 담배를 피우지 않아(요).

geu-neun dam-bae-reul pi-u-ji a-na(-yo)

■ I quit smoking all together.

담배를 완전히 끊었어(요).

dam-bae-reul wan-jeon-hi ggeu-neo-sseo(-yo)

Chapter 4

Looks & Appearance

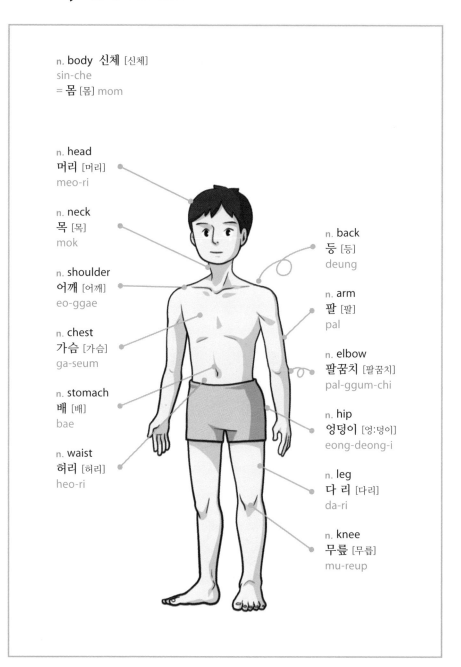

n. body 신체 [신체]
sin-che
= 몸 [몸] mom

n. head
머리 [머리]
meo-ri

n. neck
목 [목]
mok

n. shoulder
어깨 [어깨]
eo-ggae

n. chest
가슴 [가슴]
ga-seum

n. stomach
배 [배]
bae

n. waist
허리 [허리]
heo-ri

n. back
등 [등]
deung

n. arm
팔 [팔]
pal

n. elbow
팔꿈치 [팔꿈치]
pal-ggum-chi

n. hip
엉덩이 [엉:덩이]
eong-deong-i

n. leg
다 리 [다리]
da-ri

n. knee
무릎 [무릅]
mu-reup

n. hand
손 [손] son

n. wrist 손목 [손목]
son-mok

n. finger
손가락 [손까락]
son-gga-rak

n. nail 손톱 [손톱]
son-top

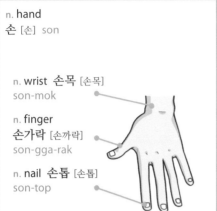

n. foot, feet
발 [발] bal

n. ankle 발목 [발목]
bal-mok

n. toe
발가락 [발까락]
bal-gga-rak

n. toenail
발톱 [발톱]
bal-top

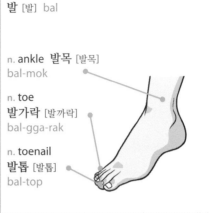

n. face
얼굴 [얼굴] eol-gul

n. forehead
이마 [이마] i-ma

n. eyebrow
눈썹 [눈썹]
nun-sseop

n. eye
눈 [눈] nun

n. nose
코 [코] ko

n. mouth
입 [입] ip

n. lip
입술 [입쑬]
ip-ssul

n. ear
귀 [귀] gwi

n. cheek
볼 [볼] bol

n. chin
턱 [턱] teok

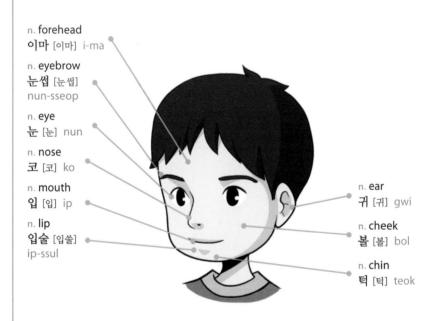

Physical Characteristics

■ He has broad shoulders.

그의 어깨는 넓어(요).

geu-e eo-ggae-neun neol-beo(-yo)

■ You have long legs.

너는 롱다리구나.

neo-neun rong-da-ri-gu-na

■ I don't like my piano legs.

내 무다리가 싫어(요).

nae mu-da-ri-ga si-reo(-yo)

Tip: 무다리 [mu-da-ri] means fat and thick legs like daikon radish.

■ He is an old man doubled over with age.

그는 나이가 들어서 허리가 굽었어(요).

geu-neun na-i-ga deu-reo-seo heo-ri-ga gu-beo-sseo(-yo)

■ I am left-handed.

나는 왼손잡이예요.

na-neun oen-son-ja-bi-ye-yo

Tip: 오른손잡이 [o-reun-son-ja-bi] means right-handed.

■ He's flat-footed.

그는 평발이에요.

geu-neun pyeong-ba-ri-e-yo

Height

■ How tall are you?

키가 얼마예요?

ki-ga eol-ma-ye-yo?

■ I'm 170 centimeters.

170cm예요.

baek-chil-ssip-ssen-ti-mi-teo-ye-yo

170이에요.

baek-chil-ssi-bi-e-yo

Tip: When talking about height, people just say the number without saying "centimeters."

■ He's of average height.

그는 키가 평균이에요.

geu-neun ki-ga pyeong-gyu-ni-e-yo

■ You're rather tall.

키가 큰 편이네(요).

ki-ga keun pyeo-ni-ne(-yo)

■ He is a little short.

그는 키가 좀 작아(요).

geu-neun ki-ga jom ja-ga(-yo)

■ She is tall and slim.

그녀는 키가 크고 날씬해(요).

geu-nyeo-neun ki-ga keu-go nal-ssin-hae(-yo)

Weight 1

- How much do you weigh?
  몸무게가 얼마나 나가(요)?
  mom-mu-ge-ga eol-ma-na na-ga(-yo)?

- I've gained some weight recently.
  요즘 체중이 늘었어(요).
  yo-jeum che-jung-i neu-reo-sseo(-yo)

- I'm afraid I'm a little overweight.
  살찐 거 같아(요).
  sal-jjin geo ga-ta(-yo)

- You lost weight, didn't you?
  너 살 빠졌는데, 그렇지?
  neo sal bba-jeon-neun-de, geu-reo-chi?

- She is very thin, nothing but skin and bone.
  그녀는 너무 말라서, 뼈밖에 없어(요).
  geu-nyeo-neun neo-mu mal-ra-seo, bbyeo-ba-gge eop-sseo(-yo)

- I'm trying to slim down by going on a diet.
  날씬해지려고 다이어트 중이에요.
  nal-ssin-hae-ji-ryeo-go da-i-eo-teu jung-i-e-yo

Weight 2

- If you want to lose weight, don't eat so much candy.
  살을 빼고 싶으면, 단 걸 많이 먹지 마(세요).
  sa-reul bbae-go si-peu-myeon, dan geol ma-ni meok-jji ma(-se-yo)

- I'd like to put on some weight.
  몸 좀 키우려고(요).
  mom jom ki-u-ryeo-go(-yo)

- You'd better slim down.
  살 좀 빼는 게 좋겠어(요).
  sal jom bbae-neun ge jo-ke-sseo(-yo)

- I've been working on my weight.
  체중 조절을 하고 있어(요).
  che-jung jo-jeo-reul ha-go i-sseo(-yo)

- He has a pot belly.
  그는 똥배가 나왔어(요).
  geu-neun ddong-bbae-ga na-wa-sseo(-yo)

- He has love handles.
  그는 옆구리에 군살이 있어(요).
  geu-neun yeop-ggu-ri-e gun-sa-ri i-sseo(-yo)

Different Appearances

■ He has an average body.
그는 표준 체형이에요.
geu-neun pyo-jun che-hyeong-i-e-yo

■ He's well-built.
그는 멋진 체형이에요.
geu-neun meot-jjin che-hyeong-i-e-yo

■ You are in fine shape.
건강해 보여(요).
geon-gang-hae bo-yeo(-yo)

■ You're beautiful just the way you are.
있는 그대로 아름다워(요).
in-neun geu-dae-ro a-reum-da-wo(-yo)

■ He is a little fat.
그는 좀 뚱뚱해(요).
geu-neun jom ddung-ddung-hae(-yo)

■ That kid is chubby.
그[저] 아이는 통통해(요).
geu[jeo] a-i-neun tong-tong-hae(-yo)

■ Don't be misled by appearances.
외모에 속으면 안 돼(요).
oe-mo-e so-geu-myeon an dwae(-yo)

Talchum

Talchum (탈춤 "Mask Dance") is a type of traditional performance where dancers cover their faces with various masks. It was originally performed in both shamanistic and harvest rituals before its evolution as popular entertainment. It was also adapted for the court but was discontinued during the Joseon Dynasty (1392–1897).

Styles and characteristics vary from region to region though many of the narratives were united in their criticism of the monks and noble classes who oppressed the common people.

Some famous Korean traditional mask dances include Hahoe Byeolsingut (하회별신굿 "exorcism"), Bongsan Talchum (봉산탈춤 "Bongsan Mask Dance") and the Bukcheong Sajanoreum (북청사자놀음 "Korean Lion Dance").

Face Shapes

- I have a round face.
  얼굴이 둥근형이에요.
  eol-gu-ri dung-geun-hyeong-i-e-yo

- I have an oval face.
  얼굴이 달걀형이에요.
  eol-gu-ri dal-gyal-hyeong-i-e-yo

  얼굴이 계란형이에요.
  eol-gu-ri gye-ran-hyeong-i-e-yo

- He has a square jaw.
  그는 사각턱이에요.
  geu-neun sa-gak-teo-gi-e-yo

- My face is a little chubby.
  내 얼굴은 통통해(요).
  nae eol-gu-reun tong-tong-hae(-yo)

- What hairstyle is best for my face shape?
  내 얼굴에 어떤 헤어스타일이
  가장 좋을까(요)?
  nae eol-gu-re eo-ddeon he-eo-seu-ta-i-ri
  ga-jang jo-eul-gga(-yo)?

- These glasses don't compliment my face shape.
  이 안경은 내 얼굴형에 어울리지
  않아(요).
  i an-gyeong-eun nae eol-gul-hyeong-e
  eo-ul-ri-ji a-na(-yo)

Looks

- She has a baby face.
  그녀는 동안이에요.
  geu-nyeo-neun dong-a-ni-e-yo

- I look young for my age.
  나는 나이보다 어려 보여(요).
  na-neun na-i-bo-da eo-ryeo bo-yeo(-yo)

- He looks old.
  그는 나이 들어 보여(요).
  geu-neun na-i deu-reo bo-yeo(-yo)

- He has a broad forehead.
  그의 이마는 넓어(요).
  geu-e i-ma-neun neol-beo(-yo)

- I have dimples when I smile.
  웃을 때 보조개가 있어(요).
  u-seul ddae bo-jo-gae-ga i-sseo(-yo)

- I like a man with thick eyebrows.
  눈썹이 짙은 남자가 좋아(요).
  nun-sseo-bi ji-teun nam-ja-ga jo-a(-yo)

- My elder sister and I don't look alike.
  우리 언니[누나]와 나는
  안 닮았어(요).
  u-ri eon-ni[nu-na]-wa na-neun
  an dal-ma-sseo(-yo)

Skin

- She has a fair complexion.
그녀의 피부는 하얘(요).
geu-nyeo-e pi-bu-neun ha-yae(-yo)

- She is dark-skinned.
그녀의 피부는 까매(요).
geu-nyeo-e pi-bu-neun gga-mae(-yo)

- I got sunburned.
피부가 햇볕에 탔어(요).
pi-bu-ga hat-bbyeo-te ta-sseo(-yo)

- I wish my skin had more elasticity.
내 피부가 더 탄력 있으면 좋겠어(요).
nae pi-bu-ga deo tal-ryeok i-sseu-myeon jo-ke-sseo(-yo)

- Your skin is oily.
피부가 지성이군(요).
pi-bu-ga ji-seong-i-gun(-yo)

- My skin is very dry. I use a lot of moisturizer.
피부가 아주 건성이라서 수분크림을 많이 발라(요).
pi-bu-ga a-ju geon-seong-i-ra-seo su-bun-keu-ri-meul ma-ni bal-ra(-yo)

Skin Problems 1

- My face is peeling.
얼굴에 각질이 생겼어(요).
eol-gu-re gak-jji-ri saeng-gyeo-sseo(-yo)

- My skin is chapped.
피부가 텄어(요).
pi-bu-ga teo-sseo(-yo)

- I worry about my pores.
모공 때문에 고민이에요.
mo-gong ddae-mu-ne go-mi-ni-e-yo

- A rash broke out all over my face.
얼굴에 온통 두드러기가 났어(요).
eol-gu-re on-tong du-deu-reo-gi-ga na-sseo(-yo)

- I suffer from eczema.
습진 때문에 고통에 시달려(요).
seup-jjin ddae-mu-ne go-tong-e si-dal-ryeo(-yo)

- I have sensitive skin, so I can't wear cosmetics.
피부가 예민해서, 화장품을 쓸 수 없어(요).
pi-bu-ga ye-min-hae-seo, hwa-jang-pu-meul sseul ssu eop-sseo(-yo)

Skin Problems 2

- I have a skin allergy.
  피부에 알레르기가 있어(요).
  pi-bu-e al-re-reu-gi-ga i-sseo(-yo)

- There are pimples on my face.
  얼굴에 여드름이 났어(요).
  eol-gu-re yeo-deu-reu-mi na-sseo(-yo)

- I have too many spots on my face.
  얼굴에 점이 많아(요).
  eol-gu-re jeo-mi ma-na(-yo)

- I've always had freckles.
  주근깨가 늘 있었어(요).
  ju-geun-ggae-ga neul i-sseo-sseo(-yo)

- Recently I've gotten some liver spots.
  요즘 검버섯이 많이 생겼어(요).
  yo-jeum geom-beo-seo-si ma-ni saeng-gyeo-sseo(-yo)

- Your face is wrinkle-free.
  얼굴에 주름이 하나도 없네(요).
  eol-gu-re ju-reu-mi ha-na-do eom-ne(-yo)

Eyes 1

- I have double eyelids.
  쌍꺼풀이 있어(요).
  ssang-ggeo-pu-ri i-sseo(-yo)

- I have inner double eyelids.
  속쌍꺼풀이에요.
  sok-ssang-ggeo-pu-ri-e-yo

- If you have double eyelids, your eyes look bigger.
  쌍꺼풀이 있으면, 눈이 더 커 보여(요).
  ssang-ggeo-pu-ri i-sseu-myeon, nu-ni deo keo bo-yeo(-yo)

- I have long eyelashes.
  내 속눈썹은 길어(요).
  nae song-nun-sseo-beun gi-reo(-yo)

- She has beautiful big eyes.
  그녀는 눈이 크고 예뻐(요).
  geu-nyeo-neun nu-ni keu-go ye-bbeo(-yo)

- He has big bright eyes.
  그는 눈이 부리부리해(요).
  geu-neun nu-ni bu-ri-bu-ri-hae(-yo)

Eyes 2

I have bulging eyeballs.

눈이 좀 튀어나왔어(요).

nu-ni jom twi-eo-na-wa-sseo(-yo)

My eyes are far apart from each other.

내 두 눈은 많이 떨어져 있어(요).

nae du nu-neun ma-ni ddeo-reo-jeo i-sseo(-yo)

Her eyes are close together.

그녀는 눈이 가까이 몰려 있어(요).

geu-nyeo-nuen nu-ni ga-gga-i mol-ryeo i-sseo(-yo)

My eyes slant downward.

눈꼬리가 처졌어(요).

nun-ggo-ri-ga cheo-jeo-sseo(-yo)

I have small eyes.

눈이 작아(요).

nu-ni ja-ga(-yo)

Eyesight

He is color-blind.

그는 색맹이에요.

geu-neun saeng-maeng-i-e-yo

How is your eyesight?

시력은 어때(요)?

si-ryeo-geun eo-ddae(-yo)?

I have twenty-twenty vision.

시력이 좋아(요).

si-ryeo-gi jo-a(-yo)

I am nearsighted so I wear glasses.

근시라서 안경을 써(요).

geun-si-ra-seo an-gyeong-eul sseo(-yo)

Byeong-ho has poor eyesight, and he is astigmatic.

병호는 시력이 나쁜데다가, 난시예요.

byeong-ho-neun si-ryeo-gi na-bbeun-de-da-ga, nan-si-ye-yo

Do you wear contacts?

콘택트렌즈 해(요)?

kon-taek-teu-ren-jeu hae(-yo)?

Nose

- I have a sharp nose.
  내 콧대는 높아(요).
  nae kot-ddae-neun no-pa(-yo)

- His nose is flat.
  그는 코가 평평해(요).
  geu-neun ko-ga
  pyeong-pyeong-hae(-yo)

- She has a hooked nose.
  그녀는 매부리코예요.
  geu-nyeo-neun mae-bu-ri-ko-ye-yo

- I think my nose is a bit flat.
  내 코는 좀 낮은 것 같아(요).
  nae ko-neun jom na-jeun geot
  ga-ta(-yo)

- People say he has the perfect
  nose.
  사람들은 그가 완벽한 코를
  가졌다고 해(요).
  sa-ram-deu-reun geu-ga wan-byeo-kan
  ko-reul ga-jeot-dda-go hae(-yo)

Ears

- I can't hear well out of this ear.
  이 귀로 잘 들을 수 없어(요).
  i gwi-ro jal deu-reul ssu eop-sseo(-yo)

- He has poor hearing.
  그는 귀가 좀 어두워(요).
  geu-neun gwi-ga jom eo-du-wo(-yo)

- My ears are full of wax.
  귀지가 많이 있어(요).
  gwi-ji-ga ma-ni i-sseo(-yo)

- He wears a hearing aid.
  그는 보청기를 달고 있어(요).
  geu-neun bo-cheong-gi-reul dal-go
  i-sseo(-yo)

- Where did you get your ears
  pierced?
  어디에서 귀 뚫었어(요)?
  eo-di-e-seo gwi ddu-reo-sseo(-yo)?

- I have an ear infection.
  중이염에 걸렸어(요).
  jung-i-yeo-me geol-ryeo-sseo(-yo)

Mouth & Lips

- His mouth is big.
  그는 입이 커(요).
  geu-neun i-bi keo(-yo)

- She has a very small mouth.
  그녀는 입이 유난히 작아(요).
  geu-nyeo-neun i-bi yu-nan-hi ja-ga(-yo)

- She has a lovely mouth.
  그녀는 입매가 예뻐(요).
  geu-nyeo-neun im-mae-ga
  ye-bbeo(-yo)

- His lips are full.
  그는 입술이 두꺼워(요).
  geu-neun ip-ssu-ri du-ggeo-wo(-yo)

- My lips are thin.
  입술이 얇아(요).
  ip-ssu-ri yal-ba(-yo)

- My lips often crack.
  입술이 자주 터(요).
  ip-ssu-ri ja-ju teo(-yo)

Oral

- I have a gum problem.
  잇몸이 별로 좋지 않아(요).
  in-mo-mi byeol-ro jo-chi a-na(-yo)

- My gums are so swollen that
  I can't eat anything.
  잇몸이 너무 부어서 아무것도
  먹을 수 없어(요).
  in-mo-mi neo-mu bu-eo-seo
  a-mu-geot-ddo meo-geul ssu
  eop-sseo(-yo)

- My gums ache when I drink
  cold water.
  찬물을 마시면 잇몸이 시려(요).
  chan-mu-reul ma-si-myeon in-mo-mi
  si-ryeo(-yo)

- Recently my gums bleed a lot.
  최근 잇몸에서 피가 많이 나(요).
  choe-geun in-mo-me-seo pi-ga ma-ni
  na(-yo)

- Your breath smells bad.
  네 입냄새가 지독해(요).
  ne im-naem-sae-ga ji-do-kae(-yo)

- Gargle with mouthwash.
  구강청정제로 헹구세요.
  gu-gang-cheong-jeong-je-ro
  heng-gu-se-yo

Teeth

- Her teeth are so white.
  그녀는 이가 새하얘(요).
  geu-nyeo-neun i-ga sae-ha-yae(-yo)

- I have straight teeth.
  이가 고르게 났어(요).
  i-ga go-reu-ge na-sseo(-yo)

- I had my wisdom teeth taken out.
  사랑니를 뽑았어(요).
  sa-rang-ni-reul bbo-ba-sseo(-yo)

- I have a cavity.
  충치가 생겼어(요).
  chung-chi-ga saeng-gyeo-sseo(-yo)

- I have a few fillings.
  이를 때운 것이 몇 개 있어(요).
  i-reul ddae-un geo-si myeot gae
  i-sseo(-yo)

- I have a double tooth.
  덧니가 하나 있어(요).
  deon-ni-ga ha-na i-sseo(-yo)

- Do you floss regularly?
  정기적으로 치실질 해(요)?
  jeong-gi-jeo-geu-ro chi-sil-jil hae(-yo)?

Hair

- My hair has begun to turn gray recently.
  요즘 흰머리가 나기 시작했어(요).
  yo-jeum hin-meo-ri-ga na-gi
  si-ja-kae-sseo(-yo)

- He is bald.
  그는 대머리예요.
  geu-neun dae-meo-ri-ye-yo

- My hair is damaged.
  머릿결이 상했어(요).
  meo-rit-ggeo-ri sang-hae-sseo(-yo)

- I have split ends.
  머리끝이 갈라졌어(요).
  meo-ri-ggeu-chi gal-ra-jeo-sseo(-yo)

- My hair loss is turning into a serious problem.
  머리카락이 자꾸 빠져서 큰일이에요.
  meo-ri-ka-ra-gi ja-ggu bba-jeo-seo
  keu-ni-ri-e-yo

- Her hair is very healthy looking.
  그녀의 머릿결은 아주 건강해 보여(요).
  geu-nyeo-e meo-rit-ggyeo-reun a-ju
  geon-gang-hae bo-yeo(-yo)

Hairstyles

■ She likes ponytails.
그녀는 포니테일 스타일을
좋아해(요).
geu-nyeo-neun po-ni-te-il seu-ta-i-reul
jo-a-hae(-yo)

■ My elder sister wears her hair in
a braid.
언니[누나]는 머리를 땋았어(요).
eon-ni[nu-na]-neun meo-ri-reul
dda-a-sseo(-yo)

■ I have short hair.
짧은 머리예요.
jjal-beun meo-ri-ye-yo

■ What color is your hair?
네 머리는 무슨 색이니?
ne meo-ri-neun mu-seun sae-gi-ni?

■ He has brown hair.
그의 머리는 갈색이에요.
geu-e meo-ri-neun gal-ssae-gi-e-yo

■ I changed my hairstyle.
헤어스타일을 바꿨어(요).
he-eo-seu-ta-i-reul ba-ggwo-sseo(-yo)

Beards & Mustaches

■ My dad had a mustache.
우리 아빠는 콧수염이
있었어(요).
u-ri a-bba-neun kot-ssu-yeo-mi
i-sseo-sseo(-yo)

■ He has mutton chops.
그는 구레나룻이 있어(요).
geu-neun gu-re-na-ru-si i-sseo(-yo)

■ He has a goatee.
그는 턱밑에 수염을 길렀어(요).
geu-neun teong-mi-te su-yeo-meul
gil-reo-sseo(-yo)

■ Grandfather has a white beard.
할아버지는 하얀 수염이
있어(요).
ha-ra-beo-ji-neun ha-yan su-yeo-mi
i-sseo(-yo)

■ Do you want to grow a beard?
수염을 기르고 싶어(요)?
su-yeo-meul gi-reu-go si-peo(-yo)?

Style 1	**Style 2**

■ The kid looks so cute.
아이가 귀엽게 생겼어(요).
a-i-ga gwi-yeop-gge
saeng-gyeo-sseo(-yo)

■ He looks quite intelligent.
그는 꽤 지적으로 보여(요).
geu-neun ggwae ji-jjeo-geu-ro
bo-yeo(-yo)

■ That guy is so hot.
저 남자는 섹시한데(요).
jeo nam-ja-neun sek-ssi-han-de(-yo)

■ He is good-looking.
그는 잘생겼어(요).
geu-neun jal-saeng-gyeo-sseo(-yo)

■ He is a handsome guy.
그는 미남이에요.
geu-neun mi-na-mi-e-yo

■ She is a real knockout.
그녀는 정말 미인이에요.
geu-nyeo-neun jeong-mal mi-i-ni-e-yo

■ She's curvy.
그녀는 글래머예요.
geu-nyeo-neun geul-rae-meo-ye-yo

■ She's very plain looking.
그녀는 수수하게 생겼어(요).
geu-nyeo-neun su-su-ha-ge
saeng-gyeo-sseo(-yo)

■ You look great today.
오늘 멋져 보여(요).
o-neul meot-jjeo bo-yeo(-yo)

■ I'm a bit of a tomboy.
나는 말괄량이예요.
na-neun mal-gwal-ryang-i-ye-yo

■ He looks the same as always.
그는 항상 그 모습 그대로인 것
같아(요).
geu-neun hang-sang geu mo-seup
geu-dae-ro-in geot ga-ta(-yo)

■ He's a man with taste.
그는 멋을 아는 남자예요.
geu-neun meo-seul a-neun nam-ja-ye-yo

■ She's out of style.
그녀는 촌스러워(요).
geu-nyeo-neun chon-sseu-reo-wo(-yo)

■ You look sharp.
세련되어 보이는데(요).
se-ryeon-doe-eo bo-i-neun-de(-yo)

Resemblance

■ You look like someone I know.

당신은 내가 아는 사람이랑
닮았어(요).

dang-si-neun nae-ga a-neun sa-ra-mi-
rang dal-ma-sseo(-yo)

■ My sister resembles my father
around the eyes.

여동생은 아빠 눈을 닮았어(요).

yeo-dong-saeng-eun a-bba nu-neul
dal-ma-sseo(-yo)

■ Do you look more like your dad
or your mom?

넌 아빠를 닮았니 엄마를 닮았니?

neon a-bba-reul dal-mat-ni eom-ma-reul
dal-mat-ni?

■ Sang-hee looks exactly like her
mother.

상희는 엄마와 붕어빵이에요.

sang-hi-neun eom-ma-wa
bung-eo-bbang-i-e-yo

Tip: 붕어빵 [bung-eo-bbang] **is carp-shaped
bread (i.e., bread that looks like a fish) so this
phrase is used to say two things look similar.**

■ Do people say you look like
Seo-jun Park?

남들이 박서준을 닮았다고
하지(요)?

nam-deu-ri bak-sseo-ju-neul dal-ma-
dda-go ha-ji(-yo)?

Tip: 박서준 [Park Seo-jun] **is a Korean actor.**

Ugly Looking

■ He is butt-ugly.

그는 너무 못났어(요).

geu-neun neo-mu mon-na-sseo(-yo)

■ She is ugly.

그녀는 못생겼어(요).

geu-nyeo-neun mot-ssaeng-gyeo-
sseo(-yo)

■ She has a nice personality.

그녀는 성격만 좋아(요).

geu-nyeo-neun seong-ggyeong-man
jo-a(-yo)

Tip: This sentence means she looks ugly.
It has an indirect meaning.

■ She is short on looks.

그녀는 외모가 좀 떨어져(요).

geu-nyeo-neun oe-mo-ga jom
ddeo-reo-jeo(-yo)

■ His looks are just passable.

그의 외모는 그저그래(요).

geu-e oe-mo-neun geu-jeo-geu-rae(-yo)

■ He is a man of disagreeable
appearance.

그는 별로 호감이 가지 않는
외모예요.

geu-neun byeol-ro ho-ga-mi ga-ji
an-neun oe-mo-ye-yo

Clothes 옷 ot

n. clothes 옷 [옫] ot	n. suit 양복 [양복] yang-bok	n. jacket 재킷 [재킫] jae-kit
	n. dress shirt 와이셔츠 [와이셔츠] wa-i-syeo-cheu	n. tie 넥타이 [넥타이] nek-ta-i
n. sweater 스웨터 [스웨터] seu-we-teo	n. jacket 점퍼 [점퍼] jeom-peo	n. cardigan 카디건 [카디건] ka-di-geon
n. overcoat 외투 [외:투/웨:투] oe-tu/we-tu	n. padded jacket 패딩 점퍼 [패딩 점퍼] pae-ding jeom-peo	n. pants, trousers 바지 [바지] ba-ji
n. blouse 블라우스 [블라우스] beul-ra-u-seu	n. dress 원피스 [원피스] won-pi-seu	n. skirt 치마 [치마] chi-ma
n. pajamas 잠옷 [자몯] ja-mot	n. underwear 속옷 [소:곧] so-got	n. briefs, underpants 팬티 [팬티] paen-ti
n. sportswear 운동복 [운:동복] un-dong-bok	n. swimsuit 수영복 [수영복] su-yeong-bok	n. raincoat 비옷 [비옫] bi-ot

n. cap, hat 모자 [모자]
mo-ja

n. muffler 목도리 [목또리]
mok-ddo-ri

n. scarf 스카프 [스카프]
seu-ka-peu

n. gloves 장갑 [장:갑]
jang-gap

n. belt 허리띠 [허리띠]
heo-ri-ddi

n. suspenders 멜빵 [멜:빵]
mel-bbang

n. shoes 신발 [신발]
sin-bal

n. dress shoes 구두 [구두]
gu-du

n. sneakers
운동화 [운:동화]
un-dong-hwa

n. slides 슬리퍼 [슬리퍼]
seul-ri-peo

n. sandals 샌들 [샌들]
saen-deul

n. slippers 실내화 [실래화]
sil-rae-hwa

n. bag 가방 [가방]
ga-bang

n. handbag 핸드백 [핸드백]
haen-deu-baek

n. backpack 배낭 [배:낭]
bae-nang

n. suitcase, trunk
트렁크 [트렁크]
teu-reong-keu

n. wallet, purse
지갑 [지갑]
ji-gap

n. glasses 안경 [안:경]
an-gyeong

n. ring 반지 [반지]
ban-ji

n. necklace
목걸이 [목꺼리]
mok-ggeo-ri

n. earrings
귀걸이 [귀거리]
gwi-geo-ri

Dress 1

- She only wears the latest fashions.
그녀는 최신 유행하는 옷만 입어(요).
geu-nyeo-neun choe-sin yu-haeng-ha-neun on-man i-beo(-yo)

- It's in vogue now.
이것은 유행하는 중이에요.
i-geo-seun yu-haeng-ha-neun jung-i-e-yo

- This is the latest style.
이것은 최신 스타일이에요.
i-geo-seun choe-sin seu-ta-i-ri-e-yo

- She doesn't care much about clothes.
그녀는 옷차림에 별로 신경을 쓰지 않아(요).
geu-nyeo-neun ot-cha-ri-me byeol-ro sin-gyeong-eul sseu-ji a-na(-yo)

- He never dresses up.
그는 절대 차려입지 않아(요).
geu-neun jeol-ddae cha-ryeo-ip-jji a-na(-yo)

Dress 2

- He always wears a suit.
그는 항상 정장을 입어(요).
geu-neun hang-sang jeong-jang-eul i-beo(-yo)

- You look good in everything.
아무거나 잘 어울리는데(요).
a-mu-geo-na jal eo-ul-ri-neun-de(-yo)

- You're out of fashion if you don't wear this style of jeans.
이런 청바지를 입지 않으면 유행에 뒤떨어져(요).
i-reon cheong-ba-ji-reul ip-jji a-neu-myeon yu-haeng-e dwi-ddeo-reo-jeo(-yo)

- She only wears designer clothes.
그녀는 명품만 입어(요).
geu-nyeo-neun myeong-pum-man i-beo(-yo)

- Did you pick an outfit for the Christmas party?
크리스마스 파티에 입을 옷 골랐어(요)?
keu-ri-seu-ma-seu pa-ti-e i-beul ot gol-ra-sseo(-yo)?

Makeup 1

■ She wears too much makeup.

그녀는 화장이 너무 진해(요).

geu-nyeo-neun hwa-jang-i neo-mu jin-hae(-yo)

■ I'm almost done with my makeup.

화장이 곧 끝나가(요).

hwa-jang-i got ggeun-na-ga(-yo)

■ She puts on her makeup in the car when she goes to work.

그녀는 출근할 때 차에서 화장해(요).

geu-nyeo-neun chul-geun-hal ddae cha-e-seo hwa-jang-hae(-yo)

■ She looks pretty without any makeup.

그녀는 화장을 안 해도 예뻐(요).

geu-nyeo-neun hwa-jang-eul an hae-do ye-bbeo(-yo)

■ Don't forget to wear lipstick.

립스틱 바르는 거 잊지 마(요).

lip-sseu-tik ba-reu-neun geo it-jji ma(-yo)

■ My eyeshadow isn't blending.

아이섀도가 잘 발라지지 않았어(요).

a-i-syae-do-ga jal bal-ra-ji-ji a-na-sseo(-yo)

The DMZ

The Korean Demilitarized Zone (DMZ) divides North and South Korea and stretches across the 38th parallel.

When the Korean War (1950–1953) concluded with an armistice agreement, a land border known as the Military Demarcation Line was established there. As the name states, the two-and-a-half mile (4 km)–wide strip is demilitarized though not the land beyond it.

The Joint Security Area (JSA or Panmunjeom 판문점) within the DMZ serves as a site for diplomatic meetings; this is where soldiers from North and South face off.

Interestingly, the natural environment inside the DMZ has been preserved for about seventy years, and so has high scientific value.

You can take a tour to the DMZ. Be sure to check out Imjingak Park (임진각), Unification Bridge (통일대교 [tong-il-dae-gyo]), the Third Tunnel (제3땅굴 [je-sam-ddang-ggul]) and Dora Observatory (도라 전망대 [do-ra jeon-mang-dae]).

Makeup 2

- Your makeup is smeared.
화장이 다 번졌어(요).
hwa-jang-i da beon-jeo-sseo(-yo)

- Her makeup is caked on.
그녀의 화장이 떡졌어(요).
geu-nyeo-e hwa-jang-i ddeok-jjeo-sseo(-yo)

- Which makeup brand do you use?
무슨 브랜드(의) 화장품을
써(요)?
mu-seun beu-raen-deu(-e) hwa-jang-pu-meul sseo(-yo)?

- I spend too much on makeup.
화장품을 사는 데 돈을 너무
많이 써(요).
hwa-jang-pu-meul sa-neun de do-neul neo-mu ma-ni sseo(-yo)

- Did you take off all your makeup?
화장을 다 지웠어(요)?
hwa-jang-eul da ji-wo-sseo(-yo)?

- I slept with my makeup on yesterday.
어제 화장을 안 지우고
잠들었어(요).
eo-je hwa-jang-eul an ji-u-go jam-deu-reo-sseo(-yo)

Plastic Surgery

- I want to get plastic surgery.
성형수술 하고 싶어(요).
seong-hyeong-su-sul ha-go si-peo(-yo)

- I got double-eyelid surgery.
쌍꺼풀 수술을 했어(요).
ssang-ggeo-pul su-su-reul hae-sseo(-yo)

- There was a problem when I had my nose done.
코 성형수술이 잘못 됐어(요).
ko seong-hyeong-su-su-ri jal-mot dwae-sseo(-yo)

- I had facial contouring surgery.
안면 윤곽 수술을 했어(요).
an-myeon yun-gwak su-su-reul hae-sseo(-yo)

- I had the size of my jaw reduced.
턱을 깎았어(요).
teo-geul gga-gga-sseo(-yo)

- You don't look like you had plastic surgery.
성형수술한 티가 안 나는데(요).
seong-hyeong-su-sul-han ti-ga an na-neun-de(-yo)

Chapter 5

Out & About

Restaurants & Cafés 음식점 & 카페 eum-sik-jjeom & ka-pe

n. restaurant 음식점 [음:식쩜] eum-sik-jjeom
= 식당 [식땅]
sik-ddang

n. dish, cooking
요리 [요리]
yo-ri

n. menu
메뉴판 [메뉴판]
me-nyu-pan

n. reservation, booking
예약 [예:약]
ye-yak

n. recommendation
추천 [추천]
chu-cheon

n. order
주문 [주:문]
ju-mun

n. takeout, takeaway
테이크아웃 [테이크아웉]
te-i-keu-a-ut

n. bill 계산서 [계:산서/게:산서]
gye-san-seo/ge-san-seo

n. appetizer
애피타이저 [애피타이저]
ae-pi-ta-i-jeo

n. main dish
주요리 [주요리]
ju-yo-ri

n. side dish
반찬 [반찬]
ban-chan

n. dessert 후식 [후:식]
hu-sik
= 디저트 [디저트]
di-jeo-teu

n. rice 밥 [밥]
bap

n. bibimbap
비빔밥 [비빔빱]
bi-bim-bbap

n. soup 국 [국]
guk

n. stew, casserole
찌개 [찌개]
jji-gae

n. namul (vegetables mixed with seasonings)
나물 [나물]
na-mul

n. dried meat or fish
마른반찬 [마른반찬]
ma-reun-ban-chan

n. bulgogi, barbecued beef
불고기 [불고기]
bul-go-gi

n. tteokbokki stir-fried rice cake
떡볶이 [떡뽀끼]
ddeok-bbo-ggi

n. bread
빵 [빵]
bbang

n. cookie, biscuit
과자 [과자]
gwa-ja

n. cake 케이크 [케이크]
ke-i-keu

n. ice cream
아이스크림 [아이스크림]
a-i-seu-keu-rim

n. chocolate
초콜릿 [초콜릳]
cho-kol-rit

n. candy
사탕 [사탕]
sa-tang

adj. delicious, tasty
맛있다 [마딛따/마싣따]
ma-dit-dda/
ma-sit-dda

adj. salty 짜다 [짜다]
jja-da

adj. sweet 달다 [달다]
dal-da

adj. hot, spicy 맵다 [맵따]
maep-dda

adj. sour 시다 [시다]
si-da

adj. bitter 쓰다 [쓰다]
sseu-da

n. spoon 숟가락 [숟까락]
sut-gga-rak

n. chopsticks
젓가락 [저까락/젇까락]
jeo-gga-rak/jeot-gga-rak

n. fork
포크 [포크]
po-keu

n. café, coffee shop
카페 [카페] ka-pe
= 커피숍 [커피숍]
keo-pi-syop

n. coffee 커피 [커피]
keo-pi

n. tea 차 [차] cha

n. beverage, drink
음료 [음:뇨]
eum-nyo
= 음료수 [음:뇨수]
eum-nyo-su

n. juice 주스 [주스]
ju-seu

n. carbonated water
탄산수 [탄:산수]
tan-san-su

Recommending Restaurants

■ I'd like to have a light meal.
간단하게 먹고 싶은데(요).
gan-dan-ha-ge meok-ggo si-peun-de(-yo)

■ Is there a good restaurant around here?
이 근처에 맛있는 음식점 있어(요)?
i geun-cheo-e ma-din-neun eum-sik-jjeom i-sseo(-yo)?

■ Can you recommend a nice restaurant?
괜찮은 음식점을 추천해 주세요.
gwaen-cha-neun eum-sik-jjeo-meul chu-cheon-hae ju-se-yo

■ Is there a restaurant open at this time?
이 시간에 문을 연 음식점이 있어(요)?
i si-ga-ne mu-neul yeon eum-sik-jjeo-mi i-sseo(-yo)?

■ Where is the main area for restaurants?
음식점이 많은 곳이 어디예요?
eum-sik-jjeo-mi ma-neun go-si eo-di-ye-yo?

Reservations

■ Shall I book a table at the restaurant?
음식점을 예약할까(요)?
eum-sik-jjeo-meul ye-ya-kal-gga(-yo)?

■ I'll make a reservation.
예약할게(요).
ye-ya-kal-gge(-yo)

■ Do we need a reservation?
예약해야 해(요)?
ye-ya-kae-ya hae(-yo)?

■ I'd like a table for three at seven o'clock.
7시에 3인석 예약하려고(요).
il-gop-ssi-e sa-min-seok ye-ya-ka-ryeo-go(-yo)

■ I want to change my reservation.
예약을 바꿔 주세요.
ye-ya-geul ba-ggwo ju-se-yo

■ Cancel my reservation, please.
예약을 취소해 주세요.
ye-yak-geul chwi-so-hae ju-se-yo

Getting a Table

■ How large is your party?

몇 분이세요?

meot bu-ni-se-yo?

■ We have a party of five.

다섯 명입니다.

da-seot myeong-im-ni-da

■ Those tables are reserved.

그 테이블들은 예약석입니다.

geu te-i-beul-deu-reun
ye-yak-sseo-gim-ni-da

■ I'm afraid there are no tables available now.

죄송하지만, 지금은 자리가 없습니다.

joe-song-ha-ji-man, ji-geu-meun ja-ri-ga
eop-sseum-ni-da

■ About how long will we have to wait?

얼마나 기다려야 해(요)?

eol-ma-na gi-da-ryeo-ya hae(-yo)?

■ There's a twenty-minute wait.

20분 정도 기다리셔야 합니다.

i-sip-bbun jeong-do gi-da-ri-syeo-ya
ham-ni-da

Best Korean Food Part 1

1. Bibimbap (비빔밥)
Bibimbap is a delicious, low-calorie dish anyone who's ever set foot in Korea will know. Ingredients may vary but tradition dictates you will find the following: rice, vegetables, beef, gochujang (고추장 hot chili paste), and a fried egg. Veggies like bean sprouts, carrots and cucumber are cut in strips and arranged on top in attractively colored sections. The city of Jeonju (전주) is especially known for its bibimbap.

2. Sundubu Jjigae (순두부찌개 soft tofu stew) **& Kimchi jjigae** (김치찌개 kimchi stew)
Jjigae (찌개) is a kind of stew, usually served with rice. Sundubu jjigae is a Korean comfort food made with soft tofu, vegetables and chilli paste. Meat (pork or beef), seafood (mussels, clams, etc.) or a raw egg may also be added. Kimchi jjigae is classic Korean cuisine with kimchi, pork or tuna, tofu, and vegetables.

3. Samgyeopsal (삼겹살, Korean BBQ)
Samgyeopsal is a kind of pork BBQ, a favorite dish in Korea. The dish is simple: thick unmarinated slices of pork belly are set on a grill at your table, heated via charcoal or gas. Customers usually perform the cooking honors themselves, then wrap the strips of pork in lettuce along with garlic, onion and spicy ssamjang sauce (쌈장). Meat lovers should also try bulgogi (불고기 Korean BBQ beef) and galbi (갈비 grilled ribs).

The Menu

▪ Can I see the menu, please?

메뉴 좀 볼 수 있어요?

me-nyu jom bol ssu i-sseo(-yo)?

▪ What would you recommend?

추천 메뉴가 뭐예요?

chu-cheon me-nyu-ga mwo-ye-yo?

▪ We need a little more time to look at the menu.

메뉴를 좀 더 보고 싶은데요.

me-nyu-reul jom deo bo-go
si-peun-de(-yo)

▪ Could you take our orders a little later?

이따가 주문할게요.

i-dda-ga ju-mun-hal-gge-yo

▪ What's your specialty?

여기 특선 요리는 뭔가요?

yeo-gi teuk-sseon yo-ri-neun
mwon-ga-yo?

▪ We specialize in beoseot-jeongol.

버섯전골은 우리 가게의 간판 메뉴입니다.

beo-seot-jjeon-go-reun u-ri ga-ge-e
gan-pan me-nyu-im-ni-da

Tip: Beoseot-jeongol is a mushroom hot pot.

Ordering 1

▪ Have you been served?

주문하시겠어요?

ju-mun-ha-si-ge-sseo-yo?

▪ Can I order now?

지금 주문해도 돼요?

ji-geum ju-mun-hae-do dwae-yo?

▪ What would you like?

뭘 주문하시겠습니까?

mwol ju-mun-ha-si-get-sseum-ni-gga?

▪ We'd like to order drinks first.

먼저 음료부터 시킬게요.

meon-jeo eum-nyo-bu-teo si-kil-gge-yo

▪ We are ready to order.

주문하고 싶은데요.

ju-mun-ha-go si-peun-de-yo

▪ I'd like this one, please.

이것으로 주세요.

i-geo-seu-ro ju-se-yo

▪ Okay, I'll have that.

좋아요, 그걸로 할게요.

jo-a-yo, geu-geol-ro hal-gge-yo

▪ The same for me, please.

저도 같은 것으로 주세요.

jeo-do ga-teun geo-seu-ro ju-se-yo

Ordering 2

■ Let me check your order.

주문 확인하겠습니다.

ju-mun hwa-gin-ha-get-sseum-ni-da

■ Anything else?

더 필요하신 것 없으세요?

deo pi-ryo-ha-sin geot eop-sseu-se-yo?

■ Which options would you like
for your jeukseok tteokbokki?

즉석 떡볶이에 어떤 사리를
하시겠어요?

jeuk-sseok ddeok-bbo-ggi-e eo-ddeon
sa-ri-reul ha-si-ge-sseo-yo?

Tip: Jeukseok tteokbokki is a kind of stew
that diners cook themselves. It may contain
ramyeon (instant noodles), chewy noodles, fish
cakes, cheese, boiled eggs and so on.

■ Please add a portion of ramyeon
and a portion of chewy noodles.

라면사리 하나, 쫄면사리 하나
추가해 주세요.

ra-myeon-sa-ri ha-na, jjol-myeon-sa-ri
ha-na chu-ga-hae ju-se-yo

■ I'd like a cheese gimbap and a
tuna gimbap.

치즈김밥 하나, 참치김밥 하나
주세요.

chi-jeu-gim-bbap ha-na,
cham-chi-gim-bbap ha-na ju-se-yo

Ordering 3

■ Which one do you want,
mul-naengmyeon or
bibim-naengmyeon?

물냉면으로 드릴까요
비빔냉면으로 드릴까요?

mul-raeng-myeo-neu-ro deu-ril-gga-yo
bi-bim-naeng-myeo-neu-ro
deu-ril-gga-yo?

Tip: Naengmyeon is a kind of cold noodle dish,
popular in summer. "Mul-naengmyeon" are
noodles served in a cold broth and "bibim-
naengmyeon" are spicy noodles.

■ You can enjoy a cup of insam-ju
if you order a samgye-tang.

삼계탕을 시키면 인삼주가
서비스로 나옵니다.

sam-gye-tang-eul si-ki-myeon in-sam-
ju-ga seo-bi-seu-ro na-om-ni-da

Tip: Insam-ju is ginseng wine. Samgye-tang is
Korean ginseng chicken soup.

■ Please keep the bibimbap and
red pepper paste separate.

비빔밥에 고추장을 따로 주세요.

bi-bim-bba-be go-chu-jang-eul dda-ro
ju-se-yo

Ordering 4

■ I'd like a sundubu-jjigae.

순두부찌개 하나 주세요.

sun-du-bu-jji-gae ha-na ju-se-yo

Tip: Sundubu-jjigae is a spicy soft-tofu stew.

■ Don't put scallions in the
seolleong-tang.

설렁탕에 파를 넣지 마세요.

seol-reong-tang-e pa-reul neo-chi
ma-se-yo

Tip: Seolleong-tang is a Korean broth made
from ox bones, brisket or other cuts of meat.
The seasoning is generally done at the table
according to personal taste, often by adding salt.

■ Three servings of pork belly,
please.

삼겹살 3인분 주세요.

sam-gyeop-ssal sa-min-bun ju-se-yo

■ Two servings of soondae, please.
And put the livers on the side.

순대 2인분 주세요.
간도 주세요.

sun-dae i-in-bun ju-se-yo. gan-do
ju-se-yo

Tip: Soondae is a type of sausage, similar
to blood pudding. Authentic soondae is pig
intestine with a stuffing of cellophane noodles,
vegetables and meat, but even if you eat the
street-vendor version, which uses a synthetic
replacement for the pig intestine, you will still
be able to enjoy the lungs and liver on the side.

Beverages

■ What would you like to drink?

어떤 음료로 하시겠어요?

eo-ddeon eum-nyo-ro ha-si-ge-sseo-yo?

■ A bottle of soju.

소주 한 병 주세요.

so-ju han byeong ju-se-yo

■ Water is self-service.

물은 셀프입니다.

mu-reun sel-peu-im-ni-da

■ Water's fine with me.

물이면 됩니다.

mu-ri-myeon doem-ni-da

■ Just coffee, please.

커피만 주세요.

keo-pi-man ju-se-yo

■ I'd like a daechu-cha.

대추차 주세요.

dae-chu-cha ju-se-yo

Tip: Daechu-cha is a kind of Korean traditional
tea. "Daechu" means jujube.

Special Requests

■ Don't add salt, please.

소금을 넣지 마세요.

so-geu-meul neo-chi ma-se-yo

■ Don't add red pepper paste,
please.

고추장을 넣지 마세요.

go-chu-jang-eul neo-chi ma-se-yo

■ Don't make it too spicy, please.

너무 맵게 하지 마세요.

neo-mu maep-gge ha-ji ma-se-yo

■ Can I have more rice?

밥 좀 더 주세요.

bap jom deo ju-se-yo

■ Please refill the side dishes.

반찬 더 주세요.

ban-chan deo ju-se-yo

Server Q&A

■ What are the ingredients in this?

이 음식의 재료는 뭐예요?

i eum-si-ge jae-ryo-neun mwo-ye-yo?

■ How is it cooked?

이것은 어떻게 한 거죠?

i-geo-seun eo-ddeo-ke han geo-jyo?

■ I dropped my chopsticks.

젓가락을 떨어뜨렸어요.

jeot-gga-ra-geul
ddeo-reo-ddeu-ryeo-sseo-yo

Tip: Koreans mostly use a spoon and chopsticks
when they have a meal.

■ Could you clean the table, please?

테이블 좀 치워 주세요.

te-i-beul jom chi-wo ju-se-yo

■ Do you have any dishes without
meat? I'm vegetarian.

고기가 안 들어간 음식 있어요?
저는 채식주의자거든요.

go-gi-ga an deu-reo-gan eum-sik i-sseo-
yo? jeo-neun chae-sik-jju-i-ja-geo-deun-yo

Complaints

▪ My order hasn't come yet.

주문한 요리가 아직 안
나왔어(요).

ju-mun-han yo-ri-ga a-jik an na-wa-
sseo(-yo)

▪ This is not what I ordered.

이건 제가 주문한 요리가
아닌데요.

i-geon je-ga ju-mun-han yo-ri-ga
a-nin-de-yo

▪ I'm afraid this meat is not done
enough.

고기가 완전히 익지 않았어(요).

go-gi-ga wan-jeon-hi ik-jji a-na-sseo(-yo)

▪ There's something strange in it.

여기에 뭔가 이상한 게 들어
있어(요).

yeo-gi-e mwon-ga i-sang-han ge deu-
reo i-sseo(-yo)

▪ It tastes a little strange.

맛이 좀 이상한데(요).

ma-si jom i-sang-han-de(-yo)

▪ I'm afraid this bread is stale.

이 빵은 상한 것 같은데(요).

i bbang-eun sang-han geot
ga-teun-de(-yo)

Personal Taste

▪ Did you enjoy your meal?

식사는 어떠셨어요?

sik-ssa-neun eo-ddeo-syeo-sseo-yo?

▪ It's the best meal I've ever had.

이렇게 맛있는 음식은 처음
먹어봤어(요).

i-reo-ke ma-din-neun eum-si-geun
cheo-eum meo-geo-bwa-sseo(-yo)

▪ It's a little too sweet for me.

좀 달았어(요).

jom da-ra-sseo(-yo)

▪ It's a little salty.

맛이 좀 짰어(요).

ma-si jom jja-sseo(-yo)

▪ It's a little spicy.

좀 매웠어(요).

jom mae-wo-sseo(-yo)

▪ Sorry, but it's not really to my
taste.

죄송하지만, 제 입맛에 맞지
않아요.

joe-song-ha-ji-man, je im-ma-se mat-jji
a-na-yo

Paying the Bill 1

■ The check, please.
계산서 주세요.
gye-san-seo ju-se-yo

■ Where is the cashier?
어디에서 계산하나요?
eo-di-e-seo gye-san-ha-na-yo?

■ Let's go Dutch for lunch.
점심은 각자 내자.
jeom-si-meun gak-jja nae-ja

점심은 더치페이하자.
jeom-si-meun deo-chi-pe-i-ha-ja

■ I'll treat you today.
오늘 내가 한턱낼게(요).
o-neul nae-ga han-teong-nael-gge(-yo)

오늘 내가 쏠게(요).
o-neul nae-ga ssol-gge(-yo)

■ How much is it in all?
다 얼마예요?
da eol-ma-ye-yo?

■ The total comes to 54,000 won.
총 5만 4천 원입니다.
chong o-man sa-cheon won-im-ni-da

Paying the Bill 2

■ Will you pay by cash or credit card?
현금으로 하시겠어요
신용카드로 하시겠어요?
hyeon-geu-meu-ro ha-si-ge-sseo-yo
si-nyong-ka-deu-ro ha-si-ge-sseo-yo?

■ By credit card, please.
카드로 할게요.
ka-deu-ro hal-gge-yo

■ Can I pay by credit card?
신용카드로 해도 돼요?
si-nyong-ka-deu-ro hae-do dwae-yo?

■ I'd like to pay in cash.
현금으로 할게요.
hyeon-geu-meu-ro hal-gge-yo

■ Here is your change.
거스름돈입니다.
geo-seu-reum-ddo-nim-ni-da

잔돈입니다.
jan-do-nim-ni-da

■ Can I have a receipt, please?
영수증 주세요.
yeong-su-jeung ju-se-yo

■ Here is your receipt.
영수증입니다.
yeong-su-jeung-im-ni-da

Coffee

■ **Shall we have a cup of iced coffee?**

함께 아이스커피 할래(요)?

ham-gge a-i-seu-keo-pi hal-rae(-yo)?

■ **Let's talk over a cup of coffee.**

우리 커피 마시면서 얘기해(요).

u-ri keo-pi ma-si-myeon-seo
yae-gi-hae(-yo)

■ **I'd like an espresso.**

에스프레소 주세요.

e-seu-peu-re-so ju-se-yo

■ **I'll have a decaf latte, please.**

디카페인 카페라테 주세요.

di-ka-pe-in ka-pe-ra-te ju-se-yo

■ **Would you like some sugar or cream in your coffee?**

커피에 설탕과 크림을 넣으세요?

keo-pi-e seol-tang-gwa keu-ri-meul
neo-eu-se-yo?

■ **Hold the whipped cream on the caffè mocha.**

카페모카에 휘핑크림은
빼 주세요.

ka-pe-mo-ka-e hwi-ping-keu-ri-meun
bbae ju-se-yo

Fast Food

■ **Next, please.**

다음 손님, 주문하세요.

da-eum son-nim, ju-mun-ha-se-yo

■ **With no mayo.**

마요네즈를 넣지 마세요.

ma-yo-ne-jeu-reul neo-chi ma-se-yo

■ **For here or to go?**

여기에서 드실 건가요 가져가실
건가요?

yeo-gi-e-seo deu-sil ggeon-ga-yo
ga-jeo-ga-sil ggeon-ga-yo?

■ **Does the burger come with cheese?**

햄버거 안에 치즈가 있나요?

haem-beo-geo a-ne chi-jeu-ga in-na-yo?

■ **The set includes a drink and French fries.**

세트에 음료수와 감자튀김이
포함됩니다.

se-teu-e eum-nyo-su-wa gam-ja-twi-gi-
mi po-ham-doem-ni-da

■ **We'll have that ready in a minute.**

1분 안에 다 됩니다.

il-bun a-ne da doem-ni-da

Food Delivery

■ Let's order some pizza!

우리 피자 시켜 먹자!

u-ri pi-ja si-kyeo meok-jja!

■ I'd like to order two jjajangmyeon, one jjambbong and tangsuyuk.

짜장면 둘, 짬뽕 하나, 탕수육 하나 시킬게요.

jja-jang-myeon dul, jjam-bbong ha-na, tang-su-yuk ha-na si-kil-gge-yo

Tip: Jjajangmyeon (noodles in black bean sauce), jjambbong (spicy noodle soup), and tangsuyuk (sweet-and-sour beef or pork) are popular delivery foods in Korea.

■ Do you deliver to Han-il Apartment?

한일아파트로 배달되나요?

ha-nil-a-pa-teu-ro bae-dal-doe-na-yo?

■ How soon will the pizza get here?

피자 배달하는 데 얼마나 걸려요?

pi-ja bae-dal-ha-neun de eol-ma-na geol-ryeo-yo?

■ Can you deliver it in half an hour or less?

30분 내에 배달되나요?

sam-sip-bbun nae-e bae-dal-doe-na-yo?

Best Korean Food Part 2

1. Gimbap (김밥 Korean-style sushi)
Gimbap is a popular and portable Korean street food, consisting of rice, meat or ham, spinach, yellow pickled radish, and stir-fried carrots rolled up in dried seaweed. The roll is then cut into small bite-sized discs. Gimbap can be made with many different kinds of filling.

2. Tteokbokki (떡볶이)
Tteokbokki, the Korean street food made of sweet and chewy rice cakes and fish cakes, is everywhere. Eaten as a snack or a full meal, it is cheap and delicious but fairly spicy as it is often swimming in gochujang (고추장 hot chili paste). It's often served with twigim (튀김 fried food) and soondae (순대, Korean sausage).

3. Jjajangmyeon (짜장면)
Myeon (면) are wheat-flour noodles. Jjajang (짜장) is black-bean sauce. Together, the pair form a much-loved dish, the Korean incarnation of an older Chinese food. Expect some familiar ingredients in the sauce, such as onion and pork, but a flavor unlike most Korean foods.

4. Fried Chicken (치킨)
Plain or seasoned, with beer (치맥 [chi-maek]), and often ordered as a delivery food, fried chicken in Korea is barely ever a stone's throw away. Domestic fried-chicken franchises outweigh Popeyes and KFC by an obscene number, serving up flavors the Colonel never dreamed of.

Going Shopping 1

■ I'm a shopaholic.

난 쇼핑광이에요.

nan syo-ping-gwang-i-e-yo

■ You really like luxury goods, don't you?

넌 명품만 밝히는구나, 그렇지?

neon myoeng-pum-man bal-ki-neun-gu-na, geu-reo-chi?

■ I'm an impulsive shopper.

나는 충동구매자예요.

na-neun chung-dong-gu-mae-ja-ye-yo

■ What time does the Mega Mall open?

메가몰은 몇 시에 열어(요)?

me-ga-mo-reun myeot si-e yeo-reo(-yo)?

■ What time does the Mega Mall close?

메가몰은 몇 시에 닫아(요)?

me-ga-mo-reun myeot si-e da-da(-yo)?

■ Why don't we go shopping together?

같이 쇼핑하러 가지 않을래(요)?

ga-chi syo-ping-ha-reo ga-ji a-neul-rae(-yo)?

Going Shopping 2

■ I like hanging out with my friends in the shopping mall.

난 친구들과 쇼핑센터에서 돌아다니기를 좋아해(요).

nan chin-gu-deul-gwa syo-ping-sen-teo-e-seo do-ra-da-ni-gi-reul jo-a-hae(-yo)

■ We went shopping for gifts.

우리는 선물을 사려고 쇼핑했어(요).

u-ri-neun seon-mu-reul sa-ryeo-go syo-ping-hae-sseo(-yo)

■ This neighborhood is great for shopping.

이 근처는 쇼핑하기 아주 좋아(요).

i geun-cheo-neun syo-ping-ha-gi a-ju jo-a(-yo)

■ We do our shopping at midnight.

우리는 심야에 쇼핑해(요).

u-ri-neun si-mya-e syo-ping-hae(-yo)

Tip: There are night markets in most cities and big towns in Korea.

■ It's convenient to buy things online.

온라인 쇼핑이 편리해(요).

ol-ra-in syo-ping-i pyeol-ri-hae(-yo)

Clothing Shops 1

■ May I help you?
뭘 도와드릴까요?
mwol do-wa-deu-ril-gga-yo?

■ I'm just looking around.
그냥 좀 둘러볼게요.
geu-nyang jom dul-reo-bol-gge-yo

■ What styles are popular now?
요즘 어떤 스타일이 유행하죠?
yo-jeum eo-ddeon seu-ta-i-ri
yu-haeng-ha-jyo?

■ This seems to be out of fashion.
이건 이미 유행이 지난 것
같은데(요).
i-geon i-mi yu-haeng-i ji-nan geot
ga-teun-de(-yo)

■ Can I try this on?
한번 입어 봐도 될까요?
han-beon i-beo bwa-do doel-gga-yo?

■ Where is the fitting room?
탈의실이 어디예요?
ta-ri-si-ri eo-di-ye-yo?

Clothing Shops 2

■ What size are you?
사이즈가 어떻게 되세요?
sa-i-jeu-ga eo-ddeo-ke doe-se-yo?

■ Mediums don't fit me.
I think I need a large.
미디엄 사이즈는 맞지 않아요.
라지 사이즈를 입어야 할 거
같아요.
mi-di-eom sa-i-jeu-neun mat-jji a-na-yo.
ra-ji sa-i-jeu-reul i-beo-ya hal ggeo
ga-ta-yo

■ Does it come in a larger size?
더 큰 사이즈 있어요?
deo keun sa-i-jeu i-sseo-yo?

■ Do you have other styles?
다른 스타일 있어요?
da-reun seu-ta-il i-sseo-yo?

■ Do you have other colors?
다른 색 있어요?
da-reun saek i-sseo-yo?

■ Do you have this in red?
이거 빨간색 있어요?
i-geo bbal-gan-saek i-sseo-yo?

Clothing Shops 3

- That looks great on you!

정말 어울리네!

jeong-mal eo-ul-ri-ne!

너한테 딱인데!

neo-han-te dda-gin-de!

- Which one is the dress that the mannequin is wearing?

저 마네킹이 입은 원피스는 어떤 거죠?

jeo ma-ne-king-i i-beun won-pi-seu-neun eo-ddeon geo-jyo?

- This is just what I'm looking for.

이것은 바로 제가 찾던 거예요.

i-geo-seun ba-ro je-ga chat-ddeon geo-ye-yo

- You should go with that one.

저 옷을 사는 게 좋겠어(요).

jeo o-seul sa-neun ge jo-ke-sseo(-yo)

- I'll look around at a few more places and then decide.

몇 군데 더 돌아보고 결정하자.

myeot gun-de deo do-ra-bo-go gyeol-jjeong-ha-ja

The Mall

- Where can I find the electrical appliances?

전자제품은 어디에 있어요?

jeon-ja-je-pu-meun eo-di-e i-sseo-yo?

- Is the supermarket in the basement?

슈퍼마켓은 지하에 있어요?

syu-peo-ma-ke-seun ji-ha-e i-sseo-yo?

- I think we'd better get a shopping cart.

쇼핑 카트를 가져오는 게 낫겠어(요).

syo-ping ka-teu-reul ga-jeo-o-neun ge nat-gge-sseo(-yo)

- Do you sell these individually?

낱개 판매하나요?

nat-ggae pan-mae-ha-na-yo?

- Can I taste a sample?

시식해도 돼요?

si-si-kae-do dwae-yo?

- Do you have this in stock?

이거 재고 있어요?

i-geo jae-go i-sseo-yo?

Sales & Discounts 1

- Are you currently having a sale?
지금 할인하고 있어요?
ji-geum ha-rin-ha-go i-sseo-yo?

- When is it going to be on sale?
언제 할인해요?
eon-je ha-rin-hae-yo?

- When does the sale end?
할인은 언제 끝나요?
ha-ri-neun eon-je ggeun-na-yo?

- The sale ended yesterday.
할인은 어제 끝났어요.
ha-ri-neun eo-je ggeun-na-sseo-yo

- The summer sales are on now.
지금은 여름 할인합니다.
ji-geu-meun yeo-reum ha-rin-ham-ni-da

- We are having a clearance sale.
재고 정리 할인 중입니다.
jae-go jeong-ri ha-rin jung-im-ni-da

- The winter sale will go on for a week.
겨울 할인이 일주일 동안 계속됩니다.
gyeo-ul ha-ri-ni il-jju-il dong-an gye-sok-doem-ni-da

Sales & Discounts 2

- Do you know when this item will go on sale again?
이 상품은 언제 또 할인해요?
i sang-pu-meun eon-je ddo ha-rin-hae-yo?

- Which items are on sale?
어떤 상품들이 할인하고 있어요?
eo-ddeon sang-pum-deu-ri ha-rin-ha-go i-sseo-yo?

- Sale prices are good through May 31st.
이 할인 가격은 5월 31일까지입니다.
i ha-rin ga-gyeo-geun o-wol sam-si-bi-il-gga-ji-im-ni-da

- The spring sale starts this Friday.
봄 할인은 이번 주 금요일부터 시작합니다.
bom ha-ri-neun i-beon ju geu-myo-il-bu-teo si-ja-kam-ni-da

- The sale is from December 20th to the 31st.
할인은 12월 20일부터 31일까지입니다.
ha-ri-neun si-bi-wol i-si-bil-bu-teo sam-si-bi-ril-gga-ji-im-ni-da

Sales & Discounts 3

■ Everything's 20 percent off.

전 상품은 20퍼센트 할인합니다.

jeon sang-pu-meun i-sip-peo-sen-teu
ha-rin-ham-ni-da

Tip: Percent is also read 프로 [peu-ro].

■ There's a 25-percent-off sale
today.

오늘은 25퍼센트 할인합니다.

o-neu-reun i-si-bo-peo-sen-teu
ha-rin-ham-ni-da

■ The regular price is 80,000 won
but it's on sale for 64,000 won.

정가는 8만 원인데, 할인해서
6만 4천 원입니다.

jeong-gga-neun pal-man wo-nin-de,
ha-rin-hae-seo yung-man sa-cheon
wo-nim-ni-da

■ Buy one, get the second
half-price.

한 벌 사시면, 다른 한 벌은
50퍼센트 할인해 드려요.

han beol sa-si-myeon, da-reun han
beo-reun o-sip-peo-sen-teu ha-rin-hae
deu-ryeo-yo

■ T-shirts are on sale. Buy three
and get the fourth free.

티셔츠가 할인 중입니다.
세 벌 사시면, 한 벌 드립니다.

ti-syeo-cheu-ga ha-rin jung-im-ni-da. se
beol sa-si-myeon, han beol deu-rim-ni-da

On Installment

■ Can I buy it on an installment
plan?

할부로 살 수 있어요?

hal-bu-ro sal ssu i-sseo-yo?

■ Would you like to pay in full or
in installments?

일시불이에요 할부예요?

il-ssi-bu-ri-e-yo hal-bu-ye-yo?

■ How many installments would
you like to make?

몇 개월 할부로 하시겠어요?

myeot gae-wol hal-bu-ro
ha-si-ge-sseo-yo?

■ I'd like to make three no-interest
payments.

3개월 무이자 할부로 할게요.

sam-gae-wol mu-i-ja hal-bu-ro hal-gge-yo

■ If you put 50 percent down, we'll
sell it in installments.

계약금으로 50퍼센트를 내시면,
잔금을 할부로 해 드립니다.

gye-yak-ggeu-meu-ro
o-sip-peo-sen-teu-reul nae-si-myeon,
jan-geu-meul hal-bu-ro hae deu-rim-
ni-da

■ How much do I pay per month?

한 달에 얼마씩 내나요?

han da-re eol-ma-ssik nae-na-yo?

Delivery

■ Could you deliver them to my house?

집까지 배송해 줄 수 있어요?

jip-gga-ji bae-song-hae jul ssu i-sseo-yo?

■ Does the price include the delivery charge?

배송비가 포함된 가격인가요?

bae-song-bi-ga po-ham-doen ga-gyeo-gin-ga-yo?

■ It's free delivery for all purchases over 50,000 won.

5만 원 이상 구입하면 무료 배송입니다.

o-man won i-sang gu-i-pa-myeon mu-ryo bae-song-im-ni-da

■ If I purchase it now, can I get it today?

지금 구입하면, 오늘 받을 수 있어요?

ji-geum gu-i-pa-myeon, o-neul ba-deul ssu i-sseo-yo?

■ When will it be delivered?

언제 배달해 주세요?

eon-je bae-dal-hae ju-se-yo?

■ We can deliver overnight.

구매한 다음 날 보내 드립니다.

gu-mae-han da-eum nal bo-nae deu-rim-ni-da

Refunds & Exchanges

■ I'd like to get a refund for this.

반품해 주세요.

ban-pum-hae ju-se-yo

■ When should I return this by?

언제까지 반품해야 해요?

eon-je-gga-ji ban-pum-hae-ya hae-yo?

■ Within two weeks from the day you bought it.

구매일로부터 2주 내입니다.

gu-mae-il-ro-bu-teo i-ju nae-im-ni-da

■ You can't return it without the receipt.

영수증이 없으면, 반품이 안 됩니다.

yeong-su-jeung-i eop-sseu-myeon, ban-pu-mi an doem-ni-da

■ No refund, no return.

환불 및 반품 불가.

hwan-bul mit ban-pum bul-ga

■ We're not allowed to make exchanges or give refunds for items bought on sale.

할인 기간에 구입한 물건은 교환이나 환불이 안 됩니다.

ha-rin gi-gan-e gu-i-pan mul-geo-neun gyo-hwa-ni-na hwan-bu-ri an doem-ni-da

n. hospital, clinic
병원 [병:원]
byeong-won

n. doctor
의사 [의사]
ui-sa

n. nurse
간호사 [간호사]
gan-ho-sa

n. patient
환자 [환:자]
hwan-ja

n. examination
진찰 [진:찰]
jin-chal

n. symptom
증세 [증세]
jeung-se
= 증상 [증상]
jeung-sang

n. pain, agony
고통 [고통]
go-tong

v. to be hurt
다치다 [다치다]
da-chi-da

n. injury, wound, cut
부상 [부:상]
bu-sang
= 상처 [상처]
sang-cheo

n. pharmacy
약국 [약꾹]
yak-gguk

n. medicine 약 [약] yak

n. painkiller, analgesic
진통제 [진:통제]
jin-tong-je

n. fever reducer
해열제 [해:열쩨]
hae-yeol-jje

n. digestive medicine
소화제 [소화제]
so-hwa-je

n. sleeping pill
수면제 [수면제]
su-myeon-je

n. Band-Aid,
sticking plaster
반창고 [반창고]
ban-chang-go

Appointments 1

- **Where is the reception desk, please?**
  접수처가 어디예요?
  jeop-ssu-cheo-ga eo-di-ye-yo?

- **I'd like to make an appointment to see the doctor.**
  진찰을 예약하고 싶은데요.
  jin-cha-reul ye-ya-ka-go si-peun-de-yo

- **Have you ever visited here before?**
  저희 병원에 처음 오신 건가요?
  jeo-hi byeong-wo-ne cheo-eum o-sin geon-ga-yo?

- **Today is my first visit.**
  오늘이 처음인데요.
  o-neu-ri cheo-eu-min-de-yo

- **I'd like to get a physical exam.**
  건강검진을 받고 싶은데요.
  geon-gang-geom-ji-neul bat-ggo si-peun-de-yo

- **What are your consultation hours?**
  진료 시간이 어떻게 됩니까?
  jil-ryo si-ga-ni eo-ddeo-ke doem-ni-gga?

Appointments 2

- **I have an appointment to see Dr. Jeong at one o'clock.**
  1시에 정 선생님께 진료 예약을 했어요.
  han-si-e jeong seon-saeng-nim-gge jil-ryo ye-ya-geul hae-sseo-yo

- **Is Dr. Kim open for consultation on Tuesdays?**
  김 선생님 화요일에도 진료하시나요?
  gim seon-saeng-nim hwa-yo-i-re-do jil-ryo-ha-si-na-yo?

- **Until what time do you give consultations today?**
  오늘 몇 시까지 진료해요?
  o-neul myeot si-gga-ji jil-ryo-hae-yo?

- **I don't have an appointment. Can I still get in?**
  예약을 하지 않았는데요. 진찰받을 수 있나요?
  ye-ya-geul ha-ji a-nan-neun-de-yo. jin-chal-ba-deul ssu in-na-yo?

- **The doctor is booked up today.**
  오늘 진료 예약은 마감됐습니다.
  o-neul jil-ryo ye-ya-geun ma-gam-dwaet-sseum-ni-da

Medical Treatments

■ What's the matter?
어디가 불편하세요?
eo-di-ga bul-pyeon-ha-se-yo?
어디가 안 좋으세요?
eo-di-ga an jo-eu-se-yo?

■ What are your symptoms?
어떤 증상이 있으세요?
eo-ddeon jeung-sang-i i-sseu-se-yo?

■ Have you ever suffered from this before?
전에 이 병을 앓은 적 있으세요?
jeo-ne i byeong-eul a-reun jeok i-sseu-se-yo?

■ Let's take your temperature.
체온을 좀 재 보겠습니다.
che-o-neul jom jae bo-get-sseum-ni-da

■ Take a deep breath.
심호흡하세요.
sim-ho-heu-pa-se-yo

■ Would you please lift up your shirt? I'll examine you.
셔츠를 걷어 보세요.
진찰하겠습니다.
syeo-cheu-reul geo-deo bo-se-yo.
jin-chal-ha-get-sseum-ni-da

At the Doctor's Office 1

■ I have a swollen foot.
발이 부었어요.
ba-ri bu-eo-sseo-yo

■ I broke my leg in a car accident.
교통사고로 다리가 부러졌어요.
gyo-tong-sa-go-ro da-ri-ga bu-reo-jeo-sseo-yo

■ I fell down and skinned my knees.
넘어져서 무릎이 까졌어요.
neo-meo-jeo-seo mu-reu-pi gga-jeo-sseo-yo

■ I have a backache.
허리가 아파요.
heo-ri-ga a-pa-yo

■ I sprained my ankle.
발목이 삐었어요.
bal-mo-gi bbi-eo-sseo-yo

■ My shoulders are stiff.
어깨가 결려요.
eo-ggae-ga gyeol-ryeo-yo

At the Doctor's Office 2

■ When can my cast come off?

깁스는 언제 풀 수 있어요?

gip-sseu-neun eon-je pul ssu i-sseo-yo?

■ I cut my finger with a knife.

칼에 손가락을 베었어요.

ka-re son-gga-ra-geul be-eo-sseo-yo

■ I'm black and blue all over.

온몸에 멍이 들었어요.

on-mo-me meong-i deu-reo-sseo-yo

■ I had an appendectomy.

지난주에 맹장수술을 했어요.

ji-nan-ju-e maeng-jang-su-su-reul hae-sseo-yo

■ This is a simple operation. Don't worry.

이것은 간단한 수술이에요. 걱정하지 마세요.

i-geo-seun gan-dan-han su-su-ri-e-yo. geok-jjeong-ha-ji ma-se-yo

■ I had metal pins inserted into the fractured leg.

골절된 다리에 철심을 박았어요.

gol-jjeol-doen da-ri-e cheol-ssi-meul ba-ga-sseo-yo

Hanbok Traditional Dress

As Korea's traditional clothing, the hanbok (한복) has a long history of about 1,600 years.

Men's hanbok consists of a vest, jeogori (저고리 top jacket), and a loose pair of pants comfortable for sitting on the floor. Women also wear a jeogori (shorter than the men's), a skirt, an undershirt and a pair of pantaloons. Colors and materials historically signified the social status of the wearer. There are special hanbok for weddings and funerals too.

These days, most Koreans wear hanbok during festivals, Seollal (설날, Lunar New Year's Day), chuseok (추석, Korean Thanksgiving Day) and so on.

As many foreigners have shown interest in the hanbok, rental shops have sprung up to fill the need.

Many of Seoul's major palaces grant free admission to hanbok-wearing visitors, from Gyeongbokgung Palace (경복궁) to the Royal Tombs of the Joseon Dynasty.

Colds

- I seem to have caught a cold.
  감기에 걸린 것 같아요.
  gam-gi-e geol-rin geot ga-ta-yo

- I have a stuffy nose.
  코가 막혔어요.
  ko-ga ma-kyeo-sseo-yo

- I have a runny nose.
  콧물이 나요.
  kon-mu-ri na-yo

- I've had a persistent cough for over a month.
  한 달 이상 기침감기를 앓았어요.
  han dal i-sang gi-chim-gam-gi-reul a-ra-sseo-yo

- My throat hurts when I swallow.
  침을 삼킬 때마다 목이 아파요.
  chi-meul sam-kil ddae-ma-da mo-gi a-pa-yo

- There's a lot of flu going around.
  독감이 유행하고 있어요.
  dok-gga-mi yu-haeng-ha-go i-sseo-yo

Fevers

- I have a fever.
  열이 나요.
  yeo-ri na-yo

- I have a fever of 102°F (39°C).
  열이 화씨 102도 섭씨 39도 까지 나요.
  yeo-ri hwa-si-baek-yi-do seop-si-sam-sip-ggu-do-gga-ji na-yo

- I have a terrible headache.
  머리가 깨질 듯 아파요.
  meo-ri-ga ggae-jil ddeut a-pa-yo

- The fever hasn't left me.
  열이 내리지 않아요.
  yeo-ri nae-ri-ji a-na-yo

- I have a fever and my whole body aches.
  열이 나고 온몸이 아파요.
  yeo-ri na-go on-mo-mi a-pa-yo

- Did you take a fever reducer?
  해열제 먹었어요?
  hae-yeol-jje meo-geo-sseo-yo?

- I have a fever and my throat is sore.
  열도 나고 목도 아파요.
  yeol-do na-go mok-ddo a-pa-yo

Digestive System 1

■ My stomach hurts.

배가 아파요.

bae-ga a-pa-yo

■ I have a pain in my abdomen.

아랫배가 아파요.

a-raet-bbae-ga a-pa-yo

■ I am having trouble with my stomach.

속이 안 좋아요.

so-gi an jo-a-yo

■ I think I have food poisoning.

식중독에 걸린 거 같아요.

sik-jjung-do-ge geol-rin geo ga-ta-yo

■ I feel like vomiting.

구역질이 나요.

gu-yeok-jji-ri na-yo

■ I throw up when I eat.

먹으면 토해요.

meo-geu-myeon to-hae-yo

Digestive System 2

■ I've got the runs.

배탈이 났어요.

bae-ta-ri na-sseo-yo

■ I'm constipated.

변비예요.

byeon-bi-ye-yo

■ I've had no bowel movement for a few days.

요즘 며칠 계속 변을 못 봤어요.

yo-jeum myeo-chil gye-sok byeo-neul mot bwa-sseo-yo

■ I've had diarrhea since yesterday.

어제부터 설사했어요.

eo-je-bu-teo seol-ssa-hae-sseo-yo

■ I had diarrhea all day long yesterday.

어제 종일 설사했어요.

eo-je jong-il seol-ssa-hae-sseo-yo

■ I am suffering from chronic indigestion.

만성 소화불량을 겪고 있어요.

man-seong so-hwa-bul-ryang-eul gyeok-ggo i-sseo-yo

Toothache

▨ I have a severe toothache.
이가 몹시 아파요.
i-ga mop-ssi a-pa-yo

▨ This back tooth hurts me.
어금니가 아파요.
eo-geum-ni-ga a-pa-yo

▨ I have a slight toothache.
치통이 약간 있어요.
chi-tong-i yak-ggan i-sseo-yo

▨ I have a toothache whenever
I eat. I can't eat anything.
먹으면 이가 아파서요.
아무것도 못 먹어요.
meo-geu-myeon i-ga a-pa-seo-yo.
a-mu-geot-ddo mot meo-geo-yo

▨ I can't chew on this side of my
mouth.
치통 때문에 이쪽으로 씹을 수
없어요.
chi-tong ddae-mu-ne i-jjo-geu-ro ssi-
beul ssu eop-sseo-yo

At the Dentist 1

▨ I have a loose tooth.
이 하나가 흔들려요.
i ha-na-ga heun-deul-ryeo-yo

▨ This tooth should be taken out.
이를 빼야 할 것 같아요.
i-reul bbae-ya hal ggeot ga-ta-yo

▨ How much is a filling?
이를 때우는 데 얼마예요?
i-reul ddae-u-neun de eol-ma-ye-yo?

▨ It's better not to extract your
wisdom tooth yet.
아직 사랑니를 뽑지 않는 것이
좋겠어요.
a-jik sa-rang-ni-reul bbop-jji an-neun
geo-si jo-ke-sseo-yo

▨ My gums bleed whenever I floss.
치실을 쓸 때마다 잇몸에서 피가
나요.
chi-si-reul sseul ddae-ma-da in-mo-me-
seo pi-ga na-yo

▨ When will I get my braces off?
언제 치아 교정기를 빼요?
eon-je chi-a-gyo-jeong-gi-reul bbae-yo?

At the Dentist 2

- I think I have a cavity.
  충치가 생긴 것 같아요.
  chung-chi-ga saeng-gin geot ga-ta-yo

- It looks like you have two small cavities.
  충치 두 개가 있는데, 심하지는 않아요.
  chung-chi du gae-ga in-neun-de, sim-ha-ji-neun a-na-yo

- I need a filling.
  이 충치는 때워야겠어요.
  i chung-chi-neun ddae-wo-ya-ge-sseo-yo

- I want to bleach my teeth.
  치아 미백을 받고 싶어요.
  chi-a mi-bae-geul bat-ggo si-peo-yo

- Can you recommend a good dentist?
  좋은 치과 의사 선생님을 추천해 줄 수 있어(요)?
  jo-eun chi-gwa ui-sa seon-saeng-ni-meul chu-cheon-hae jul ssu i-sseo(-yo)?

Jeju

The volcanic island, Jeju (제주) sits off the southern coast of Korea and is the largest island in the country. Its natural splendor and subtropical climate are a magnet for tourists, both domestic and international.

Jeju boasts some unique descriptors such as "samda (삼다)," meaning "three abundances (stones, wind, and women)" and "sammu (삼무)," which translates to the "three nothings (lack of thieves, fences or gates, and beggars)."

Two treasured things that it does have, and which you'll want to experience, are Jeju tangerines and Halla-san, South Korea's iconic highest mountain. A national park surrounds it and it can be hiked during daylight hours. Did I mention it's a volcano? No worries. It hasn't erupted for at least five thousand years.

Other interests are the remarkable female shellfish divers, the "haenyeo (해녀)," and the "dolhareubang (돌하르방)" guardian statues carved from basalt. "Dol (돌)" means stone and "hareubang (하르방)" means grandfather.

Other Ailments

■ I'm allergic to pollen.

꽃가루에 알레르기가 있어요.

ggot-gga-ru-e al-re-reu-gi-ga i-sseo-yo

■ I suffer from anemia.

빈혈이 있어요.

bin-hyeo-ri i-sseo-yo

■ I often get nose bleeds.

코피가 자주 나요.

ko-pi-ga ja-ju na-yo

■ I have high blood pressure.

고혈압이 있어요.

go-hyeo-ra-bi i-sseo-yo

■ I've got a strange rash.

두드러기가 났어요.

du-deu-reo-gi-ga na-sseo-yo

■ I have an asthma attack.

천식 발작이 있어요.

cheon-sik bal-jja-gi i-sseo-yo

■ I've got eczema on my hand.

손에 습진이 생겼어요.

so-ne seup-jji-ni saeng-gyeo-sseo-yo

■ I missed a monthly period.

생리를 건너뛰었어요.

saeng-ri-reul geon-neo-ddwi-eo-sseo-yo

Hospitalization

■ I've come to be admitted.

입원 수속을 하려고 합니다.

i-bwon su-so-geul ha-ryeo-go ham-ni-da

■ Do I have to stay here overnight?

입원해야 하나요?

i-bwon-hae-ya ha-na-yo?

■ You should be admitted right away.

바로 입원 수속하세요.

ba-ro i-bwon su-so-ka-se-yo

■ How long will I have to be in the hospital?

얼마나 입원해야 하나요?

eol-ma-na i-bwon-hae-ya ha-na-yo?

■ Will my insurance policy cover my stay here?

입원하면 의료보험이 적용되나요?

i-bwon-ha-myeon ui-ryo-bo-heo-mi jeo-gyong-doe-na-yo?

■ I would like to have a private room if possible.

가능하면 1인실로 해 주세요.

ga-neung-ha-myeon i-rin-sil-ro hae ju-se-yo

Operations

■ The patient is seriously ill.

지금 환자의 상태가 위급합니다.

ji-geum hwan-ja-e sang-tae-ga
wi-geu-pam-ni-da

■ I'm afraid he won't last the
month.

아마 이 달을 넘기지 못할
겁니다.

a-ma i da-reul neom-gi-ji mo-tal
ggeom-ni-da

■ Do I need surgery? /
Do I need an operation?

수술해야 하나요?

su-sul-hae-ya ha-na-yo?

■ Have you ever had an operation?

수술한 적 있어요?

su-sul-han jeok i-sseo-yo?

■ I had a C-section.

제왕절개 수술을 했습니다.

je-wang-jeol-gae su-su-reul
haet-sseum-ni-da

Tip: "Natural birth" is 자연분만 [ja-yeon-bun-man].

■ What's the recovery time?

회복 기간은 어떻게 돼요?

hoe-gok gi-ga-neun eo-ddeo-ke
dwae-yo?

Medical Costs & Insurance

■ How much will it be for this visit?

진찰비가 얼마예요?

jin-chal-bi-ga eol-ma-ye-yo?

■ Do you have health insurance?

건강보험 있어요?

geon-gang-bo-heom i-sseo-yo?

■ I don't have health insurance.

건강보험에 가입하지 않았어요.

geon-gang-bo-heo-me ga-i-pa-ji
a-na-sseo-yo

■ Does my insurance cover all the
costs?

모든 비용은 보험 적용이 돼요?

mo-deun bi-yong-eun bo-heom
jeo-gyong-i dwae-yo?

■ Some kinds of medicine are not
covered by insurance.

일부 의약품은 보험 적용이
안 됩니다.

il-bu ui-yak-pu-meun bo-heom jeo-
gyong-i an doem-ni-da

■ It covers only half of the costs.

반액만 보험 적용이 됩니다.

ba-naeng-man bo-heom jeo-gyong-i
doem-ni-da

Visiting the Sick

■ Please take good care of yourself!

몸조심 해(요)!

mom-jo-sim hae(-yo)!

■ I hope you get well soon.

속히 회복되길 바랍니다.

so-ki hoe-bok-ddoe-gil ba-ram-ni-da

■ Good luck!

건강하세요!

geon-gang-ha-se-yo!

■ I'm sorry to hear you've been sick.

편찮으시다니 유감입니다.

pyeon-cha-neu-si-da-ni yu-ga-mim-ni-da

Tip: 편찮다 [pyeon-chan-ta] is the polite word for 아프다 [a-peu-da], to be sick.

■ I hope it's nothing serious.

병이 심각하지 않기를 바라(요).

byeong-i sim-ga-ka-ji an-ki-reul ba-ra(-yo)

■ I'm glad you're feeling better!

회복되셨다니, 다행입니다!

hoe-bok-ddoe-syeot-dda-ni,
da-haeng-im-ni-da!

Prescriptions

■ I'll prescribe some medicine.

처방전을 써 드릴게요.

cheo-bang-jeo-neul sseo deu-ril-gge-yo

■ I'll prescribe some medicine for three days.

3일치 처방전을 드릴게요.

sa-mil-chi cheo-bang-jeo-neul
deu-ril-gge-yo

■ Are you taking any medication?

현재 복용하는 약이 있어요?

hyeon-jae bo-gyong-ha-neun ya-gi
i-sseo-yo?

■ Are you allergic to any medicine?

알레르기 있는 약 있어요?

al-re-reu-gi in-neun yak i-sseo-yo?

■ It will make you feel a little drowsy.

이 약은 먹으면 졸릴 수 있습니다.

i ya-geun meo-geu-myeon jol-ril ssu
it-sseum-ni-da

■ Does this medicine have any side effects?

이 약은 어떤 부작용이 있습니까?

i ya-geun eo-ddeon bu-ja-gyong-i
it-sseum-ni-gga?

The Pharmacy 1

- Can I get this prescription filled?

  이 처방전대로 조제해 주세요.

  i cheo-bang-jeon-dae-ro jo-je-hae ju-se-yo

- You can't buy this without a prescription.

  처방전이 없으면 약을 살 수 없습니다.

  cheo-bang-jeo-ni eop-sseu-myeon ya-geul sal ssu eop-sseum-ni-da

- May I have some sleeping pills?

  수면제 좀 주세요.

  su-myeon-je jom ju-se-yo

- Do you have any painkillers?

  진통제 있어요?

  jin-tong-je i-sseo-yo?

- Some ointment, please.

  연고 주세요.

  yeon-go ju-se-yo

- How should I take this medicine?

  이 약은 어떻게 먹죠?

  i ya-geun eo-ddeo-ke meok-jjyo?

The Pharmacy 2

- How many should I take per day?

  하루에 몇 알씩 먹어요?

  ha-ru-e myeot al-ssik meo-geo-yo?

- Take one every four hours.

  4시간마다 한 알씩 먹어요.

  ne si-gan-ma-da han al-ssik meo-geo-yo

- Take this medicine one capsule at a time.

  이 약은 한 번에 한 알씩 먹어요.

  i ya-geun han beo-ne han al-ssik meo-geo-yo

- Three times a day before meals.

  하루에 세 번, 식사 전에 먹습니다.

  ha-ru-e se beon, sik-ssa jeo-ne meok-sseum-ni-da

- Could you recommend a supplement to strengthen immunity?

  면역력을 강화하는 영양제 추천해 주세요.

  myeo-nyeong-nyeo-geul gang-hwa-ha-neun yeong-yang-je chu-cheon-hae ju-se-yo

🎧 Banks 은행 eun-haeng

n. bank 은행 [은행] eun-haeng 	**n. money 돈** [돈:] don **n. cash** 현금 [현:금] hyeon-geum 	**n. bill, note** 지폐 [지폐/지페] ji-pye/ji-pe
	n. coin 동전 [동전] dong-jeon 	**n. deposit, savings** 저축 [저:축] jeo-chuk = 저금 [저:금] jeo-geum = 예금 [예:금] ye-geum
	n. bankbook, passbook 통장 [통장] tong-jang 	**n. credit transfer** 이체 [이체] i-che
	n. deposit 입금 [입끔] ip-ggeum 	**n. withdrawal** 출금 [출금] chul-geum
	n. loan 대출 [대:출] dae-chul 	**n. interest 이자** [이:자] i-ja
	n. exchange 환전 [환:전] hwan-jeon 	**n. ATM** 에이티엠 [에이티엠] e-i-ti-em
	n. Internet banking 인터넷 뱅킹 [인터넫 뱅킹] in-teo-net baeng-king 	**n. password, PIN** 비밀번호 [비:밀번호] bi-mil-beon-ho

The Bank 1

- Please take a number.

번호표를 뽑으세요.

beon-ho-pyo-reul bbo-beu-se-yo

- I'd like to open a bank account.

계좌를 개설하려고 하는데요.

gye-jwa-reul gae-seol-ha-ryeo-go
ha-neun-de-yo

- What type of account do you want?

어떤 종류의 예금을
하시겠습니까?

eo-ddeon jong-nyu-e ye-geu-meul
ha-si-get-sseum-ni-gga?

- I want to start Internet banking.

인터넷뱅킹을 신청하고
싶은데요.

in-teo-net-baeng-king-eul
sin-cheong-ha-go si-peun-de-yo

- Would you like to apply for a debit card, too?

체크카드도 만드실 건가요?

che-keu-ka-deu-do man-deu-sil
ggeon-ga-yo?

- Could you endorse this check, please?

이 수표에 이서해 주시겠어요?

i su-pyo-e i-seo-hae ju-si-ge-sseo-yo?

The Bank 2

- A savings account or a checking account?

저축 예금인가요 아니면
당좌 예금인가요?

jeo-chuk ye-geu-min-ga-yo a-ni-myeon
dang-jwa ye-geu-min-ga-yo?

- What's the interest rate?

이율은 얼마죠?

i-yu-reun eol-ma-jyo?

- I'd like to close my bank account.

계좌를 해지하려고요.

gye-jwa-reul hae-ji-ha-ryeo-go-yo

- I'd like to check my transactions for last month.

제 계좌의 거래 내역을 확인하고
싶어요.

je gye-jwa-e geo-rae nae-yeo-geul
hwa-gin-ha-go si-peo-yo

- Could you break this (into smaller bills)?

잔돈으로 교환할 수 있어요?

jan-do-neu-ro gyo-hwan-hal
ssu i-sseo-yo?

- I'd like to get an e-passbook.

전자통장으로 바꾸고 싶어요.

jeon-ja-tong-jang-eu-ro ba-ggu-go
si-peo-yo

Deposits & Withdrawals

■ How much do you want to deposit today?

오늘 얼마를 예금하시겠어요?

o-neul eol-ma-reul
ye-geum-ha-si-ge-sseo-yo?

■ I'd like to make a deposit of 1,000,000 won.

100만 원을 예금하려고요.

baeng-man wo-neul
ye-geum-ha-ryeo-go-yo

■ How much do you want to withdraw?

얼마를 인출하실 거예요?

eol-ma-reul in-chul-ha-sil ggeo-ye-yo?

■ I want to withdraw 300,000 won.

30만 원을 인출하려는데요.

sam-sim-man wo-neul
in-chul-ha-ryeo-neun-de-yo

■ I'd like to set up an automatic withdrawal for my electric bill.

전기요금을 자동이체로 지정해 주세요.

jeon-gi-yo-geu-meul ja-dong-i-che-ro
ji-jeong-hae ju-se-yo

Remittances

■ Please transfer the funds to this account.

이 계좌로 송금해 주세요.

i gye-jwa-ro song-geum-hae ju-se-yo

■ We need your bank's name and address, your bank account number and the bank routing number.

은행 이름과 주소, 계좌번호와 송금번호를 알려 주세요.

eun-haeng i-reum-gwa ju-so,
gye-jwa-beon-ho-wa
song-geum-beon-ho-reul al-ryeo ju-se-yo

■ I'd like to make a remittance to the US

미국으로 송금하려고 합니다.

mi-gu-geu-ro song-geum-ha-ryeo-go
ham-ni-da

■ Is there a bank fee for transferring money? How much?

송금 수수료가 있어요? 얼마예요?

song-geum su-su-ryo-ga i-sseo-yo?
eol-ma-ye-yo?

■ There's an 800 won charge.

수수료는 800원입니다.

su-su-ryo-neun pal-bae-gwo-nim-ni-da

ATMs

- Where are the ATMs?

ATM은 어디에 있어요?

e-i-ti-e-meun eo-di-e i-sseo-yo?

- How do I make a deposit?

어떻게 입금해요?

eo-ddeo-ke ip-ggeum-hae-yo?

- Please insert your card here.

카드를 여기에 넣으세요.

ka-deu-reul yeo-gi-e neo-eu-se-yo

- Please enter your PIN number.

비밀번호를 누르세요.

bi-mil-beon-ho-reul nu-reu-se-yo

- Please press the account balance key.

잔액조회 버튼을 누르세요.

ja-naek-jjo-hoe beo-teu-neul
nu-reu-se-yo

- The ATM ate my card.

ATM이 카드를 먹어 버렸어요.

e-i-ti-e-mi ka-deu-reul meo-geo
beo-ryeo-sseo-yo

Tteokbokki Recipe

How to cook **tteokbokki** (떡볶이)
rice cake:

- **Ingredients** (4 servings)
1½ cups (360 ml) water
7 large dried anchovies with heads
 and intestines removed
6 x 8 inch (15 x 20 cm) piece dried
 kombu
3 tablespoons hot pepper paste
1 tablespoon hot pepper flakes
2 tablespoons sugar
1 lb (450 g) tteokbokki rice cakes
3 scallions, chopped
2 hardboiled eggs, shelled (optional)
5 oz (150 g) Korean fish cake
 (optional)

- **Directions**
① Put the water, anchovies and
kombu in a shallow pot. Boil for 15
minutes over medium-high heat
without the lid.
② Combine the hot pepper paste,
hot pepper flakes and sugar in a
small bowl.
③ Remove the anchovies and kelp
from the pot. Put in the rice cakes,
the pepper and sugar mixture, the
scallions, and the hardboiled eggs
and fish cakes, if using.
④ When the pot starts to boil, stir
gently with a wooden spoon. Keep
stirring until the rice cake turns soft
and the sauce thickens and looks
shiny, which should take about
10–15 minutes. If the rice cake is not
soft enough, add more water and
continue stirring until soft.

Credit Cards

■ When will my card be issued?

신용카드가 언제 발급되나요?

si-nyong-ka-deu-ga eon-je
bal-geup-ddoe-na-yo?

■ What is the expiry date of this
credit card?

이 카드의 유효기간은
언제까지예요?

i ka-deu-e yu-hyo-gi-ga-neun
eon-je-gga-ji-ye-yo?

■ How much is the limit for this
card?

사용 한도액이 어떻게 되나요?

sa-yong han-do-ae-gi eo-ddeo-ke
doe-na-yo?

■ I want to check my latest credit
card statement.

최근 신용카드 사용내역을
확인하고 싶은데요.

choe-geun si-nyong-ka-deu
sa-yong-nae-yeo-geul hwa-gin-ha-go
si-peun-de-yo

■ I had my credit card stolen.
Please cancel it.

신용카드를 도난당했어요.
해지해 주세요.

si-nyong-ka-deu-reul
do-nan-dang-hae-sseo-yo.
hae-ji-hae ju-se-yo

Foreign Exchange

■ Do you exchange foreign
currency?

환전할 수 있어요?

hwan-jeon-hal ssu i-sseo-yo?

■ I'd like to exchange US dollars
for Korean won.

달러를 원화로 바꾸고 싶어요.

dal-reo-reul won-hwa-ro ba-ggu-go
si-peo-yo

■ How would you like your bills?

어떻게 환전해 드릴까요?

eo-ddeo-ke hwan-jeon-hae
deu-ril-gga-yo?

■ Please give it to me in
10,000 won bills.

전액 만 원짜리로 주세요.

jeo-naek man won-jja-ri-ro ju-se-yo

■ We get a 2 percent commission
of the exchanged amount.

환전 비용의 2%를 수수료로
받습니다.

hwan-jeon bi-yong-e i-peo-sen-teu-reul
su-su-ryo-ro bat-sseum-ni-da

■ There is a money changer across
the street.

길 건너편에 환전소가 있습니다.

gil geon-neo-pyeo-ne hwan-jeon-so-ga
it-sseum-ni-da

Exchange Rates

- What's today's rate for Korean won?

  오늘 원화의 환율은 얼마예요?

  o-neul won-hwa-e hwa-nyu-reun
  eol-ma-ye-yo?

- Today's exchange rate is 92 cents US to 1,000 won.

  오늘 환율은 천 원에 0.92달러입니다.

  o-neul hwa-nyu-reun cheon wo-ne
  yeong-jjeom-gu-i-dal-reo-im-ni-da

- What's the rate for Korean won to Euros?

  원화를 유로로 환전하는 환율이 어떻게 돼요?

  won-hwa-reul yu-ro-ro hwan-jeon-ha-
  neun hwa-nyu-ri eo-ddeo-ke dwae-yo?

- Has the won risen against the pound?

  파운드에 대한 원 환율이 올랐어요?

  pa-un-deu-e dae-han won hwa-nyu-ri
  ol-ra-sseo-yo?

- Should I exchange some money now?

  지금 환전해야 할까요?

  ji-geum hwan-jeon-hae-ya hal-gga-yo?

Loans

- Can foreigners get loans at this bank?

  외국인이 이 은행에서 대출할 수 있어요?

  oe-gu-gi-ni i eun-haeng-e-seo dae-chul-
  hal ssu i-sseo-yo?

- I'd like to discuss a bank loan.

  대출 문제로 상담하고 싶은데요.

  dae-chul mun-je-ro sang-dam-ha-go
  si-peun-de-yo

- Has my loan been approved?

  제 대출이 승인되었나요?

  je dae-chu-ri seung-in-doe-eon-na-yo?

- I'm going to take out a loan to pay my tuition.

  학자금 대출을 신청하고 싶은데요.

  hak-jja-geum dae-chu-reul
  sin-cheong-ha-go si-peun-de-yo

- I put my house up as collateral for the loan.

  집을 담보로 대출을 받았어요.

  ji-beul dam-bo-ro dae-chu-reul
  ba-da-sseo-yo

- I got a loan at 4 percent interest.

  4부 이자로 대출을 받았어요.

  sa-bu i-ja-ro dae-chu-reul ba-da-sseo-yo

Sending Letters 1

- How much is the postage for this letter?

  이 편지 요금은 얼마예요?

  i pyeon-ji yo-geu-meun eol-ma-ye-yo?

- By express or regular mail?

  빠른우편인가요
  보통우편인가요?

  bba-reu-nu-pyeo-nin-ga-yo
  bo-tong-u-pyeo-nin-ga-yo?

- How much is it to send this letter by express mail?

  빠른우편으로 보내는 데
  얼마인가요?

  bba-reu-nu-pyeo-neu-ro bo-nae-neun
  de eol-ma-in-ga-yo?

- Please register this letter.

  등기우편으로 해 주세요.

  deun-ggi-u-pyeo-neu-ro hae ju-se-yo

- By airmail or surface mail?

  항공편인가요 배편인가요?

  hang-gong-pyeo-nin-ga-yo
  bae-pyeo-nin-ga-yo?

- Could I have three 330 won stamps?

  330원짜리 우표 세 장 주세요.

  sam-baek-ssam-si-bwon-jja-ri u-pyo se
  jang ju-se-yo

Sending Letters 2

- What is the zip code?

  우편번호가 뭐예요?

  u-pyeon-beon-ho-ga mwo-ye-yo?

- Postage will be paid by the addressee.

  우편 요금은 착불입니다.

  u-pyeon yo-geu-meun
  chak-bbu-rim-ni-da

- How long does it take to reach Seoul?

  서울까지 가는 데 얼마나
  걸려요?

  seo-ul-gga-ji ga-neun de eol-ma-na
  geol-ryeo-yo?

- It will take three days to get there.

  사흘 후에 도착합니다.

  sa-heul hu-e do-cha-kam-ni-da

  Tip: 사흘 [sa-heul] **means three days.**

- Where do I write the addressee's name and address?

  수신인의 이름과 주소를 어디에
  쓰면 돼요?

  su-si-ni-ne i-reum-gwa ju-so-reul eo-di-e
  sseu-myeon dwae-yo?

- I want to send this letter to Daegu.

  이 편지를 대구로 보내려고요.

  i pyeon-ji-reul dae-gu-ro bo-nae-ryeo-
  go-yo

Packages

- Could you weigh this parcel?

  소포 무게를 달아주세요.

  so-po mu-ge-reul da-ra-ju-se-yo

- Please wrap this parcel in package paper.

  이 소포를 포장해 주세요.

  i so-po-reul po-jang-hae ju-se-yo

- What does your parcel contain?

  소포 안에는 뭐죠?

  so-po a-ne-neun mwo-jyo?

- Please be careful, this parcel is fragile.

  조심해 주세요, 깨지기 쉬운 물건입니다.

  jo-sim-hae ju-se-yo, ggae-ji-gi swi-un mul-geo-nim-ni-da

- Please insure this parcel just in case.

  만일을 대비해 소포를 보험에 가입해 주세요.

  ma-ni-reul dae-bi-hae so-po-reul bo-heo-me ga-i-pae ju-se-yo

The Hair Salon

- I need a new hairstyle.

  새로운 헤어스타일을 하고 싶어요.

  sae-ro-un he-eo-seu-ta-i-reul ha-go si-peo-yo

- How would you like your hair?

  어떤 헤어스타일을 원하세요?

  eo-ddeon he-eo-seu-ta-i-reul won-ha-se-yo?

- May I show you a hairstyle book?

  헤어스타일 책을 보여 드릴까요?

  he-eo-seu-ta-il chae-geul bo-yeo deu-ril-gga-yo?

- Could you recommend something for me?

  좀 추천해 주시겠어요?

  jom chu-cheon-hae ju-si-ge-sseo-yo?

- I want to look like the model in this photo.

  이 사진의 모델 헤어스타일을 하고 싶어요.

  i sa-ji-e mo-del he-eo-seu-ta-i-reul ha-go si-peo-yo

- I'll leave it up to you.

  알아서 어울리게 해 주세요.

  a-ra-seo eo-ul-ri-ge hae ju-se-yo

Haircuts 1

- I need to get my hair cut.

  커트하려고요.

  keo-teu-ha-ryeo-go-yo

- How do you want it cut?

  어떻게 잘라 드릴까요?

  eo-ddeo-ke jal-ra deu-ril-gga-yo?

- Leave it this long, please.

  이 정도 자르려고요.

  i jeong-do ja-reu-ryeo-go-yo

- Can you cut it shoulder length?

  어깨 길이로 잘라 주세요.

  eo-ggae gi-ri-ro jal-ra ju-se-yo

- I'd like to have my hair cut short.

  머리를 짧게 자르고 싶어요.

  meo-ri-reul jjal-gge ja-reu-go si-peo-yo

  Tip: 머리 [meo-ri] usually means "head," but the word is used at a hair salon to refer to one's hair.

- Please take a few inches off the ends.

  머리끝을 살짝 다듬어 주세요.

  meo-ri-ggeu-teul sal-jjak da-deu-meo ju-se-yo

Haircuts 2

- I want a crew cut.

  스포츠형으로 잘라 주세요.

  seu-po-cheu-hyeong-eu-ro jal-ra ju-se-yo

- I'd like a bob cut.

  단발머리를 하고 싶어요.

  dan-bal-meo-ri-reul ha-go si-peo-yo

- I'd like to have bangs, too.

  앞머리도 잘라 주세요.

  am-meo-ri-do jal-ra ju-se-yo

- I'd like to keep my bangs.

  앞머리는 그대로 두세요.

  am-meo-ri-neun geu-dae-ro du-se-yo

- I want my hair layered.

  머리에 층을 내 주세요.

  meo-ri-e cheung-eul nae ju-se-yo

- Don't cut it too short.

  너무 짧게 자르지 마세요.

  neo-mu jjal-gge ja-reu-ji ma-se-yo

Perms

■ I want to get a perm.

파마하려고요.

pa-ma-ha-ryeo-go-yo

■ What kind of perm do you want?

어떤 스타일로 파마하시겠어요?

eo-ddeon seu-ta-il-ro
pa-ma-ha-si-ge-sseo-yo?

■ I'd like my hair wavy.

웨이브 파마로 해 주세요.

we-i-beu pa-ma-ro hae ju-se-yo

■ I want to get rid of my curls.

스트레이트 파마로 해 주세요.

seu-teu-re-i-teu pa-ma-ro hae ju-se-yo

■ Don't curl my hair too much, please.

너무 곱슬거리지 않게 해
주세요.

neo-mu gop-sseul-geo-ri-ji an-ke hae
ju-se-yo

■ Your perm came out nicely.

파마가 잘 나왔네요.

pa-ma-ga jal na-wan-ne-yo

Holidays

• Seollal

Seollal (설날, Lunar New Year's Day) is the most important of the traditional festivals. At the start of the lunar calendar (dates vary between Jan and Feb), Koreans from far and wide will return home to celebrate with loved ones present and acknowledge those past. Expect customs of all types, from folk games and hanboks (한복) to tteokguk (떡국, rice cake soup). "Sebae (세배)" is a traditional ritual of respect. Here young people bow to their elders with wishes of good fortune. They are rewarded with gifts of pocket money (세뱃돈 [se-baet-ddon]).

Also known as Great Full Moon, **Daeboreum** (대보름) celebrates the first full moon of the lunar calendar, 15 days after Seollal. The day boasts a host of customs, some naturally involving food. People eat a special dish called ogok-bap (오곡밥), made with five kinds of grain.

• Chuseok

Chuseok (추석) is a three-day lunar harvest festival that draws obvious comparisons with Thanksgiving Day. Typically held in September or October. Members convey their wishes of thanks together while enjoying the full moon. The chuseok food of choice is unquestionably songpyeon (송편), a kind of rice cake steamed over pine needles. "Song (송)" in Korean means pine tree.

Coloring

■ I'd like to have my hair dyed, please.

염색하려고요.

yeom-sae-ka-ryeo-go-yo

■ What color do you want your hair dyed?

어떤 색으로 염색하시겠어요?

eo-ddeon sae-geu-ro
yeom-sae-ka-si-ge-sseo-yo?

■ Can you color my hair brown?

갈색으로 염색해 주세요.

gal-ssae-geu-ro yeom-sae-kae ju-se-yo

■ Highlighting makes you look younger.

밝게 염색하면 어려 보여요.

bal-gge yeom-sae-ka-myeon eo-ryeo
bo-yeo-yo

■ Can you hide the gray hair with coloring?

흰머리를 염색해 주세요.

hin-meo-ri-reul yeom-sae-kae ju-se-yo

■ Your hair has been seriously damaged by too much coloring.

염색을 자주 해서 머릿결이
심하게 손상됐어요.

yeom-sae-geul ja-ju hae-seo
meo-rit-ggyeo-ri sim-ha-ge
son-sang-dwae-sseo-yo

Putting in the Laundry

■ I'm going to take these clothes to the cleaner's.

이 옷은 내가 세탁소에 맡길게요.

i o-seun nae-ga se-tak-sso-e mat-ggil-
gge-yo

■ Can you put this suit in at the laundry?

이 양복을 세탁소에 맡겨 주세요.

i yang-bo-geul se-tak-sso-e mat-ggyeo
ju-se-yo

■ I'd like these pants to be pressed.

이 바지를 다려 주세요.

i ba-ji-reul da-ryeo ju-se-yo

■ Could I get this cardigan dry-cleaned?

이 카디건을 드라이클리닝 해
주세요.

i ka-di-geo-neul deu-ra-i-keul-ri-ning
hae ju-se-yo

■ I'll need this suit cleaned by next Monday.

다음 주 월요일까지 세탁해
주세요.

da-eum ju wo-ryo-il-gga-ji se-ta-kae
ju-se-yo

Collecting the Laundry

■ When can I get it back?

언제 찾을 수 있어요?

eon-je cha-jeul ssu i-sseo-yo?

■ I want to pick up my laundry.

옷 찾으러 왔어요.

ot cha-jeu-reo wa-sseo-yo

■ Is my laundry ready?

제 옷은 세탁이 다 됐나요?

je o-seun se-ta-gi da dwaen-na-yo?

■ Here's my laundry receipt.

여기 세탁물 보관증입니다.

yeo-gi se-tang-mul
bo-gwan-jjeung-im-ni-da

■ What's the charge for cleaning?

세탁비는 얼마예요?

se-tak-bbi-neun eol-ma-ye-yo?

■ How much is it to dry-clean this coat?

이 코트 드라이클리닝 비용은 얼마예요?

i ko-teu deu-ra-i-keul-ri-ning bi-yong-eun eol-ma-ye-yo?

Getting Stains Out

■ Please take out this stain.

얼룩을 제거해 주세요.

eol-ru-geul je-geo-hae ju-se-yo

■ Could you take out the stains on these pants?

이 바지의 얼룩을 제거해 주세요.

i ba-ji-e eol-ru-geul je-geo-hae ju-se-yo

■ I spilled coffee all over my skirt.

커피를 치마에 쏟았어요.

keo-pi-reul chi-ma-e sso-da-sseo-yo

■ The dry-cleaner can remove the stain.

드라이클리닝을 하면 얼룩을 지울 수 있어요.

deu-ra-i-keul-ri-ning-eul ha-myeon eol-ru-geul ji-ul ssu i-sseo-yo

■ This stain won't wash out.

이 얼룩은 빨아서 지워지지 않아요.

i eol-ru-geun bba-ra-seo ji-wo-ji-ji a-na-yo

■ The stain didn't come out.

얼룩이 제대로 빠지지 않았어요.

eol-ru-gi je-dae-ro bba-ji-ji a-na-sseo-yo

Mending

- Do you mend clothes?
  옷을 수선할 수 있나요?
  o-seul su-seon-hal ssu in-na-yo?

- Could you mend this jacket?
  이 재킷을 좀 수선해 주세요.
  i jae-ki-seul jom su-seon-hae ju-se-yo

- I'd like to have these pants shortened.
  이 바지를 좀 줄여 주세요.
  i ba-ji-reul jom ju-ryeo ju-se-yo

- Could you lengthen these pants?
  이 바지 기장을 좀 늘여 주세요.
  i ba-ji gi-jang-eul jom neu-ryeo ju-se-yo

- I'm sorry I can't fix that.
  죄송하지만, 수선할 수 없어요.
  joe-song-ha-ji-man, su-seon-hal ssu eop-sseo-yo

- This zipper fell off. Can you replace it?
  지퍼가 떨어졌어요.
  좀 고쳐 주세요.
  ji-peo-ga ddeo-reo-jeo-sseo-yo.
  jom go-cheo ju-se-yo

Rental Cars 1

- I plan to rent a car for this Saturday.
  이번 주 토요일에 차를 빌리려고요.
  i-beon ju to-yo-i-re cha-reul bil-ri-ryeo-go-yo

- Can I pick up a rental car at the airport?
  공항에서 렌터카를 받을 수 있어요?
  gong-hang-e-seo ren-teo-ka-reul ba-deul ssu i-sseo-yo?

- What kind of car do you want?
  어떤 차를 빌리시겠어요?
  eo-ddeon cha-reul bil-ri-si-ge-sseo-yo?

- I want a compact car.
  소형차를 빌리려고 합니다.
  so-hyeong-cha-reul bil-ri-ryeo-go ham-ni-da

- How long will you need it?
  얼마나 빌리실 겁니까?
  eol-ma-na bil-ri-sil ggeom-ni-gga?

- I'd like to rent a car for five days.
  5일 동안 빌리려고요.
  o-il dong-an bil-ri-ryeo-go-yo

Rental Cars 2

■ What's your rental fee?

렌탈 요금은 얼마입니까?

ren-tal yo-geu-meun eol-ma-im-ni-gga?

■ 65,000 won per day.

하루에 6만 5천 원입니다.

ha-ru-e yung-man o-cheon wo-nim-ni-da

■ Do you want insurance?

보험에 가입하시겠어요?

bo-heo-me ga-i-pa-si-ge-sseo-yo?

■ With full coverage, please.

종합 보험에 가입해 주세요.

jong-hap bo-heo-me ga-i-pae ju-se-yo

■ Where should I leave the car?

차를 어디로 반납하나요?

cha-reul eo-di-ro ban-na-pa-na-yo?

■ You can return the car to any branch in the country.

전국 지점 어느 곳으로나 반납이 가능합니다.

jeon-guk ji-jeom eo-neu go-seu-ro-na ban-na-bi ga-neung-ham-ni-da

Gas Stations 1

■ Is there a gas station around here?

이 근처에 주유소가 있어(요)?

i geun-cheo-e ju-yu-so-ga i-sseo(-yo)?

■ Let's pull up to that gas station.

주유소에 들릅시다.

ju-yu-so-e deul-reup-ssi-da

■ Can you direct me to the nearest gas station?

가장 가까운 주유소는 어디예요?

ga-jang ga-gga-un ju-yu-so-neun eo-di-ye-yo?

■ Do you have enough gas?

기름이 충분해(요)?

gi-reu-mi chung-bun-hae(-yo)?

■ We're running low on gas.

기름이 떨어져 가는데(요).

gi-reu-mi ddeo-reo-jeo ga-neun-de(-yo)

■ Pull over at the next gas station.

다음 주유소에서 차를 세워(요).

da-eum ju-yu-so-e-seo cha-reul se-wo(-yo)

Gas Stations 2

- I need some gas.
  기름을 넣어야 해(요).
  gi-reu-meul neo-eo-ya hae(-yo)

- The tank is almost empty.
  기름이 거의 떨어졌어(요).
  gi-reu-mi geo-i ddeo-reo-jeo-sseo(-yo)

- This is a self-service gas station.
  이 주유소는 셀프 주유입니다.
  i ju-yu-so-neun sel-peu ju-yu-im-ni-da

- Do I have to pump the gas myself?
  내가 직접 주유해야 하나요?
  nae-ga jik-jjeop ju-yu-hae-ya ha-na-yo?

- Fill it up, please.
  기름 가득 넣어 주세요.
  gi-reum ga-deuk neo-eo ju-se-yo

- Fill it up with regular gas, please.
  일반 휘발유요, 가득 넣어
  주세요.
  il-ban hwi-bal-ryu-yo, ga-deuk neo-eo
  ju-se-yo

- Give me 50,000 won worth,
  please.
  5만 원어치 넣어 주세요.
  o-mam wo-neo-chi neo-eo ju-se-yo

Washing & Servicing Cars

- Wash it down, please.
  세차해 주세요.
  se-cha-hae ju-se-yo

- Could you wash and wax
  the car?
  세차하고, 왁스를 발라 주세요.
  se-cha-ha-go, wak-sseu-reul bal-ra ju-
  se-yo

- How much is it to wash the car?
  세차하는 데 얼마예요?
  se-cha-ha-neun de eol-ma-ye-yo?

- Check the oil, please.
  엔진오일 좀 봐 주세요.
  en-ji-no-il jom bwa ju-se-yo

- Check the windshield wipers,
  please.
  앞 유리 와이퍼 좀 점검해 주세요.
  ap yu-ri wa-i-peo jom jeom-geom-hae
  ju-se-yo

- Is there enough washer fluid?
  워셔액이 충분한가요?
  wo-syeo-ae-gi chung-bun-han-ga-yo?

- Would you check my tires?
  타이어 좀 점검해 주세요.
  ta-i-eo jom jeom-geom-hae ju-se-yo

The Bookstore

- This bookstore has a large number of books for children.

  이 서점에는 아동 도서가 많이 있어(요).

  i seo-joe-me-nuen a-dong do-seo-ga ma-ni i-sseo(-yo)

- That bookstore specializes in computer books.

  저 서점은 컴퓨터 서적을 전문적으로 취급해(요).

  jeo seo-jeo-meun keom-pyu-teo seo-jeo-geul jeon-mun-jjeo-geu-ro chwi-geu-pae(-yo)

- You can buy that book anywhere.

  그 책은 어디서나 살 수 있어(요).

  geu chae-geun eo-di-seo-na sal ssu i-sseo(-yo)

- There's a good secondhand bookstore not far from here.

  근처에 괜찮은 헌책방이 있어(요).

  geun-cheo-e gwaen-cha-neun heon-chaek-bbang-i i-sseo(-yo)

  근처에 괜찮은 중고 서점이 있어(요).

  geun-cheo-e gwaen-cha-neun jung-go seo-jeo-mi i-sseo(-yo)

- This is my favorite bookstore.

  여기는 내 단골 책방이에요.

  yeo-gi-neun nae dan-gol chaek-bbang-i-e-yo

Looking for Books 1

- Excuse me, do you have *Toji*?

  실례지만, 〈토지〉라는 책이 있나요?

  sil-rye-ji-man, <to-ji>-ra-neun chae-gi in-na-yo?

- Where are the books on history?

  역사에 관한 책은 어디 있죠?

  yeok-ssa-e gwan-han chae-geun eo-di it-jjyo?

- Do you know who wrote *The Great Gatsby*?

  〈위대한 개츠비〉 누가 썼는지 알아(요)?

  <wi-dae-han gae-cheu-bi> nu-ga sseon-neun-ji a-ra(-yo)?

- Do you have a foreign-language section?

  외국어 코너 있어요?

  oe-gu-geo ko-neo i-sseo-yo?

- What's the title of the book?

  책 제목이 뭐예요?

  chaek je-mo-gi mwo-ye-yo?

- I can't find the book that I'm looking for.

  제가 사려는 책을 찾을 수 없어요.

  je-ga sa-ryeo-neun chae-geul cha-jeul ssu eop-sseo-yo

Looking for Books 2

- I'm calling to see if you have any copies of *Korean Grammar* left.

  〈한국어 문법〉책이 있는지 물어보려고 전화했어요.

  <han-gu-geo mun-bbeop> chae-gi in-neun-ji mu-reo-bo-ryeo-go jeon-hwa-hae-sseo-yo

- When will the book come out?

  그 책은 언제 나옵니까?

  geu chae-geun eon-je na-om-ni-gga?

- The book will be on sale soon.

  그 책은 곧 판매됩니다.

  geu chae-geun got pan-mae-doem-ni-da

- The book came out in September.

  이 책은 9월에 출간됐어요.

  i chae-geun gu-wo-re chul-gan-dwae-sseo-yo

- The book is out of print.

  이 책은 절판됐습니다.

  i chae-geun jeol-pan-dwaet-sseum-ni-da

- Could you give me the title of the book you want?

  원하는 책 제목을 알려 주시겠어요?

  won-ha-neun chaek je-mo-geul al-ryeo ju-si-ge-sseo-yo?

Books Online

- If I ordered it today, when would I get it?

  오늘 주문하면, 언제 받을 수 있어요?

  o-neul ju-mun-ha-myeon, eon-je ba-deul ssu i-sseo-yo?

- Are the books online much cheaper?

  인터넷 서점에서 사는 책은 많이 싸(요)?

  in-teo-net seo-jeo-me-seo sa-neun chae-geun ma-ni ssa(-yo)?

- What's the current bestseller?

  요즘 베스트셀러는 뭐예요?

  yo-jeum be-seu-teu-sel-reo-neun mwo-ye-yo?

- Why don't you buy it online?

  인터넷 서점에서 사는 게 어때(요)?

  in-teo-net seo-jeo-me-seo sa-neun ge eo-ddae(-yo)?

- They sell paper books and e-books.

  종이책과 이북을 팔고 있어(요).

  jong-i-chaek-ggwa i-bu-geul pal-go i-sseo(-yo)

Paying for Books

■ I bought *The Korean Cookbook* for 18,000 won.

〈한국 요리책〉을 만 8천 원에 샀어(요).

<han-guk yo-ri-chae>-geul man pal-cheon wo-ne sa-sseo(-yo)

■ The book will cost somewhere around 10,000 won.

그 책은 아마 만 원쯤 할 걸(요).

geu chae-geun a-ma man won-jjeum hal ggeol(-yo)

■ The regular price is 20,000 won but you get a 10 percent discount.

원래 2만 원인데, 권 당 10% 할인해 드립니다.

wol-rae i-man wo-nin-de, gwon dang sip-peo-sen-teu ha-rin-hae deu-rim-ni-da

■ We will exchange the book if there's any problem or damage.

파본은 교환해 드립니다.

pa-bo-neun gyo-hwan-hae deu-rim-ni-da

■ I bought the books on impulse as they were so cheap.

책이 싸길래 충동구매 해 버렸어(요).

chae-gi ssa-gil-rae chung-dong-gu-mae hae beo-ryeo-sseo(-yo)

The Library 1

■ The book I need isn't in the library.

제가 필요한 책이 도서관에 없어요.

je-ga pi-ryo-han chae-gi do-seo-gwa-ne eop-sseo-yo

■ You should be quiet in the library.

도서관에서는 조용히 해야 해(요).

do-seo-gwa-ne-seo-neun jo-yong-hi hae-ya hae(-yo)

■ Don't use your phone in the library.

도서관에서는 휴대폰을 사용하면 안 돼(요).

do-seo-gwa-ne-seo-neun hyu-dae-po-neul sa-yong-ha-myeon an dwae(-yo)

■ This library has a collection of 30,000 volumes.

이 도서관은 3만 권의 책을 소장하고 있어(요).

i do-seo-gwa-neun sam-man gwo-ne chae-geul so-jang-ha-go i-sseo(-yo)

■ I'd like to get a library card.

도서관 카드를 만들려고요.

do-seo-gwan ka-deu-reul man-deul-ryeo-go-yo

The Library 2

■ He is borrowing books from the library.

그는 도서관에서 책을 빌리고 있어(요).

geu-neun do-seo-gwa-ne-seo chae-geul bil-ri-go i-sseo(-yo)

■ We were reading books in the library.

우리는 도서관에서 책을 읽고 있었어(요).

u-ri-neun do-seo-gwa-ne-seo chae-geul il-ggo i-sseo-sseo(-yo)

■ Where can I find the magazines?

잡지가 어디에 있어(요)?

jap-jji-ga eo-di-e i-sseo(-yo)?

■ Is there a photocopier I can use?

복사기를 쓸 수 있어요?

bok-ssa-gi-reul sseul ssu i-sseo-yo?

■ The library is going to close in a half hour.

도서관은 30분 후에 문을 닫아(요).

do-seo-gwa-neun sam-sip-bbun hu-e mu-neul da-da(-yo)

Borrowing Books

■ How many books can I borrow at one time?

한 번에 몇 권 빌릴 수 있어요?

han beo-ne myeot gwon bil-ril ssu i-sseo-yo?

■ I'd like to explain about borrowing and returning books.

대출과 반납에 관련된 규정을 설명해 드릴게요.

dae-chul-gwa ban-na-be gwal-ryeon-doen gyu-jeong-eul seol-myeong-hae deu-ril-gge-yo

■ You can borrow up to five books.

다섯 권까지 대출할 수 있습니다.

da-seot gwon-gga-ji dae-chul-hal ssu it-sseum-ni-da

■ I'd like to borrow four books.

네 권을 대출하려고요.

ne gwo-neul dae-chul-ha-ryeo-go-yo

■ How can I borrow a book?

대출하려면 어떻게 해야 하죠?

dae-chul-ha-ryeo-myeon eo-ddeo-ke hae-ya ha-jyo?

■ I forgot my card.
Can I still borrow a book?

제 카드를 깜박했는데요.
그래도 책을 대출할 수 있어요?

je ka-deu-reul ggam-ba-kaen-neun-de-yo.
geu-rae-do chae-geul dae-chul-hal ssu i-sseo-yo?

Returning Books

- The library books need to be returned by tomorrow.

  도서관 책은 내일까지 반납해야 해(요).

  do-seo-gwan chae-geun nae-il-gga-ji ban-na-pae-ya hae(-yo)

- I have to go to the library to return some books due today.

  오늘까지 반납해야 하는 책이 있어서, 도서관에 가야 해(요).

  o-neul-gga-ji ban-na-pae-ya ha-neun chae-gi i-sseo-seo, do-seo-gwa-ne ga-ya hae(-yo)

- This book is on loan until next Monday.

  이 책은 다음 주 월요일까지 대출되어 있습니다.

  i chae-geun da-eum ju wo-ryo-il-gga-ji dae-chul-doe-eo it-sseum-ni-da

- What happens if I lose a book?

  책을 잃어버리면 어떻게 돼죠?

  chae-geul i-reo-beo-ri-myeon eo-ddeo-ke dwae-jyo?

- Could I renew this book?

  이 책을 연장할 수 있어요?

  i chae-geul yeon-jang-hal ssu i-sseo-yo?

National Holidays

In Korea, there are five government-designated national holidays.

Independence Movement Day (Samiljeol 삼일절, March 1) commemorates the March First Movement, when mass protests took place against the Japanese occupation of Korea in the early twentieth century.

Constitution Day (Jeheonjeol 제헌절, July 17) is the anniversary of the proclamation of the South Korean constitution in 1948. It has not been a "no work" public holiday since 2008.

National Liberation Day (Gwangbokjeol 광복절, August 15) celebrates Korea's liberation from Japanese rule in 1945.

National Foundation Day (Gaecheonjeol 개천절, October 3) marks the founding of the first Korean kingdom of Gojoseon (고조선) in 2333 BC.

Finally, **Hangul Day** (Hangeullal 한글날, October 9) commemorates the creation of the Korean writing system. It had not been a day off since 1990 but was reinstated as a national holiday in 2013.

On national holidays the Korean flag (Taegeukgi 태극기) is flown.

Church 1

- I go to church on Sundays.

  일요일마다 교회에 가(요).

  i-ryo-il-ma-da gyo-hoe-e ga(-yo)

- I always attend a Sunday worship service.

  주일 예배는 꼭 참석해(요).

  ju-il ye-bae-neun ggok cham-seo-kae(-yo)

- Is there anything different about a Korean service?

  한국어 예배에는 뭐 다른 게 있어(요)?

  han-gu-geo ye-bae-e-neun mwo da-reun ge i-sseo(-yo)?

- What was the topic of today's sermon?

  오늘 설교의 주제가 뭐예요?

  o-neul seol-gyo-e ju-je-ga mwo-ye-yo?

- What scripture is today's sermon based on?

  오늘 예배의 성경 구절은 뭐예요?

  o-neul ye-bae-e seong-gyeong gu-jeo-reun mwo-ye-yo?

- Turn to the Gospel according to John, chapter 3, verse 16.

  요한복음 3장 16절을 펴세요.

  yo-han-bo-geum sam-jang sim-nyuk-jjeo-reul pyeo-se-yo

Church 2

- The pastor's sermon was touching today.

  오늘 목사님의 설교는 감동적이었어(요).

  o-neul mok-ssa-ni-me seol-gyo-neun gam-dong-jeo-gi-eo-sseo(-yo)

- The sermon was so long that I got sleepy.

  설교가 길어서 졸렸어(요).

  seol-gyo-ga gi-reo-seo jol-ryeo-sseo(-yo)

- I don't have any money for the collection.

  돈이 없어서 헌금을 못 냈어(요).

  do-ni eop-sseo-seo heon-geu-meul mot nae-sseo(-yo)

- How long have you attended this church?

  이 교회를 얼마나 다녔어(요)?

  i gyo-hoe-reul eol-ma-na da-nyeo-sseo(-yo)?

- Christmas and Easter are important church festivals.

  성탄절과 부활절은 교회의 큰 행사예요.

  seong-tan-jeol-gwa bu-hwal-jjeo-reun gyo-hoe-e keun haeng-sa-ye-yo

Church 3

- She sings in the church choir.
그녀는 교회 성가대에서
노래해(요).
geu-nyeo-neun gyo-hoe seong-ga-dae-
e-seo no-rae-hae(-yo)

- Let us kneel in prayer.
무릎 꿇고 기도합시다.
mu-reup ggul-ko gi-do-hap-ssi-da

- I pray in Jesus' name. Amen.
예수님의 이름으로 기도합니다.
아멘.
ye-su-ni-me i-reu-meu-ro gi-do-ham-ni-
da. a-men

- My prayer was answered.
기도가 응답되었어(요).
gi-do-ga eung-dap-ddoe-eo-sseo(-yo)

- Do you mind if I say a prayer
before eating?
식사 전에 기도해도 될까요?
sik-ssa jeo-ne gi-do-hae-do doel-gga-yo?

- We give thanks to God before
this meal.
우리는 식사 전에 감사
기도해(요).
u-ri-neun sik-ssa jeo-ne gam-sa gi-do-
hae(-yo)

Public Holidays

There are several public holidays in
Korea including Seollal (설날, Lunar
New Year's Day, celebrated for three
days), chuseok (추석, Mid-autumn
Festival, celebrated for three days),
Buddha's Birthday (석가탄신일 [seok-
gga-tan-si-nil], April 8 of the lunar
calendar, late April or early May),
Children's Day (어린이날 [eo-ri-ni-nal],
May 5), Memorial Day (현충일 [hyeon-
chung-il], June 6) and Christmas Day
(크리스마스 [keu-ri-seu-ma-seu]).

There are fifteen such holidays
throughout the year where
employees are entitled to time off
by law.

Parents' Day (어버이날 [eo-beo-i-nal],
May 8), Teachers' Day (스승의 날
[seu-seung-e nal], May 15) and Arbor
Day (식목일 [sing-mo-gil], April 5) are
not days off. Labor Day (근로자의 날
[geul-ro-ja-e nal], May 1) is a day off
for workers only.

The Korean government introduced
a substitute holiday since 2014, but
only for public officers.

Church 4

- Myeong-jin prayed the rosary.

  명진이는 묵주 기도를 했어(요).

  myeong-ji-ni-neun muk-jju gi-do-reul
  hae-sseo(-yo)

- I made the sign of the cross and prayed.

  십자가를 그리고 기도했어(요).

  sip-jja-ga-reul geu-ri-go
  gi-do-hae-sseo(-yo)

- The priest celebrated Mass.

  신부님은 미사를 올렸어(요).

  sin-bu-ni-meun mi-sa-reul
  ol-ryeo-sseo(-yo)

- The memorial Mass will be held at the Catholic cathedral tomorrow at 5 p.m.

  추모 미사는 내일 오후 5시에 성당에서 드립니다.

  chu-mo mi-sa-neun nae-il o-hu da-seot-
  ssi-e seong-dang-e-seo deu-rim-ni-da

- He has come to make his confession.

  그는 고해성사를 하러 왔어(요).

  geu-neun go-hae-seong-sa-reul ha-reo
  wa-sseo(-yo)

- I confessed to the priest.

  신부님께 고해성사를 했어(요).

  sin-bu-nim-gge go-hae-seong-sa-reul
  hae-sseo(-yo)

Temples

- My grandmother goes to a temple to worship.

  할머니는 불공드리러 절에 가셔(요).

  hal-meo-ni-neun bul-gong-deu-ri-reo
  jeo-re ga-syeo(-yo)

- Where should I do a temple stay?

  템플스테이 하러 어디로 가야 할까요?

  tem-peul-seu-te-i ha-reo eo-di-ro ga-ya
  hal-gga-yo?

- I feel soothed whenever I go to the temple.

  그 절에 가면 마음이 안정돼(요).

  geu jeo-re ga-myeon ma-eu-mi
  an-jeong-dwae(-yo)

- Can we meet a Buddhist monk here?

  여기에서 스님을 뵐 수 있을까요?

  yeo-gi-e-seo seu-ni-meul boel ssu
  i-sseul-gga-yo?

- When the monk sounds a wooden gong, everyone bows to Buddha.

  스님이 목탁을 두드리면, 모두 부처님께 절을 합니다.

  seu-ni-mi mok-ta-geul du-deu-ri-myeon,
  mo-du bu-cheo-nim-gge jeo-reul ham-
  ni-da

Mosques

▪ Do you know any Korean Muslims?

한국 무슬림 알아(요)?

han-guk mu-seul-rim a-ra(-yo)?

▪ Muslims visit mosques to pray.

무슬림들은 기도하기 위해 모스크에 가(요).

mu-seul-rim-deu-reun gi-do-ha-gi wi-hae mo-seu-keu-e ga(-yo)

▪ The masjid or mosque is the place of Muslim worship.

회교 사원이나 모스크는 무슬림의 예배처예요.

hoe-gyo sa-wo-ni-na mo-seu-keu-neun mu-seul-ri-me ye-bae-cheo-ye-yo

▪ There is a mosque in Itaewon. Do you know any others?

이태원에 모스크가 있잖아(요). 다른 곳 알아(요)?

i-tae-wo-ne mo-seu-keu-ga it-jja-na(-yo). da-reun got a-ra(-yo)?

▪ What should I wear to the mosque?

모스크에 들어갈 때는 어떻게 입어야 해(요)?

mo-seu-keu-e deu-reo-gal ddae-neun eo-ddeo-ke i-beo-ya hae(-yo)?

Movie Theaters 1

▪ I'll meet you in front of the theater at 6:30!

6시 반에 극장 입구에서 만나(요)!

yeo-seot-ssi ba-ne geuk-jjang ip-ggu-e-seo man-na(-yo)!

▪ Which theater do you want to go to?

어느 극장으로 갈 거예요?

eo-neu geuk-jjang-eu-ro gal ggeo-ye-yo?

▪ That movie is showing at the CC Theater.

저 영화는 CC극장에서 상영해(요).

jeo yeong-hwa-neun ssi-ssi-geuk-jjang-e-seo sang-yeong-hae(-yo)

▪ Where would you like to sit?

어떤 좌석으로 드릴까요?

eo-ddeon jwa-seo-geu-ro deu-ril-gga-yo?

▪ I'd like to sit in the front row.

앞쪽 좌석으로 주세요.

ap-jjok jwa-seo-geu-ro ju-se-yo

▪ I can't see very well. Do you want to move?

잘 안 보여(요). 옮길래(요)?

jal an bo-yeo(-yo). om-gil-rae(-yo)?

Movie Theaters 2

▪ There are a lot of multiplex theaters in Korea.

한국에는 복합 영화 상영관이 많이 있어(요).

han-gu-ge-neun bo-kap yeong-hwa sang-yeong-gwa-ni ma-ni i-sseo(-yo)

▪ Did you book tickets for the 3D theater?

3D 상영관으로 예매했어(요)?

sseu-ri-di sang-yeong-gwa-neu-ro ye-mae-hae-sseo(-yo)?

▪ At 4D theaters, audiences can experience the wind blowing, see chairs moving, or smell certain odors during key moments in the film.

4D 상영관에서는 주요 장면에서 바람이 불거나 의자가 움직이거나 냄새가 나(요).

po-di sang-yeong-gwa-ne-seo-neun ju-yo jang-myeo-ne-seo ba-ra-mi bul-geo-na ui-ja-ga um-ji-gi-geo-na naem-sae-ga na(-yo)

▪ I arrived at the theater too late and missed the beginning.

극장에 너무 늦게 도착해서, 영화를 처음부터 못 봤어(요).

geuk-jjang-e neo-mu neut-gge do-cha-kae-seo, yeong-hwa-reul cheo-eum-bu-teo mot bwa-sseo(-yo)

Movie Tickets

▪ It's getting late. We should probably get our tickets.

늦겠어(요). 우리 표를 사 둬야 할 걸(요).

neut-gge-sseo(-yo).
u-ri pyo-reul sa dwo-ya hal ggeol(-yo)

▪ You can't get a refund now. The movie's already started.

지금은 환불할 수 없어(요). 영화가 이미 시작했거든(요).

ji-geu-meun hwan-bul-hal ssu eop-sseo(-yo). yeong-hwa-ga i-mi si-ja-kaet-ggeo-deun(-yo)

▪ Do you have any tickets left for the seven o'clock show?

7시 표 아직 있어(요)?

il-gop-ssi pyo a-jik i-sseo(-yo)?

▪ I bought the tickets so you get the popcorn.

예매는 내가 했으니까, 팝콘은 네가 사라.

ye-mae-neun nae-ga hae-sseu-ni-gga, pap-ko-neun ne-ga sa-ra

▪ Two tickets for the 2:30, please.

2시 반 표 두 장 주세요.

du-si ban pyo du jang ju-se-yo

Theater Etiquette

■ Can I bring some bread into the theater?

영화관에 빵을 좀 가져가도 될까(요)?

yeong-hwa-gwa-ne bbang-eul jom ga-jeo-ga-do doel-gga(-yo)?

■ Food is not allowed in the theater.

영화관에서 음식을 먹을 수 없습니다.

yeong-hwa-gwa-ne-seo eum-si-geul meo-geul ssu eop-sseum-ni-da

■ Turn your phone off before the movie starts.

영화 시작 전에 휴대폰을 꺼 두세요.

yeong-hwa si-jak jeo-ne hyu-dae-po-neul ggeo du-se-yo

■ Be quiet, please.

조용히 해 주세요.

jo-yong-hi hae ju-se-yo

■ Please don't kick my seat.

제 자리를 차지 마세요.

je ja-ri-reul cha-ji ma-se-yo

■ Don't take photos while the movie is showing.

상영 중 촬영 금지.

sang-yeong jung chwa-ryeong geum-ji

Musicals

■ The performance starts in twenty minutes.

공연은 20분 후에 시작합니다.

gong-yeo-neun i-sip-bbun hu-e si-ja-kam-ni-da

■ It's a musical for people of all ages.

이 뮤지컬은 모든 관람객이 볼 수 있어(요).

i myu-ji-keo-reun mo-deun gwal-ram-gae-gi bol ssu i-sseo(-yo)

■ What time is the matinee?

마티네는 언제예요?

ma-ti-ne-neun eon-je-ye-yo?

■ The musical will play for two days, on Saturday and Sunday.

그 뮤지컬은 토요일과 일요일 양일간 공연될 예정입니다.

geu myu-ji-keo-reun to-yo-il-gwa i-ryo-il yang-il-gan gong-yeon-doel ye-jeong-im-ni-da

■ How long is the intermission?

중간 쉬는 시간은 얼마나 돼죠?

jung-gan swi-neun si-ga-neun eol-ma-na dwae-jyo?

Other Theaters

■ This play is showing three times a day.

이 연극은 하루에 3회 공연해(요).

i yeon-geu-geun ha-ru-e sam-hoe gong-yeon-hae(-yo)

■ *Romeo and Juliet* is showing at the National Theater.

〈로미오와 줄리엣〉은 지금 국립극장에서 공연 중이에요.

<ro-mi-o-wa jul-ri-e>-seun ji-geum gung-nip-geuk-jjang-e-seo gong-yeon jung-i-e-yo

■ It's showing regularly at the Civic Center.

시민회관에서 정기 공연이 있어(요).

si-min-hoe-gwa-ne-seo jeong-gi gong-yeo-ni i-sseo(-yo)

■ Let's go out to dinner and then see *Nanta*.

저녁 식사하고, 〈난타〉 보러 가자.

jeo-nyeok sik-ssa-ha-go, <nan-ta> bo-reo ga-ja

Tip: Nanta is a Korean non-verbal comedy show where the actors perform with various knives and kitchen tools.

■ I'll be at the concert hall soon.

음악회 홀에 곧 도착할 거예요.

eu-ma-koe ho-re got do-cha-kal ggeo-ye-yo

Bars & Pubs 1

■ I often get a drink after work.

퇴근 후에 종종 술집에 가(요).

toe-geun hu-e jong-jong sul-jji-be ga(-yo)

■ This bar is my hangout.

이 술집은 내 단골이에요.

i sul-jji-beun nae dan-go-ri-e-yo

■ Shall we get a drink at my go-to bar?

단골집에 가서 한잔 할까(요)?

dan-gol-jji-be ga-seo han-jan hal-gga(-yo)?

■ This bar is pretty decent!

이 술집 괜찮은데(요)!

i sul-jjip gwaen-cha-neun-de(-yo)!

■ I know a cozy place. Do you want to go?

아늑한 술집 하나 알고 있는데(요). 갈래(요)?

a-neu-kan sul-jjip ha-na al-go in-neun-de(-yo). gal-rae(-yo)?

■ Do you want to go outside for a smoke?

담배 피우러 나갈래(요)?

dam-bae pi-u-reo na-gal-rae(-yo)?

Tip: These days many bars are nonsmoking. If you want to smoke, go outside or find a smoking area.

Bars & Pubs 2

■ Let's get a beer!

맥주 한잔 하자!

maek-jju han-jan ha-ja!

■ I'll buy you a beer when we're done!

일 끝나고 내가 맥주 한잔 쏠게(요)!

il ggeun-na-go nae-ga maek-jju han-jan ssol-gge(-yo)!

■ That bar has live jazz on the weekends.

이 술집은 주말마다 라이브 재즈 공연이 있어(요).

i sul-jji-beun ju-mal-ma-da ra-i-beu jae-jeu gong-yeo-ni i-sseo(-yo)

■ What's a good place for live music?

라이브 뮤직이 좋은 곳이 어디예요?

ra-i-beu myu-ji-gi jo-eun go-si eo-di-ye-yo?

■ Let's go somewhere else!

어디 다른 데로 가자!

eo-di da-reun de-ro ga-ja!

Arirang

The Korean folk song "Arirang" (아리랑)" tells a centuries-old tale of one couple's love and separation. It is considered by many an apt metaphor for the struggles of the Korean people past and present. There are reportedly a staggering 3,600 variations of 60 versions of the song, with the best known being "Jeongseon Arirang (정선 아리랑)" "Jindo Arirang (진도 아리랑)" and "Miryang Arirang (밀양 아리랑)." Any version of Arirang though is welcomed by Koreans all over the world. The song has also made the UNESCO Intangible Cultural Heritage list twice, once via a South Korean submission in 2012 and again in 2014 after a submission from North Korea, a testament to its importance across the peninsula. In 2015, the South Korean Cultural Heritage Administration added the song to its record of intangible cultural assets.

아리랑, 아리랑, 아라리요.
아리랑 고개로 넘어간다.

a-ri-rang, a-ri-rang, a-ra-ri-yo.
a-ri-rang go-gae-ro neo-meo-gan-da

Arirang, Arirang, Arariyo.
You are going over Arirang hill.

나를 버리고 가시는 님은
십 리도 못 가서 발병 난다.

na-reul beo-ri-go ga-si-neun ni-meun
sim ri-do mot ga-seo bal-bbyeong nan-da

My love, you are leaving me. Your feet will be sore before you go ten li.
* (*One li is about a third of a mile / 0.4 km.)

Bar Talk 1

■ Cheers!
건배!
geon-bae!

■ Bottoms up!
원샷!
won-syat!

■ May I propose a toast?
건배할까(요)?
geon-bae-hal-gga(-yo)?

■ Congratulations on getting
married! Cheers!
두 분의 결혼을 축하하며, 건배!
du bu-ne gyeol-ho-neul chu-ka-ha-
myeo, geon-bae!

■ Can I have another?
한 잔 더 해도 될까(요)?
han jan deo hae-do doel-gga(-yo)?

■ Do you want one more shot?
한 잔 더 할래(요)?
han jan deo hal-rae(-yo)?

■ Let's drink some more!
좀 더 마시자!
jom deo ma-si-ja!

■ Could I pour you a glass?
한 잔 따라 드릴까요?
han jan dda-ra deu-ril-gga-yo?

Bar Talk 2

■ Let's hit the bottle!
오늘 실컷 마셔(요)!
o-neul sil-keot ma-syeo(-yo)!

■ Would you like another beer or a
shot of whiskey?
맥주 마실래(요) 위스키
마실래(요)?
maek-jju ma-sil-rae(-yo) wi-seu-ki
ma-sil-rae(-yo)?

■ Which do you like, red wine or
white wine?
레드와인 좋아해(요)
화이트와인 좋아해(요)?
re-deu-wa-in jo-a-hae(-yo) hwa-i-teu-
wa-in jo-a-hae(-yo)?

■ Two draft beers, please.
생맥주 두 잔 주세요.
saeng-maek-jju du jan ju-se-yo

■ On second thought, make it a
beer.
다시 생각해 보니, 맥주가
좋아(요).
da-si saeng-ga-kae bo-ni, maek-jju-ga
jo-a(-yo)

■ I can't drink hard liquor.
독한 술은 마실 수 없어(요).
do-kan su-reun ma-sil ssu eop-sseo(-yo)

Bar Snacks

■ What bar snacks do you have?

무슨 안주가 있어(요)?

mu-seun an-ju-ga i-sseo(-yo)?

■ Let's order some more side
dishes!

안주 더 시켜(요)!

an-ju deo si-kyeo(-yo)!

■ This goes very well with wine.

이것은 와인과 어울리는
안주예요.

i-geo-seun wa-in-gwa eo-ul-ri-neun
an-ju-ye-yo

■ What would you like to have
with your beer?

맥주랑 같이 뭘 드실래요?

maek-jju-rang ga-chi mwol deu-sil-rae-
yo?

■ What's good to eat with
makgeolli?

막걸리 와 먹기에 어떤 안주가
좋아(요)?

mak-ggeol-ri wa meok-ggi-e eo-ddeon
an-ju-ga jo-a(-yo)?

■ Stir-fried eel is great with soju.

소주 안주로는 꼼장어 볶음이
최고지(요).

so-ju an-ju-ro-neun ggom-jang-eo
bo-ggeu-mi choe-go-ji(-yo)

The Art Gallery

■ When is the Daehan Art Gallery
open?

대한미술관은 언제 열어(요)?

dae-han-mi-sul-gwa-neun eon-je
yeo-reo(-yo)?

■ The gallery waives its admission
fee on Sundays.

그 미술관은 일요일에 무료
입장이에요.

geu mi-sul-gwa-neun i-ryo-i-re mu-ryo
ip-jjang-i-e-yo

■ Is there an entrance fee?

입장료를 받아(요)?

ip-jjang-nyo-reul ba-da(-yo)?

■ Do you like abstract art?
There's an exhibition now at the
National Museum.

"추상 미술" 좋아해(요)? 지금
국립미술관에 전시회가 있어(요).

"chu-sang mi-sul" jo-a-hae(-yo)?
ji-geum gung-nip-mi-sul-gwa-ne
jeon-si-hoe-ga i-sseo(-yo)

■ There's nothing to see in this art
museum.

이 미술관에는 볼 만한 것이
아무것도 없어(요).

i mi-sul-gwa-ne-neun bol man-han geo-
si a-mu-geot-ddo eop-sseo(-yo)

Museums 1

- One ticket, please
표 한 장 주세요.
pyo han jang ju-se-yo

- When does the museum open?
박물관은 언제 열어(요)?
bang-mul-gwa-neun eon-je yeo-reo(-yo)?

- There are many things to see in this museum.
이 박물관에는 다양한 볼거리가 있어(요).
i bang-mul-gwa-ne-neun da-yang-han bol-ggeo-ri-ga i-sseo(-yo)

- Does this museum have an activity program?
이 박물관에는 활동 프로그램이 있어요?
i bang-mul-gwa-ne-neun hwal-ddong peu-ro-geu-rae-mi i-sseo-yo?

- This museum has weekend programs for kids.
이 박물관에는 어린이들을 위한 주말 프로그램이 있어(요).
i bang-mul-gwa-ne-neun eo-ri-ni-deu-reul wi-han ju-mal peu-ro-geu-rae-mi i-sseo(-yo)

Museums 2

- Do they have audio guides?
오디오 가이드 있어요?
o-di-o ga-i-deu i-sseo-yo?

- Admission to the museum is half price after 5 p.m.
오후 5시 이후에는 박물관 입장료가 50% 할인됩니다.
o-hu da-seot-ssi i-hu-e-neun bang-mul-gwan ip-jjang-nyo-ga o-sip-peo-sen-teu ha-rin-doem-ni-da

- This museum houses many rare articles.
이 박물관은 희귀 자료를 다수 소장하고 있어(요).
i bang-mul-gwa-neun hi-gwi ja-ryo-reul da-su so-jang-ha-go i-sseo(-yo)

- I'm disappointed that the museum is closed.
박물관이 휴관이어서 실망이에요.
bang-mul-gwa-ni hyu-gwa-ni-eo-seo sil-mang-i-e-yo

- Does Busan have a science museum?
부산에 과학 박물관 있어(요)?
bu-sa-ne gwa-hak bang-mul-gwan i-sseo(-yo)?

Amusement Parks

- Do you like going to amusement parks?

  놀이동산에 가는 거 좋아해(요)?

  no-ri-dong-sa-ne ga-neun geo jo-a-hae(-yo)?

- What kinds of rides do you like?

  어떤 놀이기구를 좋아해(요)?

  eo-ddeon no-ri-gi-gu-reul jo-a-hae(-yo)?

- You're not scared to ride the roller coaster?

  롤러코스터 타는 것 안 무서워(요)?

  rol-reo-ko-seu-teo ta-neun geot an mu-seo-wo(-yo)?

- The merry-go-round is Ye-na's favorite ride.

  예나는 회전목마를 가장 좋아해(요).

  ye-na-neun hoe-jeon-mong-ma-reul ga-jang jo-a-hae(-yo)

- This ticket holder is entitled to enter all areas of the amusement park.

  이 표가 있으면, 놀이동산의 모든 것을 이용할 수 있어(요).

  i pyo-ga i-sseu-myeon, no-ri-dong-sa-ne mo-deun geo-seul i-yong-hal ssu i-sseo(-yo)

The Fitness Center

- How's that gym that you go to?

  다니는 헬스클럽은 어때(요)?

  da-ni-neun hel-seu-keul-reo-beun eo-ddae(-yo)?

- I'll sign up for the gym next month.

  다음 달에 헬스클럽에 등록할 거예요.

  da-eum da-re hel-seu-keul-reo-be deung-no-kal ggeo-ye-yo

- I work out at the gym twice a week.

  일주일에 두 번 헬스클럽에서 운동해(요).

  il-jju-i-re du beon hel-seu-keul-reo-be-seo un-dong-hae(-yo)

- Do they have spinning? Pilates?

  자전거 타기 해(요)?
  필라테스 해(요)?

  ja-jeon-geo ta-gi hae(-yo)?
  pil-ra-te-seu hae(-yo)?

- I need to renew my gym membership.

  헬스클럽 회원권을 갱신해야 해(요).

  hel-seu-keul-reop hoe-won-ggwo-neul gaeng-sin-hae-ya hae(-yo)

Chapter 6

Feelings & Character

Feelings & Character 감정 & 성격 gam-jeong & seong-gyeok

adj. pleased
기쁘다 [기쁘다]
gi-bbeu-da

adj. joyful 즐겁다 [즐겁따]
jeul-geop-dda

adj. cheerful
유쾌하다 [유쾌하다]
yu-kwae-ha-da

adj. fun
재미있다 [재미읻따]
jae-mi-it-dda

adj. interested
흥미진진하다 [흥:미진진하다]
heung-mi-jin-jin-ha-da

adj. excited
흥분하다 [흥분하다]
heung-bun-ha-da

adj. happy
행복하다 [행:보카다]
haeng-bo-ka-da

adj. satisfied
v. satisfy
만족하다 [만조카다]
man-jo-ka-da

adj. relieved
안심 [안심]
an-sim

adj. trustworthy
믿다 [믿따]
mit-dda

adj. good
착하다 [차카다]
cha-ka-da

adj. kind 친절하다
[친절하다]
chin-jeol-
ha-da

adj. polite
공손하다 [공손하다]
gong-son-ha-da

adj. honest
정직하다 [정:지카다]
jeong-ji-ka-da

adj. friendly
다정하다 [다정하다]
da-jeong-ha-da

adj. calm, composed
침착하다 [침차카다]
chim-cha-ka-da

adj. sad
슬프다 [슬프다]
seul-peu-da

adj. gloomy
우울하다 [우울하다]
u-ul-ha-da

adj. in pain
괴롭다 [괴롭따/궤롭따]
goe-rop-dda/
gwe-rop-dda

adj. miserable
비참하다 [비:참하다]
bi-cham-ha-da

adj. disappointed
실망하다 [실망하다]
sil-mang-ha-da

adj. embarrassed
부끄럽다 [부끄럽따]
bu-ggeu-reop-dda

adj. jumpy
초조하다 [초조하다]
cho-jo-ha-da

adj. nervous
긴장하다 [긴장하다]
gin-jang-ha-da

adj. bad 나쁘다 [나쁘다]
na-bbeu-da

adj. arrogant
거만하다 [거:만하다]
geo-man-ha-da
= 건방지다 [건방지다]
geon-bang-ji-da

adj. idle, lazy
게으르다 [게으르다]
ge-eu-reu-da

adj. angry
화나다 [화:나다]
hwa-na-da

adj. annoying
짜증스럽다 [짜증스럽따]
jja-jeung-seu-reop-dda

adj. anxious
불안하다 [불안하다]
bu-ran-ha-da

adj. afraid
무섭다 [무섭따]
mu-seop-dda

adj. fearful
두렵다 [두렵따]
du-ryeop-dda

adj. scared
겁나다 [겁나다]
geom-na-da

Pleased 1

- I'm overjoyed!

  아주 기뻐(요)!

  a-ju gi-bbeo(-yo)!

- I'm so glad!

  기분이 정말 좋아(요)!

  gi-bu-ni jeong-mal jo-a(-yo)!

- I'm about ready to jump out of my skin!

  펄쩍 뛸 듯이 기뻐(요)!

  peol-jjeok ddwil ddeu-si gi-bbeo(-yo)!

- I jumped for joy!

  날 듯이 기뻤어(요)!

  nal ddeu-si gi-bbeo-sseo(-yo)!

- I feel like humming!

  콧노래를 부르고 싶은 기분이에요!

  kon-no-rae-reul bu-reu-go si-peun gi-bu-ni-e-yo!

- I'm so pleased, I don't know what to say!

  기뻐서 말이 안 나와(요)!

  gi-bbeo-seo ma-ri an na-wa(-yo)!

Pleased 2

- I'm happy I could do this for you!

  당신을 위해 이렇게 할 수 있어서 기뻐요!

  dang-si-neul wi-hae i-reo-ke hal ssu i-sseo-seo gi-bbeo-yo!

- I'm pleased to hear that!

  그 말을 들으니 기뻐(요)!

  geu ma-reul deu-reu-ni gi-bbeo(-yo)!

- I'm very glad to see you!

  당신을 뵙게 돼서 정말 기뻐요!

  dang-si-neul boep-gge dwae-seo jeong-mal gi-bbeo-yo!

- It was great to spend time together!

  당신과 함께 있어 즐거워요!

  dang-sin-gwa ham-gge i-sseo jeul-geo-wo-yo!

- Nothing could be more wonderful in my life!

  내 평생에 가장 기뻤어(요)!

  nae pyeong-saeng-e ga-jang gi-bbeo-sseo(-yo)!

- I'm pumped!

  아주 들떴어(요)!

  a-ju deul-ddeo-sseo(-yo)!

Having Fun

■ **How fun!**
아주 재미있어(요)!
a-ju jae-mi-i-sseo(-yo)!

■ **What a good time!**
정말 즐거워(요)!
jeong-mal jeul-geo-wo(-yo)!

■ **It's so funny that I can't stop laughing!**
아주 재미있어서 웃음을 멈출 수 없어(요)!
a-ju jae-mi-i-sseo-seo u-seu-meul meom-chul ssu eop-sseo(-yo)!

■ **I had the time of my life!**
즐거운 시간을 보냈어(요)!
jeul-geo-un si-ga-neul bo-nae-sseo(-yo)!

■ **The party was a lot of fun!**
그 파티는 아주 재미있었어(요)!
geu pa-ti-neun a-ju jae-mi-i-sseo-sseo(-yo)!

■ **The book I'm reading is interesting!**
읽고 있는 책이 재미있어(요)!
il-ggo in-neun chae-gi jae-mi-i-sseo(-yo)!

Happy

■ **I'm happy!**
행복해(요)!
haeng-bo-kae(-yo)!

■ **I've never been happier in my life!**
내 인생에서 지금보다 더 행복한 적은 없어(요)!
nae in-saeng-e-seo ji-geum-bo-da deo haeng-bo-kan jeo-geun eop-sseo(-yo)!

내 인생에서 최고로 행복해(요)!
nae in-saeng-e-seo choe-go-ro haeng-bo-kae(-yo)!

■ **I'm very happy for you!**
당신 때문에 아주 행복해요!
dang-sin ddae-mu-ne a-ju haeng-bo-kae-yo!

■ **It's just too good to be true!**
꿈만 같아(요)!
ggum-man ga-ta(-yo)!

■ **I was so happy at that time.**
그때는 아주 행복했지(요).
geu-ddae-neun a-ju haeng-bo-kaet-jji(-yo)

■ **I am unhappy with him.**
그 사람 때문에 행복하지 않아(요).
geu sa-ram ddae-mu-ne haeng-bo-ka-ji a-na(-yo)

Relieved

■ What a relief!

안심했어(요)!

an-sim-hae-sseo(-yo)!

■ I'm relieved to hear the news.

그 소식을 듣고 나서,
안심했어(요).

geu so-si-geul deut-ggo na-seo,
an-sim-hae-sseo(-yo)

■ Now I can put myself at ease!

이제 안심할 수 있어(요)!

i-je an-sim-hal ssu i-sseo(-yo)!

■ It's never as bad as you think!

네가 생각하는 것처럼 결코
나쁘진 않아(요)!

ne-ga saeng-ga-ka-neun geot-cheo-
reom gyeol-ko na-bbeu-jin a-na(-yo)!

■ I can assure you that the worst is over!

고비를 넘겼으니 안심이 돼(요)!

go-bi-reul neom-gyeo-sseu-ni an-si-mi
dwae(-yo)!

■ You can put that matter to rest.

그 문제는 안심해도 돼(요).

geu mun-je-neun an-sim-hae-do
dwae(-yo)

Relationship Slang

- 남사친/여사친 [nam-sa-chin/yeo-sa-chin] male friend/female friend
- 남친/여친 [nam-chin / yeo-chin] boyfriend/girlfriend
- 품절남/품절녀 [pum-jeol-ram/pum-jeol-ryeo] man/woman who just got married
- 모쏠 [mo-ssol] someone who has never had a boyfriend or girlfriend
- 밀당 [mil-ddang] push and pull in a relationship
- 썸 [sseom] an attraction between two people as they get to know each other
- 까도남/까도녀 [gga-do-nam/gga-do-nyeo] a type of man/woman who is usually arrogant and rich
- 훈남 [hun-nam] a handsome, well-mannered guy
- 베프 [be-peu] best friend
- 케미 [ke-mi] chemistry between two people
- 꿀잼 [ggul-jaem] something that is fun, funny or interesting
- 노잼 [no-jaem] something that is not fun, funny or interesting
- 심쿵 [sim-kung] an emotional heart attack you feel when you see or think about your crush or someone you find extremely attractive

Satisfied

- I'm very content.
  정말 만족스러워(요).
  jeong-mal man-jok-sseu-reo-wo(-yo)

- I'm very satisfied.
  매우 만족해(요).
  mae-u man-jo-kae(-yo)

- He was tickled at the idea.
  그는 그 아이디어에
  만족했어(요).
  geu-neun geu a-i-di-eo-e
  man-jo-kae-sseo(-yo)

- It was a result right enough.
  흡족한 결과예요.
  heup-jjo-kan gyeol-gwa-ye-yo

- She's pretty satisfied.
  그녀는 아주 만족해(요).
  geu-nyeo-neun a-ju man-jo-kae(-yo)

- I'm satisfied with my new car.
  새로 산 차가 마음에 들어(요).
  sae-ro san cha-ga ma-eu-me deu-reo(-yo)

Surprised 1

- Oh my God!
  맙소사!
  map-sso-sa!

  어머!
  eo-meo!

- What a surprise!
  놀라운 걸!
  nol-ra-un geol!

- No way!
  말도 안 돼(요)!
  mal-do an dwae(-yo)!

  설마!
  seol-ma!

  그럴리가!
  geu-reol-ri-ga!

- That's awesome!
  굉장해(요)!
  goeng-jang-hae(-yo)!

- I couldn't believe my eyes!
  내 눈을 믿을 수 없어(요)!
  nae nu-neul mi-deul ssu eop-sseo(-yo)!

- You scared me!
  (너 때문에) 놀랐잖아(요)!
  (neo ddae-mu-ne) nol-rat-jja-na(-yo)!

Surprised 2

■ I was completely surprised!
깜짝 놀랐어(요)!
ggam-jjak nol-ra-sseo(-yo)!

■ I was very surprised to hear that!
그 소식을 듣고 매우 놀랐어(요)!
geu so-si-geul deut-ggo mae-u
nol-ra-sseo(-yo)!

■ I'm dumbstruck!
놀라서 말도 안 나와(요)!
nol-ra-seo mal-do an na-wa(-yo)!

■ It was totally unexpected!
전혀 예상 밖이에요!
jeon-hyeo ye-sang ba-ggi-e-yo!

■ That's a bolt from the blue!
마른하늘에 날벼락이에요!
ma-reun-ha-neu-re nal-byeo-ra-gi-e-yo!

■ I could hardly believe my ears!
내 귀를 의심했어(요)!
nae gwi-reul ui-sim-hae-sseo(-yo)!

LESSON 2 **Bad Feelings**

Sad

■ I'm sad.
슬퍼(요).
seul-peo(-yo)

■ I feel blue.
우울해(요).
u-ul-hae(-yo)

■ I'm distressed.
너무 괴로워(요).
neo-mu goe-ro-wo(-yo)

■ I'm heartbroken.
마음이 아파(요).
ma-eu-mi a-pa(-yo)

■ I'm so sad I could cry!
슬퍼서 울고 싶어(요)!
seul-peo-seo ul-go si-peo(-yo)!

■ I cried my eyes out.
엄청 울었어(요).
eom-cheong u-reo-sseo(-yo)

■ I heard a sad story.
구슬픈 이야기를 들었어(요).
gu-seul-peun i-ya-gi-reul
deu-reo-sseo(-yo)

Angry 1

■ I'm pissed off!
너무 화나(요)!
neo-mu hwa-na(-yo)!

■ He ticked me off.
그 때문에 열받았어(요).
geu ddae-mu-ne yeol-ba-da-sseo(-yo)

■ Damn it!
젠장!
jen-jang!

제기랄!
je-gi-ral!

■ I'm extremely unhappy about this.
정말 불쾌해(요).
jeong-mal bul-kwae-hae(-yo)

■ What are you so angry about?
뭐 때문에 그렇게 화났어(요)?
mwo ddae-mu-ne geu-reo-ke hwa-na-sseo(-yo)?

■ Don't upset her.
그녀를 화나게 하지 마(세요).
geu-nyeo-reul hwa-na-ge ha-ji ma(-se-yo)

■ I can't stand it any more.
더 이상 참을 수 없어(요).
deo i-sang cha-meul ssu eop-sseo(-yo)

Angry 2

■ My patience is worn out.
내 인내심의 한계가 다 됐어(요).
nae in-nae-si-me han-gye-ga da dwae-sseo(-yo)

■ I was angry because Tae-min ruined my plan.
태민이가 내 계획을 망쳐 놔서 화났어(요).
tae-mi-ni-ga nae gye-hoe-geul mang-cheo nwa-seo hwa-na-sseo(-yo)

■ She doesn't get angry easily.
그녀는 쉽게 화내지 않아(요).
geu-nyeo-neun swip-gge hwa-nae-ji a-na(-yo)

■ Chae-hun has every right to be angry.
채훈이가 화날 법도 하군(요).
chae-hu-ni-ga hwa-nal bbeop-ddo ha-gun(-yo)

■ I didn't mean to upset you.
당신을 화나게 하려고 했던 건 아니었어요.
dang-si-neul hwa-na-ge ha-ryeo-go haet-ddeon geon a-ni-eo-sseo-yo

Disappointed 1

- How very disappointing!
  실망스러워(요)!
  sil-mang-seu-reo-wo(-yo)!

- We were disappointed at the news!
  우리는 그 소식을 듣고 실망했어(요)!
  u-ri-neun geu so-si-geul deut-ggo sil-mang-hae-sseo(-yo)!

- I'm disappointed in you!
  너한테 실망했어(요)!
  neo-han-te sil-mang-hae-sseo(-yo)!

- It was a waste of time!
  그야말로 시간을 낭비한 거예요!
  geu-ya-mal-ro si-ga-neul nang-bi-han geo-ye-yo!

- All my efforts were wasted!
  노력이 전부 허사가 됐어(요)!
  no-ryeo-gi jeon-bu heo-sa-ga dwae-sseo(-yo)!

- If you know, you might be disappointed.
  알게 되면, 실망할 거예요.
  al-ge doe-myeon, sil-mang-hal ggeo-ye-yo

Disappointed 2

- Don't let me down.
  나를 실망시키지 마(세요).
  na-reul sil-mang-si-ki-ji ma(se-yo)

- I was disappointed that I had to return empty-handed.
  허탕을 치고 돌아와서 낙담했어(요).
  heo-tang-eul chi-go do-ra-wa-seo nak-ddam-hae-sseo(-yo)

- I'm pretty bummed out right now.
  지금 아주 불쾌하거든(요).
  ji-geum a-ju bul-kwae-ha-geo-deun(-yo)

- It was disappointing to lose yesterday.
  어제 져서 실망했어(요).
  eo-je jeo-seo sil-mang-hae-sseo(-yo)

- I'm really sorry!
  정말 유감이에요!
  jeong-mal yu-ga-mi-e-yo!

- This sucks!
  형편없어(요)!
  hyeong-pyeo-neop-sseo(-yo)!

Despairing

■ The result was disappointing.
결과가 아주 절망적이에요.
gyeol-gwa-ga a-ju jeol-mang-jeo-gi-e-yo

■ For a moment I felt hopeless.
잠시 동안 절망스러웠지(요).
jam-si dong-an jeol-mang-seu-reo-wot-jji(-yo)

■ There is no hope anymore!
더 이상 희망이 없어(요)!
deo i-sang hi-mang-i eop-sseo(-yo)!

■ He's been in low spirits for weeks.
그는 몇 주 동안 풀이 죽어
있었어(요).
geu-neun myeot ju dong-an pu-ri ju-geo
i-sseo-sseo(-yo)

■ His wife's death drove him to despair.
아내의 죽음으로 그는 절망에
싸였어(요).
a-nae-e ju-geu-meu-ro geu-neun
jeol-mang-e ssa-yeo-sseo(-yo)

■ They're in despair over the money they've lost.
그들은 잃어버린 돈 때문에
절망에 빠져 있어(요).
geu-deu-reun i-reo-beo-rin don ddae-
mu-ne jeol-mang-e bba-jeo i-sseo-yo)

Hating

■ Yu-jeong was so full of hatred.
유정이는 증오심으로 가득 차
있어(요).
yu-jeong-i-neun jeung-o-si-meu-ro ga-
deuk cha i-sseo(-yo)

■ I feel so full of hate.
증오심이 치밀어 오르네(요).
jeung-o-si-mi chi-mi-reo o-reu-ne(-yo)

■ Someone should be punished for this!
어떤 사람들은 이것 때문에
벌 받아야 해(요)!
eo-ddeon sa-ram-deu-reun i-geot
ddae-mu-ne beol ba-da-ya hae(-yo)!

■ Beom-jun looked at me with hatred in his eyes.
범준이는 혐오감 가득한 눈길로
날 보고 있었어(요).
beom-ju-ni-neun hyeo-mo-gam ga-deu-
kan nun-ggil-ro nal bo-go i-sseo-sseo(-yo)

■ I have an aversion to stupidity.
어리석음을 아주 혐오해(요).
eo-ri-seo-geu-meul a-ju hyeo-mo-hae(-yo)

■ Why do you have it in for your teacher so badly?
왜 그렇게 선생님을 미워해(요)?
wae geu-reo-ke seon-saeng-ni-meul
mi-wo-hae(-yo)?

Reacting to Unfairness

■ I'm innocent of the charge.

억울해(요).

eo-gul-hae(-yo)

■ This is so unfair!

이건 아주 불공평해(요)!

i-geon a-ju bul-gong-pyeong-hae(-yo)!

■ He was arrested on a false charge.

그는 억울하게 체포됐어(요).

geu-neun eo-gul-ha-ge
che-po-dwae-sseo(-yo)

■ This is an injustice!

이건 부당해(요)!

i-geon bu-dang-hae(-yo)!

■ Why are you treating me this way?

왜 나한테 이렇게 대해(요)?

wae na-han-te i-reo-ke dae-hae(-yo)?

■ I was indignant at the way I was treated.

나를 대우하는 거에
분개했어(요).

na-reul dae-u-ha-neun geo-e
bun-gae-hae-sseo(-yo)

Everyday Slang

- 대박 [dae-bak] awesome
- 행쇼 [haeng-syo] Let's be happy.
- 멘붕 [men-bung] mental breakdown
- 헐 [heol] OMG; something shocking or surprising
- 뭥미 [mwong-mi] What is it?
- 꿀팁 [ggul-tip] a great tip
- 불금 [bul-geum] TGIF
- 웃프다 [ut-peu-da] funny but sad at the same time
- 득템 [deuk-tem] an item you get for free or as a great bargain
- 깜놀 [ggam-nol] Surprise!
- 아점 [a-jeom] brunch
- 금사빠 [geum-sa-bba] a person who falls in love easily
- 넘사벽 [neom-sa-byeok] something or someone that cannot be overcome
- 지못미 [ji-mon-mi] I'm sorry I couldn't help you look better in that situation.
- 비번 [bi-beon] password
- 안물/안궁 [a-mul/an-gung] I didn't ask. / I'm not interested.
- 노답 [no-dap] no answer, no solution
- 왕따 [wang-dda] outcast; a person who has no friends and is bullied by everybody at school or in a particular group
- 알바 [al-ba] part-time job. Short for "아르바이트 [a-reu-ba-i-teu]"
- 당근 [dang-geun] of course

Worried 1

■ What's the matter with you?

무슨 일이야?

mu-seun i-ri-ya?

무슨 일이에요?

mu-seun i-ri-e-yo?

무슨 일 있어(요)?

mu-seun il i-sseo(-yo)?

■ What's worrying you?

걱정거리가 있어(요)?

geok-jjeong-ggeo-ri-ga i-sseo(-yo)?

■ What are you fretting over?

왜 그렇게 초조하고 불안한
거예요?

wae geu-reo-ke cho-jo-ha-go bu-ran-han
geo-ye-yo?

■ You look under the weather
today.

오늘 네 기분이 안 좋아
보이는데(요).

o-neul ne gi-bu-ni an jo-a
bo-i-neun-de(-yo)

■ I was concerned to hear the
news.

그 소식을 듣고 걱정했어(요).

geu so-si-geul deut-ggo
geok-jjeong-hae-sseo(-yo)

Worried 2

■ I'm really concerned.

정말 걱정돼(요).

jeong-mal geok-jjeong-dwae(-yo)

■ I'm on edge right now.

지금 너무 초조해(요).

ji-geum neo-mu cho-jo-hae(-yo)

■ My heart is pounding like a drum.

가슴이 쿵쾅쿵쾅 뛰어(요).

ga-seu-mi kung-kwang-kung-kwang
ddwi-eo(-yo)

■ What should I do now?

이제 어떡하지?

i-je eo-ddeo-ka-ji?

이제 어떡해(요)?

i-je eo-ddeo-kae(-yo)?

■ Don't worry about it.

걱정할 거 없어(요).

geok-jjeong-hal ggeo eop-sseo(-yo)

■ Everything will be all right.

다 잘될 거예요.

da jal-doel ggeo-ye-yo

Bored

■ **I'm very bored! / It's not fun!**

정말 심심해(요)!

jeong-mal sim-sim-hae(-yo)!

정말 재미없어(요)!

jeong-mal jae-mi-eop-sseo(-yo)!

정말 지루해(요)!

jeong-mal ji-ru-hae(-yo)!

정말 지겨워(요)!

jeong-mal ji-gyeo-wo(-yo)!

■ **I'm bored to death.**

심심해서 죽겠어(요).

sim-sim-hae-seo juk-gge-sseo(-yo)

■ **I'm fed up with it.**

이젠 질렸어(요).

i-jen jil-ryeo-sseo(-yo)

이젠 싫증 났어(요).

i-jen sil-jjeung na-sseo(-yo)

■ **I'm going to fall asleep.**

잠들 거 같아(요).

jam-deul ggeo ga-ta(-yo)

■ **I need some stimulation.**

뭔가 자극이 필요해(요).

mwon-ga ja-geu-gi pi-ryo-hae(-yo)

■ **That was mind-numbing.**

그건 너무 지루해(요).

geu-geon neo-mu ji-ru-hae(-yo)

Ashamed

■ **I'm ashamed of myself.**

내 자신이 창피해(요).

nae ja-si-ni chang-pi-hae(-yo)

■ **I feel terrible for what I did.**

내가 한 일 때문에 끔찍해(요).

nae-ga han il ddae-mu-ne ggeum-jji-kae(-yo)

■ **I'm very shy by nature.**

천성적으로 수줍음을 타(요).

cheon-seong-jeo-geu-ro su-ju-beu-meul ta(-yo)

■ **She turned red with shame.**

그녀는 창피해서 얼굴이 빨개졌어(요).

geu-nyeo-neun chang-pi-hae-seo eol-gu-ri bbal-gae-jeo-sseo(-yo)

■ **Don't cry! The shame of it!**

울지 마(요)! 창피하잖아(요)!

ul-ji ma(-yo)! chang-pi-ha-ja-na(-yo)!

■ **Why are you so embarrassed?**

왜 그렇게 쑥스러워(요)?

wae geu-reo-ke ssuk-sseu-reo-wo(-yo)?

Afraid

■ I'm scared.
두려워(요).
du-ryeo-wo(-yo)

■ I was too scared to do anything.
무서워서 아무것도 할 수
없었어(요).
mu-seo-wo-seo a-mu-geot-ddo hal ssu
eop-sseo-sseo(-yo)

■ It made my skin crawl.
소름이 끼쳤어(요).
so-reu-mi ggi-cheo-sseo(-yo)

■ I dread the thought of that.
그것만 생각하면 무서워(요).
geu-geon-man saeng-ga-ka-myeon
mu-seo-wo(-yo)

■ I was scared to death.
무서워 죽는 줄 알았어(요).
mu-seo-wo jung-neun jul a-ra-sseo(-yo)

■ Don't be frightened!
무서워하지 마(세요)!
mu-seo-wo-ha-ji ma(-se-yo)!

Sorry

■ What a pity!
아쉽네(요)!
a-swip-ne(-yo)!

■ That's a shame!
그거 유감이네(요)!
geu-geo yu-ga-mi-ne(-yo)!

■ All that for nothing!
그렇게 노력했는데 허사가
됐어(요)!
geu-reo-ke no-ryeo-kaen-neun-de
heo-sa-ga dwae-sseo(-yo)!

■ I should've seen you coming!
오는 걸 꼭 봤어야 했는데(요)!
o-neun geol ggok bwa-sseo-ya
haen-neun-de(-yo)!

■ That could have been avoided!
그 일은 피할 수 있었는데(요)!
geu i-reun pi-hal ssu i-sseon-neun-de(-yo)!

■ I'm sorry we couldn't meet!
우리가 만나지 못해서
아쉬워(요)!
u-ri-ga man-na-ji mo-tae-seo
a-swi-wo(-yo)!

Inconvenienced 1

- What a nuisance!
  정말 귀찮아(요)!
  jeong-mal gwi-cha-na(-yo)!

- You're bugging me.
  너 때문에 귀찮아(요).
  neo ddae-mu-ne gwi-cha-na(-yo)

- Don't bother me.
  날 귀찮게 하지 마(세요).
  nal gwi-chan-ke ha-ji ma(-se-yo)

- He's a pain in the neck.
  그는 정말 골칫덩어리예요.
  geu-neun jeong-mal
  gol-chit-ddeong-eo-ri-ye-yo

- Here we go again!
  또 시작이야!
  ddo si-ja-gi-ya!

- That's the last thing I want to do.
  그건 내가 정말 하고 싶지 않은
  일이에요.
  geu-geon nae-ga jeong-mal ha-go sip-jji
  a-neun i-ri-e-yo

- I don't want to be disturbed.
  방해받고 싶지 않아(요).
  bang-hae-bat-ggo sip-jji a-na(-yo)

Inconvenienced 2

- I'm sorry to disturb you on the
  weekend.
  주말에 귀찮게 해서 죄송합니다.
  ju-ma-re gwi-chan-ke hae-seo
  joe-song-ham-ni-da

- We are cursed with a plague of
  mosquitoes.
  모기 때문에 참 성가시네(요).
  mo-gi ddae-mu-ne cham
  seong-ga-si-ne(-yo)

- I find it maddening that my car
  breaks down a lot.
  자동차가 자주 고장 나서
  성가셔(요).
  ja-dong-cha-ga ja-ju go-jang na-seo
  seong-ga-syeo(-yo)

- Noisy children are a nuisance.
  시끄러운 아이들은 성가셔(요).
  si-ggeu-reo-un a-i-deu-reun
  seong-ga-syeo(-yo)

- Stop bothering me while I'm
  trying to study.
  공부하려고 할 때 성가시게 굴지
  마(세요).
  gong-bu-ha-ryeo-go hal ddae
  seong-ga-si-ge gul-ji ma(-se-yo)

Annoyed

■ How irritating!

정말 짜증 나(요)!

jeong-mal jja-jeung na(-yo)!

■ He really annoyed me!

그 사람 때문에 짜증 나
죽겠어(요)!

geu sa-ram ddae-mu-ne jja-jeung na
ju-gge-sseo(-yo)!

■ I'm peed off with you!

너랑 있으면 짜증 나(요)!

neo-rang i-sseu-myeon jja-jeung na(-yo)!

■ The woman in front of me was
very annoying.

내 앞에 앉은 여자 때문에
짜증 났어(요).

nae a-pe an-jeun yeo-ja ddae-mu-ne
jja-jeung na-sseo(-yo)

■ It was annoying that someone
called at night!

한밤중에 누가 전화해서
짜증이 났어(요)!

han-bam-jung-e nu-ga jeon-hwa-hae-
seo jja-jeung-i na-sseo(-yo)!

Nervous

■ I'm a little nervous right now.

지금 좀 긴장되는데(요).

ji-geum jom gin-jang-doe-neun-de(-yo)

■ Why are you shaking?

왜 떨고 있어(요)?

wae ddeol-go i-sseo(-yo)?

■ I've got butterflies in my
stomach.

마음이 조마조마해(요).

ma-eu-mi jo-ma-jo-ma-hae(-yo)

■ I feel like I have ants in my pants.

안절부절이에요.

an-jeol-bu-jeo-ri-e-yo

■ Try not to be so nervous!

그렇게 긴장하지 마(세요)!

geu-reo-ke gin-jang-ha-ji ma(-se-yo)!

■ What makes you nervous?

뭐 때문에 그렇게 긴장했어(요)?

mwo ddae-mu-ne geu-reo-ke
gin-jang-hae-sseo(-yo)?

■ Do you have any phobias?

무슨 공포증 있어(요)?

mu-seun gong-po-jjeung i-sseo(-yo)?

Regretful 1

- I regret it now.
  지금 후회해(요).
  ji-geum hu-hoe-hae(-yo)

- I hope you don't regret your decision.
  당신 결정에 후회하지 않기를 바라(요).
  dang-sin gyeol-jjeong-e hu-hoe-ha-ji an-ki-reul ba-ra(-yo)

- Don't you feel guilty?
  죄책감 안 들어(요)?
  joe-chaek-ggam an deu-reo(-yo)?

- I feel awfully sorry.
  후회막심이에요.
  hu-hoe-mak-ssi-mi-e-yo

- Someday you'll regret it.
  나중에 후회하게 될 거예요.
  na-jung-e hu-hoe-ha-ge doel ggeo-ye-yo

- If you don't go, you'll regret it.
  가지 않으면, 후회하게 될 거예요.
  ga-ji a-neu-myeon, hu-hoe-ha-ge doel ggeo-ye-yo

Kimchi

Nothing says Korea like kimchi (김치), the side-dish of salted and fermented vegetables served with most meals.

The most common ingredient is usually cabbage or radish, but kimchi can be made with a wide range of vegetables—both roots and greens—creating endless varieties. Seasonings include chili powder, scallions, garlic, ginger, and salted seafood.

Traditionally, kimchi was placed in pots and stored underground to shelter it from summer heat and winter cold. In the modern era, kimchi refrigerators do a comparable job without the manual labor.

Not all kimchi is spicy or red. There is white kimchi (백김치 [baek-ggim-chi]), for example. But kimchi is always rich in dietary fiber and vitamin C.

There is a kimchi museum in the Coex Mall in Seoul where you can learn about the history of this Korean staple food.

Regretful 2

■ **No regrets!**
후회 없어(요)!
hu-hoe eop-sseo(-yo)!

■ **I don't have any regrets.**
후회하지 않아(요).
hu-hoe-ha-ji a-na(-yo)

■ **I've never regretted anything.**
후회한 적 없어(요).
hu-hoe-han jeok eop-sseo(-yo)

■ **I regretted my words soon after.**
내가 한 말을 바로 후회했어(요).
nae-ga han ma-reul ba-ro
hu-hoe-hae-sseo(-yo)

■ **Jong-su deeply regrets what he has done.**
종수는 자기가 한 일에 대해
후회막급했어(요).
jong-su-neun ja-gi-ga han i-re dae-hae
hu-hoe-mak-ggeu-pae-sseo(-yo)

■ **Lock the stable door after the horse has bolted.**
소 잃고 외양간 고친다.
so il-ko oe-yang-ggan go-chin-da

Tip: This is one of many Korean proverbs about regret.

Regretful 3

■ **I would have apologized to him.**
그에게 사과했으면 좋았을걸(요).
geu-e-ge sa-gwa-hae-sseu-myeon
jo-a-sseul-ggeol(-yo)

■ **I regret that I didn't take your advice.**
네 충고를 듣지 않은 것을
후회하고 있어(요).
ne chung-go-reul deut-jji a-neun geo-
seul hu-hoe-ha-go i-sseo(-yo)

■ **The time will come when you'll regret this.**
언젠가 후회할 때가 올 거예요.
eon-jen-ga hu-hoe-hal ddae-ga ol ggeo-
ye-yo

■ **I always felt bad about that.**
그것에 대해 항상 안타깝다고
생각해(요).
geu-geo-se dae-hae hang-sang
an-ta-ggap-dda-go saeng-ga-kae(-yo)

■ **Follow your conscience.**
네 양심을 따라라.
ne yang-si-meul dda-ra-ra

■ **Repent for your sins.**
네 죄를 뉘우쳐라.
ne joe-reul nwi-u-cheo-ra

Fed Up

■ Stop your bellyaching.

불평 좀 그만해라!

bul-pyeong jom geu-man-hae-ra!

■ You're always complaining!

넌 항상 불평하는구나!

neon hang-sang bul-pyoeng-ha-neun-gu-na!

■ Do you have something against me?

나한테 무슨 불만 있어(요)?

na-han-te mu-seun bul-man i-sseo(-yo)?

■ What are you complaining about?

뭐가 불만이야?

mwo-ga bul-ma-ni-ya?

뭐가 불만이에요?

mwo-ga bul-ma-ni-e-yo?

■ We have nothing to complain about.

우리는 아무런 불만이 없어(요).

u-ri-neun a-mu-reon bul-ma-ni eop-sseo(-yo)

■ Don't complain. If you don't like it, leave!

불평하지 마(세요).
싫으면 나가(요)!

bul-pyoeng-ha-ji ma(-se-yo).
si-reu-myeon na-ga(-yo)!

Moody

■ She is a bag of nerves.

그녀는 아주 신경질적이에요.

geu-nyeo-neun a-ju sin-gyeong-jil-jjeo-gi-e-yo

■ She's prone to mood swings.

그녀는 좀 다혈질이에요.

geu-nyeo-neun jom da-hyeol-jji-ri-e-yo

■ You've been acting very snippy lately.

넌 요즘 아주 신경질적으로 행동하고 있어(요).

neon yo-jeum a-ju sin-gyeong-jil-jjeo-geu-ro haeng-dong-ha-go i-sseo(-yo)

■ Don't throw a fit.

신경질 부리지 마(세요).

sin-gyeong-jil bu-ri-ji ma(se-yo)

■ Some women are moody during pregnancy.

어떤 여자들은 임신했을 때 기분 변화가 심해(요).

eo-ddeon yeo-ja-deu-reun im-sin-hae-sseul ddae gi-bun byeon-hwa-ga sim-hae(-yo)

Optimistic

■ He's an optimistic person.

그는 낙천적인 사람이에요.

geu-neun nak-cheon-jeo-gin
sa-ra-mi-e-yo

■ Stay positive!

긍정적이어야 해(요)!

geung-jeong-jeo-gi-eo-ya hae(-yo)!

■ He has an optimistic philosophy
of life.

그는 낙천적인 인생철학을
가지고 있어(요).

geu-neun nak-cheon-jeo-gin in-saeng-
cheol-ha-geul ga-ji-go i-sseo(-yo)

■ I am fond of optimistic people.

나는 낙천적인 사람을 좋아해(요).

na-neun nak-cheon-jeo-gin sa-ra-meul
jo-a-hae(-yo)

■ After all her troubles, Su-yeon is
still optimistic.

온갖 어려움에도, 수연이는
여전히 낙천적이에요.

on-gat eo-ryeo-u-me-do, su-yeo-ni-
neun yeo-jeon-hi nak-cheon-jeo-gi-e-yo

■ Cheol-min is an easygoing
person by nature.

철민이는 천성적으로
천하태평이에요.

cheol-mi-ni-neun cheon-seong-jeo-geu-
ro cheon-ha-tae-pyeong-i-e-yo

Good

■ He is good-natured.

그는 착해(요).

geu-neun cha-kae(-yo)

■ She is a kind-hearted woman.

그녀는 인정 많은 여자예요.

geu-nyeo-neun in-jeong ma-neun
yeo-ja-ye-yo

■ He has a good heart but no
common sense.

그는 착하지만, 눈치가 없어(요).

geu-neun cha-ka-ji-man, nun-chi-ga
eop-sseo(-yo)

■ Nam-ho has a rough manner
but deep down he is quite nice.

남호는 태도가 거칠지만, 마음은
착해(요).

nam-ho-neun tae-do-ga geo-chil-ji-
man, ma-eu-meun cha-kae(-yo)

■ That's a good boy [girl]!

착하지!

cha-ka-ji!

Gentle & Kind

■ He is a gentle guy.
그는 온후한 사나이예요.
geu-neun on-hu-han sa-na-i-ye-yo

■ My new neighbor is very friendly.
새 이웃은 매우 친절해(요).
sae i-u-seun mae-u chin-jeol-hae(-yo)

■ She is very kind and sweet.
그녀는 매우 친절하고
다정해(요).
geu-nyeo-neun mae-u chin-jeol-ha-go
da-jeong-hae(-yo)

■ Try to be kind to strangers.
모르는 사람들에게 친절해라.
mo-reu-neun sa-ram-deu-re-ge
chin-jeol-hae-ra

■ She wouldn't hurt a fly.
그녀는 파리 한 마리도 해치지
않아(요).
geu-nyeo-neun pa-ri han ma-ri-do hae-
chi-ji a-na(-yo)

■ Seo-jin is really sweet to his girlfriend.
서진이는 여자 친구에게 정말
다정해(요).
seo-ji-ni-neun yeo-ja chin-gu-e-ge
jeong-mal da-jeong-hae(-yo)

Outgoing

■ He is outgoing.
그는 외향적이에요.
geu-neun oe-hyang-jeo-gi-e-yo

■ I'm cheerful and sociable.
나는 쾌활하고 사교적이에요.
na-neun kwae-hwal-ha-go
sa-gyo-jeo-gi-e-yo

■ I'm enterprising.
나는 진취적이에요.
na-neun jin-chwi-jeo-gi-e-yo

■ Na-yun has an extrovert personality.
나윤이는 외향적인 성격을
가졌어(요).
na-yu-ni-neun oe-hyang-jeo-gin
seong-ggyeo-geul ga-jeo-sseo(-yo)

■ She is very passionate about everything she does.
그녀는 매사에 적극적이에요.
geu-nyeo-neun mae-sa-e
jeok-ggeuk-jjeo-gi-e-yo

■ While Min-hyeok is an introvert, his wife is an extrovert.
민혁이는 내성적인 반면, 그의
부인은 외향적이에요.
min-hyeo-gi-neun nae-seong-jeo-gin
ban-myeon, geu-e bu-i-neun
oe-hyang-jeo-gi-e-yo

Naive

■ She's so naive.

그녀는 아주 순수해(요).

geu-nyeo-neun a-ju sun-su-hae(-yo)

■ It's so naive of you to believe him.

그를 믿다니, 너도 참 순진하구나.

geul-reul mit-dda-ni, neo-do cham sun-jin-ha-gu-na

■ Why are you so naive?

어쩌면 그렇게 순진해(요)?

eo-jjeo-myeon geu-reo-ke sun-jin-hae(-yo)?

■ Don't be so gullible.

너무 믿지 마(세요).

neo-mu mit-jji ma(-se-yo)

■ He is a babe in the woods in that way.

그는 어수룩해서 그쪽 방면으로 잘 속아(요).

geu-neun eo-su-ru-kae-seo geu-jjok bang-myeo-neu-ro jal so-ga(-yo)

Introverted

■ I'm kind of an introvert.

성격이 좀 내성적이에요.

seong-ggyeo-gi jom nae-seong-jeo-gi-e-yo

■ I tend to be withdrawn.

나는 소극적인 편이에요.

na-neun so-geuk-jjeo-gin pyeo-ni-e-yo

■ Maybe he lacks confidence.

그는 아마도 자신감이 부족한 거 같아(요).

geu-neun a-ma-do ja-sin-ga-mi bu-jo-kan geo ga-ta(-yo)

■ I need time to open up.

마음을 여는 데 시간이 걸려(요).

ma-eu-meul yeo-neun de si-ga-ni geol-ryeo(-yo)

■ I'm shy by nature.

천성적으로 수줍음을 잘 타(요).

cheon-seong-jeo-geu-ro su-ju-beu-meul jal ta(-yo)

■ I'm shy around strangers.

낯을 가리는 편이에요.

na-cheul ga-ri-neun pyeo-ni-e-yo

Indecisive

■ He's too indecisive.
그는 너무 우유부단해(요).
geu-neun neo-mu u-yu-bu-dan-hae(-yo)

■ Don't be so wishy-washy.
그렇게 우유부단하지 마(세요).
geu-reo-ke u-yu-bu-dan-ha-ji ma(-se-yo)

■ He is a weak-willed man.
그는 의지가 약해(요).
geu-neun ui-ji-ga ya-kae(-yo)

■ You're too indecisive.
Make a decision.
넌 너무 우유부단해(요).
결정을 내려(요).
neon neo-mu u-yu-bu-dan-hae(-yo).
gyeol-jjeong-eul nae-ryeo(-yo)

■ He is always hesitant to make a decision.
그는 결정을 내리는 데 항상
주저해(요).
geu-neun gyeol-jjeong-eul nae-ri-neun
de hang-sang ju-jeo-hae(-yo)

■ You can't sit on the fence forever.
언제나 중립적인 태도를 취할
수 없어(요).
eon-je-na jung-nip-jjeo-gin tae-do-reul
chwi-hal ssu eop-sseo(-yo)

Gimjang: Making Kimchi

The ingredients needed to make kimchi were traditionally not available in the winter. Enter gimjang (김장), the activity of preparing and storing kimchi for the winter months. Gimjang takes place in late fall, before the cold sets in. The work is labor-intensive and traditionally relatives and neighbors would lend a hand for the two-to-three-day process. It was a kind of cooperative culture where everyone in the neighborhood could share the process and the finished product.

As with kimchi, the flavor and recipes for gimjang can vary regionally. Kimchi recipes in the north of the country tend not to be salty, while southern kimchi makes more use of pepper powder, garlic and ginger. Northerners also ready begin gimjang earlier than southerners.

Gimjang was designated a UNESCO Intangible Cultural Heritage in 2013. It is an example of Korean community culture and a chance for family and neighbors to be together.

Pessimistic

▪ You're too pessimistic.
넌 너무 비관적이야.
neon neo-mu bi-gwan-jeo-gi-ya

▪ He has a pessimistic point of view.
그는 모든 일에 비관적이에요.
geu-neun mo-deun i-re
bi-gwan-jeo-gi-e-yo

▪ I have a pessimistic view of politics.
정치에 대해 비관적인 견해를
갖고 있어(요).
jeong-chi-e dae-hae bi-gwan-jeo-gin
gyeon-hae-reul gat-ggo i-sseo(-yo)

▪ I have a negative outlook on life.
내 인생관은 소극적이고
비관적인 편이에요.
nae in-saeng-gwa-neun so-geuk-jjeo-gi-
go bi-gwan-jeo-gin pyeo-ni-e-yo

▪ Don't be so negative.
너무 비관적으로 보지 마(세요).
neo-mu bi-gwan-jeo-geu-ro bo-ji
ma(-se-yo)

▪ Your negativity is bringing me
down.
네 부정적인 성향이 나를
우울하게 해(요).
ne bu-jeong-jeo-gin seong-hyang-i na-
reul u-ul-ha-ge hae(-yo)

Selfish

▪ He is so egotistical.
그는 아주 이기적이에요.
geu-neun a-ju i-gi-jeo-gi-e-yo

▪ You are self-seeking.
너는 너밖에 몰라(요).
neo-neun neo-ba-gge mol-ra(-yo)

▪ Don't be so self-centered.
그렇게 이기적으로 굴지 마(세요).
geu-reo-ke i-gi-jeo-geu-ro gul-ji
ma(-se-yo)

▪ He's such a prima donna.
그는 그렇게 잘난 줄 알아(요).
geu-neun geu-reo-ke jal-ran jul a-ra(-yo)

▪ He has a huge ego.
그는 자아가 강해(요).
geu-neun ja-a-ga gang-hae(-yo)

▪ Do-jun is a bit narcissistic.
도준이는 자기애가 좀 강해(요).
do-ju-ni-neun ja-gi-ae-ga jom gang-
hae(-yo)

Preferences

■ I would prefer a window seat.

창가석이 더 좋아(요).

chang-gga-seo-gi deo jo-a(-yo)

■ It's probably just a personal preference.

단순한 개인적인 취향이라고나 할까(요).

dan-sun-han gae-in-jeo-gin chwi-hyang-i-ra-go-na hal-gga(-yo)

■ We prefer a small car.

우리는 소형차를 선호해(요).

u-ri-neun so-hyeong-cha-reul seon-ho-hae(-yo)

■ I prefer tea to coffee.

커피보다 차를 더 좋아해(요).

keo-pi-bo-da cha-reul deo jo-a-hae(-yo)

■ A preference for sons has caused an imbalance in the gender ratio.

남아선호사상은 성비의 불균형을 초래했어(요).

na-ma-seon-ho-sa-sang-eun seong-bi-e bul-gyun-hyeong-eul cho-rae-hae-sseo(-yo)

Tastes

■ That picture appeals to me.

저 그림이 마음에 들어(요).

jeo geu-ri-mi ma-eu-me deu-reo(-yo)

■ Geun-ho has old-fashioned tastes.

근호는 구식이고 멋이 없어(요).

geun-ho-neun gu-si-gi-go meo-si eop-sseo(-yo)

■ I don't understand Chang-su's taste in women.

창수의 여자 보는 눈을 이해할 수 없어(요).

chang-su-e yeo-ja bo-neun nu-neul i-hae-hal ssu eop-sseo(-yo)

■ Taste in art is a subjective matter.

예술에 관한 취향은 주관적인 문제예요.

ye-su-re gwan-han chi-hyang-eun ju-gwan-jeo-gin mun-je-ye-yo

■ I have a taste for soju.

소주는 내 기호에 맞아(요).

so-ju-neun nae gi-ho-e ma-ja(-yo)

■ Do you have any food preferences?

특별히 즐기는 음식이 있어(요)?

teuk-bbyeol-hi jeul-gi-neun eum-si-gi i-sseo(-yo)?

Likes

- I'm fond of music.
  음악을 좋아해(요).
  eu-ma-geul jo-a-hae(-yo)

- I have a passion for sports.
  특히 운동을 좋아해(요).
  teu-ki un-dong-eul jo-a-hae(-yo)

- Why do you like Korean TV dramas?
  왜 한국 드라마를 좋아해(요)?
  wae han-guk deu-ra-ma-reul jo-a-hae(-yo)?

- BTS is my favorite Korean celebrity group.
  방탄소년단은 내가 좋아하는 한국 연예인이에요.
  bang-tan-so-nyeon-da-neun nae-ga jo-a-ha-neun han-guk yeo-nye-i-ni-e-yo

- I hope you like it here.
  이곳을 마음에 들어하면 좋겠어(요).
  i-go-seul ma-eu-me deu-reo-ha-myeon jo-ke-sseo(-yo)

- I like playing tennis and golf.
  테니스와 골프를 즐겨(요).
  te-ni-seu-wa gol-peu-reul jeul-gyeo(-yo)

Dislikes

- I don't like it very much.
  그다지 안 좋아해(요).
  geu-da-ji an jo-a-hae(-yo)

- My husband has a dislike for fish.
  남편은 생선을 싫어해(요).
  nam-pyeo-neun saeng-seo-neul si-reo-hae(-yo)

- I dislike this kind of food.
  이런 요리를 싫어해(요).
  i-reon yo-ri-reul si-reo-hae(-yo)

- He seems to dislike me for no particular reason.
  그는 이렇다 할 이유도 없이 나를 싫어하는 것 같아(요).
  geu-neun i-reo-ta hal i-yu-do eop-ssi na-reul si-reo-ha-neun geot ga-ta(-yo)

- I can't stand a liar.
  거짓말쟁이는 참을 수 없어(요).
  geo-jin-mal-jaeng-i-neun cha-meul ssu eop-sseo(-yo)

- I dislike living in a large city.
  대도시에 사는 것을 싫어해(요).
  dae-do-si-e sa-neun geo-seul si-reo-hae(-yo)

Chapter 7

Falling in Love

Love & Farewell 사랑 & 이별 sa-rang & i-byeol

v. meet **만나다** [만나다] man-na-da n. meeting **만남** [만남] man-nam 	n. boyfriend **남자 친구** [남자 친구] nam-ja chin-gu	n. girlfriend **여자 친구** [여자 친구] yeo-ja chin-gu
	v. like **좋아하다** [조:아하다] jo-a-ha-da	n. ideal type **이상형** [이:상형] i-sang-hyeong
	n. date **데이트** [데이트] de-i-teu = **교제** [교제] gyo-je	v. make a friend **사귀다** [사귀다] sa-gwi-da
v. to love **사랑하다** [사랑하다] sa-rang-ha-da n. love **사랑** [사랑] sa-rang 	n. sweetheart **애인** [애:인] ae-in	v. have a crush on **반하다** [반:하다] ban-ha-da
	n. kiss, peck **뽀뽀** [뽀뽀] bbo-bbo n. kiss **키스** [키스] ki-seu	n. hug, cuddle **포옹** [포:옹] po-ong v. to hug, cuddle **껴안다** [껴안따] ggyeo-an-dda
v. break up **헤어지다** [헤어지다] he-eo-ji-da n. farewell **이별** [이:별] i-byeol 	n. jealousy **질투** [질투] jil-tu	n. trouble **갈등** [갈뜽] gal-ddeung
	n. betrayal **배신** [배:신] bae-sin	v. trick, cheat **속이다** [소기다] so-gi-da n. lie **거짓말** [거:진말] geo-jin-mal

Blind Dating 1

■ **Are you seeing anyone?**

만나는 사람 있어(요)?

man-na-neun sa-ram i-sseo(-yo)?

■ **I don't have a girlfriend.**

여자 친구 없어(요).

yeo-ja chin-gu eop-sseo(-yo)

■ **I'm single.**

난 혼자예요.

nan hon-ja-ye-yo

미혼이에요.

mi-ho-ni-e-yo

■ **He is just a male friend.**

쟤는 남사친이에요.

jyae-neun nam-sa-chi-ni-e-yo

Tip: 남사친 [nam-sa-chin] **means "male friend" not "boyfriend."** 여사친 [yeo-sa-chin] **means "female friend" not "girlfriend."**

■ **Set me up for a blind date!**

소개팅 시켜 줘(요)!

so-gae-ting si-kyeo jwo(-yo)!

■ **This is a meeting with a prospective marriage partner.**

이건 맞선이에요.

i-geon mat-sseo-ni-e-yo

Blind Dating 2

■ **I'll hook you up with a nice guy.**

좋은 남자 한 명 소개시켜 줄게(요).

jo-eun nam-ja han myeong so-gae-si-kyeo jul-gge(-yo)

■ **What type of girl [guy] do you prefer?**

어떤 스타일 좋아해(요)?

eo-ddeon seu-ta-il jo-a-hae(-yo)?

■ **I don't care who it is.**

어떻든 다 괜찮아(요).

eo-ddeo-teun da gwaen-cha-na(-yo)

■ **Does she have a boyfriend?**

저 여자애는 남자 친구 있어(요)?

jeo yeo-ja-ae-neun nam-ja chin-gu i-sseo(-yo)?

■ **Could you introduce that guy to me?**

나한테 저 남자애를 소개시켜 줄 수 있어(요)?

na-han-te jeo nam-ja-ae-reul so-gae-si-kyeo jul ssu i-sseo(-yo)?

■ **She's a famous matchmaker.**

그 여자는 유명한 중매쟁이예요.

geu yeo-ja-neun yu-myeong-han jung-mae-jaeng-i-ye-yo

Blind Dating 3

- He's not really my type.
  그는 내 취향이 아니에요.
  geu-neun nae chwi-hyang-i a-ni-e-yo

- I was head over heels.
  완전 반했어(요).
  wan-jeon ban-hae-sseo(-yo)

- She is the girl of my dreams.
  그녀는 내 이상형이에요.
  geu-nyeo-neun nae i-sang-hyeong-i-e-yo

- He's Prince Charming.
  그는 백마 탄 왕자님이에요.
  geu-neun bang-ma tan wang-ja-ni-mi-
  e-yo

- I'm absolutely crazy about him.
  그에게 완전히 빠졌어(요).
  geu-e-ge wan-jeon-hi bba-jeo-sseo(-yo)

- Beauty is in the eye of the
  beholder.
  제 눈에 안경.
  je nu-ne an-gyeong

- You are the apple of my eye.
  눈에 콩깍지가 씌었군(요).
  nu-ne kong-ggak-jji-ga ssi-eot-ggun(-yo)

Blind Dating 4

- I'm lovesick.
  상사병에 걸렸어(요).
  sang-sa-bbyeong-e geol-ryeo-sseo(-yo)

- You got a thing for her!
  넌 그녀를 좋아하는구나!
  neon geu-nyeo-reul jo-a-ha-neun-gu-na!

- This is a sure signal that she
  likes you.
  이건 분명히 그녀가 널
  좋아한다는 신호예요.
  i-geon bun-myeong-hi geu-nyeo-ga
  neol jo-a-han-da-neun sin-ho-ye-yo

- He's a stand-up guy!
  그는 믿을 만한 남자예요!
  geu-neun mi-deul man-han
  nam-ja-ye-yo!

- Are you going to ask her out
  again?
  그녀에게 다시 데이트 신청할
  거예요?
  geu-nyeo-e-ge da-si de-i-teu
  sin-cheong-hal ggeo-ye-yo?

- What was your first impression?
  첫인상이 어땠어(요)?
  cheo-din-sang-i eo-ddae-sseo(-yo)?

Dating 1

- How was your date?

  데이트 어땠어(요)?

  de-i-teu eo-ddae-sseo(-yo)?

- Let's call it a date.

  이걸 데이트라고 치죠.

  i-geol de-i-teu-ra-go chi-jyo

- When we met, it was love at first sight.

  우리는 만나자마자, 서로 한눈에 반했어(요).

  u-ri-neun man-na-ja-ma-ja, seo-ro han-nu-ne ban-hae-sseo(-yo)

- We have a lot of chemistry.

  우리는 통하는 게 많아(요).

  u-ri-neun tong-ha-neun ge ma-na(-yo)

- They are still at the dating stage.

  그들은 아직 그냥 만나는 단계일 뿐이에요.

  geu-deu-reun a-jik geu-nyang man-na-neun dan-gye-il bbu-ni-e-yo

- Na-yeon doesn't feel the same way.

  나연이를 짝사랑하고 있어(요).

  na-yeo-ni-reul jjak-ssa-rang-ha-go i-sseo(-yo)

Dating 2

- I'm seeing a guy from work.

  회사에 사귀는 남자 친구가 있어(요).

  hoe-sa-e sa-gwi-neun nam-ja chin-gu-ga i-sseo(-yo)

- She and I have been on three dates.

  그녀와 나는 데이트를 세 번 했어(요).

  geu-nyeo-wa na-neun de-i-teu-reul se beon hae-sseo(-yo)

- He has a really heavy date with So-yeon today.

  그는 오늘 소연이와 정말 중요한 데이트가 있어(요).

  geu-neun o-neul so-yeo-ni-wa jeong-mal jung-yo-han de-i-teu-ga i-sseo(-yo)

- Did Jae-yun ask you on a date?

  재윤이가 데이트 신청했어(요)?

  jae-yu-ni-ga de-i-teu sin-cheong-hae-sseo(-yo)?

- They've been dating for quite a while already.

  그들은 이미 오랫동안 사귀어 왔어(요).

  geu-deu-reun i-mi o-raet-ddong-an sa-gwi-eo wa-sseo(-yo)

Dating 3

- We really hit it off.
  우리는 열애 중이에요.
  u-ri-neun yeo-rae jung-i-e-yo

- This is the best way to get a girl.
  이건 여자를 꼬시기에 가장 좋은 방법이에요.
  i-geon yeo-ja-reul ggo-si-gi-e ga-jang jo-eun bang-beo-bi-e-yo

- Are you attracted to her?
  그녀에게 끌리는 거예요?
  geu-nyeo-e-ge ggeul-ri-neun geo-ye-yo?

- Do you want to get back together with her?
  그녀와 다시 사귀고 싶어(요)?
  geu-nyeo-wa da-si sa-gwi-go si-peo(-yo)?

- We don't have much in common.
  우리는 공통점이 많지 않아(요).
  u-ri-neun gong-tong-jjeo-mi man-chi a-na(-yo)

- There's a bit of friction between us.
  우리 사이에 갈등이 좀 있어(요).
  u-ri sa-i-e gal-ddeung-i jom i-sseo(-yo)

Love 1

- I love you.
  사랑해(요).
  sa-rang-hae(-yo)

- I like you.
  좋아해(요).
  jo-a-hae(-yo)

- I loved her from the moment I set eyes on her.
  그녀를 처음 본 순간부터 사랑했어(요).
  geu-nyeo-reul cheo-eum bon sun-gan-bu-teo sa-rang-hae-sseo(-yo)

- I can't get enough of her.
  그녀가 계속 보고 싶어(요).
  geu-nyeo-ga gye-sok bo-go si-peo(-yo)

- I can't live without you.
  너 없이 못 살아(요).
  neo eop-ssi mot sa-ra(-yo)

- He is really into me.
  그는 나한테 푹 빠졌어(요).
  geu-neun na-han-te puk bba-jeo-sseo(-yo)

- I will love you for the rest of my life.
  죽을 때까지 당신을 사랑할 거예요.
  ju-geul ddae-gga-ji dang-si-neul sa-rang-hal ggeo-ye-yo

Love 2

- Darling! / Sweetheart!

  자기야!

  ja-gi-ya!

  여보!

  yeo-bo!

  당신!

  dang-sin!

  Tip: The above words are all gender neutral.

- I was meant to love you.

  당신은 내 운명의 사랑이에요.

  dang-si-neun nae un-myeong-e
  sa-rang-i-e-yo

- We were meant to be together.

  우리는 천생연분이에요.

  u-ri-neun cheon-saeng-yeon-bu-ni-e-yo

- I love you more every day.

  날이 갈수록 당신을 더 많이
  사랑해(요).

  na-ri gal-ssu-rok dang-si-neul deo ma-ni
  sa-rang-hae(-yo)

- Your kiss is the sweetest thing
  I've ever felt.

  당신의 키스는 최고로 달콤해요.

  dang-si-ne ki-seu-neun choe-go-ro
  dal-kom-hae-yo

Love 3

- The only way I can be happy is if
  I'm with you.

  당신과 함께 있을 때만
  행복해요.

  dang-sin-gwa ham-gge i-sseul ddae-
  man haeng-bo-kae-yo

- He loves Gyu-rin just the way
  she is.

  그는 규린이의 있는 그대로의
  모습을 사랑해(요).

  geu-neun gyu-ri-ni-e in-neun geu-dae-
  ro-e mo-seu-beul sa-rang-hae(-yo)

- I believe that our love is eternal.

  우리의 사랑은 영원할 거라고
  믿어(요).

  u-ri-e sa-rang-eun yeong-won-hal
  ggeo-ra-go mi-deo(-yo)

- I love you more than words can
  express.

  당신을 얼마나 사랑하는지 말로
  표현할 수 없어요.

  dang-si-neul eol-ma-na sa-rang-ha-
  neun-ji mal-ro pyo-hyeon-hal ssu eop-
  sseo-yo

- You don't know how much
  I love you.

  내가 널 얼마나 사랑하는지 너는
  몰라(요).

  nae-ga neol eol-ma-na sa-rang-ha-
  neun-ji neo-neun mol-ra(-yo)

Jealousy & Betrayal

■ Why do you keep looking at her?

왜 쟤를 쳐다보는 거예요?

wae jyae-reul cheo-da-bo-neun geo-
ye-yo?

■ How many girlfriends do you have!

여자 친구가 얼마나 많은 거야!

yeo-ja chin-gu-ga eol-ma-na ma-neun
geo-ya!

■ He has commitment issues.

그는 한 사람에게 정착하지
못해(요).

geu-neun han sa-ra-me-ge jeong-cha-
ka-ji mo-tae(-yo)

■ You manipulated me.

넌 날 가지고 놀았어(요).

neon nal ga-ji-go no-ra-sseo(-yo)

■ You hurt my feelings.

넌 내게 상처를 줬어(요).

neon nae-ge sang-cheo-reul
jwo-sseo(-yo)

■ She cheated multiple times.

그녀는 바람을 여러 번
피웠어(요).

geu-nyeo-neun ba-ra-meul yeo-reo
beon pi-wo-sseo(-yo)

Conflicts 1

■ Our relationship is on the edge.

우리 관계는 위기에 빠졌어(요).

u-ri gwan-gye-neun wi-gi-e
bba-jeo-sseo(-yo)

■ I admit that our relationship is not in good shape.

우리 관계가 좋지 않다는 걸
인정해(요).

u-ri gwan-gye-ga jo-chi an-ta-neun geol
in-jeong-hae(-yo)

■ There's no way to fix our relationship.

우리 사이가 회복될 답이
없어(요).

u-ri sa-i-ga hoe-bok-ddoel da-bi
eop-sseo(-yo)

■ Our relationship was doomed from the start.

우리 관계는 처음부터 문제가
있었어(요).

u-ri gwan-gye-neun cheo-eum-bu-teo
mun-je-ga i-sseo-sseo(-yo)

■ Where did our relationship go wrong?

우리 관계가 어디서부터 잘못된
걸까(요)?

u-ri gwan-gye-ga eo-di-seo-bu-teo
jal-mot-ddoen geol-gga(-yo)?

Conflicts 2

- What's happening with your relationship with Hyo-jeong these days?

  요즘 효정이하고 사이에 무슨 일 있어(요)?

  yo-jeum hyo-jeong-i-ha-go sa-i-e mu-seun il i-sseo(-yo)?

- Deep down inside you still love me, don't you?

  솔직히 넌 아직 날 사랑하는 거 맞지(요)?

  sol-jji-ki neon a-jik nal sa-rang-ha-neun geo mat-jji(-yo)?

- Anyway, we're finished.

  어쨌든, 우리는 끝이야.

  eo-jjaet-ddeun, u-ri-neun ggeu-chi-ya

- I'm fed up with you.

  너한테 질렸어(요).

  neo-han-te jil-ryeo-sseo(-yo)

- Please don't ignore me.

  날 무시하지 말아줘(요).

  nal mu-si-ha-ji ma-ra-jwo(-yo)

- Let's talk this over.

  진지하게 얘기해 보자.

  jin-ji-ha-ge yae-gi-hae bo-ja

The Pyebaek Ceremony

If you haven't been invited to a pyebaek ceremony, don't be offended. Traditionally, this post-wedding custom was for the bride and her groom's family only. In it, the bride bows to her parents-in law and other new relations after arriving at her husband's home. She then presents them with gifts, jujubes and chestnut or snacks and wine, setting them in front of her parents-in-law. When they return the favor by throwing jujubes and chestnuts back to their daughter-in-law, it expresses their hopes for an extended family, namely children.

Current wedding culture differs of course. Newlyweds may still change into hanboks for pyebaek though most couples will now bow to the bride's parents too. Parents and relatives also contribute money towards the new couple's honeymoon.

Breakups 1

■ We broke up on bad terms.

우리는 안 좋게 헤어졌어(요).

u-ri-neun an jo-ke he-eo-jeo-sseo(-yo)

■ We're not involved any more.

우리는 더 이상 연애하지
않아(요).

u-ri-neun deo i-sang yeo-nae-ha-ji
a-na(-yo)

■ They broke up about two
weeks ago.

그들은 약 2주 전에 깨졌어(요).

geu-deu-reun yak i-ju jeo-ne
ggae-jeo-sseo(-yo)

■ We parted ways.

우리는 헤어졌어(요).

u-ri-neun he-eo-jeo-sseo(-yo)

우리는 깨졌어(요).

u-ri-neun ggae-jeo-sseo(-yo)

■ I broke up with him.

그와 헤어졌어(요).

geu-wa he-eo-jeo-sseo(-yo)

■ I still remember his words when
we parted.

이별할 때 그가 한 말을 아직도
기억해(요).

i-byeol-hal ddae geu-ga han ma-reul
a-jik-ddo gi-eo-kae(-yo)

Breakups 2

■ I dumped him.

그를 차 버렸어(요).

geu-reul cha beo-ryeo-sseo(-yo)

■ Just give it time.

시간이 해결해 줄 거예요.

si-ga-ni hae-gyeol-hae jul ggeo-ye-yo

■ Did you hear that they split up?

걔네들 헤어졌다는 소식
들었어(요)?

gyae-ne-deul he-eo-jeot-dda-neun so-
sik deu-reo-sseo(-yo)?

■ This breakup is killing me.

이번 이별로 죽을 지경이에요.

i-beon i-byeol-ro ju-geul ji-gyeong-i-e-yo

■ I think it's better if we stayed
friends.

그냥 친구로 남는 게 더 좋을 거
같아(요).

geu-nyang chin-gu-ro nam-neun ge deo
jo-eul ggeo ga-ta(-yo)

■ I'm just not in that place right
now.

지금 연애하고 싶은 마음이
아니에요.

ji-geum yeo-nae-ha-go si-peun
ma-eu-mi a-ni-e-yo

n. proposal
청혼 [청혼]
cheong-hon

n. engagement
약혼 [야콘]
ya-kon

n. fiancé, fiancée
약혼자 [야콘자] ya-kon-ja
n. fiancée 약혼녀 [야콘녀]
ya-kon-nyeo

---

n. marriage 결혼 [결혼]
gyeol-hon
n. wedding ceremony
결혼식 [결혼식]
gyeol-hon-sik

n. groom 신랑 [실랑]
sil-rang

n. bride 신부 [신부]
sin-bu

---

n. wedding invitation
청첩장 [청첩짱]
cheng-cheop-jjang

n. wedding ring
결혼반지 [결혼반지]
gyeol-hon-ban-ji

n. bridal bouquet
부케 [부케]
bu-ke

---

n. wedding dress
웨딩드레스 [웨딩드레스]
we-ding-deu-re-seu

n. husband
남편 [남편]
nam-pyeon

n. wife 아내 [아내] a-nae
n. wife, ma'am
부인 [부인]
bu-in

---

n. pregnancy 임신 [임:신]
im-sin
n. expecting mom
임산부 [임:산부]
im-san-bu

n. giving birth to
출산 [출싼] chul-ssan
n. parenting
육아 [유가]
yu-ga

n. baby 아기 [아기]
a-gi

---

n. nursing 수유 [수유]
su-yu
n. breast milk
모유 [모:유]
mo-yu

n. powdered milk
분유 [부뉴] bu-nyu
n. nursing bottle
젖병 [전뼝]
jeot-bbyeong

n. diaper 기저귀 [기저귀]
gi-jeo-gwi

---

n. stroller, baby carriage
유모차 [유모차]
yu-mo-cha

v. bring up, raise
기르다 [기르다]
gi-reu-da
= 키우다 [키우다]
ki-u-da

v. take care of
보살피다 [보살피다]
bo-sal-pi-da
= 돌보다 [돌:보다]
dol-bo-da

Marriage Proposal

■ Dae-seong proposed to me!

대성이는 나에게 청혼했어(요)!

dae-seong-i-neun na-e-ge
cheong-hon-hae-sseo(-yo)!

■ Will you marry me?

나랑 결혼해 줄래(요)?

na-rang gyeol-hon-hae jul-rae(-yo)?

■ I accepted his proposal.

그의 청혼을 받아들였어(요).

geu-e cheong-ho-neul
ba-da-deu-ryeo-sseo(-yo)

■ I declined his proposal.

그의 청혼을 거절했어(요).

geu-e cheong-ho-neul
geo-jeol-hae-sseo(-yo)

■ I'll propose marriage to her in public.

나는 그녀에게 공개적으로
청혼할 거예요.

na-neun geu-nyeo-e-ge gong-gae-jeo-
geu-ro cheong-hon-hal ggeo-ye-yo

■ I'm going to pop the question tonight.

오늘 밤에 청혼할 거예요.

o-neul ba-me cheong-hon-hal
ggeo-ye-yo

Wedding Plans

■ Where will you go for your honeymoon?

신혼여행은 어디로 갈 거예요?

sin-hon-nyeo-haeng-eun eo-di-ro gal
ggeo-ye-yo?

■ We are going to Jeju-do for our honeymoon.

제주도로 갈 거예요.

je-ju-do-ro gal ggeo-ye-yo

■ When are you going to be married?

언제 결혼해(요)?

eon-je gyeol-hon-hae(-yo)?

■ Where are you going to have the wedding?

결혼식은 어디서 하길 원해(요)?

gyeol-hon-si-geun eo-di-seo ha-gil
won-hae(-yo)?

■ We want to get married in a church.

우리는 교회에서 결혼하고
싶어(요).

u-ri-neun gyo-hoe-e-seo gyeol-hon-ha-
go si-peo(-yo)

■ We're going to have our wedding reception at a hotel.

피로연은 호텔에서 하려고 해(요).

pi-ro-yeo-neun ho-te-re-seo ha-ryeo-go
hae(-yo)

Wedding Invitations

■ Please come to my wedding.

결혼식에 꼭 참석해 줘(요).

gyeol-hon-si-ge ggok cham-seo-kae
jwo(-yo)

■ This is my wedding invitation.

이것은 내 청첩장이에요.

i-geo-seun nae cheong-cheop-jjang-i-
e-yo

■ How many people did you invite?

얼마나 많이 초대했어(요)?

eol-ma-na ma-ni cho-dae-hae-sseo(-yo)?

■ I'm afraid I can't come to your
wedding.

네 결혼식에 못 갈 거 같아(요).

ne gyeol-hon-si-ge mot gal ggeo
ga-ta(-yo)

■ We sent out hundreds of
invitations to the wedding.

우리는 청첩장 몇 백 장을
보냈어(요).

u-ri-neun cheong-cheop-jjang myeot
baek jang-eul bo-nae-sseo(-yo)

■ We invited all our relatives and
friends to the wedding.

친척 친구들 모두 결혼식에
초대했어(요).

chin-cheok chin-gu-deul mo-du
gyeol-hon-si-ge cho-dae-hae-sseo(-yo)

The Wedding Ceremony 1

■ Who will get the bridal
bouquet?

누가 부케를 받아(요)?

nu-ga bu-ke-reul ba-da(-yo)?

■ Before the wedding, she covers
her face with a wedding veil.

결혼식 전에, 신부는 얼굴에
면사포를 덮었어(요).

gyeol-hon-sik jeo-ne, sin-bu-neun
eol-gu-re myeon-sa-po-reul
deo-peo-sseo(-yo)

■ A wedding ring symbolizes the
union of husband and wife.

결혼반지는 부부의 결합을
상징해(요).

gyeol-hon-ban-ji-neun bu-bu-e
gyeol-ha-beul sang-jing-hae(-yo)

■ They are taking marital vows!

그들은 결혼 서약을 하고
있어(요)!

geu-deu-reun gyeol-hon seo-ya-geul
ha-go i-sseo(-yo)!

■ Who is officiating your wedding?

누가 결혼식 주례이신가요?

nu-ga gyeol-hon-sik ju-rye-i-sin-ga-yo?

The Wedding Ceremony 2

- I wish you both the best!

  행복하시길 바랍니다!

  haeng-bo-ka-si-gil ba-ram-ni-da!

  백년해로하세요!

  baeng-nyeon-hae-ro-ha-se-yo!

  Tip: 백년해로 [baeng-nyeon-hae-ro] means "to stay together forever and ever." It's a phrase used to express a blessing for a married couple at the wedding ceremony.

- You make a lovely couple!

  잘 어울리는 한 쌍이네(요)!

  jal eo-ul-ri-neun han ssang-i-ne(-yo)!

- What a beautiful bride!

  신부가 정말 예뻐(요)!

  sin-bu-ga jeong-mal ye-bbeo(-yo)!

- I love her dress!

  신부 드레스가 예뻐(요)!

  sin-bu deu-re-seu-ga ye-bbeo(-yo)!

- Who is the bridesmaid?

  저 신부 들러리는 누구예요?

  jeo sin-bu deul-reo-ri-neun nu-gu-ye-yo?

- There were a lot of guests at the wedding.

  이 결혼식의 하객은 아주 많아(요).

  i gyeol-hon-si-ge ha-gae-geun a-ju ma-na(-yo)

The Wedding Ceremony 3

- The bride threw the bouquet to her friend.

  신부가 친구에게 부케를 던졌어(요).

  sin-bu-ga chin-gu-e-ge bu-ke-reul deon-jeo-sseo(-yo)

- Where did they take their wedding pictures?

  그들은 웨딩 사진을 어디에서 찍었대(요)?

  geu-deu-reun we-ding sa-ji-neul eo-di-e-seo jji-geot-ddae(-yo)?

- I gave 100,000 won as a wedding gift.

  축의금으로 10만 원을 냈어(요).

  chu-gi-geu-meu-ro sim-man wo-neul nae-sseo(-yo)

- "Pyebaek" is a traditional ceremony where the bride bows down before her parents-in-law and the groom's relatives.

  "폐백"은 신부가 신랑의 부모님과 친척들에게 절하는 전통 의식입니다.

  "pye-bae"-geun sin-bu-ga sil-rang-e bu-mo-nim-gwa chin-cheok-ddeu-re-ge jeol-ha-neun jeon-tong ui-si-gim-ni-da

Married Life

■ How is married life treating you?

결혼 생활 어때(요)?

gyeol-hon saeng-hwal eo-ddae(-yo)?

■ Are you happily married?

결혼 생활은 행복해(요)?

gyeol-hon saeng-hwa-reun
haeng-bo-kae(-yo)?

■ I've been married for eight years.

결혼한 지 이미 8년이에요.

geol-hon-han ji i-mi pal-ryeo-ni-e-yo

■ She is married now with two kids.

그녀는 결혼 후 아이 둘을
낳았어(요).

geu-nyeo-neun gyeol-hon hu a-i du-reul
na-a-sseo(-yo)

■ Their marriage is hanging by a
thread.

그들의 결혼 생활은 위기일발
상황이었어(요).

geu-deu-re gyeol-hon saeng-hwa-reun
wi-gi-il-bal sang-hwang-i-eo-sseo(-yo)

■ Our twentieth anniversary is
coming up soon.

곧 결혼 20주년 기념일이에요.

got gyeol-hon i-sip-jju-nyeon
gi-nyeo-mi-ri-e-yo

Korean Traditional Love Story
Chunhyangjeon (춘향전)

The setting of the story is Namwon (남원), a southern city. Mong-ryong Yi (이몽룡), the son of a nobleman, sees Chun-hyang Seong (성춘향) on a swing and falls helplessly in love with her. She is a lower class gisaeng (기생), or geisha, but despite their difference in class, they're in love and want to marry.

Things are blissful between them until one day Mong-ryong has to move to the capital city Hanyang (한양), where his father has been relocated. His father's replacement in Namwon is Byeon (변), a man who has a liking for geisha. He propositions Chun-hyang but she repeatedly declines. Her rejection makes Byeon angry. He imprisons her and plans to punish her on his birthday.

On the day of Byeon's birthday, Mong-ryong returns from the capital in the guise of an insane beggar and ridicules Byeon in poetry. Chun-hyang does not recognize Mong-ryong. To test Chun-hyang's fidelity, he propositions her. She turns him down. He reveals himself to her and they live happily ever after.

Separation & Divorce

■ I'm separated now.

지금 별거 중이에요.

ji-geum byeol-geo jung-i-e-yo

■ Technically they are not divorced, just separated.

따지자면, 그들은 이혼한 것이 아니라 별거 중이에요.

dda-ji-ja-myeon, geu-deu-reun i-hon-han geo-si a-ni-ra byeol-geo jung-i-e-yo

■ They finally got divorced.

그들은 결국 이혼했어(요).

geu-deu-reun gyeol-guk i-hon-hae-sseo(-yo)

■ Do you want to get a divorce?

이혼하고 싶어(요)?

i-hon-ha-go si-peo(-yo)?

■ More elderly couples are getting divorced these days.

요즘 황혼 이혼율이 갈수록 높아지고 있어(요).

yo-jeum hwang-hon i-hon-nyu-ri gal-ssu-rok no-pa-ji-go i-sseo(-yo)

■ Let's get a divorce!

우리 이혼하자!

u-ri i-hon-ha-ja!

Pregnancy

■ The pregnancy wasn't planned.

계획된 임신은 아니었어(요).

gye-hoek-ddoen im-si-neun a-ni-eo-sseo(-yo)

■ My wife is expecting.

아내가 임신했어(요).

a-nae-ga im-sin-hae-sseo(-yo)

■ She's eight months pregnant.

그녀는 임신한 지 8개월이에요.

geu-nyeo-neun im-sin-han ji pal-gae-wo-ri-e-yo

■ When is the baby due?

출산 예정일이 언제예요?

chul-ssan ye-jeong-i-ri eon-je-ye-yo?

■ Tae-hee wanted to check whether she was pregnant or not.

태희는 자신이 임신했는지 확인하고 싶었어(요).

tae-hi-neun ja-si-ni im-sin-haen-neun-ji hwa-gin-ha-go si-peo-sseo(-yo)

■ They were trying to conceive via artificial insemination.

그들은 인공 수정으로 임신하려고 노력했어(요).

geu-deu-reun in-gong su-jeong-eu-ro im-sin-ha-ryeo-go no-ryeo-kae-sseo(-yo)

Parenting 1

■ It's time to feed the baby.
젖을 먹일 시간이에요.
jeo-jeul meo-gil si-ga-ni-e-yo

■ Did you feed the baby?
아기에게 우유 먹였어(요)?
a-gi-e-ge u-yu meo-gyeo-sseo(-yo)?

■ Do you breastfeed your baby?
아이에게 모유를 먹여(요)?
a-i-e-ge mo-yu-reul meo-gyeo(-yo)?

■ Parenting is a lot of hard work.
육아는 많이 힘들어(요).
yu-ga-neun ma-ni him-deu-reo(-yo)

■ Breastfeeding is very difficult, especially for working mothers.
모유 수유는 특히 직장 여성에게는 어려운 일이에요.
mo-yu su-yu-neun teu-ki jik-jjang yeo-seong-e-ge-neun eo-ryeo-un i-ri-e-yo

■ You should start weaning the baby from the bottle at around five months.
아기가 5개월이 되면 이유식을 시작해야 해(요).
a-gi-ga o-gae-wo-ri doe-myeon i-yu-si-geul si-ja-kae-ya hae(-yo)

Parenting 2

■ I will look after the baby.
내가 아기를 돌볼게(요).
nae-ga a-gi-reul dol-bol-gge(-yo)

■ Please push the stroller.
유모차 좀 밀어 줘(요).
yu-mo-cha jom mi-reo jwo(-yo)

■ I've found someone to babysit on Friday.
금요일에 아이 볼 사람을 구했어(요).
geu-myo-i-re a-i bol sa-ra-meul gu-hae-sseo(-yo)

■ Would you mind changing the diaper?
기저귀 좀 갈아 줄래(요)?
gi-jeo-gwi jom ga-ra jul-rae(-yo)?

■ Can you help me give the baby a bath?
아기 목욕 시키는 데 도와줄 수 있어(요)?
a-gi mo-gyok si-ki-neun de do-wa-jul ssu i-sseo(-yo)?

■ I can't put the baby to sleep.
아기를 재울 수 없어(요).
a-gi-reul jae-ul ssu eop-sseo(-yo)

Chapter 8

School Life

School 학교 hak-ggyo

n. school
학교 [학꾜]
hak-ggyo

n. elementary school,
primary school
초등학교 [초등학꾜]
cho-deung-hak-ggyo

n. middle school,
junior high school
중학교 [중학꾜]
jung-hak-ggyo

n. high school,
senior high school
고등학교 [고등학꾜]
go-deung-hak-ggyo

n. college, university
대학교 [대:학꾜]
dae-hak-ggyo

n. enrollment, admission
입학 [이팍]
i-pak

n. graduation
졸업 [조럽]
jo-reop

n. class, lecture, course,
lesson 수업 [수업] su-eop
= 강의 [강:의/강:이]
gang-ui/gang-i

n. study 공부 [공부]
gong-bu
v. learn
배우다 [배우다]
bae-u-da

n. student
학생 [학쌩]
hak-ssaeng

v. teach
가르치다 [가르치다]
ga-reu-chi-da

n. teacher 교사 [교:사]
gyo-sa
= 선생 [선생]
seon-saeng

n. attendance
출석 [출썩]
chul-sseok

n. lateness, tardiness
지각 [지각]
ji-gak

n. absence 결석 [결썩]
gyeol-sseok

n. question 질문 [질문] jil-mun v. ask 묻다 [묻:따] mut-dda = 물어보다 [무러보다] mu-reo-bo-da	n. answer 대답 [대:답] dae-dap = 답 [답] dap	n. notebook 공책 [공책] gong-chaek = 노트 [노트] no-teu
n. pencil 연필 [연필] yeon-pil	n. eraser 지우개 [지우개] ji-u-gae	n. taking notes 필기 [필기] pil-gi
n. homework 숙제 [숙쩨] suk-jje n. assignment 과제 [과제] gwa-je	n. submission 제출 [제출] je-chul	n. grade, achievement 성적 [성적] seong-jeok
n. examination, exam, test 시험 [시험] si-heom	a. easy 쉽다 [쉽:따] swip-dda	adj. difficult 어렵다 [어렵따] eo-ryeop-dda
n. passing the exam 합격 [합격] hap-ggeok	n. evaluation 평가 [평:까] pyeong-gga	n. degree 학위 [하귀] ha-gwi
n. scholarship 장학금 [장:학끔] jang-hak-ggeum	n. summer break 여름방학 [여름방학] yeo-reum-bang-hak	n. winter break 겨울방학 [겨울방학] gyeo-ul-bang-hak

Going to School 1

■ How long does it take you to walk to school?

학교까지 걸어서 얼마나 걸려(요)?

hak-ggyo-gga-ji geo-reo-seo eol-ma-na geol-ryeo(-yo)?

■ I usually walk to school.

보통 걸어서 등교해(요).

bo-tong geo-reo-seo deung-gyo-hae(-yo)

■ Are you going to ride your bicycle?

자전거 타고 가(요)?

ja-jeon-geo ta-go ga(-yo)?

■ I take the school bus to school.

스쿨버스를 타고 등교해(요).

seu-kul-beo-seu-reul ta-go deung-gyo-hae(-yo)

■ Kyoung-mi drives her children to school.

경미는 아이들을 차로 학교에 데려다 줘(요).

gyeong-mi-neun a-i-deu-reul cha-ro hak-ggyo-e de-ryeo-da jwo(-yo)

Going to School 2

■ The students must attend school in uniform.

학교갈 때 교복을 입어야 해(요).

hak-ggyo-gal ddae gyo-bo-geul i-beo-ya hae(-yo)

■ I go to school with my friend every morning.

매일 아침 친구와 함께 등교해(요).

mae-il a-chim chin-gu-wa ham-gge deung-gyo-hae(-yo)

■ He tried to be on time for school.

그는 제 시간에 학교에 가려고 노력했어(요).

geu-neun je si-ga-ne hak-ggyo-e ga-ryeo-go no-ryeo-kae-sseo(-yo)

■ I'm going to stop by a stationery store on the way to school.

등굣길에 문방구를 들를 거예요.

deung-gyo-ggi-re mun-bang-gu-reul deul-reul ggeo-ye-yo

■ What time do you go to school?

몇 시에 등교해(요)?

myeot si-e deung-gyo-hae(-yo)?

After School

- My mom came to the school to pick me up.

  엄마가 나를 데리러 학교에 오셨어(요).

  eom-ma-ga na-reul de-ri-reo hak-ggyo-e o-syeo-sseo(-yo)

- Do you have any plans after school?

  학교 끝나고 뭐 해(요)?

  hak-ggyo ggeun-na-go mwo hae(-yo)?

  방과 후에 뭐 해(요)?

  bang-gwa hu-e mwo hae(-yo)?

- Why don't we go home together after school?

  학교 끝나고 우리 집에 같이 갈래(요)?

  hak-ggyo ggeun-na-go u-ri ji-be ga-chi gal-rae(-yo)?

- Hang around a little after school!

  학교 끝나고 놀다 가자!

  hak-ggyo ggeun-na-go nol-da ga-ja!

- What programs are there after school?

  방과 후 프로그램으로 어떤 게 있어(요)?

  bang-gwa hu peu-ro-geu-rae-meu-ro eo-ddeon ge i-sseo(-yo)?

Entrance 1

- Kyeong-su matriculated into the university last spring.

  경수는 작년 봄에 대학에 입학했어(요).

  gyeong-su-neun jang-nyeon bo-me dae-ha-ge i-pa-kae-sseo(-yo)

- He got through the entrance examination.

  그는 입학시험의 관문을 통과했어(요).

  geu-neun i-pak-ssi-heo-me gwan-mu-neul tong-gwa-hae-sseo(-yo)

- She entered university this year.

  그녀는 올해 대학에 합격했어(요).

  geu-nyeo-neun ol-hae dae-ha-ge hap-ggyeo-kae-sseo(-yo)

- I start at Seoul National University in the spring.

  봄에 서울대에 진학해(요).

  bo-me seo-ul-dae-e jin-ha-kae(-yo)

  Tip: Seoul National University is widely considered the top university in Korea.

- I was admitted into an university without an examination.

  시험을 안 치고 대학에 입학했어(요).

  si-heo-meul an chi-go dae-ha-ge i-pa-kae-sseo(-yo)

Entrance 2

- He took the entrance exam calmly.

그는 침착하게 입학시험을 치렀어(요).

geu-neun chim-cha-ka-ge i-pak-ssi-heo-meul chi-reo-sseo(-yo)

- I want to have my son enrolled at this school.

우리 아들을 이 학교에 입학시키고 싶어(요).

u-ri a-deu-reul i hak-ggyo-e i-pak-ssi-ki-go si-peo(-yo)

- What kind of documents are required for admission?

입학할 때 어떤 서류가 필요해(요)?

i-pa-kal ddae eo-ddeon seo-ryu-ga pi-ryo-hae(-yo)?

- Did you know that you can download the entrance application form from the website?

입학 지원서를 웹사이트에서 다운로드할 수 있는 걸 알고 있었어(요)?

i-pak ji-won-seo-reul wep-ssa-i-teu-e-seo da-un-ro-deu-hal ssu in-neun geol al-go i-sseo-sseo(-yo)?

The Korean School System

As in many Western nations, Korean schooling is a twelve year stretch: six years of elementary school, three years of middle school and three years of high school.

Elementary and middle school are compulsory. High school is not, though of OECD countries, South Korea leads the way in the percentage of its students who do graduate from high school. Many children also get a jump-start by attending kindergarten from ages three to five. Unlike the West however, the school year begins in March and ends in February of the following year.

There are two vacations per year, summer vacation (about mid-July to mid-August) and winter vacation (about the middle or end of December to the end of January or early February).

Entrance 3

- There's a difference between the school that I want to go to and the school that I can go to.

가고 싶은 학교와 갈 수 있는 학교는 원래 다른 거예요.

ga-go si-peun hak-ggyo-wa gal ssu in-neun hak-gyo-neun wol-rae da-reun geo-ye-yo

- He gave up the idea of going to college.

그는 대학 진학을 단념했어(요).

geu-neun dae-hak jin-ha-geul dan-nyeom-hae-sseo(-yo)

- It's harder to get in because of the number of applicants.

지원자가 많아서 들어가기 어려워졌어(요).

ji-won-ja-ga ma-na-seo deu-reo-ga-gi eo-ryeo-wo-jeo-sseo(-yo)

- Each college has different guidelines for its applicants.

각 대학마다 다양한 지원 요강이 있습니다.

gak dae-hak-ma-da da-yang-han ji-won yo-gang-i it-sseum-ni-da

- He has been admitted into the MBA program.

그는 MBA에 들어갔어(요).

geu-neun em-bi-e-i-e deu-reo-ga-sseo(-yo)

Freshman Year

- There's an orientation for new students tomorrow morning.

내일 아침 신입생 오리엔테이션이 있어(요).

nae-il a-chim si-nip-ssaeng o-ri-en-te-i-syeo-ni i-sseo(-yo)

- A welcome party was held for freshmen at the Student Union.

신입생 환영회가 학생회관에서 열렸어(요).

si-nip-ssaeng hwa-nyeong-hoe-ga hak-ssaeng-hoe-gwa-ne-seo yeol-ryeo-sseo(-yo)

- Freshmen, we welcome you to our university!

우리 대학에 온 신입생 여러분을 환영합니다!

u-ri dae-ha-ge on si-nip-ssaeng yeo-reo-bu-neul hwa-nyeong-ham-ni-da!

- Don't haze freshmen.

신입생 못살게 굴지 마(세요).

sin-ip-ssaeng mot-ssal-ge gul-ji ma(-se-yo)

- As a senior, you have to help freshmen.

선배로서, 신입생을 도와줘야 해(요).

seon-bae-ro-seo, si-nip-ssaeng-eul do-wa-jwo-ya hae(-yo)

Graduation 1

▪ There's only one semester left before graduation.

졸업까지 한 학기밖에 안 남았어(요).

jo-reop-gga-ji han hak-ggi-ba-gge
an na-ma-sseo(-yo)

▪ He's just fresh out of college.

그는 막 대학을 졸업했어(요).

geu-neun mak dae-ha-geul
jo-reo-pae-sseo(-yo)

▪ When did you graduate from university?

언제 대학 졸업했어(요)?

eon-je dae-hak jo-reo-pae-sseo(-yo)?

▪ Do you expect to graduate next year?

내년에 졸업해(요)?

nae-nyeo-ne jo-reo-pae(-yo)?

▪ What school did you graduate from?

어느 학교를 졸업했어(요)?

eo-neu hak-ggyo-reul
jo-reo-pae-sseo(-yo)?

▪ What are you going to do after you graduate?

졸업하면 뭐 할 거예요?

jo-reo-pa-myeon mwo hal ggeo-ye-yo?

Graduation 2

▪ Na-hyeon was attending a graduation party.

나현이는 졸업 파티에 참석 중이었어(요).

na-hyeo-ni-neun jo-reop pa-ti-e
cham-seok jung-i-eo-sseo(-yo)

▪ What did you get for a graduation present?

졸업 선물로 뭘 받았어(요)?

jo-reop seon-mul-ro mwol
ba-da-sseo(-yo)?

▪ I'm not sure what to do after graduation.

졸업 후에 뭘 해야 할지 모르겠어(요).

jo-reop hu-e mwol hae-ya hal-jji
mo-reu-ge-sseo(-yo)

▪ Tell me what you plan to do after graduation.

졸업 후 포부를 말해 주세요.

jo-reop hu po-bu-reul mal-hae ju-se-yo

▪ Now that I've finished school, I'm thinking of moving out.

졸업한 이상, 나가서 살려고(요).

jo-reo-pan i-sang, na-ga-seo
sal-ryeo-go(-yo)

Graduation Record

■ I need two more English credits to graduate.

졸업하려면 영어 2학점이 더 필요해(요).

jo-reo-pa-ryeo-myeon yeong-eo
i-hak-jjeo-mi deo pi-ryo-hae(-yo)

■ Congratulations on graduating first in your class!

수석 졸업을 축하해(요)!

su-seok jo-reo-beul chu-ka-hae(-yo)!

■ Dong-min graduated with honors.

동민이는 우수한 성적으로 졸업했어(요).

dong-mi-ni-neun u-su-han seong-jeo-
geu-ro jo-reo-pae-sseo(-yo)

■ He graduated one year ahead of me.

그는 나보다 1년 일찍 졸업했어(요).

geu-neun na-bo-da il-ryeon il-jjik
jo-reo-pae-sseo(-yo)

■ I need this class to graduate.

이 과목을 이수해야 졸업할 수 있어(요).

i gwa-mo-geul i-su-hae-ya jo-reo-pal ssu
i-sseo(-yo)

Classes 1

■ Class starts at nine.

9시에 수업이 시작해(요).

a-hop-ssi-e su-eo-bi si-ja-kae(-yo)

■ Did the teacher check the attendance?

선생님이 출석 체크했어(요)?

seon-saeng-ni-mi chul-sseok che-keu-
hae-sseo(-yo)?

Tip: Koreans don't address a teacher by their name they just use the respectful term 선생님 [seon-saeng-nim] "Teacher."

■ We have a ten-minute break.

쉬는 시간은 10분이에요.

swi-neun si-ga-neun sip-bbu-ni-e-yo

■ That's all for today.

오늘은 이것으로 수업을 마치겠습니다.

o-neu-reun i-geo-seu-ro su-eo-beul
ma-chi-get-sseum-ni-da

■ School finishes at five o'clock.

학교는 5시에 끝나(요).

hak-ggyo-neun da-seot-ssi-e ggeun-
na(-yo)

Classes 2

- How much did we cover in the last class?

  지난 시간에 어디까지 했죠?

  ji-nan si-ga-ne eo-di-gga-ji haet-jjyo?

- I'm sorry I'm late for class.

  수업에 늦어서 죄송합니다.

  su-eo-be neu-jeo-seo
  joe-song-ham-ni-da

- Everybody should speak in Korean in this class.

  이 수업은 모두 한국어로 말해야 합니다.

  i su-eo-beun mo-du han-gu-geo-ro
  mal-hae-ya ham-ni-da

- What's your favorite subject?

  좋아하는 과목이 뭐예요?

  jo-a-ha-neun gwa-mo-gi mwo-ye-yo?

- Did you hear the bell?

  벨소리 들었어(요)?

  bel-so-ri deu-reo-sseo(-yo)?

- Next Tuesday is our school's eighth anniversary, so no classes.

  다음 주 화요일은 제8회 개교기념일이라서, 수업이 없습니다.

  da-eum ju hwa-yo-i-reun je-pal-hoe
  gae-gyo-gi-nyeo-mi-ri-ra-seo su-eo-bi
  eop-sseum-ni-da

Class Schedule 1

- What subject is the next class?

  다음 수업은 무슨 과목이에요?

  da-eum su-eo-beun mu-seun
  gwa-mo-gi-e-yo?

- How many classes are you taking this semester?

  이번 학기에 몇 과목 들어(요)?

  i-beon hak-ggi-e myeot gwa-mok
  deu-reo(-yo)?

- Have you registered for your classes yet?

  벌써 수강 신청했어(요)?

  beol-sseo su-gang
  sin-cheong-hae-sseo(-yo)?

- I have a class at 2 p.m.

  오후 2시에 수업이 있어(요).

  o-hu du-si-e su-eo-bi i-sseo(-yo)

- We have four Korean lessons a week.

  일주일에 한국어 수업이 4시간 있어(요).

  il-jju-i-re han-gu-geo su-eo-bi ne-si-gan
  i-sseo(-yo)

- After lunch, we had history class.

  점심시간 후에, 역사 수업이 있었어(요).

  jeom-sim-si-gan hu-e, yeok-ssa su-eo-bi
  i-sseo-sseo(-yo)

Class Schedule 2

■ Do you have the schedule for this semester?

이번 학기 수업 시간표 갖고 있어(요)?

i-beon hak-ggi su-eop si-gan-pyo gat-ggo i-sseo(-yo)?

■ The classes are full today.

오늘 수업이 꽉 찼어(요).

o-neul su-eo-bi ggwak cha-sseo(-yo)

■ How's your Korean class going?

한국어 수업 잘 돼가(요)?

han-gu-geo su-eop jal dwae-ga(-yo)?

■ What day is your class scheduled for?

수업이 무슨 요일이에요?

su-eo-bi mu-seun yo-i-ri-e-yo?

■ I don't know what classes to take.

어떤 수업을 들어야 할지 모르겠어(요).

eo-ddeon su-eo-beul deu-reo-ya hal-jji mo-reu-ge-sseo(-yo)

■ We had a class off-campus today.

오늘은 학교 밖에서 수업했어(요).

o-neu-reun hak-ggyo ba-gge-seo su-eo-pae-sseo(-yo)

Levels of Difficulty

■ The lesson didn't sink in.

이 수업은 잘 못 알아듣겠어(요).

i su-eo-beun jal mot a-ra-deut-gge-sseo(-yo)

■ That lesson went over my head.

저 수업은 너무 어려워(요).

jeo su-eo-beun neo-mu eo-ryeo-wo(-yo)

■ I know my geometry inside out.

기하학 수업을 완전히 이해하고 있어(요).

gi-ha-hak su-eo-beul wan-jeon-hi i-hae-ha-go i-sseo(-yo)

■ Math is a pain in the ass.

수학 수업은 지겨웠어(요).

su-hak su-eo-beun ji-gyeo-wo-sseo(-yo)

■ I need a good private tutor.

좋은 개인 과외 선생님이 필요해(요).

jo-eun gae-in gwa-oe seon-saeng-ni-mi pi-ryo-hae(-yo)

■ Do you want to make a study group?

스터디 그룹을 만들고 싶어(요)?

seu-teo-di geu-ru-beul man-deul-go si-peo(-yo)?

Attitudes in Class

- He doesn't like students using their phones in class.

  선생님은 학생들이 수업 시간에 휴대폰 쓰는 걸 안 좋아하셔(요).

  seon-saeng-ni-meun hak-ssaeng-deu-ri su-eop si-ga-ne hyu-dae-pon sseu-neun geol an jo-a-ha-syeo(-yo)

- She's always sleeping in class.

  그녀는 수업 시간에 늘 자(요).

  geu-nyeo-neun su-eop si-ga-ne neul ja(-yo)

- Why weren't you in class yesterday?

  어제 수업에 왜 안 왔어(요)?

  eo-je su-eo-be wae an wa-sseo(-yo)?

- He is always late for class.

  그는 수업에 항상 늦어(요).

  geu-neun su-eo-be hang-sang neu-jeo(-yo)

- Min-ji made some excuse to skip class.

  민지는 아프다는 핑계로 수업을 빠졌어(요).

  min-ji-neun a-peu-da-neun ping-gye-ro su-eo-beul bba-jeo-sseo(-yo)

CSAT (College Scholastic Ability Test)

Whether you know it as CSAT or Suneung (수능, 수학능력시험 [su-hak-neung-nyeok-ssi-heom]), the meaning is the same. On the second or third Thursday in November, upwards of 600,000 South Korean high-school students bear down for this mother of university entrance exams. There are similarities to the SAT but length is not one. The CSAT runs eight hours to the SAT's possible four.

All CSAT questions are derived from the Korean high school curriculum; textbooks are standardized across the country.

There are six sections: National Language (Korean), Mathematics, English, Korean History, Subordinate Subjects (Social Studies/Sciences/ Vocational Education), and Second Foreign Languages/Chinese Characters and Classics.

The implications of test day on Korean life are stunning. Businesses open late. Public transportation ramps up to reduce congestion. Even airplanes put on the brakes during the listening exam. Parents might be seen praying for success.

Homework 1

■ How long does it take to finish your homework?

숙제 다 하려면 얼마나 걸려(요)?

suk-jje da ha-ryeo-myeon eol-ma-na geol-ryeo(-yo)?

■ It took her two hours to finish her homework.

그녀는 숙제하는 데 두 시간 걸렸어(요).

geu-nyeo-neun suk-jje-ha-neun de du si-gan geol-ryeo-sseo(-yo)

■ I should get my assignment done right now.

난 지금 당장 숙제를 다 해야 해(요).

nan ji-geum dang-jang suk-jje-reul da hae-ya hae(-yo)

■ You can submit the assignment online.

온라인으로 숙제를 제출할 수 있어(요).

ol-ra-i-neu-ro suk-jje-reul je-chul-hal ssu i-sseo(-yo)

■ I'm behind in my homework.

숙제가 밀려 있어(요).

suk-jje-ga mil-ryeo i-sseo(-yo)

Homework 2

■ Be sure to do your homework.

숙제는 꼭 해라.

suk-jje-neun ggok hae-ra

■ I breezed through my assignment.

숙제를 쉽게 끝냈어(요).

suk-jje-reul swip-gge ggeun-nae-sseo(-yo)

■ I was up late last night doing my math homework.

어제 수학 숙제를 하느라 밤늦게까지 있었어(요).

eo-je su-hak suk-jje-reul ha-neu-ra bam-neut-gge-gga-ji i-sseo-sseo(-yo)

■ I stayed up all night doing my assignment.

숙제하느라 밤을 꼴딱 샜어(요).

suk-jje-ha-neu-ra ba-meul ggol-ddak sae-sseo(-yo)

■ So much homework, so little time.

숙제는 너무 많고, 시간은 너무 부족해(요).

suk-jje-neun neo-mu man-ko, si-ga-neun neo-mu bu-jo-kae(-yo)

Homework 3

- I have to do a lot of homework, too.

  해야 할 숙제도 많은데(요).

  hae-ya hal suk-jje-do ma-neun-de(-yo)

- Oh no! I forgot to bring my homework.

  오, 이런! 숙제 갖고 오는 걸 잊어버렸어(요).

  o, i-reon! suk-jje gat-ggo o-neun geol i-jeo-beo-ryeo-sseo(-yo)

- Could you help me with my homework?

  내 숙제를 도와줄 수 있어(요)?

  nae suk-jje-reul do-wa-jul ssu i-sseo(-yo)?

- I can't put this off any longer.

  숙제를 더 이상 미룰 수 없어(요).

  suk-jje-reul deo i-sang mi-rul ssu eop-sseo(-yo)

- I have a lot more homework today than usual.

  오늘은 평소보다 숙제가 훨씬 많아(요).

  o-neu-reun pyeong-so-bo-da suk-jje-ga hwol-ssin ma-na(-yo)

- Do your homework before you go to sleep!

  숙제하고 자렴!

  suk-jje-ha-go ja-ryeom!

Homework 4

- Don't you have homework?

  오늘 숙제 없어(요)?

  o-neul suk-jje eop-sseo(-yo)?

- That is not an easy assignment.

  쉬운 숙제가 아닌데(요).

  swi-un suk-jje-ga a-nin-de(-yo)

- Your homework is to write the corrections.

  네 숙제는 틀린 것을 다시 쓰는 거야.

  ne suk-jje-neun teul-rin geo-seul da-si sseu-neun geo-ya

- I need to borrow some books for my homework.

  숙제 때문에, 도서관에서 책을 빌려야 해(요).

  suk-jje ddae-mu-ne, do-seo-gwa-ne-seo chae-geul bil-ryeo-ya hae(-yo)

- It's stressful that we have so much homework.

  숙제가 너무 많아 스트레스예요.

  suk-jje-ga neo-mu ma-na seu-teu-re-seu-ye-yo

- I forgot the due date for my homework.

  숙제 제출하는 날을 잊어버렸어(요).

  suk-jje je-chul-ha-neun na-reul i-jeo-beo-ryeo-sseo(-yo)

Evaluating Assignments

■ I'm a bit disappointed with the evaluation of my assignment.

내 과제 평가 때문에 좀
실망했어(요).

nae gwa-je pyeong-gga ddae-mu-ne jom
sil-mang-hae-sseo(-yo)

■ The teacher praised Ji-eun for her assignment.

선생님은 지은이의 과제를
칭찬했어(요).

seon-saeng-ni-meun ji-eu-ni-e gwa-je-
reul ching-chan-hae-sseo(-yo)

■ I'll evaluate your assignments by group.

숙제는 그룹별로 평가할게요.

suk-jje-neun geu-rup-bbyeol-ro
pyeong-gga-hal-gge-yo

■ Can I talk to you about my assignment?

제 과제에 대해 얘기할 수
있어요?

je gwa-je-e dae-hae yae-gi-hal ssu
i-sseo-yo?

■ I totally goofed up the assignment.

과제를 망쳤어(요).

gwa-je-reul mang-cheo-sseo(-yo)

Before the Exam 1

■ The examination is only one week off.

시험 날짜가 일주일 후로
다가왔어(요).

si-heom nal-jja-ga il-jju-il hu-ro
da-ga-wa-sseo(-yo)

■ Have you studied for the test tomorrow?

내일 시험 공부했어(요)?

nae-il si-heom gong-bu-hae-sseo(-yo)?

■ They are busy preparing for the exam.

그들은 시험 준비하느라
바빠(요).

geu-deu-reun si-heom jun-bi-ha-neu-ra
ba-bba(-yo)

■ Min-jeong is really nervous about this exam.

민정이는 시험 생각으로 정말
긴장하고 있어(요).

min-jeong-i-neun si-heom saeng-
ga-geu-ro jeong-mal gin-jang-ha-go
i-sseo(-yo)

■ Can you tell me what the test will cover?

시험 범위가 어디까지예요?

si-heom beo-mwi-ga eo-di-gga-ji-ye-yo?

Before the Exam 2

■ He always crams before the exam.

그는 늘 시험 전에 벼락치기로 준비해(요).

geu-neun neul si-heom jeo-ne byeo-rak-chi-gi-ro jun-bi-hae(-yo)

■ The final test is just around the corner.

곧 기말고사예요.

got gi-mal-go-sa-ye-yo

■ Next week we have midterm exams.

다음 주에 중간고사가 있어(요).

da-eum ju-e jung-gan-go-sa-ga i-sseo(-yo)

■ Final exams are in two weeks.

기말고사가 2주 후에 있어(요).

gi-mal-go-sa-ga i-ju hu-e i-sseo(-yo)

■ Students avoid eating seaweed before important exams.

중요한 시험을 앞두고 학생들은 미역국 먹기를 꺼려(요).

jung-yo-han si-heo-meul ap-ddu-go hak-ssaeng-deu-reun mi-yeok-gguk meok-ggi-reul ggeo-ryeo(-yo)

Tip: There is a common myth in Korea that having seaweed soup before an exam will lead to failure.

Ondol

Ondol (온돌) is the below-floor heating system best appreciated when the temperature dips.

The ancient Korean invention served the dual purpose of generating heat for cooking and keeping people comfortable, by warming up an entire room from below.

In today's ondol heating system, water is heated and circulated in pipes under the floor. In days past however, they used wood as fuel. The resulting smoke moved through a passageway, heating stones below the floor to make the house warm. Given that Koreans make use of the floor of their homes for any number of activities, it makes perfect sense.

The jjimjilbang (찜질방), or Korean bathhouse, uses the ondol concept for their steam rooms.

After the Exam

■ The examination is over.
시험이 끝났어(요).
si-heo-mi ggeun-na-sse(-yo)

■ That test was a joke.
그 시험은 매우 쉬웠어(요).
geu si-heo-meun mae-u swi-wo-sseo(-yo)

■ That question was in the exam.
그 문제가 시험에서 나왔어(요).
geu mun-je-ga si-heo-me-seo
na-wa-sseo(-yo)

■ I'm so relieved that's over.
시험이 끝나서 긴장이
풀렸어(요).
si-heo-mi ggeun-na-seo gin-jang-i
pul-ryeo-sseo(-yo)

■ I'm confident I did well.
시험 잘 봤어(요).
si-heom jal bwa-sseo(-yo)

■ I killed that exam.
시험에서 내 실력을 충분히
발휘했어(요).
si-heo-me-seo nae sil-ryeo-geul
chung-bun-hi bal-hwi-hae-sseo(-yo)

Exam Results

■ He aced it.
그는 우수한 성적을 받았어(요).
geu-neun u-su-han seong-jeo-geul
ba-da-sseo(-yo)

■ She's feeling a little on edge.
그녀는 초조해(요).
geu-nyeo-neun cho-jo-hae(-yo)

■ He is concerned about the
results.
그는 시험 결과 때문에 마음을
졸이고 있어(요).
geu-neun si-heom gyeol-gwa ddae-mu-
ne ma-eu-meul jo-ri-go i-sseo(-yo)

■ I'm disappointed with the result
of the test.
시험 결과를 보고 맥이
빠졌어(요).
si-heom gyeol-gwa-reul bo-go mae-gi
bba-jeo-sseo(-yo)

■ This is going to hurt my GPA.
이건 내 평균을 깎을 거예요.
i-geon nae pyeong-gyu-neul gga-ggeul
ggeo-ye-yo

■ Do I have to retake it?
다시 해야 돼(요)?
da-si hae-ya dwae(-yo)?

Report Cards

■ He failed physics.

그는 물리가 낙제였어(요).

geu-neun mul-ri-ga nak-jje-yeo-sseo(-yo)

■ I didn't do very well in math.

수학 시험을 망쳤어(요).

su-hak si-heo-meul mang-cheo-sseo(-yo)

■ I don't want an F appearing on my transcript.

성적표에 F가 나오게 하고 싶지 않아(요).

seong-jeok-pyo-e e-peu-ga na-o-ge ha-go sip-jji an-na(-yo)

■ My dad isn't going to be happy about this report card.

아빠는 내 성적표 때문에 화나셨어(요).

a-bba-neun nae seong-jeok-pyo ddae-mu-ne hwa-na-syeo-sseo(-yo)

■ Ho-jin had a bad report this term.

호진이는 이번 학기에 안 좋은 성적표를 받았어(요).

ho-ji-ni-neun i-beon hak-ggi-e an jo-eun seong-jeok-pyo-reul ba-da-sseo(-yo)

Good Grades

■ My parents expect straight As.

부모님은 전 과목 A를 기대하셔(요).

bu-mo-ni-meun jeon gwa-mok e-i-reul gi-dae-ha-syeo(-yo)

■ His grades are in the top fifth of his class.

그의 성적은 늘 반에서 다섯 손가락 안에 들어(요).

geu-e seong-jeo-geun neul ba-ne-seo da-seot son-gga-rak a-ne deu-reo(-yo)

■ Su-bin got the highest mark in the history exam.

수빈이는 역사 시험에서 가장 높은 성적을 받았어(요).

su-bi-ni-neun yeok-ssa si-heo-me-seo ga-jang no-peun seong-jeo-geul ba-da-sseo(-yo)

■ They're about equal in English.

그들은 영어 성적에서 어깨를 나란히 해(요).

geu-deu-reun yeong-eo seong-jeo-ge-seo eo-ggae-reul na-ran-hi hae(-yo)

■ I got full marks in the exam.

시험에서 만점을 받았어(요).

si-heo-me-seo man-jjeo-meul ba-da-sseo(-yo)

Bad Grades

■ Mun-ho is falling a bit behind.

문호는 성적이 뒤처졌어(요).

mun-ho-neun seong-jeo-gi
dwi-cheo-jeo-sseo(-yo)

■ The grade is lower than I was expecting.

성적이 예상 이하예요.

seong-jeo-gi ye-sang i-ha-ye-yo

■ I'm terribly concerned about your low grades.

뒤떨어진 네 성적 때문에 정말 걱정이구나.

dwi-ddeo-reo-jin ne seong-jeok ddae-mu-ne jeong-mal geok-jjeong-i-gu-na

■ Her grades were low again this semester.

그녀는 이번 학기도 성적이 좋지 않아(요).

geu-nyeo-neun i-beon hak-ggi-do seong-jeo-gi jo-chi a-na(-yo)

■ I got a zero in the exam.

시험에서 0점을 받았어(요).

si-heo-me-seo yeong-jjeo-meul ba-da-sseo(-yo)

Tip: 0점 "zero" can be read as [yeong-jjeom] or [bbang-jjeom].

Scholarships

■ What kind of scholarship did you get?

무슨 장학금을 받았어(요)?

mu-seun jang-hak-ggeu-meul ba-da-sseo(-yo)?

■ You might qualify for a scholarship.

너는 장학금을 받을 수 있을 거예요.

neo-neun jang-hak-ggeu-meul ba-deul ssu i-sseul ggeo-ye-yo

■ I'm afraid I can't get a scholarship.

장학금을 받지 못할까봐 걱정이에요.

jang-hak-ggeu-meul bat-jji mo-tal-gga-bwa geok-jjeong-i-e-yo

■ I have to work harder to keep my scholarship.

장학금을 계속 받기 위해서는 열심히 공부해야 해(요).

jang-hak-ggeu-meul gye-sok bat-ggi wi-hae-seo-neun yeol-ssim-hi gong-bu-hae-ya hae(-yo)

■ It's just a one-time scholarship.

단지 1회성 장학금이에요.

dan-ji il-hoe-sseong jang-hak-ggeu-mi-e-yo

Before Vacation

- Summer vacation is getting close.

곧 여름방학이에요.

got yeo-reum-bang-ha-gi-e-yo

- When does your vacation begin?

방학이 언제 시작해(요)?

bang-ha-gi eon-je si-ja-kae(-yo)?

- They are looking forward to the vacation.

그들은 방학이 오기를 기대하고 있어(요).

geu-deu-reun bang-ha-gi o-gi-reul gi-dae-ha-go i-sseo(-yo)

- I can't wait for my vacation.

어서 방학이 왔으면 좋겠어(요).

eo-seo bang-ha-gi wa-sseu-myeon jo-ke-sseo(-yo)

- Have a fun vacation, everyone!

즐거운 방학 보내요, 여러분!

jeul-geo-un bang-hak bo-nae-yo, yeo-reo-bun!

- Vacation starts in three days!

3일만 있으면 방학이야!

sa-mil-man i-sseu-myeon bang-ha-gi-ya!

Vacation Plans

- What are you planning for your summer break?

여름방학에 뭘 할 거예요?

yeo-reum-bang-ha-ge mwol hal ggeo-ye-yo?

- They're going to Gangwon-do for a few days.

그들은 강원도로 며칠 동안 갈 거예요.

geu-deu-reun gang-won-do-ro myeo-chil dong-an gal ggeo-ye-yo

- I'm going to visit my grandma during the break.

방학 동안 할머니네 갈 거예요.

bang-hak dong-an hal-meo-ni-ne gal ggeo-ye-yo

- I plan to do some volunteer work.

봉사 활동을 하려고 해(요).

bong-sa hwal-ddong-eul ha-ryeo-go hae(-yo)

- Let's read a lot of books during winter break.

겨울방학 동안 책을 많이 읽자.

gyeo-ul-bang-hak dong-an chae-geul ma-ni il-jja

After Vacation

■ Did you have a good winter break?
겨울방학 잘 보냈어(요)?
gyeo-ul-bang-hak jal bo-nae-sseo(-yo)?

■ She had a good time on her vacation.
그녀는 방학을 즐겁게 보냈어(요).
geu-nyeo-neun bang-ha-geul jeul-geop-gge bo-nae-sseo(-yo)

■ She spent her whole vacation at the beach.
그녀는 방학 내내 바닷가에서 보냈어(요).
geu-nyeo-neun bang-hak nae-nae ba-dat-gga-e-seo bo-nae-sseo(-yo)

■ I wasted the entire vacation in front of the TV.
방학 내내 텔레비전만 보고, 허송세월을 보냈어(요).
bang-hak nae-nae tel-re-bi-jeon-man bo-go, heo-song-se-wo-reul bo-nae-sseo(-yo)

■ Su-ho put on a lot of weight after the vacation.
수호는 방학이 지나고 몸무게가 많이 늘었어(요).
su-ho-neun bang-ha-gi ji-na-go mom-mu-ge-ga ma-ni neu-reo-sseo(-yo)

Field Trips 1

■ We are going on a school trip this Friday.
이번 주 금요일에 학교 소풍을 가(요).
i-beon ju geu-myo-i-re hak-ggyo so-pung-eul ga(-yo)

■ We are having a picnic tomorrow!
내일 소풍 간다!
nae-il so-pung gan-da!

■ A picnic will be fun.
소풍 가면 재미있을 거야.
so-pung ga-myeon jae-mi-i-sseul ggeo-ya

■ We went for an outing to the mountains.
우리는 산으로 소풍을 갔어(요).
u-ri-neun sa-neu-ro so-pung-eul ga-sseo(-yo)

■ The kids are pretty excited about the field trip.
아이들은 소풍으로 아주 들떠 있어(요).
a-i-deu-reun so-pung-eu-ro a-ju deul-ddeo i-sseo(-yo)

Field Trips 2

▪ I hope the weather stays fine.

날씨가 좋으면 좋겠어(요).

nal-ssi-ga jo-eu-myeon jo-ke-sseo(-yo)

▪ Bring a packed lunch and some water for the picnic.

소풍에 도시락과 물을 가져 오세요.

so-pung-e do-si-rak-ggwa mu-reul ga-jeo o-se-yo

▪ I'll probably bring a couple of gimbaps.

아마 김밥을 좀 싸 갈 거예요.

a-ma gim-bba-beul jom ssa gal ggeo-ye-yo

Tip: 김밥 [gim-bbap] is a typical picnic item in Korea.

▪ The rain ruined the picnic.

비가 와서, 소풍을 망쳤어(요).

bi-ga wa-seo, so-pung-eul mang-cheo-sseo(-yo)

▪ The trip was canceled because of rain.

비 때문에 소풍이 취소됐어(요).

bi ddae-mu-ne so-pung-i chwi-so-dwae-sseo(-yo)

Everland & Lotte World

Everland (에버랜드) and Lotte World (롯데월드) are Korean amusement parks.

Everland is the nation's largest outdoor theme park and caters to a gamut of tastes with roller coasters, parades and animals to pet and view. There are seasonal festivals too and the very sizeable water park "Caribbean Bay" is close by.

Lotte World has a family-Disney vibe and is located in Jamsil (잠실), Seoul. It is the world's largest indoor amusement park but also has an outdoor section with roller coasters, swings and tower drop rides. The world under the roof is crammed with rides, shows and even a skating rink. When you've had your fill there's always shopping or you can take a walk around Seokchon Lake (석촌 호수 [seok-chon ho-su]).

Field Days 1

■ Our school Sports Day is next week.

우리 학교는 다음 주에 운동회를 해(요).

u-ri hak-ggyo-neun da-eum ju-e
un-dong-hoe-reul hae(-yo)

■ If it rains, Sports Day will be postponed.

비가 오면, 운동회는 연기될 거예요.

bi-ga o-myeon, un-dong-hoe-neun
yeon-gi-doel ggeo-ye-yo

■ The athletic meet will be held on April 5.

4월 5일에 운동회가 열려(요).

sa-wol o-i-re un-dong-hoe-ga
yeol-ryeo(-yo)

■ We're determined to win this event.

우리는 이번 행사에서 이기기로 결심했어(요).

u-ri-neun i-beon haeng-sa-e-seo i-gi-gi-
ro gyeol-ssim-hae-sseo(-yo)

■ What event are you going to participate in?

무슨 종목에 참가할 거예요?

mu-seun jong-mo-ge cham-ga-hal
ggeo-ye-yo?

Field Days 2

■ Tug-of-war is a favorite activity on field day.

줄다리기는 운동회에서 인기 있는 활동이에요.

jul-da-ri-gi-neun un-dong-hoe-e-seo
in-ggi in-neun hwal-ddong-i-e-yo

■ I was selected as a 100m runner.

100미터 달리기 선수로 뽑혔어(요).

baeng-mi-teo dal-ri-gi seon-su-ro
bbo-pyeo-sseo(-yo)

■ He was the last runner in the 400m relay.

그는 400미터 계주에서 최종 주자로 뛰었어(요).

geu-neun sa-baeng-mi-teo gye-ju-e-seo
choe-jong ju-ja-ro ddwi-eo-sseo(-yo)

■ Students are practicing cheering for the fall field day.

가을 운동회를 위한 학생들의 응원 연습이 한창이에요.

ga-eul un-dong-hoe-reul wi-han
hak-ssaeng-deu-re eung-won yeon-seu-
bi han-chang-i-e-yo

Chapter 9

Work, Work, Work!

n. work 일 [일:] il
v. work, do one's job
일하다 [일:하다] il-ha-da

n. company
회사 [회:사/훼:사]
hoe-sa/hwe-sa

n. office 사무실 [사:무실]
sa-mu-sil

n. worker
회사원 [회:사원/
훼:사원]
hoe-sa-won/
hwe-sa-won

n. president 사장 [사장]
sa-jang
n. staff
사원 [사원]
sa-won

n. going to work
출근 [출근]
chul-geun

n. getting off work
퇴근 [퇴:근/퉤:근]
toe-geun/
twe-geun

n. overtime 야근 [야:근]
ya-geun

n. meeting, conference
회의 [회:의/훼:이]
hoe-ui/hwe-i

n. presentation
발표 [발표]
bal-pyo

n. document
서류 [서류]
seo-ryu
= 문서 [문서]
mun-seo

n. wage 임금 [임:금]
im-geum
n. salary 봉급 [봉:급]
bong-geup
n. allowance, wage
급여 [그벼] geu-byeo

n. bonus 상여금 [상여금]
sang-yeo-geum
= 보너스 [보너스]
bo-neo-seu

n. extra pay
수당 [수당]
su-dang

n. vacation,
holiday, leave
휴가 [휴가]
hyu-ga

n. sick leave
병가 [병:가]
byeong-ga

n. parental leave,
paternity leave,
maternity leave
출산 휴가 [출싼 휴가]
chul-ssan hyu-ga

n. retirement 퇴직 [퇴:직/퉤:직] toe-jik/twe-jik	n. resignation 사직 [사직] sa-jik	n. dismissal 해고 [해:고] hae-go
n. job hunting 구직 [구직] gu-jik n. recruitment 구인 [구인] gu-in	n. resume 이력서 [이:력써] i-ryeok-sseo n. profile 프로필 [프로필] peu-ro-pil	n. letter of self-introduction 자기소개서 [자기소개서] ja-gi-so-gae-seo
n. career, work experience 경력 [경녁] gyeong-nyeok	n. written test 필기시험 [필기시험] pil-gi-si-heom	n. interview 면접시험 [면:접씨험] myeon-jeop-ssi-heom

Going to Work 1

■ I have to be at work by eight
o'clock.

8시까지 출근해(요).

yeo-deol-si-gga-ji chul-geun-hae(-yo)

■ He punched in on time.

그는 제 시간에 출근해(요).

geu-neun je si-ga-ne chul-geun-hae(-yo)

■ We'd better get to work thirty
minutes early tomorrow.

내일 30분 일찍 출근하는 게
좋겠어(요).

nae-il sam-sip-bbun il-jjik
chul-geun-ha-neun ge jo-ke-sseo(-yo)

■ Congratulations on your new
job. When do you start?

취직한 거 축하해(요).
언제부터 출근해(요)?

chwi-ji-kan geo chu-ka-hae(-yo).
eon-je-bu-teo chul-geun-hae(-yo)?

■ Hyeon-taek comes in early
every day.

현택 씨는 매일 일찍 출근해(요).

hyeon-taek ssi-neun mae-il il-jjik
chul-geun-hae(-yo)

Going to Work 2

■ Are you going to work now?

출근하는 중이에요?

chul-geun-ha-neun jung-i-e-yo?

■ How do you get to work?

당신은 어떻게 출근해요?

dang-si-neun eo-ddeo-ke
chul-geun-hae-yo?

■ I carpool with a coworker.

동료와 카풀해(요).

dong-nyo-wa ka-pul-hae(-yo)

■ I wear suits to work.

정장을 입고 출근해(요).

jeong-jang-eul ip-ggo
chul-geun-hae(-yo)

■ Sorry I'm late. My bus broke
down on the way in this
morning.

늦게 와서 죄송해요.
출근하는 길에 버스가
고장 났어요.

neut-gge wa-seo joe-song-hae-yo.
chul-geun-ha-neun gi-re beo-seu-ga
go-jang na-sseo-yo

Going to Work 3

■ Please tell me when Na-yeon gets in.

나연 씨가 언제 출근하는지 알려 주세요.

na-yeon ssi-ga eon-je chul-geun-ha-neun-ji al-ryeo ju-se-yo

■ Why didn't you get to work on time?

왜 제 시간에 출근하지 않죠?

wae je si-ga-ne chul-geun-ha-ji an-chyo?

■ I can't come in today.

오늘 출근하지 못할 거 같아(요).

o-neul chul-geun-ha-ji mo-tal ggeo ga-ta(-yo)

■ I am off on weekends.

주말에는 출근하지 않아(요).

ju-ma-re-neun chul-geun-ha-ji a-na(-yo)

■ May I come in one hour late tomorrow morning?

내일 한 시간 늦게 출근해도 될까(요)?

nae-il han si-gan neut-gge chul-geun-hae-do doel-gga(-yo)?

Getting Off Work 1

■ What time do you think you'll get off?

몇 시에 퇴근할 수 있어(요)?

myeot si-e toe-geun-hal ssu i-sseo(-yo)?

■ What time do you get off?

언제 퇴근해(요)?

eon-je toe-geun-hae(-yo)?

■ I'm off at seven o'clock sharp.

7시 정각에 퇴근해(요).

il-gop-ssi jeong-ga-ge toe-geun-hae(-yo)

■ He doesn't leave until ten.

그는 10시가 넘어서야 퇴근해(요).

geu-neun yeol-ssi-ga neo-meo-seo-ya toe-geun-hae(-yo)

■ He just called it a day.

그는 막 퇴근했어(요).

geu-neun mak toe-geun-hae-sseo(-yo)

Getting Off Work 2

■ Unless there's anything else,
I'm leaving for the day.

무슨 다른 일이 없으면,
퇴근할게(요).

mu-seun da-reun i-ri eop-sseu-myeon,
toe-geun-hal-gge(-yo)

■ Okay, see you after work.

네, 퇴근하고 봐(요).

ne, toe-geun-ha-go bwa(-yo)

■ How about a drink after?

퇴근하고 한잔 어때(요)?

toe-geun-ha-go han-jan eo-ddae(-yo)?

■ Do you often go for a drink
after work?

퇴근하고 종종 술 마시러 가(요)?

toe-teun-ha-go jong-jong sul ma-si-reo
ga(-yo)?

■ I'm starving. Let's grab a bite
after work.

좀 배고픈데.
퇴근하고 간단하게 좀 먹자.

jom bae-go-peun-de.
toe-geun-ha-go gan-dan-ha-ge jom
meok-jja

Leaving Early

■ Is it okay if I leave work early
today?

오늘 좀 일찍 퇴근하면 어때(요)?

o-neul jom il-jjik toe-geun-ha-myeon
eo-ddae(-yo)?

■ Jong-seok got off work early.

종석 씨는 일찍 퇴근했어(요).

jong-seok ssi-neun il-jjik
toe-geun-hae-sseo(-yo)

■ Deputy manager Park took off
early yesterday.

박 대리는 어제 조퇴했어(요).

bak dae-ri-neun eo-je jo-toe-hae-sseo(-yo)

■ Yesterday I wasn't feeling well,
so I left work early.

어제 몸이 별로 안 좋아서,
조퇴했어(요).

eo-je mo-mi byeol-ro an jo-a-seo,
jo-toe-hae-sseo(-yo)

■ I had to leave early because of a
doctor's appointment.

병원 예약 때문에 조퇴했어(요).

byeong-won ye-yak ddae-mu-ne
jo-toe-hae-sseo(-yo)

Jobs 직업 ji-geop

n. job, occupation, profession 직업 [지겁] ji-geop	n. teacher 교사 [교:사] gyo-sa	n. police officer 경찰 [경:찰] gyeong-chal
n. firefighter 소방관 [소방관] so-bang-gwan	n. engineer 엔지니어 [엔지니어] en-ji-ni-eo	n. programmer 프로그래머 [프로그래머] peu-ro-geu-rae-meo
n. cook 요리사 [요리사] yo-ri-sa n. chef 주방장 [주방장] ju-bang-jang	n. baker 제빵사 [제:빵사] je-bbang-sa	n. merchant, trader, seller 상인 [상인] sang-in
n. hairdresser, beautician 미용사 [미:용사] mi-yong-sa	n. pharmacist 약사 [약싸] yak-ssa	n. reporter 기자 [기자] gi-ja

In Charge 1

■ I'm in charge of marketing.
마케팅을 담당합니다.
ma-ke-ting-eul dam-dang-ham-ni-da

■ I'm in sales.
영업 쪽 일을 합니다.
yeong-eop jjok i-reul ham-ni-da

■ I work with Jeong-min.
정민 씨와 함께 일합니다.
jeong-min ssi-wa ham-gge il-ham-ni-da

■ I'm a section chief.
과장입니다.
gwa-jang-im-ni-da

■ What kind of work experience
do you have?
어떠한 업무 경험을 갖고 있어요?
eo-ddeo-han eom-mu gyeong-heo-
meul gat-ggo i-sseo-yo?

■ Sales is not my area.
영업은 제 분야가 아닙니다.
yeong-eo-beun je bu-nya-ga
a-nim-ni-da

■ The task exceeds his ability.
이 일은 그가 감당할 수
없어(요).
i i-reun geu-ga gam-dang-hal ssu
eop-sseo(-yo)

In Charge 2

■ He's highly qualified with good
interpersonal skills.
그는 업무 능력도 뛰어나고
인간관계도 좋아(요).
geu-neun eom-mu neung-nyeok-ddo
ddwi-eo-na-go in-gan-gwan-gye-do
jo-a(-yo)

■ I'm in charge of this project.
제가 이 프로젝트를 담당하고
있습니다.
je-ga i peu-ro-jek-teu-reul dam-dang-
ha-go it-sseum-ni-da

■ Editing is not my area.
I'm in design.
편집은 제 담당이 아닙니다.
디자인을 담당하고 있어요.
pyeon-ji-beun je dam-dang-i a-nim-ni-da.
di-ja-i-neul dam-dang-ha-go i-sseo-yo

■ Who is in charge of accounting?
누가 회계 업무를 담당하나요?
nu-ga hoe-gye eom-mu-reul
dam-dang-ha-na-yo?

■ Myeong-ho Kim will replace me
in export services.
김명호 씨가 제 대신 수출
업무를 담당할 겁니다.
kim-myeong-ho ssi-ga je dae-sin su-chul
eom-mu-reul dam-dang-hal ggeom-ni-da

Busy at Work 1

■ I work hard.

열심히 일해(요).

yeol-ssim-hi il-hae(-yo)

■ All I have time for these days is work and sleep.

요즘 잠자는 것을 빼고는 일만 해(요).

yo-jeum jam-ja-neun geo-seul bbae-go-neun il-man hae(-yo)

■ I'm tied up at work.

요즘 일이 바빠(요).

yo-jeum i-ri ba-bba(-yo)

■ I've got a pretty tight schedule today.

오늘 일정은 빡빡한 편이에요.

o-neul il-jjeong-eun bbak-bba-kan pyeo-ni-e-yo

■ I have a lot of work that I have to finish today.

오늘 끝내야 할 일이 많아(요).

o-neul ggeun-nae-ya hal i-ri ma-na(-yo)

Korean Money

The won is the official currency of South Korea.

· Coins

10 won

50 won

100 won

500 won

There are 1 won and 5 won coins too, but due to inflation, no one uses them much these days. The 10 won coin is rarely used.

· Bank Notes

1,000 won

5,000 won

10,000 won

50,000 won

The 50,000 won note, released in 2009, bears a portrait of Saimdang Shin (신사임당). She was the mother of I Yi (이이), the Confucian scholar illustrated on the 5,000 won note.

Busy at Work 2

■ I'm going to pull an all-nighter.

바빠서 밤을 샐 거예요.

ba-bba-seo ba-meul sael ggeo-ye-yo

■ We are short of workers.

요즘 일손이 부족해(요).

yo-jeum il-sso-ni bu-jo-kae(-yo)

■ I'm afraid we can't make the deadline.

마감 기한까지 다 할 수 없어(요).

ma-gam gi-han-gga-ji da hal ssu eop-sseo(-yo)

■ She waded through a mountain of paperwork.

그녀는 산더미 같은 서류 업무를 겨우 다 했어(요).

geu-nyeo-neun san-ddeo-mi ga-teun seo-ryu eom-mu-reul gyeo-u da hae-sseo(-yo)

■ Hui-seong is jaded from years of overwork.

희성 씨는 과도한 업무 때문에 죽을 지경이에요.

hi-seong ssi-neun gwa-do-han eom-mu ddae-mu-ne ju-geul ji-gyeong-i-e-yo

Checking Progress 1

■ Back to work.

돌아가서 네 일을 하세요.

do-ra-ga-seo ne i-reul ha-se-yo

■ Finish this by the end of the day.

오늘 중으로 이것을 끝내(세요).

o-neul jung-eu-ro i-geo-seul ggeun-nae(-se-yo)

■ Keep up the good work.

계속 수고들 해(요).

gye-sok su-go-deul hae(-yo)

Tip: Korean bosses often say this to encourage their employees.

■ Are you ready for today's presentation?

오늘 프레젠테이션 준비 다 됐어(요)?

o-neul peu-re-jen-te-i-syeon jun-bi da dwae-sseo(-yo)?

■ What's happening to the new project?

새 프로젝트는 어떻게 진행되고 있어(요)?

sae peu-ro-jek-teu-neun eo-ddeo-ke jin-haeng-doe-go i-sseo(-yo)?

■ How's the project going?

이 프로젝트는 잘되고 있어(요)?

i peu-ro-jek-teu-neun jal-doe-go i-sseo(-yo)?

Checking Progress 2

■ What's the best way to handle this problem?

이 문제를 처리하는 데 가장 좋은 방법은 뭘까(요)?

i mun-je-reul cheo-ri-ha-neun de ga-jang jo-eun bang-beo-beun mwol-gga(-yo)?

■ Send the papers over this afternoon.

오늘 오후에 그 서류를 보내 주세요.

o-neul o-hu-e geu seo-ryu-reul bo-nae ju-se-yo

■ Can you put the survey results on my desk?

시장 조사 결과를 내 책상에 둘래(요)?

si-jang jo-sa gyeol-gwa-reul nae chaek-ssang-e dul-rae(-yo)?

■ Would you sort out these files?

이 서류철들을 정리해 주실래요?

i seo-ryu-cheol-deu-reul jeong-ri-hae ju-sil-rae-yo?

■ Could you make five copies?

다섯 부 복사해 줄 수 있어(요)?

da-seot bu bok-ssa-hae jul ssu i-sseo(-yo)?

Replying to Requests

■ When do you need it?

언제 필요하시죠?

eon-je pi-ryo-ha-si-jyo?

■ I'm on it.

바로 하겠습니다.

ba-ro ha-get-sseum-ni-da

■ It shouldn't be a problem.

문제 없습니다.

mun-je eop-sseum-ni-da

■ Everything is under control.

잘되고 있습니다.

jal-doe-go it-sseum-ni-da

■ I'll give it my best shot.

최선을 다하겠습니다.

choe-seo-neul da-ha-get-sseum-ni-da

■ I'll try to get the hang of things quickly.

업무를 속히 파악하도록 노력하겠습니다.

eom-mu-reul so-ki pa-a-ka-do-rok no-ryeo-ka-get-sseum-ni-da

■ We're waiting for the manager's decision.

저희는 부장님의 결정을 기다리고 있습니다.

jeo-hi-neun bu-jang-ni-me gyeol-jjeong-eul gi-da-ri-go it-sseum-ni-da

The Work of Others

- He's attending to business in Busan.

  그는 업무차 부산에 있습니다.

  geu-neun eom-mu-cha bu-sa-ne
  it-sseum-ni-da

- He's at a conference.
  He'll be back Tuesday.

  그는 콘퍼런스에 갔어요.
  화요일에 돌아옵니다.

  geu-neun kon-peo-reon-seu-e ga-sseo-yo.
  hwa-yo-i-re do-ra-om-ni-da

- She's away on business and I'm taking over for her now.

  그녀는 업무 때문에 출장 중이라,
  제가 대신 업무를 합니다.

  geu-nyeo-neun eom-mu ddae-mu-ne
  chul-jjang jung-i-ra, je-ga dae-sin
  eom-mu-reul ham-ni-da

- When is a good time to call?

  언제 통화하기 좋아(요)?

  eon-je tong-hwa-ha-gi jo-a(-yo)?

- Tell me the do's and don'ts of your job.

  이 일의 준수 사항과 금지
  사항을 말씀해 주세요.

  i i-re jun-su sa-hang-gwa geum-ji
  sa-hang-eul mal-sseum-hae ju-se-yo

Working Conditions

- We don't work Saturdays.

  토요일에는 근무하지 않습니다.

  to-yo-i-re-neun geun-mu-ha-ji
  an-sseum-ni-da

- We're open five days a week.

  주 5일 근무합니다.

  ju o-il geun-mu-ham-ni-da

- Because there are more holidays, we have fewer working days.

  휴일이 늘어나서, 근무 일수가
  줄어들었습니다.

  hyu-i-ri neu-reo-na-seo, geun-mu il-ssu-
  ga ju-reo-deu-reot-sseum-ni-da

- The office dress code is business formal.

  사무실에서는 정장을 입어야
  합니다.

  sa-mu-si-re-seo-neun jeong-jang-eul
  i-beo-ya ham-ni-da

- We have flexible working hours.

  업무 시간은 자유로운 편이에요.

  eom-mu si-ga-neun ja-yu-ro-un pyeo-
  ni-e-yo

Get-togethers

■ We're having a staff dinner this evening.
오늘 저녁에 회식이 있어(요).
o-neul jeo-nyeo-ge hoe-si-gi i-sseo(-yo)

■ Let's discuss it over dinner.
저녁에 식사하면서 토론합시다.
jeo-nyeo-ge sik-ssa-ha-myeon-seo
to-ron-hap-ssi-da

■ They say a company dinner is also an extension of work.
회식도 업무의 연장이래(요).
hoe-sik-ddo eom-mu-e
yeon-jang-i-rae(-yo)

■ Did you dine with them somewhere last week?
지난주에 당신은 그들과 회식했어요?
ji-nan-ju-e dang-si-neun geu-deul-gwa
hoe-si-kae-sseo-yo?

■ A group of us from work are going out to dinner on Friday.
직장 동료들끼리 금요일 저녁에 회식을 할 거예요.
jik-jjang dong-nyo-deul-ggi-ri geu-myo-il
jeo-nyeo-ge hoe-si-geul hal ggeo-ye-yo

■ I'd like to propose a toast.
다같이 건배하죠.
da-ga-chi geon-bae-ha-jyo

Salary 1

■ When do we get paid?
급여일이 언제예요?
geu-byeo-i-ri eon-je-ye-yo?

■ I get paid on the 25th of the month.
매월 25일에 급여가 나옵니다.
mae-wol i-si-bo-i-re geu-byeo-ga
na-om-ni-da

■ He has a very decent salary.
그는 월급을 아주 많이 받아(요).
geu-neun wol-geu-beul a-ju ma-ni
ba-da(-yo)

■ It's difficult to survive on my salary.
이 급여로는 살기 빠듯해(요).
i geu-byeo-ro-neun sal-gi bba-deu-tae(-yo)

■ Your raises are outlined in the contract.
월급 인상은 계약에 준합니다.
wol-geup in-sang-eun gye-ya-ge
jun-ham-ni-da

■ I got a raise this month.
이번 달에 월급이 올랐어(요).
i-beon da-re wol-geu-bi ol-ra-sseo(-yo)

■ I get paid by the hour.
시급으로 받아(요).
si-geu-beu-ro ba-da(-yo)

Salary 2

- I just got paid yesterday.
  I'm loaded.

  어제 급여를 막 받았거든(요).
  주머니 사정이 좋아(요).

  eo-je geu-byeo-reul mak
  ba-dat-ggeo-deun(-yo).
  ju-meo-ni sa-jeong-i jo-a(-yo)

- Taxes are deducted from my
  salary.

  급여에서 세금을 공제합니다.

  geu-byeo-e-seo se-geu-meul
  gong-je-ham-ni-da

- Have you ever asked for a raise?

  월급을 올려 달라고 한 적
  있어(요)?

  wol-geu-beul ol-ryeo dal-ra-go han jeok
  i-sseo(-yo)?

- He got a pay cut.

  그는 감봉됐어(요).

  geu-neun gam-bong-dwae-sseo(-yo)

- What's a fair salary for this job?

  이 일의 적절한 급여는 뭐죠?

  i i-re jeok-jjeol-han geu-byeo-neun
  mwo-jyo?

Benefits

- Do you get paid overtime?

  잔업 수당 있어(요)?

  ja-neop su-dang i-sseo(-yo)?

- You are paid extra for overtime.

  초과 근무를 하면 수당이
  있어(요).

  cho-gwa geun-mu-reul ha-myeon su-
  dang-i i-sseo(-yo)

- I worked extra hours without
  being paid.

  야근을 했는데 잔업 수당을 받지
  못했어(요).

  ya-geu-neul haen-neun-de ja-neop
  su-dang-eul bat-jji mo-tae-sseo(-yo)

- I claimed unemployment
  benefit.

  실업 수당을 신청했어(요).

  si-reop su-dang-eul sin-cheong-hae-
  sseo(-yo)

- Chang-min forgot to bill for
  some extra work he did.

  창민이는 잔업 수당 청구하는 걸
  잊어버렸어(요).

  chang-mi-ni-neun ja-neop su-dang
  cheong-gu-ha-neun geol
  i-jeo-beo-ryeo-sseo(-yo)

Bonuses

■ I get five bonuses a year.

1년에 다섯 번 상여금을
받아(요).

il-ryeo-ne da-seot beon sang-yeo-geu-
meul ba-da(-yo)

■ Our bonuses are based on profit.

수익이 좋아야 상여금이
나옵니다.

su-i-gi jo-a-ya sang-yeo-geu-mi
na-om-ni-da

■ He received a special bonus.

그는 특별 상여금을 받았어(요).

geu-neun teuk-bbyeol sang-yeo-geu-
meul ba-da-sseo(-yo)

■ My boss is so cheap that he never gives bonuses.

사장님이 인색해서, 상여금을
절대 안 줄 거예요.

sa-jang-ni-mi in-sae-kae-seo,
sang-yeo-geu-meul jeol-ddae an jul
ggeo-ye-yo

■ The company gave an across-the-board salary increase of 5 percent.

회사는 전 직원에게 5퍼센트
인상된 상여금을 지급했습니다.

hoe-sa-neun jeon ji-gwo-ne-ge
o-peo-sen-teu in-sang-doen
sang-yeo-geu-meul ji-geu-paet-sseum-
ni-da

Celebrations

There are two special celebrations for babies in Korea. One is **baegil** (백일, the one-hundredth day after the baby's birth) and the other "dol" (돌, the first birthday).

When times weren't so prosperous, the chances of reaching one's first birthday were much lower. Parents used to invite relatives, friends and neighbors to celebrate what we consider today early milestones.

Doljabi (돌잡이) is an eagerly awaited part of "dol," the first birthday, where a number of objects are placed before the baby, such as a book, a brush, rice, a length of yarn, and a bow (and arrow). The belief is that the baby will reveal something about their destiny depending on what they grab. The book or brush are signs of intelligence, rice means wealth, the yarn means a long life and the bow means bravery. These days, a pencil might take the place of a brush or book and money might be used in place of rice. A stethoscope might be used in the hope that the child will grow up to be a doctor.

A person's sixtieth birthday (환갑 [hwan-gap]) used to be celebrated with a party as well. With life expectancies now into the eighties though, a seventieth birthday (칠순 [chil-ssun]) is more likely to be treated as special.

Business Trips

▪ I'm going on a business trip next week.

다음 주에 출장갑니다.

da-eum ju-e chul-jjang-gam-ni-da

▪ I have a two-day business trip to Daegu.

대구로 이틀 출장갑니다.

dae-gu-ro i-teul chul-jjang-gam-ni-da

▪ I was on a business trip for a month in the US.

한 달 동안 미국으로 출장을 갔어(요).

han dal dong-an mi-gu-geu-ro chul-jjang-eul ga-sseo(-yo)

▪ Can you write it off as a business expense?

그것도 출장 경비로 청구할 수 있어(요)?

geu-geot-ddo chul-jjang gyeong-bi-ro cheong-gu-hal ssu i-sseo(-yo)?

▪ How did you like your business trip to Europe?

유럽 출장 어땠어(요)?

yu-reop chul-jjang eo-ddae-sseo(-yo)?

Stress & Complaints

▪ I'm the one who is most stressed.

스트레스를 가장 많이 받는 건 나예요.

seu-teu-re-seu-reul ga-jang ma-ni ban-neun geon na-ye-yo

▪ How well do you handle stress?

당신은 스트레스를 어떻게 관리하세요?

dang-si-neun seu-teu-re-seu-reul eo-ddeo-ke gwan-ri-ha-se-yo?

▪ All this stress is affecting my health.

이 모든 스트레스가 내 건강을 해치고 있어(요).

i mo-deun seu-teu-re-seu-ga nae geon-gang-eul hae-chi-go i-sseo(-yo)

▪ I can't work like this.

이런 식으로 일할 수 없어(요).

i-reon si-geu-ro il-hal ssu eop-sseo(-yo)

▪ I can't stand it any longer.

더 이상 못 참겠어(요).

deo i-sang mot cham-gge-sseo(-yo)

Talking About Colleagues

▪ What's it like to work with him?

그와 함께 일하기 어때(요)?

geu-wa ham-gge il-ha-gi eo-ddae(-yo)?

▪ She is always one step behind.

그녀는 일하는 것이 항상
한 박자 늦어(요).

geu-nyeo-neun il-ha-neun geo-si hang-
sang han bak-jja neu-jeo(-yo)

▪ He's so competitive.

그는 승부욕이 강해(요).

geu-neun seung-bu-yo-gi gang-hae(-yo)

▪ She is a workaholic.

그녀는 일 중독자예요.

geu-nyeo-neun il jung-dok-jja-ye-yo

▪ He got in through his connections.

그 사람은 낙하산으로
들어왔어(요).

geu sa-ra-meun na-ka-sa-neu-ro
deu-reo-wa-sseo(-yo)

Promotions 1

▪ You deserve a promotion.

당신은 승진할 만하죠.

dang-si-neun seung-jin-hal man-ha-jyo

▪ Do you think you'll get promoted this time?

이번에 승진할 수 있을 것
같아(요)?

i-beo-ne seung-jin-hal ssu i-sseul ggeot
ga-ta(-yo)?

▪ Min Dok-go got the promotion because he lives and breathes work.

독고 민 씨는 열심히 일해서
승진했어(요).

dok-ggo min ssi-neun yeol-ssim-hi
il-hae-seo seung-jin-hae-sseo(-yo)

Tip: 독고 "Dok-go" is a family name in Korea.
Most family names have only one syllable.

▪ I hear you've been promoted to sales director.

그가 영업 부장으로
승진했다면서(요).

geu-ga yeong-eop bu-jang-eu-ro
seung-jin-haet-dda-myeon-seo(-yo)

▪ I hope you will be promoted next year.

내년에 승진하기를 바랍니다.

nae-nyeo-ne seung-jin-ha-gi-reul
ba-ram-ni-da

Promotions 2

■ He got promoted under a year ago.

그는 승진한 지 1년이
안 됐어(요).

geu-neun seung-jin-han ji il-ryeo-ni
an dwae-sseo(-yo)

■ He flattered his boss to get a
promotion.

그는 승진하려고 상사한테
아부해(요).

geu-neun seung-jin-ha-ryeo-go
sang-sa-han-te a-bu-hae(-yo)

■ He cut me out of the promotion
this time.

그는 이번 승진에서 나를
제외했어(요).

geu-neun i-beon seung-ji-ne-seo na-reul
je-oe-hae-sseo(-yo)

■ His promotion has gone to his
head.

그는 승진하고 나서 잘난 척해(요).

geu-neun seung-jin-ha-go na-seo jal-ran
cheo-kae(-yo)

■ Did you hear about Seong-hui's
promotion?

성희 씨가 승진했다고
들었어(요)?

seong-hi ssi-ga seung-jin-haet-dda-go
deu-reo-sseo(-yo)?

Holidays 1

■ The manager is on leave.

과장님은 휴가 중이신데요.

gwa-jang-ni-meun hyu-ga
jung-i-sin-de-yo

■ When are you going back to
work?

휴가는 언제 끝나(요)?

hyu-ga-neun eon-je ggeun-na(-yo)?

■ Can I get the day off tomorrow?

내일 휴가 낼 수 있을까(요)?

nae-il hyu-ga nael ssu i-sseul-gga(-yo)?

■ Geon-ho deserves a promotion.
He works so hard.

건호 씨는 포상 휴가를
받을 만해(요).
아주 열심히 일하거든(요).

geon-ho ssi-neun po-sang hyu-ga-reul
ba-deul man-hae(-yo).
a-ju yeol-ssim-hi il-ha-geo-deun(-yo)

■ Hong-min's back from his
holiday.

홍민 씨는 휴가를 잘 보내고
직장에 복귀했어(요).

hong-min ssi-neun hyu-ga-reul jal
bo-nae-go jik-jjang-e
bok-ggwi-hae-sseo(-yo)

Holidays 2

■ I took a sick day today.
오늘 병가를 냈어(요).
o-neul byeong-ga-reul nae-sseo(-yo)

■ Eun-jin Hong is on maternity leave.
홍은진 씨는 출산 휴가 중이에요.
hong-eun-jin ssi-neun chul-ssan hyu-ga jung-i-e-yo

■ She can't take time off until next month.
그녀는 다음 달까지 휴가를 미뤄야 해(요).
geu-nyeo-neun da-eum dal-gga-ji hyu-ga-reul mi-rwo-ya hae(-yo)

■ I saved up some money for the holidays.
휴가 때 쓰려고 돈을 아꼈어(요).
hyu-ga ddae sseu-ryeo-go do-neul a-ggyeo-sseo(-yo)

■ I'll take a leave of absence from my job to travel.
여행을 가려고 휴직할 거예요.
yeo-haeng-eul ga-ryeo-go hyu-ji-kal ggeo-ye-yo

Korean Table Manners Part 1

• Respect Your Elders
Here's another reason to inquire as to someone's age. When sharing a communal dish at the table, show respect to your elders by letting them serve themselves first, and then waiting until they've taken their first bite before you start eating. It's a small gesture but a meaningful one and besides, your food isn't going anywhere!.

• Acknowledge the Meal
The phrase 잘 먹겠습니다 [jal meok-gget-sseum-ni-da] , which is said just before you start eating, might seem more of a mouthful than the food itself but say it anyway. It means "I will eat well" and is a way of showing gratitude for what you are about to eat and to those who made it.

• Adjust Your Tempo
Eating is regarded as a social occasion in Korea, not a race, in either direction. If you're lagging, speed up. If you're "winning," do your tablemates the courtesy of slowing down.

Before the Meeting

■ I now call this meeting to order!

이제 회의를 시작합시다!

i-je hoe-i-reul si-ja-kap-ssi-da!

■ Let's get started and talk about today's agenda!

오늘의 의제부터 진행하겠습니다!

o-neu-re ui-je-bu-teo
jin-haeng-ha-get-sseum-ni-da!

■ Should we begin with the main issue of the meeting?

회의의 주요 의제부터 시작할까요?

hoe-i-e ju-yo ui-je-bu-teo
si-ja-kal-gga-yo?

■ There are two items on the agenda.

두 가지 항목이 안건으로 있습니다.

du ga-ji hang-mo-gi an-ggeo-neu-ro
it-sseum-ni-da

■ We will discuss each topic for twenty-five minutes.

안건마다 약 25분간 토론합니다.

an-ggeon-ma-da yak i-si-bo-bun-gan
to-ron-ham-ni-da

During the Meeting 1

■ Next up.

다음.

da-eum

■ Let's see what's next on our agenda.

다음 의제를 보십시오.

da-eum ui-je-reul bo-sip-ssi-o

■ May I have your attention, please?

주목해 주시겠습니까?

ju-mo-kae ju-si-get-sseum-ni-gga?

■ Let's get down to business.

지금 본론을 말하겠습니다.

ji-geum bol-ro-neul
mal-ha-get-sseum-ni-da

■ Let's move on!

계속 진행합시다!

gye-sok jin-haeng-hap-ssi-da!

■ Does anybody have any questions?

질문 있으신 분?

jil-mun i-sseu-sin bun?

■ What's the bottom line?

요점이 뭐죠?

yo-jjeo-mi mwo-jyo?

During the Meeting 2

■ Do you have any comments on this?

이것에 대해 이견 있습니까?

i-geo-se dae-hae i-gyeon it-sseum-ni-gga?

■ Who agrees?

동의하시는 분?

dong-i-ha-si-neun bun?

■ Is there anyone who disagrees with this plan?

이 안건에 대해 반대하는 분 계십니까?

i an-ggeo-ne dae-hae ban-dae-ha-neun bun gye-sim-ni-gga?

■ I should mention one more thing.

한 가지 더 짚고 넘어가겠습니다.

han ga-ji deo jip-ggo neo-meo-ga-get-sseum-ni-da

■ The plan needs some modification.

그 계획은 수정이 좀 필요합니다.

geu gye-hoe-geun su-jeong-i jom pi-ryo-ham-ni-da

■ Can I get back to you on that?

다음에 대답해 드려도 될까요?

da-eu-me dae-da-pae deu-ryeo-do doel-gga-yo?

Concluding the Meeting

■ So what I'm saying is that there are some problems with this project.

그래서 제 말씀은 이 프로젝트에 문제가 좀 있다는 겁니다.

geu-rae-seo je mal-sseu-meun i peu-ro-jek-teu-e mun-je-ga jom it-dda-neun geom-ni-da

■ We'll take questions at the end.

질문은 마지막에 받겠습니다.

jil-mu-neun ma-ji-ma-ge bat-gget-ssem-ni-da

■ We have covered all the topics today.

오늘 모든 의제를 다 토론했습니다.

o-neul mo-deun ui-je-reul da to-ron-haet-sseum-ni-da

■ The meeting is over.

이상으로 회의를 마칩니다.

i-sang-eu-ro hoe-i-reul ma-chim-ni-da

■ The meeting is adjourned.

회의를 연기하겠습니다.

hoe-i-reul yeon-gi-ha-get-sseum-ni-da

Meeting Clients 1

■ Here's my card.

이것은 제 명함입니다.

i-geo-seun je myeong-ha-mim-ni-da

■ I'm so glad you took time to visit our company.

시간 내어 저희 회사를 방문해 주셔서 기쁩니다.

si-gan nae-eo jeo-hi hoe-sa-reul
bang-mun-hae ju-syeo-seo
gi-bbeum-ni-da

■ Could I meet the person in charge?

담당자를 만날 수 있어요?

dam-dang-ja-reul man-nal ssu i-sseo-yo?

■ Anytime.

언제든지요.

eon-je-deun-ji-yo

■ I'm here to meet Ho-jun Hwang.

황호준 씨를 만나러 왔습니다.

hwang-ho-jun ssi-reul man-na-reo
wat-sseum-ni-da

■ The head of the department will be right out.

부장님이 곧 나오실 겁니다.

bu-jang-ni-mi got na-o-sil ggeom-ni-da

Meeting Clients 2

■ He's been expecting you.

그가 기다리고 있습니다.

geu-ga gi-da-ri-go it-sseum-ni-da

■ He will see you now.

(방으로) 들어가 보세요.

(bang-eu-ro) deu-reo-ga bo-se-yo

■ Then let's meet at three o'clock.

그럼 오후 3시에 만납시다.

geu-reom o-hu se-si-e man-nap-ssi-da

■ Can I come to meet you tomorrow?

내일 만나러 가도 됩니까?

nae-il man-na-reo ga-do doem-ni-gga?

■ Mun-seong Kim is in charge of new accounts.

김문성 씨가 새 거래처를 관리합니다.

gim-mun-seong ssi-ga sae
geo-rae-cheo-reul gwan-ri-ham-ni-da

Public Relations

■ Please see our company website for details.

구체적인 내용은 저희 회사의 공식 사이트를 참고하세요.

gu-che-jeo-gin nae-yong-eun jeo-hi hoe-sa-e gong-sik sa-i-teu-reul cham-go-ha-se-yo

■ Have you ever checked our homepage?

저희 회사의 홈페이지를 보신 적 있습니까?

jeo-hi hoe-sa-e hom-pe-i-ji-reul bo-sin jeok it-sseum-ni-gga?

■ This is the latest brochure.

이것은 최신 브로슈어입니다.

i-geo-seun choe-sin beu-ro-syu-eo-im-ni-da

■ Please show me the catalog.

카탈로그 좀 보여 주세요.

ka-tal-ro-geu jom bo-yeo ju-se-yo

■ We can send you the catalog first, if you like.

원하시면 카탈로그를 보내 드리겠습니다.

won-ha-si-myeon ka-tal-ro-geu-reul bo-nae deu-ri-get-sseum-ni-da

Product Information 1

■ Let me explain how this works.

어떻게 작동하는지 설명해 드리겠습니다.

eo-ddeo-ke jak-ddong-ha-neun-ji seol-myeong-hae deu-ri-get-sseum-ni-da

■ If you need product information, press "3" now.

상품 정보가 필요하면, 3번을 누르십시오.

sang-pum jeong-bo-ga pi-ryo-ha-myeon, sam-beo-neul nu-reu-sip-ssi-o

■ What are the main features?

주요 기능이 뭐죠?

ju-yo gi-neung-i mwo-jyo?

■ This is one of our popular models.

이것은 저희 회사의 가장 잘 나가는 모델 중 하나입니다.

i-geo-seun jeo-hi hoe-sa-e ga-jang jal na-ga-neun mo-del jung ha-na-im-ni-da

■ We stand behind our products.

품질을 보장합니다.

pum-ji-reul bo-jang-ham-ni-da

Product Information 2

- The newest goods are cutting edge.
이 상품은 최신식입니다.
i sang-pu-meun choe-sin-si-gim-ni-da

- It's pocket-sized.
주머니에 쏙 들어가는 작은 크기입니다.
ju-meo-ni-e ssok deu-reo-ga-neun ja-geun keu-gi-im-ni-da

- It's lightning fast.
번개처럼 빠릅니다.
beon-gae-cheo-reom bba-reum-ni-da

- We'll refund your money if you don't like it.
마음에 들지 않으시면, 환불하실 수 있습니다.
ma-eu-me deul-ji a-neu-si-myeon, hwan-bul-ha-sil ssu it-sseum-ni-da

- If there are any questions, please let us know.
문의 사항이 있으면, 저희에게 알려 주세요.
mu-ni sa-hang-i i-sseu-myeon, jeo-hi-e-ge al-ryeo ju-se-yo

Talking Business

- Price is the most important factor.
가격이 제일 중요합니다.
ga-gyeo-gi je-il jung-yo-ham-ni-da

- May I ask you what your market share is?
시장 점유율이 어떻게 되는지 알 수 있을까요?
si-jang jeo-myu-yu-ri eo-ddeo-ke doe-neun-ji al ssu i-sseul-gga-yo?

- How long is the warranty?
보증 기간은 얼마나 되나요?
bo-jeung gi-ga-neun eol-ma-na doe-na-yo?

- How long does this contract remain in effect?
이 계약은 언제까지 유효합니까?
i gye-ya-geun eon-je-gga-ji yu-hyo-ham-ni-gga?

- What's the price per unit?
상품 단가는 얼마입니까?
sang-pum dan-gga-neun eol-ma-im-ni-gga?

Ordering

■ I'd like to order 2,000 units.

2천 개를 구매하겠습니다.

i-cheon gae-reul
gu-mae-ha-get-sseum-ni-da

■ What quantity did you have in mind?

주문량이 얼마나 됩니까?

ju-mun-nyang-i eol-ma-na doem-ni-gga?

■ What is the minimum order for this product?

이 상품의 최소 주문량은 얼마입니까?

i sang-pu-me choe-so ju-mun-nyang-eun eol-ma-im-ni-gga?

■ I'd like to change my order.

제 주문을 바꾸려고 합니다.

je ju-mu-neul ba-ggu-ryeo-go ham-ni-da

■ Do you have a problem with the contract?

계약에 문제가 있습니까?

gye-ya-ge mun-je-ga it-sseum-ni-gga?

■ That's a tall order.

그 주문은 좀 곤란합니다.

geu ju-mu-neun jom gol-ran-ham-ni-da

Korean Table Manners Part 2

• Thou Shalt Not Raise Thy Bowl

However tempting it is to raise your bowl to your mouth as if it was a coffee cup, don't. That last bit of broth or rice is just as easy to navigate with a spoon and doesn't look nearly as Neanderthal.

• Utensil Use

Different utensils have different jobs, and should be held in different hands. Choose one hand for your spoon and one for your chopsticks. Holding both in one hand is bad form. In addition, avoid impaling your chopsticks vertically in your rice (or anyone else's) as this resembles a funeral rite for the deceased.

• The Politics of Pouring

With wine or beer, all the liquids of cheer, be gracious and pour for others before yourself. Also use both hands to hold the bottle if you are serving, or your glass if you are being served. Finally, as always, elders come first. Be sure to refill their empty glasses and, if you can help it, never refuse a drink they offer.

Negotiations 1

How much can you go down?

가격을 얼마나 하향 조정할 수
있습니까?

ga-gyeo-geul eol-ma-na ha-hyang
jo-jeong-hal ssu it-sseum-ni-gga?

It's hard to reduce the price
that much.

가격을 그렇게 많이 깎는 것은
곤란합니다.

ga-gyeo-geul geu-reo-ke ma-ni ggang-
neun geo-seun gol-ran-ham-ni-da

Do you have volume discounts?

수량 할인이 있습니까?

su-ryang ha-ri-ni it-sseum-ni-gga?

The price depends on quantity.

구매 수량이 얼마냐에 따라
가격이 다릅니다.

gu-mae su-ryang-i eol-ma-nya-e dda-ra
ga-gyeo-gi da-reum-ni-da

If you order 2,000 or more, you
get a 10 percent discount.

2천 개 이상 구매하면,
10퍼센트 할인해 드립니다.

i-cheon gae i-sang gu-mae-ha-myeon,
sip-peo-sen-teu ha-rin-hae deu-rim-ni-da

Negotiations 2

What's your best offer?

최고 제시액은 얼마입니까?

choe-go je-si-ae-geun eol-ma-im-ni-gga?

There's no room to negotiate.

협상의 여지가 없습니다.

hyeop-ssang-e yeo-ji-ga
eop-sseum-ni-da

This is the best deal that we
can offer.

이것은 저희측 최저 가격입니다.

i-geo-seun jeo-hi-cheuk choe-jeo
ga-gyeo-gim-ni-da

Please offer your best price.

최저 가격을 제시해 주세요.

choe-jeo ga-gyeo-geul je-si-hae ju-se-yo

I'll give you a reply this week.

이번 주중으로 답변을
드리겠습니다.

i-beon ju-jung-eu-ro dap-bbyeo-neul
deu-ri-get-sseum-ni-da

Please put your signature here.

여기에 서명해 주십시오.

yeo-gi-e seo-myeong-hae ju-sip-ssi-o

Delivery

- When will you be able to deliver them?

  언제 납품할 수 있습니까?

  eon-je nap-pum-hal ssu it-sseum-ni-gga?

- Could you deliver five units by Wednesday?

  수요일까지 5대 납품해 주실 수 있습니까?

  su-yo-il-gga-ji da-seot-ddae nap-pum-hae ju-sil ssu it-sseum-ni-gga?

- We guarantee delivery by tomorrow noon.

  내일 정오까지 납품을 보장하겠습니다.

  nae-il jeong-o-gga-ji nap-pu-meul bo-jang-ha-get-sseum-ni-da

- It will be delivered in one week at the latest.

  늦어도 일주일 안에 납품합니다.

  neu-jeo-do il-jju-il a-ne nap-pum-ham-ni-da

- Can we find another supplier?

  다른 납품 업체를 찾을 수 있습니까?

  da-reun nap-pum eop-che-reul cha-jeul ssu it-sseum-ni-gga?

Claims

- We have a problem with your product.

  귀사의 상품에 문제가 있습니다.

  gwi-sa-e sang-pu-me mun-je-ga it-sseum-ni-da

- The goods do not match what I ordered.

  그 상품은 제가 주문한 것과 다릅니다.

  geu sang-pu-meun je-ga ju-mun-han geot-ggwa da-reum-ni-da

- I'd like to make a complaint.

  저희쪽은 클레임을 제기할 것입니다.

  jeo-hi-jjo-geun keul-re-i-meul je-gi-hal ggeo-sim-ni-da

- Unfortunately, several of the pieces were damaged in transit.

  유감이지만, 상품의 일부가 운송 도중 손상되었습니다.

  yu-ga-mi-ji-man, sang-pu-me il-bu-ga un-song do-jung son-sang-doe-eot-sseum-ni-da

- I'd like to speak with the person in charge.

  책임자와 이야기하고 싶습니다.

  chae-gim-ja-wa i-ya-gi-ha-go sip-sseum-ni-da

Claims Processing

■ We'll take care of it immediately.

당장 처리하겠습니다.

dang-jang cheo-ri-ha-get-sseum-ni-da

■ I'll check into it and call you back.

조사하고 바로
연락드리겠습니다.

jo-sa-ha-go ba-ro
yeol-rak-ddeu-ri-get-sseum-ni-da

■ We'll fix this for you as soon as
we can.

가능한 빨리 수리하겠습니다.

ga-neung-han bbal-ri
su-ri-ha-get-sseum-ni-da

■ Sorry for any inconvenience this
may have caused.

불편하게 해 드려서 죄송합니다.

bul-pyeon-ha-ge hae deu-ryeo-seo
joe-song-ham-ni-da

■ Anything else I can help you
with?

도와드릴 것이 더 있나요?

do-wa-deu-ril ggeo-si deo in-na-yo?

Dismissals

■ Dong-su Jeon got fired.

전동수 씨는 해고됐어(요).

jeon-dong-su ssi-neun
hae-go-dwae-sseo(-yo)

■ Why were you laid off?

왜 해고됐어(요)?

wae hae-go-dwae-sseo(-yo)?

■ More than a hundred people
will be laid off.

100명 이상이 해고될 거예요.

baeng-myeong i-sang-i hae-go-doel
ggeo-ye-yo

■ He made a mistake so he lost
his job.

그는 실수 때문에 해고됐습니다.

geu-neun sil-ssu ddae-mu-ne
hae-go-dwaet-sseum-ni-da

■ She wasn't a good fit for the
company.

그녀는 그 회사에 맞지
않았어(요).

geu-nyeo-neun geu hoe-sa-e mat-jji
a-na-sseo(-yo)

Retirement

▪ Seon-ju Hwang has retired and is enjoying himself.

황선주 씨는 퇴직하고 한가롭게 지내고 있어(요).

hwang-seon-ju ssi-neun toe-ji-ka-go han-ga-rop-gge ji-nae-go i-sseo(-yo)

▪ Did you hear that Hong-min is going to retire?

홍민 씨가 퇴직할 거라는 소식 들었어(요)?

hong-min ssi-ga toe-ji-kal ggeo-ra-neun so-sik deu-reo-sseo(-yo)?

▪ How long until you are eligible for retirement?

정년퇴직하려면 얼마나 남았습니까?

jeong-nyeon-toe-ji-ka-ryeo-myeon eol-ma-na na-mat-sseum-ni-gga?

▪ We have to save money for retirement.

퇴직을 대비하여 저축해야 합니다.

toe-ji-geul dae-bi-ha-yeo jeo-chu-kae-ya ham-ni-da

Job Hunting

▪ He's job hunting these days.

그는 요즘 일자리를 찾고 있어(요).

geu-neun yo-jeum il-jja-ri-reul chat-ggo i-sseo(-yo)

▪ Excuse me, do you have any positions available?

실례지만, 사람을 구하나요?

sil-rye-ji-man, sa-ra-meul gu-ha-na-yo?

▪ I'm calling about the position posted online.

인터넷의 모집 공고를 보고, 전화드렸습니다.

in-teo-ne-se mo-jip gong-go-reul bo-go, jeon-hwa-deu-ryeot-sseum-ni-da

▪ I want to apply for this position.

이 자리에 지원하고 싶습니다.

i ja-ri-e ji-won-ha-go sip-sseum-ni-da

▪ Does the position require experience?

그 일에는 경력이 필요합니까?

geu i-re-neun gyeong-nyeo-gi pi-ryo-ham-ni-gga?

▪ When will you have interviews?

언제 면접입니까?

eon-je myeon-jeo-bim-ni-gga?

Resumes

- Should I drop off my resume in person?

  이력서를 직접 제출해야 하나요?

  i-ryeok-sseo-reul jik-jjeop je-chul-hae-ya ha-na-yo?

- Send your resume by e-mail.

  이력서를 이메일로 보내 주세요.

  i-ryeok-sseo-reul i-me-il-ro bo-nae ju-se-yo

- Could you proofread my resume?

  내 이력서 좀 봐 줄 수 있어(요)?

  nae i-ryeok-sseo jom bwa jul ssu i-sseo(-yo)?

- It should be simple and easy to read.

  이력서는 최대한 간단명료해야 합니다.

  i-ryeok-sseo-neun choe-dae-han gan-dan-myeong-nyo-hae-ya ham-ni-da

- Can you help me with my resume and cover letter?

  이력서와 자기소개서를 도와줄 수 있어(요)?

  i-ryeok-sseo-wa ja-gi-so-gae-seo-reul do-wa-jul ssu i-sseo(-yo)?

Job Interviews

- What kind of salary are you looking for?

  연봉은 어느 정도 원하십니까?

  yeon-bong-eun eo-neu jeong-do won-ha-sim-ni-gga?

- When would you be able to start?

  언제부터 일할 수 있습니까?

  eon-je-bu-teo il-hal ssu it-sseum-ni-gga?

- Why did you leave your last job?

  전 직장을 왜 그만뒀습니까?

  jeon jik-jjang-eul wae geu-man-dwot-sseum-ni-gga?

- Why do you want to work here?

  왜 우리 회사에 지원했습니까?

  wae u-ri hoe-sa-e ji-won-haet-sseum-ni-gga?

- Do you have any experience working for a Korean company?

  한국 회사에서 일한 경력 있어요?

  han-guk hoe-sa-e-seo il-han gyeong-nyeok i-sseo-yo?

- Please tell me about your strengths.

  당신의 장점을 설명하세요.

  dang-si-ne jang-jjeo-meul seol-myeong-ha-se-yo

Chapter 10

For My Trip

Transportation 교통 gyo-tong

n. plane, airplane 비행기 [비행기] bi-haeng-gi 	n. airport 공항 [공항] gong-hang 	n. ticket 표 [표] pyo
n. airline ticket 항공권 [항:공꿘] hang-gong-ggwon	n. ticket office 매표소 [매:표소] mae-pyo-so 	n. destination 목적지 [목쩍찌] mok-jjeok-jji = 행선지 [행선지] haeng-seon-ji
n. boarding pass, boarding card 탑승권 [탑쏭꿘] tap-sseung-ggwon	n. passport 여권 [여꿘] yeo-ggwon = 패스포트 [패스포트] pae-seu-po-teu	n. visa 비자 [비자] bi-ja
n. terminal 터미널 [터미널] teo-mi-neol 	n. departure 출발 [출발] chul-bal 	n. arrival 도착 [도:착] do-chak
n. departure gate 탑승구 [탑쏭구] tap-sseung-gu 	n. take-off 이륙 [이:륙] i-ryuk 	n. landing 착륙 [창뉵] chang-nyuk
n. luggage 수하물 [수하물] su-ha-mul 	n. duty-free shop 면세점 [면:세점] myeon-se-jeom 	n. transfer 환승 [환:승] hwan-seung

n. train 기차 [기차]
gi-cha
= 열차 [열차]
yeol-cha

n. subway, metro
지하철 [지하철]
ji-ha-cheol

n. taxi, cab
택시 [택씨]
taek-ssi

n. bus 버스 [버스]
beo-seu

n. motorcycle
오토바이 [오토바이]]
o-to-ba-i

n. bicycle, bike
자전거 [자전거]
ja-jeon-geo

Booking 1

■ **Do you have any cheaper tickets?**

할인 항공권 있어요?

ha-rin hang-gong-ggwon i-sseo-yo?

■ **What's your destination?**

목적지가 어디예요?

mok-jjeok-jji-ga eo-di-ye-yo?

■ **When would you like to leave?**

언제 떠날 예정인가요?

eon-je ddeo-nal ye-jeong-in-ga-yo?

■ **One way or round trip?**

편도인가요 왕복인가요?

pyeon-do-in-ga-yo wang-bo-gin-ga-yo?

■ **What's the cheapest one-way ticket?**

가장 싼 편도표는 얼마입니까?

ga-jang ssan pyeon-do-pyo-neun eol-ma-im-ni-gga?

■ **Then give me a round-trip ticket, please.**

그럼, 왕복표로 주세요.

geu-reom, wang-bok-pyo-ro ju-se-yo

Booking 2

■ **I'd like to book a flight for Busan.**

부산으로 가는 항공권을 예약하려고 하는데요.

bu-sa-neu-ro ga-neun hang-gong-ggwo-neul ye-ya-ka-ryeo-go ha-neun-de-yo

■ **I want to reserve a seat from Seoul to San Francisco.**

서울에서 샌프란시스코로 가는 항공권을 예약하려고요.

seo-u-re-seo saen-peu-ran-si-seu-ko-ro ga-neun hang-gong-ggwo-neul ye-ya-ka-ryeo-go-yo

■ **Is that the earliest flight you have?**

그게 가장 이른 항공편인가요?

geu-ge ga-jang i-reun hang-gong-pyeo-nin-ga-yo?

■ **A one-way ticket to Jeju, please.**

제주도행 편도표 한 장 주세요.

je-ju-do-haeng pyeon-do-pyo han jang ju-se-yo

■ **How long is the round trip good for?**

왕복표의 유효 기간은 언제까지입니까?

wang-bok-pyo-e yu-hyo gi-ga-neun eon-je-gga-ji-im-ni-gga?

Flight Issues

■ I'd like to check my reservation.

예약한 항공권을 확인하려고
하는데요.

ye-ya-kan hang-gong-ggwo-neul
hwa-gin-ha-ryeo-go ha-neun-de-yo

■ How many bags can I check?

가방을 몇 개 가져갈 수 있죠?

ga-bang-eul myeot gae ga-jeo-gal ssu
it-jjyo?

■ I'm on flight 704 to Seoul on
December 10. My reservation
number is 123456.

12월 10일 서울로 가는
704편이고, 예약 번호는
123456입니다.

si-bi-wol si-bil seo-ul-ro ga-neun
chil-gong-sa-pyeo-ni-go, ye-yak
beon-ho-neun il-i-sam-sa-o-ryu-gim-ni-da

■ Can I change my flight?

항공편을 바꿀 수 있어요?

hang-gong-pyeo-neul ba-ggul ssu
i-sseo-yo?

■ Can I change my reservation for
a later date?

제 예약 날짜를 미룰 수 있어요?

je ye-yak nal-jja-reul mi-rul ssu i-sseo-yo?

Visiting Myeong-dong

Any Korean shopper worth their salt
will know Myeong-dong (명동).

Within walking distance of Seoul
Station (서울역 [seo-ul-ryeok]), this
neighborhood of department
stores and branded shops is one
of the priciest in the world. But
don't be scared. Within the maze
of clothing, cosmetics and luxury
goods, there are bargains. You'll
find good food too, as restaurants
and food stalls are bound to exist
in any Korean destination this busy.
By some estimates, two million
people clog the streets of Myeong-
dong every day.

Other nearby attractions are
Namdaemun Market (남대문 시장
[nam-dae-mun si-jang]), N Seoul Tower
(N 서울 타워 [en seo-ul ta-wo]), also
called 남산 타워 [nam-san ta-wo],
because it is located on Namsan
Mountain (남산) and Myeong-dong
Cathedral (명동 성당 [myeong-dong
seong-dang]), Korea's first Catholic
place of worship.

Passports

■ I'd like to apply for a passport.

여권을 만들려고요.

yeo-ggwo-neul man-deul-ryeo-go-yo

■ Where can I get a passport?

여권을 발급하려면 어디로 가야
하나요?

yeo-ggwo-neul bal-geu-pa-ryeo-myeon
eo-di-ro ga-ya ha-na-yo?

■ What should I prepare to get a passport?

여권을 발급하려면 무엇을
준비해야 하나요?

yeo-ggwo-neul bal-geu-pa-ryeo-myeon
mu-eo-seul jun-bi-hae-ya ha-na-yo?

■ How long does it take to get a passport?

여권을 만드는 데 얼마나
걸려요?

yeo-ggwo-neul man-deu-neun de
eol-ma-na geol-ryeo-yo?

■ My passport expires at the end of the year.

제 여권은 올해 말로 만기가
됩니다.

je yeo-ggwo-neun ol-hae mal-ro man-
gi-ga doem-ni-da

Visas 1

■ I want to apply for a visa for the Republic of Korea.

한국 비자를 신청하려고
하는데요.

han-guk bi-ja-reul sin-cheong-ha-ryeo-
go ha-neun-de-yo

■ You don't need a visa to travel to Jeju.

제주도를 관광할 때 비자가 필요
없습니다.

je-ju-do-reul gwan-gwang-hal ddae bi-
ja-ga pi-ryo eop-sseum-ni-da

■ How long does it take to get a visa?

비자를 신청하는 데 얼마나
걸립니까?

bi-ja-reul sin-cheong-ha-neun de eol-
ma-na geol-rim-ni-gga?

■ This visa is good for thirty days only.

이 비자의 유효 기간은
30일입니다.

i bi-ja-e yu-hyo gi-ga-neun
sam-si-bi-rim-ni-da

■ I want to know if my visa has been authorized yet.

비자가 발급되었는지
물어보려고요.

bi-ja-ga bal-geup-ddoe-eon-neun-ji
mu-reo-bo-ryeo-go-yo

Visas 2

- I'm planning to go to Hong Kong for travel.
  Do I need a visa?

  홍콩으로 여행 가려는데요.
  비자가 필요합니까?

  hong-kong-eu-ro yeo-haeng
  ga-ryeo-neun-de-yo.
  bi-ja-ga pi-ryo-ham-ni-gga?

- Without a visa, you can stay in Hong Kong for ninety days.

  홍콩은 90일 간 비자
  면제입니다.

  hong-kong-eun gu-si-bil gan bi-ja
  myeon-je-im-ni-da

- Please renew your visa before it expires.

  비자 만료 기간 전에 갱신해야
  합니다.

  bi-ja mal-ryo gi-gan jeo-ne gaeng-sin-
  hae-ya ham-ni-da

- What is your visa status?

  비자가 어떤 종류입니까?

  bi-ja-ga eo-ddeon jong-nyu-im-ni-gga?

- I see you have a student visa.

  알고 보니 학생 비자였군요.

  al-go bo-ni hak-ssaeng bi-ja-yeot-ggun-
  yo

The Airport

- Please check in at least two hours before departure time.

  늦어도 이륙하기 두 시간 전에
  탑승 수속해야 합니다.

  neu-jeo-do i-ryu-ka-gi du si-gan jeo-ne
  tap-sseung su-so-kae-ya ham-ni-da

- What time did you arrive at the airport?

  공항에는 몇 시에 도착했어(요)?

  gong-hang-e-neun myeot si-e
  do-cha-kae-sseo(-yo)?

- Where is the international terminal?

  국제선 터미널은 어디입니까?

  guk-jje-seon teo-mi-neo-reun
  eo-di-im-ni-gga?

- I missed my connection because my flight was delayed.

  비행기가 연착되는 바람에,
  연결편을 놓쳤어(요).

  bi-haeng-gi-ga yeon-chak-ddoe-neun
  ba-ra-me, yeon-gyeol-pyeo-neul
  not-cheo-sseo(-yo)

- I reached the airport in the nick of time.

  공항에 아슬아슬하게
  도착했어(요).

  gong-hang-e a-seu-ra-seul-ha-ge
  do-cha-kae-sseo(-yo)

Check-in

- Where is the Asiana Airlines office?

  아시아나항공 카운터는 어디예요?

  a-si-a-na-hang-gong ka-un-teo-neun eo-di-ye-yo?

- You may proceed to the next window.

  다음 창구로 가세요.

  da-eum chang-gu-ro ga-se-yo

- I reserved a flight ticket on the Internet.

  인터넷에서 항공권을 예약했습니다.

  in-teo-ne-se-seo hang-gong-ggwo-neul ye-ya-kaet-sseum-ni-da

- I will probably pay an excess-baggage charge.

  초과 수하물 요금을 내야 할 거예요.

  cho-gwa su-ha-mul yo-geu-meul nae-ya hal ggeo-ye-yo

- When is the check-in?

  체크인 시간이 언제예요?

  che-keu-in si-ga-ni eon-je-ye-yo?

Departure Check

- May I see your passport, please?

  여권을 보여 주시겠어요?

  yeo-ggwo-neul bo-yeo ju-si-ge-sseo-yo?

- Where are you headed?

  어디에 가십니까?

  eo-di-e ga-sim-ni-gga?

- I'm on my way to Yeo-su.

  여수에 갑니다.

  yeo-su-e gam-ni-da

- When are you going to return?

  언제 귀국합니까?

  eon-je gwi-gu-kam-ni-gga?

- Who is going with you?

  일행이 있습니까?

  il-haeng-i it-sseum-ni-gga?

- I'm going with my boss.

  상사와 함께 갑니다.

  sang-sa-wa ham-gge gam-ni-da

Duty-free

■ Where are the duty-free shops?

면세점은 어디 있어(요)?

myeon-se-jeo-meun eo-di i-sseo(-yo)?

■ Duty-free shops are on the departures level.

면세점은 출발층에 있어(요).

myeon-se-jeo-meun chul-bal-cheung-e i-sseo(-yo)

■ Will we have time to do some duty-free shopping?

면세점 쇼핑할 시간 있어(요)?

myeon-se-jeom syo-ping-hal si-gan i-sseo(-yo)?

■ I think you're over the limit.

한도 초과한 거 같은데(요).

han-do cho-gwa-han geo ga-teun-de(-yo)

■ How much alcohol am I allowed to buy?

주류는 얼마나 살 수 있어(요)?

ju-ryu-neun eol-ma-na sal ssu i-sseo(-yo)?

■ I have to buy some gifts for my family at the duty-free shop in the airport.

공항 면세점에서 가족 선물을 사야 해(요).

gong-hang myeon-se-jeo-me-seo ga-jok seon-mu-reul sa-ya hae(-yo)

Boarding

■ When should I check in?

언제 탑승합니까?

eon-je tap-sseung-ham-ni-gga?

■ Which gate do I go to?

어느 탑승구로 가야 합니까?

eo-neu tap-sseung-gu-ro ga-ya ham-ni-gga?

■ We will begin boarding soon.

곧 탑승을 시작하겠습니다.

got tap-sseung-eul si-ja-ka-get-sseum-ni-da

■ May I see your boarding pass, please?

탑승권을 보여 주시겠어요?

tap-sseung-ggwo-neul bo-yeo ju-si-ge-sseo-yo?

■ Flight 605, departing at 10 a.m., has had a gate change. The new gate is B29.

오전 10시에 출발하는 605 편의 탑승구가 B29로 변경되었습니다.

o-jeon yeol-ssi-e chul-bal-ha-neun yuk-ggong-o-pyeo-ne tap-sseung-gu-ga bi-i-sip-ggu-ro byeon-gyeong-doe-eot-sseum-ni-da

Immigration

■ **This is my first visit.**
이번이 처음 방문입니다.
i-beo-ni cheo-eum bang-mu-nim-ni-da

■ **I'm here to visit my relatives.**
친척들을 만나러 왔습니다.
chin-cheok-ddeu-reul man-na-reo
wat-sseum-ni-da

■ **I'll stay for a week.**
일주일 머물 겁니다.
il-jju-il meo-mul ggeom-ni-da

■ **I'll be staying at the Seoul Hotel.**
서울 호텔에 묵을 겁니다.
seo-ul ho-te-re mu-geul ggeom-ni-da

■ **I'm just here for sightseeing.**
관광차 왔습니다.
gwan-gwang-cha wat-sseum-ni-da

■ **I'm here on business.**
사업차 왔습니다.
sa-eop-cha wat-sseum-ni-da

■ **I'm traveling with my friend.**
친구와 여행 왔습니다.
chin-gu-wa yeo-haeng wat-sseum-ni-da

Luggage

■ **Where can I pick up my luggage?**
어디에서 짐을 찾습니까?
eo-di-e-seo ji-meul chat-sseum-ni-gga?

■ **My luggage was damaged.**
제 짐이 파손됐어요.
je ji-mi pa-son-dwae-sseo-yo

■ **I can't find my luggage.**
제 짐을 못 찾겠어요.
je ji-meul mot chat-gge-sseo-yo

■ **Can you check to see where my luggage is?**
제 짐이 어디에 있는지 확인해 주세요.
je ji-mi eo-di-e in-neun-ji hwa-gin-hae ju-se-yo

■ **My luggage hasn't arrived yet.**
제 짐이 아직 도착하지 않았어요.
je ji-mi a-jik do-cha-ka-ji a-na-sseo-yo

■ **Can you deliver it to my hotel?**
호텔까지 운반해 주실 수 있어요?
ho-tel-gga-ji un-ban-hae ju-sil ssu i-sseo-yo?

Customs

- Please fill in this customs declaration.

  세관 신고서를 기입해 주세요.

  se-gwan sin-go-seo-reul gi-i-pae
  ju-se-yo

- Can I see your customs declaration?

  세관 신고서를 보여 주시겠어요?

  se-gwan sin-go-seo-reul bo-yeo
  ju-si-ge-sseo-yo?

- Anything to declare?

  신고할 물품이 있습니까?

  sin-go-hal mul-pu-mi it-sseum-ni-gga?

- Nothing to declare.

  신고할 것이 없습니다.

  sin-go-hal ggeo-si eop-sseum-ni-da

- It's for my own use.

  이것은 제가 쓰는 것입니다.

  i-geo-seun je-ga sseu-neun
  geo-sim-ni-da

- Can I bring this?

  이것을 반입할 수 있어요?

  i-geo-seul ba-ni-pal ssu i-sseo-yo?

Meeting at the Airport

- Will someone pick you up at the airport?

  누가 공항에 마중 나와(요)?

  nu-ga gong-hang-e ma-jung na-wa(-yo)?

- Can you meet me at the airport?

  공항에 마중 나올 수 있어(요)?

  gong-hang-e ma-jung na-ol ssu
  i-sseo(-yo)?

- I'll arrange for a car to meet you at the airport.

  당신을 마중하려고 차를
  예약했어요.

  dang-si-neul ma-jung-ha-ryeo-go cha-
  reul ye-ya-kae-sseo-yo

- Thanks for meeting me.

  마중하러 공항에 와서 고마워(요).

  ma-jung-ha-reo gong-hang-e wa-seo
  go-ma-wo(-yo)

- I'll be there. When do you land?

  마중 나갈게(요). 언제 내려(요)?

  ma-jung na-gal-gge(-yo).
  eon-je nae-ryeo(-yo)?

- I need to pick up my sister at the airport.

  공항에 여동생을 마중 나가야
  해(요).

  gong-hang-e yeo-dong-saeng-eul ma-
  jung na-ga-ya hae(-yo)

On Board 1

- Could you help me find my seat?
  좌석을 안내해 주시겠어요?
  jwa-seo-geul an-nae-hae ju-si-ge-sseo-yo?

- This way, please.
  Your seat is just over there.
  이쪽으로 오세요.
  바로 저기입니다.
  i-jjo-geu-ro o-se-yo. ba-ro
  jeo-gi-im-ni-da

- Can you help me with my bag?
  제 가방 좀 도와주실래요?
  je ga-bang jom do-wa-ju-sil-rae-yo?

- I don't think it'll fit in the
  overhead bin.
  그건 기내 짐칸에 들어갈 것
  같지 않은데요.
  geu-geon gi-nae jim-ka-ne deu-reo-gal
  ggeot gat-jji a-neun-de-yo

- Please fasten your seat belt.
  안전벨트를 매 주십시오.
  an-jeon-bel-teu-reul mae ju-sip-ssi-o

- Do they sell duty-free goods
  on board?
  기내에서 면세품을 판매하나요?
  gi-nae-e-seo myeon-se-pu-meul
  pan-mae-ha-na-yo?

On Board 2

- May I have a pillow and a
  blanket?
  베개와 담요를 주실래요?
  be-gae-wa dam-nyo-reul ju-sil-rae-yo?

- How long does the flight take?
  비행시간은 얼마나 돼요?
  bi-haeng-si-ga-neun eol-ma-na dwae-yo?

- What's the time difference
  between Seoul and New York?
  서울과 뉴욕의 시차는 얼마나
  돼(요)?
  seo-ul-gwa nyu-yo-ge si-cha-neun
  eol-ma-na dwae(-yo)?

- The toilet is vacant now.
  화장실이 지금 비었어(요).
  hwa-jang-si-ri ji-geum bi-eo-sseo(-yo)

- Excuse me, would you mind
  trading seats with me?
  죄송하지만, 저와 자리를
  바꿔 주실 수 있어요?
  joe-song-ha-ji-man, jeo-wa ja-ri-reul
  ba-ggwo ju-sil ssu i-sseo-yo?

- I don't like the in-flight movies.
  기내 영화가 마음에 안 들어(요).
  gi-nae yeong-hwa-ga ma-eu-me
  an deu-reo(-yo)

In-flight Meals

■ **Is there a meal on this flight?**

기내식이 나오나요?

gi-nae-si-gi na-o-na-yo?

■ **Can I get something to drink?**

음료수를 좀 주시겠어요?

eum-nyo-su-reul jom ju-si-ge-sseo-yo?

■ **Which would you prefer, beef or fish?**

소고기와 생선 중, 어떤 것으로 하시겠습니까?

so-go-gi-wa saeng-seon jung, eo-ddeon geo-seu-ro ha-si-get-sseum-ni-gga?

■ **Beef, please.**

소고기로 할게요.

so-go-gi-ro hal-gge-yo

■ **How was your meal?**

기내식 괜찮았어(요)?

gi-nae-sik gwaen-cha-na-sseo(-yo)?

■ **I'd like to have a glass of water, please.**

물 한 잔 주세요.

mul han jan ju-se-yo

Insa-dong & Samcheong-dong

In these areas of central Seoul, you can find a slice of old Korea:

Insa-dong (인사동) is where you can buy traditional Korean clothing, but there's much more too. The street and its alleyways are peppered with galleries (as many as one hundred) that showcase Korean art and antiques. Travelers will appreciate its unique souvenirs too, such as hanji (한지, Korean handmade paper) and folk crafts, and a variety of teahouses.

Samcheong-dong (삼청동) has a prized location. It stands between Gyeongbokgung Palace (경복궁, the largest of the Joseon era palaces) and Changdeokgung Palace (창덕궁) with the presidential residence (Cheong Wa Dae (청와대), The Blue House) close by. It is also the location of the Bukchon Hanok Village (북촌 한옥 마을 [buk-chon ha-nok ma-eul], a neighborhood of traditional Korean houses) and a picturesque main drag of shops and cafés both chic and European.

Accommodations 숙소 suk-sso

n. accommodation 숙소 [숙쏘] suk-sso = 숙박 시설 [숙빡 시:설] suk-bbak si-seol	**n. room** 객실 [객씰] gaek-ssil	**v. stay** 머무르다 [머무르다] meo-mu-reu-da = 묵다 [묵따] muk-dda = 체류하다 [체류하다] che-ryu-ha-da
n. hotel 호텔 [호텔] ho-tel	**n. check-in** 체크인[체크인] che-keu-in	**n. check-out** 체크아웃 [체크아욷] che-keu-a-ut
n. reservation, booking 예약 [예:약] ye-yak	**n. cancellation** 취소 [취:소] chwi-so	**n. sheet** 시트 [시트] si-teu
n. pillow 베개 [베개] be-gae	**n. towel** 수건 [수:건] su-geon	**n. soap** 비누 [비누] bi-nu
n. shampoo 샴푸 [샴푸] syam-pu **n. conditioner** 린스 [린스] rin-seu	**n. toothbrush** 칫솔 [치쏠/칟쏠] chi-ssol/chit-ssol **n. toothpaste** 치약 [치약] chi-yak	**n. razor, shaver** 면도기 [면:도기] myeon-do-gi
n. comb 빗 [빋] bit = 머리빗 [머리빋] meo-ri-bit	**n. blow-dryer, hairdryer** 드라이어 [드라이어] deu-ra-i-eo = 헤어드라이어 [헤어드라이어] he-eo-deu-ra-i-eo	**n. toilet paper** 화장지 [화장지] hwa-jang-ji = 휴지 [휴:지] hyu-ji

Booking a Room 1

- I'd like to book a room.
  방을 예약하려고 하는데요.
  bang-eul ye-ya-ka-ryeo-go
  ha-neun-de-yo

- Sorry, but we're full.
  죄송합니다만, 만실입니다.
  joe-song-ham-ni-da-man,
  man-si-rim-ni-da

- I'd like to make a reservation for two nights next week.
  다음 주에 2박을 예약하고 싶어요.
  da-eum ju-e i-ba-geul ye-ya-ka-go
  si-peo-yo

- I'd like a double room with a bath.
  욕실이 딸린 더블룸으로 하려고요.
  yok-ssi-ri ddal-rin deo-beul-ru-meu-ro
  ha-ryeo-go-yo

- Do you have a single room available?
  싱글룸 있어요?
  sing-geul-rum i-sseo-yo?

- I'd rather stay closer to downtown.
  차라리 시내에 있는 호텔에 머물겠어(요).
  cha-ra-ri si-nae-e in-neun ho-te-re
  meo-mul-ge-sseo(-yo)

Booking a Room 2

- I'd like a room with a view of the ocean.
  바다가 보이는 방으로 부탁합니다.
  ba-da-ga bo-i-neun bang-eu-ro
  bu-ta-kam-ni-da

- I'd like to stay three nights and check out Sunday morning.
  3박하고 일요일 오전에 체크아웃하려고요.
  sam-ba-ka-go i-ryo-il o-jeo-ne
  che-keu-a-u-ta-ryeo-go-yo

- What's the rate for the room?
  숙박비가 얼마예요?
  suk-bbak-bbi-ga eol-ma-ye-yo?

- Does this rate include breakfast?
  조식이 포함됐어요?
  jo-si-gi po-ham-dwae-sseo-yo?

- Do you have a cheaper room?
  좀 더 싼 방 있어(요)?
  jom deo ssan bang i-sseo(-yo)?

- It had some good reviews online.
  인터넷에 좋은 후기가 좀 있었어(요).
  in-teo-ne-se jo-eun hu-gi-ga jom
  i-sseo-sseo(-yo)

Checking In 1

- Can I check in now?

  지금 체크인할 수 있어요?

  ji-geum che-keu-in-hal ssu i-sseo-yo?

- What time is check-in?

  몇 시에 체크인할 수 있어요?

  myeot si-e che-keu-in-hal ssu i-sseo-yo?

- When is the earliest I can check in?

  가장 빨리 체크인할 수 있는 게 언제예요?

  ga-jang bbal-ri che-keu-in-hal ssu in-neun ge eon-je-ye-yo?

- Do you have a reservation?

  예약하셨습니까?

  ye-ya-ka-syeot-sseum-ni-gga?

- My name is Min-ji Go. I have a reservation for a single room.

  싱글룸 예약한 고민지입니다.

  sing-geul-rum ye-ya-kan go-min-ji-im-ni-da

- I booked online.

  인터넷에서 예약했습니다.

  in-teo-ne-se-seo ye-ya-kaet-sseum-ni-da

Checking In 2

- I need to change my check-in date.

  체크인 날짜를 변경해야 해(요).

  che-keu-in nal-jja-reul byeon-gyeong-hae-ya hae(-yo)

- I'll call the hotel and cancel.

  호텔에 전화해서 취소하겠다고 할게(요).

  ho-te-re jeon-hwa-hae-seo chwi-so-ha-get-dda-go hal-gge(-yo)

- Can I check in early?

  조기 체크인이 가능해(요)?

  jo-gi che-keu-i-ni ga-neung-hae(-yo)?

- Do you need a credit card for a damage deposit when I check in?

  체크인할 때 디포짓을 위한 신용카드가 필요해요?

  che-keu-in-hal ddae di-po-ji-seul wi-han si-nyong-ka-deu-ga pi-ryo-hae-yo?

- Could you help me with my bags?

  짐을 맡길 수 있어요?

  ji-meul mat-ggil ssu i-sseo-yo?

Checking Out

■ We'd like to check out.
체크아웃하려고요.
che-keu-a-u-ta-ryeo-go-yo

■ I'll probably check out around ten.
10시 쯤 체크아웃하려고요.
yeol-ssi jjeum che-keu-a-u-ta-ryeo-go-yo

■ Is it possible to have a late check out?
늦은 체크아웃 가능해(요)?
neu-jeun che-keu-a-ut ga-neung-hae(-yo)?

■ I already paid the hotel bill.
청구서를 지불했어요.
cheong-gu-seo-reul ji-bul-hae-sseo-yo

■ What's this item?
이 항목은 뭐죠?
i hang-mo-geun mwo-jyo?

■ I never ordered any room service.
룸서비스를 시키지 않았는데요.
rum-seo-bi-seu-reul si-ki-ji a-nan-neun-de-yo

■ I think there is a mistake here.
여기가 잘못된 것 같은데요.
yeo-gi-ga jal-mot-ddoen geot ga-teun-de-yo

Hotel Services 1

■ Do you have a laundry service?
세탁 서비스가 되나요?
se-tak seo-bi-seu-ga doe-na-yo?

■ When will the sauna open?
사우나는 언제 열어요?
sa-u-na-neun eon-je yeo-reo-yo?

■ Does the room have a security box?
방에 금고가 있어요?
bang-e geum-go-ga i-sseo-yo?

■ I'd like a wake-up call at six, please.
아침 6시에 모닝콜을 해 주세요.
a-chim yeo-seot-ssi-e mo-ning-ko-reul hae ju-se-yo

■ Can you hold my bags until my flight time?
이 짐을 비행기 시간까지 맡아 줄 수 있어요?
i ji-meul bi-haeng-gi si-gan-gga-ji ma-ta jul ssu i-sseo-yo?

■ Can I have my key?
제 방 열쇠를 주시겠어요?
je bang yeol-soe-reul ju-si-ge-sseo-yo?

Hotel Services 2

■ Is there any message for me?

제게 메시지 온 것 있어요?

je-ge me-si-ji on geot i-sseo-yo?

■ I'd like to stay one day longer.

하루 연장하려고 하는데요.

ha-ru yeon-jang-ha-ryeo-go
ha-neun-de-yo

■ Could someone change my towels?

수건을 바꿔 줄 수 있어요?

su-geo-neul ba-ggwo jul ssu i-sseo-yo?

■ What amenities do you have in this hotel?

이 호텔에 어떤 편의 시설이 있어요?

i ho-te-re eo-ddeon pyeo-ni si-seo-ri
i-sseo-yo?

■ I'm having trouble with my key card.

카드키에 문제가 있어요.

ka-deu-ki-e mun-je-ga i-sseo-yo

■ What's the Wi-Fi password?

와이파이 비밀번호가 뭐예요?

wa-i-pa-i bi-mil-beon-ho-ga mwo-ye-yo?

Trouble at the Hotel

■ I left the key in my room.

열쇠를 방에 두고 나왔어요.

yeol-soe-reul bang-e du-go
na-wa-sseo-yo

■ My room is too close to the elevator. Can I change it?

방이 엘리베이터와 너무 가까워서요. 바꿀 수 있을까요?

bang-i el-ri-be-i-teo-wa neo-mu
ga-gga-wo-seo-yo. ba-ggul
ssu i-sseul-gga-yo?

■ There's no hot water.

방에 온수가 나오지 않아요.

bang-e on-su-ga na-o-ji a-na-yo

■ The toilet doesn't flush.

변기가 막혔어요.

byeon-gi-ga ma-kyeo-sseo-yo

■ My room has not been cleaned yet.

방이 청소되어 있지 않아요.

bang-i cheong-so-doe-eo it-jji a-na-yo

■ It's very noisy next door.

옆 방이 시끄러워 죽겠어요.

yeop bang-i si-ggeu-reo-wo
juk-gge-sseo-yo

Tourist Information

■ Where is the tourist information center?

관광안내소가 어디에 있습니까?

gwan-gwang-an-nae-so-ga eo-di-e
it-sseum-ni-gga?

■ Do you have any leaflets on the town?

시내 관광 안내서 있어요?

si-nae gwan-gwang an-nae-seo
i-sseo-yo?

■ Can you recommend some interesting places around here?

근처에 가 볼 만한 관광지를
추천해 주실래요?

geun-cheo-e ga bol man-han
gwan-gwang-ji-reul chu-cheon-hae
ju-sil-rae-yo?

■ Please recommend a cheap and nice hotel.

싸고 좋은 호텔을 추천해
주세요.

ssa-go jo-eun ho-te-reul chu-cheon-hae
ju-se-yo

■ Could you draw me a map?

약도를 그려 주실 수 있어요?

yak-ddo-reul geu-ryeo ju-sil ssu
i-sseo-yo?

Dongdaemun Market & Namdaemun Market

Dongdaemun (동대문) means "Great East Gate" and is one of eight structures that led through the fortress wall that used to surround Seoul. Also called Heunginjimun (흥인지문), the gate has been deemed a national treasure since the 1960s. The area today is first and foremost a shopper's paradise with markets and malls in every direction, above ground and below, open day and night.

Follow your compass south and you'll find **Namdaemun** (남대문), the Great Southern Gate, the largest of the eight. It also goes by the name Sungnyemun (숭례문). Just east of the structure, between Seoul Station (서울역 [seo-ul-ryeok]) and Myeong-dong (명동), is the market that bears the same name. This is Korea's largest traditional market, in operation since 1964: a ten-thousand-store mini town that's as fun to walk through as it is to go shopping in.

Tour Inquiries 1

- What time does the next tour leave?

  다음 투어는 언제 출발해요?

  da-eum tu-eo-neun eon-je
  chul-bal-hae-yo?

- Do you have any one-day tours?

  당일치기 여행 있어요?

  dang-il-chi-gi yeo-haeng i-sseo-yo?

- What time and where does it leave?

  몇 시, 어디에서 출발해요?

  myeot si, eo-di-e-seo chul-bal-hae-yo?

- How long does it take?

  몇 시간 걸려요?

  myeot si-gan geol-ryeo-yo?

- What time will we be back?

  몇 시에 돌아올 수 있어요?

  myeot si-e do-ra-ol ssu i-sseo-yo?

- How much is it per person?

  1인당 비용이 얼마예요?

  i-rin-dang bi-yong-i eol-ma-ye-yo?

- Do you have a guide?

  관광 가이드가 있어요?

  gwan-gwang ga-i-deu-ga i-sseo-yo?

Tour Inquiries 2

- I'd like to book a city tour.

  시내 관광을 예약하고 싶은데요.

  si-nae gwan-gwang-eul ye-ya-ka-go
  si-peun-de-yo

- Do you have any tours to Gyeongbokgung Palace?

  경복궁 관광 투어가 있어요?

  gyeong-bok-ggung gwan-gwang
  tu-eo-ga i-sseo-yo?

  Tip: Gyeongbokgung Palace was the main royal palace of the Joseon Dynasty (1392–1897) and was first built in 1395. It is located in northern Seoul.

- Do you have a tour for night views?

  야경을 볼 수 있어요?

  ya-gyeong-eul bol ssu i-sseo-yo?

- Is lunch included?

  점심이 포함되어 있나요?

  jeom-si-mi po-ham-doe-eo in-na-yo?

- Is there one leaving in the morning?

  아침에 출발하는 것이 있어요?

  a-chi-me chul-bal-ha-neun geo-si
  i-sseo-yo?

Purchasing Tickets

- **Where can I buy a ticket?**

  어디에서 입장권을 사요?

  eo-di-e-seo ip-jjang-ggwo-neul sa-yo?

- **How much is the admission fee?**

  입장권이 얼마예요?

  ip-jjang-ggwo-ni eol-ma-ye-yo?

- **Two adults and one child, please.**

  어른 두 장, 어린이 한 장 주세요.

  eo-reun du jang, eo-ri-ni han jang ju-se-yo

- **Do you have any tickets for the one o'clock performance?**

  1시 공연, 자리 있습니까?

  han si gong-yeon, ja-ri it-sseum-ni-gga?

- **Are there any tickets left for tonight's show?**

  오늘 밤 공연 입장권 남은 게 있어요?

  o-neul bam gong-yeon ip-jjang-ggwon na-meun ge i-sseo-yo?

- **Do you have a group discount?**

  단체 할인돼요?

  dan-che ha-rin-dwae-yo?

At the Location

- **What a beautiful place!**

  정말 아름다운 곳이네요!

  jeong-mal a-reum-da-un go-si-ne-yo!

- **What a fantastic view!**

  전망이 환상적이에요!

  jeon-mang-i hwan-sang-jeo-gi-e-yo!

- **What time will it be over?**

  관람 시간은 몇 시에 끝나요?

  gwal-ram si-ga-neun myeot si-e ggeun-na-yo?

- **It's not recommended for children.**

  어린이는 이용할 수 없습니다.

  eo-ri-ni-neun i-yong-hal ssu eop-sseum-ni-da

- **Can I take a look inside?**

  내부를 둘러봐도 되나요?

  nae-bu-ruel dul-reo-bwa-do doe-na-yo?

- **Where is the souvenir shop?**

  기념품 가게는 어디 있습니까?

  gi-nyeom-pum ga-ge-neun eo-di it-sseum-ni-gga?

- **Where is the exit?**

  출구가 어디 있습니까?

  chul-gu-ga eo-di it-sseum-ni-gga?

Asking the Way 1

■ Which way do I go to get to the National Gallery?

국립미술관은 어떻게 갑니까?

gung-nip-mi-sul-gwa-neun eo-ddeo-ke gam-ni-gga?

■ Is this the right way to N Seoul Tower?

N 서울 타워에 가려면 이 길이 맞아요?

en seo-ul ta-wo-e ga-ryeo-myeon i gi-ri ma-ja-yo?

■ Please tell me the way to the bus stop.

버스 정류소로 가는 길을 알려 주세요.

beo-seu jeong-nyu-so-ro ga-neun gi-reul al-ryeo ju-se-yo

■ Is there a subway station around here?

근처에 지하철역이 있습니까?

geun-cheo-e ji-ha-cheol-ryeo-gi it-sseum-ni-gga?

■ It's far from here.
You'd better take a bus.

여기에서 멀어요.
버스를 타고 가는 편이 좋겠어요.

yeo-gi-e-seo meo-reo-yo. beo-seu-reul ta-go ga-neun pyeo-ni jo-ke-sseo-yo

Asking the Way 2

■ How far is the museum from here?

여기에서 박물관까지 멀어요?

yeo-gi-e-seo bang-mul-gwan-gga-ji meo-reo-yo?

■ Is it far from the hotel?

호텔에서 멀어요?

ho-te-re-seo meo-reo-yo?

■ Can I walk there?

걸어서 갈 수 있어요?

geo-reo-seo gal ssu i-sseo-yo?

■ How long does it take on foot?

걸어서 가면 몇 분 걸립니까?

geo-reo-seo ga-myeon myeot bun geol-rim-ni-gga?

■ It's only five minutes' walk.

걸어서 5분이면 도착합니다.

geo-reo-seo o-bu-ni-myeon do-cha-kam-ni-da

■ I'm sorry, I'm a stranger here.

죄송하지만, 저도 여기는 처음입니다.

joe-song-ha-ji-man, jeo-do yeo-gi-neun cheo-eu-mim-ni-da

Trains

Subways

- One round trip to Jeonju, please.
  전주로 가는 왕복표 한 장 주세요.
  jeon-ju-ro ga-neun wang-bok-pyo han jang ju-se-yo

- The train was thirty minutes behind schedule.
  기차가 30분 연착됐어요.
  gi-cha-ga sam-sip-bbun yeon-chak-ddwae-sseo-yo

- What time is the first train to Yongsan?
  용산행 첫 차가 몇 시에 있죠?
  yong-san-haeng cheot cha-ga myeot si-e it-jjyo?

- How often does the train come?
  배차 간격이 어떻게 돼죠?
  bae-cha gan-gyeo-gi eo-ddeo-ke dwae-jyo?

- Every thirty minutes.
  30분마다 있습니다.
  sam-sip-bbun-ma-da it-sseum-ni-da

- What time does the train for Gwangju leave?
  광주행 기차가 몇 시에 출발하죠?
  gwang-ju-haeng gi-cha-ga myeot si-e chul-bal-ha-jyo?

- Where is the ticket counter?
  매표소가 어디예요?
  mae-pyo-so-ga eo-di-ye-yo?

- Can I have a subway map?
  지하철 노선도 한 장 주실래요?
  ji-ha-cheol no-seon-do han jang ju-sil-rae-yo?

- Where should I transfer?
  어디에서 갈아타나요?
  eo-di-e-seo ga-ra-ta-na-yo?

- You should transfer to Line 2.
  2호선으로 갈아타세요.
  i-ho-seo-neu-ro ga-ra-ta-se-yo

- How much is the fare?
  요금은 얼마예요?
  yo-geu-meun eol-ma-ye-yo?

- Which exit should I take for Yeouido Park?
  여의도공원으로 가려면 몇 번 출구로 가야 해요?
  yeo-i-do-gong-wo-neu-ro ga-ryeo-myeon myeot beon chul-gu-ro ga-ya hae-yo?

Buses 1

■ **Where is the nearest bus stop?**

가장 가까운 버스 정류장이
어디예요?

ga-jang ga-gga-un beo-seu
jeong-nyu-jang-i eo-di-ye-yo?

Tip: 버스 정류장 [beo-seu jeong-nyu-jang] "**bus
stop**" can also be said 버스 정류소 [beo-seu
jeong-nyu-so].

■ **Does this bus go to the airport?**

이 버스는 공항에 갑니까?

i beo-seu-neun gong-hang-e gam-ni-gga?

■ **Could you tell me where to
get off?**

어디에서 내려야 하는지
알려 줄 수 있어요?

eo-di-e-seo nae-ryeo-ya ha-neun-ji
al-ryeo jul ssu i-sseo-yo?

■ **Is this seat vacant?**

여기에 자리 있어요?

yeo-gi-e ja-ri i-sseo-yo?

■ **I'll get off here.**

여기에서 내리겠습니다.

yeo-gi-e-seo nae-ri-get-sseum-ni-da

■ **Press this button when you
want to get off.**

버스에서 내릴 때, 이 버튼을
누르세요.

beo-seu-e-seo nae-ril ddae, i beo-teu-
neul nu-reu-se-yo

Buses 2

■ **I missed the last bus.**

막차를 놓쳤어요.

mak-cha-reul not-cheo-sseo-yo

■ **Do you sell tickets for the airport
shuttle bus?**

공항 셔틀버스 표 팔아요?

gong-hang syeo-teul-beo-seu pyo
pa-ra-yo?

■ **How often does the airport bus
operate?**

공항버스는 얼마나 자주
운행돼죠?

gong-hang-beo-seu-neun eol-ma-na
ja-ju un-haeng-dwae-jyo?

Tip: The airport bus is called "Airport
Limousine Bus" in Korea.

■ **When's the last bus to Bundang?**

분당으로 가는 막차는 몇 시에
있나요?

bun-dang-eu-ro ga-neun mak-cha-neun
myeot si-e in-na-yo?

■ **Do you ride this bus often?**

이 버스 자주 타세요?

i beo-seu ja-ju ta-se-yo?

■ **I'll go to Daejeon by express bus.**

고속버스를 타고 대전에
갈 거예요.

go-sok-bbeo-seu-reul ta-go dae-jeo-ne
gal ggeo-ye-yo

Taxis 1

■ Could you call me a taxi, please?

택시를 불러 주실래요?

taek-ssi-reul bul-reo ju-sil-rae-yo?

■ Let's catch a taxi here!

여기에서 택시를 잡자!

yeo-gi-e-seo taek-ssi-reul jap-jja!

■ I can't find a taxi.

택시를 못 잡겠어요.

taek-ssi-reul mot jap-gge-sseo-yo

■ Take me to this address, please.

이 주소로 가 주세요.

i ju-so-ro ga ju-se-yo

■ The airport, please.

공항으로 가 주세요.

gong-hang-eu-ro ga ju-se-yo

■ Please go quickly.

빨리 가 주세요.

bbal-ri ga ju-se-yo

■ Slow down, please.

천천히 가 주세요.

cheon-cheon-hi ga ju-se-yo

Traveling by Bus in Korea

Buses in Korea offer convenient travel to almost any destination. If you are taking a bus in the Seoul area, pay particular attention to bus color. Red signifies express travel from the city into the suburbs while yellow buses repeat a route in a particular district of the city. Blue buses are best for longer routes across the city via the busier streets, and green buses are local community hoppers. Electric buses are also a reality now and are clearly marked.

Bus fares are relatively cheap and can be paid using cash or a transportation card upon boarding. If transferring to another bus or subway, passengers can swipe their cards when exiting to receive a small discount.

Taxis 2

■ I called a taxi thirty minutes ago, but it hasn't arrived.

택시를 부른 지 30분이 지났는데, 아직 안 왔어(요).

taek-ssi-reul bu-reun ji sam-sip-bbu-ni ji-nat-neun-de, a-jik an wa-sseo(-yo)

■ Drop me off at the corner.

저 모퉁이에서 내릴게요.

jeo mo-tung-i-e-seo nae-ril-gge-yo

■ Can you take out my bags?

제 짐을 꺼내 주실래요?

je ji-meul ggeo-nae ju-sil-rae-yo?

■ I had a heck of a time flagging down a taxi.

택시 잡느라고 혼났어(요).

taek-ssi jap-neu-ra-go hon-na-sseo(-yo)

■ Please get a taxi on the other side of the street.

길 건너편에서 택시를 타세요.

gil geon-neo-pyeo-ne-seo taek-ssi-reul ta-se-yo

■ Keep the change.

잔돈은 가지세요.

jan-do-neun ga-ji-se-yo

Ships & Cruises

■ Where can I take a sightseeing boat?

유람선 타는 데가 어디예요?

yu-ram-seon ta-neun de-ga eo-di-ye-yo?

■ Let's go on a cruise down the Han River after lunch!

점심 먹고 한강 유람선을 타자!

jeom-sim meok-ggo han-gang yu-ram-seo-neul ta-ja!

■ I get seasick whenever I get in a boat.

배를 탈 때마다 뱃멀미를 해(요).

bae-reul tal ddae-ma-da baen-meol-mi-reul hae(-yo)

■ What time do we embark?

승선 시간은 몇 시입니까?

seung-seon si-ga-neun myeot si-im-ni-gga?

■ We just got back from a cruise.

유람선 여행에서 막 돌아왔어(요).

yu-ram-seon yeo-haeng-e-seo mak do-ra-wa-sseo(-yo)

■ How about going on a cruise?

유람선 여행은 어때(요)?

yu-ram-seon yeo-haeng-eun eo-ddae(-yo)?

Chapter 11

Tough Times

Emergencies 응급 eung-geup

n. urgency 긴급 [긴급] gin-geup **n. rescue** 구조 [구:조] gu-jo 	**n. ambulance** 구급차 [구:급차] gu-geup-cha = 앰뷸런스 [앰뷸런스] aem-byul-reon-seu 	**n. first-aid kit** 구급상자 [구:급쌍자] gu-geup-ssang-ja
	n. heart attack 심장마비 [심장마비] sim-jang-ma-bi 	**n. CPR** 심폐 소생술 [심폐 소생술/심페 소생술] sim-pye so-saeng-sul/ sim-pe so-saeng-sul
v. hurt 다치다 [다치다] da-chi-da 	**v. cure** 치료하다 [치료하다] chi-ryo-ha-da = 낫다 [낟:따] nat-dda 	**v. recover** 회복하다 [회보카다/훼보카다] hoe-bo-ka-da/ hwe-bo-ka-da

Emergency

■ This is an emergency.

응급 상황이에요.

eung-geup sang-hwang-i-e-yo

■ My friend fell and is unconscious.

친구가 쓰러져서 의식이
없어(요).

chin-gu-ga sseu-reo-jeo-seo ui-si-gi
eop-sseo(-yo)

■ I think he's having a heart
attack.

그는 심장마비인 거 같아(요).

geu-neun sim-jang-ma-bi-in geo
ga-ta(-yo)

■ We have to give first aid to him
right now.

당장 그에게 응급 처치를 해야
해(요).

dang-jang geu-e-ge eung-geup cheo-
chi-reul hae-ya hae(-yo)

■ Do you have a phone?
Quick, call 119!

휴대폰 있어(요)?
얼른, 119에 전화해(요)!

hyu-dae-pon i-sseo(-yo)?
eol-reun, il-ril-gu-e jeon-hwa-hae(-yo)!

Ambulance

■ Could you call an ambulance?

구급차를 불러 주실래요?

gu-geup-cha-reul bul-reo ju-sil-rae-yo?

■ Hurry and call an ambulance.

어서 구급차를 불러라.

eo-seo gu-geup-cha-reul bul-reo-ra

■ Don't move until the ambulance
arrives.

구급차가 오기 전에 움직이지
마(세요).

gu-geup-cha-ga o-gi jeo-ne um-ji-gi-ji
ma(-se-yo)

■ Here comes an ambulance.

구급차가 와(요).

gu-geup-cha-ga wa(-yo)

■ Is there anything I can do before
the ambulance comes?

구급차가 오기 전에 제가
뭘 할 수 있을까요?

gu-geup-cha-ga o-gi jeo-ne je-ga
mwol hal ssu i-sseul-gga-yo?

■ Luckily an ambulance arrived
shortly after.

다행히 구급차가 금방 왔어(요).

da-haeng-i gu-geup-cha-ga geum-bang
wa-sseo(-yo)

Emergency Room

- Where's the emergency room, please?

  응급실이 어디예요?

  eung-geup-ssi-ri eo-di-ye-yo?

- Go to your local hospital emergency room.

  집에서 가까운 병원 응급실로 가세요.

  ji-be-seo ga-gga-un byeong-won eung-geup-ssil-ro ga-se-yo

- Should I go to the ER now or just schedule a doctor's appointment tomorrow morning?

  지금 응급실로 가야 할까(요) 아니면 내일 아침 병원 진료를 예약할까(요)?

  ji-geum eung-geup-ssil-ro ga-ya hal-gga(-yo) a-ni-myeon nae-il a-chim byeong-won jil-ryo-reul ye-ya-kal-gga(-yo)?

- My son was rushed to the emergency room.
  He had an allergic reaction.

  우리 아들은 급하게 응급실에 갔어(요).
  알레르기 반응이 있었거든(요).

  u-ri a-deu-reun geu-pa-ge eung-geup-ssi-re ga-sseo(-yo).
  al-re-reu-gi ban-eung-i i-sseot-ggeo-deun(-yo).

Getting Lost

- I got lost.

  길을 잃었어(요).

  gi-reul i-reo-sseo(-yo)

- Where are you now?

  지금 어디에 있어(요)?

  ji-geum eo-di-e i-sseo(-yo)?

- We're going the wrong way.

  길을 잘못 들어선 거 같아(요).

  gi-reul jal-mot deu-reo-seon geo ga-ta(-yo)

- I don't know where I am.

  어디에 있는지 모르겠어(요).

  eo-di-e in-neun-ji mo-reu-ge-sseo(-yo)

- Can you tell me what you can see around you?

  주변에 뭐가 있는지 말씀해 주시겠어요?

  ju-byeo-ne mwo-ga in-neun-ji mal-sseum-hae ju-si-ge-sseo-yo?

- Where can I find this address?

  여기 주소를 어디에서 알 수 있어(요)?

  yeo-gi ju-so-reul eo-di-e-seo al ssu i-sseo(-yo)?

Missing Children

■ My daughter is missing.

내 딸을 잃어버렸어요.

nae dda-reul i-reo-beo-ryeo-sseo-yo

■ Where did you lose her?

따님을 어디에서 잃어버렸나요?

dda-ni-meul eo-di-e-seo
i-reo-beo-ryeon-na-yo?

■ What does your son look like?

아드님이 어떻게 생겼어요?

a-deu-ni-mi eo-ddeo-ke
saeng-gyeo-sseo-yo?

아드님의 인상착의를 말씀해
주세요.

a-deu-ni-me in-sang-cha-gi-reul
mal-sseum-hae ju-se-yo

■ Could you make an announcement for a missing child?

미아 방송을 해 주시겠어요?

mi-a bang-song-eul hae ju-si-ge-sseo-
yo?

■ Where's the station for lost children?

미아보호소가 어디예요?

mi-a-bo-ho-so-ga eo-di-ye-yo?

■ I want to report a missing child.

미아 신고를 하려고요.

mi-a sin-go-reul ha-ryeo-go-yo

Emergency Phone Numbers in Korea

Remember these emergency phone numbers for your safety in Korea.

119	Fire / Emergency and Ambulance
112	Police
111	National Intelligence Service
122	Coastguard
1339	Medical information center
1330	Tourism and Translation Service

Your location is automatically detected when you call 119, so you don't have to give it. Emergency responses are also very rapid; ambulances are free of charge and will quickly take people to a hospital. When a foreigner makes a 119 call, the call is diverted to a translator from the Korea National Tourist Organization. There is an emergency medical information center which is available 24/7—simply dial 1339. English-speaking doctors will supply medical information in an emergency, as well as advice on finding a pharmacy that is open or a hospital.

Losing Items

■ **Didn't you see a phone here?**

여기에서 휴대폰 못 봤어(요)?

yeo-gi-e-seo hyu-dae-pon mot
bwa-sseo(-yo)?

■ **I can't find my keys.**

내 열쇠를 찾을 수 없어(요).

nae yeol-soe-reul cha-jeul ssu
eop-sseo(-yo)

■ **I lost my bag.**

가방을 잃어버렸습니다.

ga-bang-eul i-reo-beo-ryeot-sseum-ni-da

■ **I left my wallet in a taxi.**

택시 안에 지갑을 두고
내렸어(요).

taek-ssi a-ne ji-ga-beul du-go
nae-ryeo-sseo(-yo)

■ **I don't remember where I lost it.**

어디에서 잃어버렸는지
생각나지 않아(요).

eo-di-e-seo i-reo-beo-ryeon-neun-ji
saeng-gak-na-ji a-na(-yo)

■ **You'd better hurry and report the card missing.**

빨리 카드 분실 신고를 하세요.

bbal-ri ka-deu bun-sil sin-go-reul
ha-se-yo

Lost & Found

■ **Where is the Lost and Found?**

분실물 보관소가 어디예요?

bun-sil-mul bo-gwan-so-ga eo-di-ye-yo?

■ **Fill out this lost-luggage form.**

분실물 신청서를 작성해 주세요.

bun-sil-mul sin-cheong-seo-reul
jak-sseong-hae ju-se-yo

■ **I'm here to pick up my lost luggage.**

분실한 짐을 찾으러 왔습니다.

bun-sil-han ji-meul cha-jeu-reo
wat-sseum-ni-da

■ **The Lost and Found Office is right over there.**

분실물 보관소는 바로 저기에
있어(요).

bun-sil-mul bo-gwan-so-neun ba-ro
jeo-gi-e i-sseo(-yo)

■ **You'll have to check with the Lost and Found.**

분실물 보관소에 가서 확인해
봐(요).

bun-sil-mul bo-gwan-so-e ga-seo
hwa-gin-hae bwa(-yo)

Incidents & Accidents 사건 & 사고 sa-ggeon & sa-go

n. police station 경찰서 [경ː찰써] gyeong-chal-sseo 	n. police officer 경찰 [경ː찰] gyeong-chal 	n. criminal 범죄인 [범ː죄인/범ː줴인] beom-joe-in/beom-jwe-in = 범인 [버ː민] beo-min
	n. thief 도둑 [도ː둑] do-duk 	n. robber, burglar 강도 [강ː도] gang-do
	n. pickpocket 소매치기 [소매치기] so-mae-chi-gi 	n. swindler 사기꾼 [사기꾼] sa-gi-ggun
n. traffic accident, car accident 교통사고 [교통사고] gyo-tong-sa-go 	n. collision, crash 충돌 [충돌] chung-dol 	n. tow truck 견인차 [겨닌차] gyeo-nin-cha = 레커차 [레커차] re-keo-cha 
v. declare 신고하다 [신고하다] sin-go-ha-da 	n. (traffic) violation 위반 [위반] wi-ban 	traffic sign 교통표지판 [교통표지판] gyo-tong-pyo-ji-pan

n. fine, penalty 벌금 [벌금] beol-geum = 범칙금 [범:칙끔] beom-chik-ggeum 	n. speeding 속도위반 [속또위반] sok-ddo-wi-ban 	n. drunk driving 음주 운전 [음:주 운:전] eum-ju un-jeon
n. fire station 소방서 [소방서] so-bang-seo 	n. fire truck 소방차 [소방차] so-bang-cha 	n. fire 화재 [화:재] hwa-jae = 불 [불] bul
n. explosion 폭발 [폭빨] pok-bbal 	n. earthquake 지진 [지진] ji-jin 	n. landslide 산사태 [산사태] san-sa-tae
n. avalanche 눈사태 [눈:사태] nun-sa-tae	n. tsunami 해일 [해:일] hae-il	n. flood 홍수 [홍수] hong-su

Robbery 1

- **Robber! / Thief!**
  도둑이야!
  do-du-gi-ya!

- **My wallet was stolen.**
  내 지갑을 도둑 맞았어(요).
  nae ji-ga-beul do-duk ma-ja-sseo(-yo)

- **He stole my wallet.**
  그는 내 지갑을 훔쳤어(요).
  geu-neun nae ji-ga-beul
  hum-cheo-sseo(-yo)

- **Someone took my bag.**
  누가 내 가방을 가져갔어(요).
  nu-ga nae ga-bang-eul
  ga-jeo-ga-sseo(-yo)

- **I'd like to report a robbery.**
  도둑을 신고하고 싶어(요).
  do-du-geul sin-go-ha-go si-peo(-yo)

- **Recently there have been break-ins in the neighborhood.**
  최근 이웃에 도둑이 들었어(요).
  choe-geun i-u-se do-du-gi
  deu-reo-sseo(-yo)

Robbery 2

- **It looks like we were robbed.**
  도둑맞은 거 같아(요).
  do-dung-ma-jeun geo ga-ta(-yo)

- **My house was burglarized when I was away only briefly.**
  잠시 집을 비운 사이 도둑이 들었어(요).
  jam-si ji-beul bi-un sa-i do-du-gi
  deu-reo-sseo(-yo)

- **My house was robbed last night.**
  어젯밤에 우리 집에 도둑이 들었어(요).
  eo-jet-bba-me u-ri ji-be do-du-gi
  deu-reo-sseo(-yo)

- **My bike was stolen last night.**
  지난밤에 내 자전거를 도난당했어(요).
  ji-nan-ba-me nae ja-jeon-geo-reul
  do-nan-dang-hae-sseo(-yo)

- **That's a burglar alarm.**
  그것은 도난방지 시스템이에요.
  geu-geo-seun do-nan-bang-ji
  si-seu-te-mi-e-yo

Pickpockets

■ Catch the pickpocket!
소매치기 잡아라!
so-mae-chi-gi ja-ba-ra!

■ I've been pickpocketed.
소매치기 당했어(요).
so-mae-chi-gi dang-hae-sseo(-yo)

■ Beware of pickpockets!
소매치기를 조심하세요!
so-mae-chi-gi-reul jo-sim-ha-se-yo!

■ Passengers, keep an eye on your belongings so that no one snatches them.
승객 여러분, 소매치기를 당하지 않도록 소지품에 주의하십시오.
seung-gaek yeo-reo-bun, so-mae-chi-gi-reul dang-ha-ji an-to-rok so-ji-pu-me ju-i-ha-sip-ssi-o

■ A pickpocket got his hand into my bag.
소매치기가 내 가방에 손을 넣었어(요).
so-mae-chi-gi-ga nae ga-bang-e so-neul neo-eo-sseo(-yo)

Fraud 1

■ I was scammed.
사기를 당했어(요).
sa-gi-reul dang-hae-sseo(-yo)

■ He is a con artist.
그는 사기꾼이에요.
geu-neun sa-gi-ggu-ni-e-yo

■ Don't try to scam me!
사기치지 마!
sa-gi-chi-ji ma!

■ It's obviously a scam.
그건 순전히 사기예요.
geu-geon sun-jeon-hi sa-gi-ye-yo

■ He scammed ten million won last month.
그는 지난달에 천만 원을 사기 쳤어(요).
geu-neun ji-nan-da-re cheon-man wo-neul sa-gi cheo-sseo(-yo)

■ His promise was a big lie.
그의 약속은 순 사기였어(요).
geu-e yak-sso-geun sun sa-gi-yeo-sseo(-yo)

■ That's white-collar crime.
그건 화이트칼라 범죄예요.
geu-geon hwa-i-teu-kal-ra beom-joe-ye-yo

Fraud 2

■ He conned me out of two
million won.
그는 내게 사기를 쳐서
2백만 원을 빼앗았어(요).
geu-neun nae-ge sa-gi-reul cheo-seo
i-baeng-man wo-neul bbae-a-sa-sseo(-yo)

■ He was arrested on a charge
of fraud.
그는 사기죄로 체포됐어(요).
geu-neun sa-gi-joe-ro
che-po-dwae-sseo(-yo)

■ I got ripped off by a taxi driver.
택시 기사한테 사기당했어(요).
taek-ssi gi-sa-han-te
sa-gi-dang-hae-sseo(-yo)

■ I fell for the con artist's story
hook, line and sinker.
그 사기꾼의 말을 다 믿었어(요).
geu sa-gi-ggu-ne ma-reul da
mi-deo-sseo(-yo)

■ He is a crook inside and out.
그는 완전히 사기꾼이에요.
geu-neun wan-jeon-hi sa-gi-ggu-ni-e-yo

■ Don't believe everyone you meet.
만나는 모든 사람을 믿지
마(세요).
man-na-neun mo-deun sa-ra-meul
mit-jji ma(-se-yo)

Police Reports

■ Where is the nearest police station?
여기에서 가장 가까운 경찰서가
어디예요?
yeo-gi-e-seo ga-jang ga-gga-un
gyeong-chal-sseo-ga eo-di-ye-yo?

■ Report it to the police.
경찰에 신고해라.
gyeong-cha-re sin-go-hae-ra

■ I called the police right away.
즉시 경찰에 신고했어(요).
jeuk-ssi gyeong-cha-re
sin-go-hae-sseo(-yo)

■ You'd better come down to the
station and report it.
경찰서에 가서 신고하는 게
좋겠어(요).
gyeong-chal-sseo-e ga-seo sin-go-ha-
neun ge jo-ke-sseo(-yo)

■ Why didn't you report it to the
police?
왜 경찰에 신고하지 않았어(요)?
wae gyeong-cha-re sin-go-ha-ji a-na-
sseo(-yo)?

■ Such cases must be notified to
the police.
이런 사건들은 경찰에 알려야
해(요).
i-reon sa-ggeon-deu-reun gyeong-cha-re
al-ryeo-ya hae(-yo)

Car Accidents

■ I had a car accident.
교통사고를 당했어(요).
gyo-tong-sa-go-reul dang-hae-sseo(-yo)

■ I witnessed a traffic accident.
교통사고를 목격했어(요).
gyo-tong-sa-go-reul
mok-ggyeo-kae-sseo(-yo)

■ She hit me from behind.
그녀가 뒤에서 박았어(요).
geu-nyeo-ga dwi-e-seo ba-ga-sseo(-yo)

■ When did the traffic accident happen?
그 교통사고는 언제 일어났어(요)?
geu gyo-tong-sa-go-neun eon-je
i-reo-na-sseo(-yo)?

■ This is an accident black spot.
이곳은 교통사고 다발지점이에요.
i-go-seun gyo-tong-sa-go
da-bal-ji-jeo-mi-e-yo

■ Always get their name, license number and insurance information.
항상 상대방의 이름, 면허 번호와 보험 정보를 받아야 해(요).
hang-sang sang-dae-bang-e i-reum,
myeon-heo beon-ho-wa bo-heom
jeong-bo-reul ba-da-ya hae(-yo)

Accidents 1

■ The boy fell into the water and drowned.
소년은 물에 빠져서 익사했어(요).
so-nyeo-neun mu-re bba-jeo-seo
ik-ssa-hae-sseo(-yo)

■ I heard you had a skateboard accident last week.
지난주에 스케이트보드 타다가 사고 났다면서(요).
ji-nan-ju-e seu-ke-i-teu-bo-deu ta-da-ga
sa-go nat-dda-myeon-seo(-yo)

■ He was almost killed by an electric shock.
그는 감전되어 죽을 뻔했어(요).
geu-neun gam-jeon-doe-eo ju-geul
bbeon-hae-sseo(-yo)

■ My son is unconscious after falling down the stairs.
우리 아들은 계단에서 떨어져 의식 불명이에요.
u-ri a-deu-reun gye-da-ne-seo ddeo-
reo-jeo ui-sik bul-myeong-i-e-yo

■ This morning I slipped on the ice.
오늘 아침 빙판에서 미끄러졌어(요).
o-neul a-chim bing-pa-ne-seo
mi-ggeu-reo-jeo-sseo(-yo)

Accidents 2

■ I tripped over a rock.
돌에 걸려 넘어졌어(요).
do-re geol-ryeo neo-meo-jeo-sseo(-yo)

■ I tripped on the stairs and nearly broke my neck.
계단을 헛디뎌서 목을 다칠 뻔했어(요).
gye-da-neul heot-ddi-dyeo-seo mo-geul da-chil bbeon-hae-sseo(-yo)

■ I fell off my bicycle.
자전거를 타다가 넘어졌어(요).
ja-jeon-geo-reul ta-da-ga neo-meo-jeo-sseo(-yo)

■ My grandma fell and banged her knees.
할머니가 넘어지셔서 무릎을 다치셨어(요).
hal-meo-ni-ga neo-meo-ji-syeo-seo mu-reu-peul da-chi-syeo-sseo(-yo)

■ Seung-woo lost the use of his left leg because of the accident.
승우는 사고로 왼쪽 다리를 쓰지 못해(요).
seung-u-neun sa-go-ro oen-jjok da-ri-reul sseu-ji mo-tae(-yo)

Traveling by Taxi in Korea

For certain visitors, Korean taxis will seem like a bargain—they are also very easy to find.

Regular taxis are generally orange, white or grey. Black taxis are deluxe and will set you back slightly more for the service and comfort.

Some drivers can speak English or other foreign languages and operate international taxis. The name of the second language spoken should be written on the car.

You can catch a taxi at stands in the street (most are located by bus stops), or with a simple call from your hotel, or you can flag down a taxi in the street by extending your arm with your palm down.

There are taxi apps in Korea similar to Uber. If you type your destination in Korean, a cab will be sent your way. Base fares vary depending on the area and surcharges may kick in after midnight or if you are traveling out of town.

Fire 1

- Fire!
  불이야!
  bu-ri-ya!

- Call 119!
  어서 119에 전화해(요)!
  eo-seo il-ril-gu-e jeon-hwa-hae(-yo)!

- There was a fire last night.
  어젯밤에 화재가 발생했어(요).
  eo-jet-ba-me hwa-jae-ga
  bal-ssaeng-hae-sseo(-yo)

- Last night a fire destroyed this
  building.
  이 건물은 어젯밤 화재로
  불타버렸어(요).
  i geon-mu-reun eo-jet-bbam hwa-jae-ro
  bul-ta-beo-ryeo-sseo(-yo)

- The people were evacuated
  because of the fire.
  화재가 발생하여, 사람들이
  대피했어(요).
  hwa-jae-ga bal-ssaeng-ha-yeo,
  sa-ram-deu-ri dae-pi-hae-sseo(-yo)

- Carelessness is often the cause
  of fires.
  부주의해서 화재가 자주
  발생하죠.
  bu-ju-i-hae-seo hwa-jae-ga ja-ju
  bal-ssaeng-ha-jyo

Fire 2

- That's a fire truck.
  Can you hear the siren?
  소방차예요.
  사이렌 소리 들려요?
  so-bang-cha-ye-yo.
  sa-i-ren so-ri deul-ryeo-yo?

- The firemen got to the fire in
  five minutes.
  소방관들은 5분 만에 화재
  현장에 도착했어(요).
  so-bang-gwan-deu-reun o-bun ma-ne
  hwa-jae hyeon-jang-e
  do-cha-kae-sseo(-yo)

- What caused the fire?
  그 화재 원인은 뭐예요?
  geu hwa-jae wo-ni-neun mwo-ye-yo?

- My throat and eyes were
  burning with the smoke from
  the fire.
  화재에서 발생한 연기 때문에
  목과 눈이 화끈거렸어(요).
  hwa-jae-e-seo bal-ssaeng-han yeon-gi
  ddae-mu-ne mok-ggwa nu-ni
  hwa-ggeun-geo-ryeo-sseo(-yo)

- If the fire alarm goes off, it's
  only a test.
  화재경보가 울리면, 그냥
  테스트예요.
  hwa-jae-gyeong-bo-ga ul-ri-myeon,
  geu-nyang te-seu-teu-ye-yo

Earthquakes 1

▪ Did you feel that earthquake last night?

간밤에 지진 느꼈어(요)?

gan-ba-me ji-jin neu-ggyeo-sseo(-yo)?

▪ How much damage did the earthquake do?

지진으로 얼마나 타격을 입었어(요)?

ji-ji-neu-ro eol-ma-na ta-gyeo-geul i-beo-sseo(-yo)?

▪ The village was destroyed by an earthquake.

저 마을은 지진으로 파괴됐어(요).

jeo ma-eu-reun ji-ji-neu-ro pa-goe-dwae-sseo(-yo)

▪ A 8.2 magnitude earthquake hit the region.

그 지역에 진도 8.2의 지진이 발생했어(요).

geu ji-yeo-ge jin-do pal-jjeo-mi-e ji-ji-ni bal-ssaeng-hae-sseo(-yo)

▪ What did you do when the earthquake hit the building?

지진이 일어났을 때 건물에서 어떻게 했어(요)?

ji-ji-ni i-reo-na-sseul ddae geon-mu-re-seo eo-ddeo-ke hae-sseo(-yo)?

Earthquakes 2

▪ A lot of crops were damaged by the earthquake.

지진으로 농작물이 많이 훼손됐어(요).

ji-ji-neu-ro nong-jang-mu-ri ma-ni hwe-son-dwae-sseo(-yo)

▪ Were there any aftershocks?

여진이 있었어(요)?

yeo-ji-ni i-sseo-sseo(-yo)?

▪ This building will not collapse even when an earthquake hits.

이 건물은 지진이 일어나도 괜찮아(요).

i geon-mu-reun ji-ji-ni i-reo-na-do gwaen-cha-na(-yo)

▪ The entire house shook when the earthquake occurred.

지진이 발생하자, 집 전체가 흔들거렸어(요).

ji-ji-ni bal-ssaeng-ha-ja, jip jeon-che-ga heun-deul-geo-ryeo-sseo(-yo)

▪ Are earthquakes common around here?

이 근처에 지진이 흔해(요)?

i geun-cheo-e ji-ji-ni heun-hae(-yo)?

Funerals

▪ My grandfather passed away this morning.

할아버지가 오늘 아침에 돌아가셨어(요).

ha-ra-beo-ji-ga o-neul a-chi-me
do-ra-ga-syeo-sseo(-yo)

▪ I always cry at funerals.

장례식에서는 언제나 눈물이 나(요).

jang-nye-si-ge-seo-neun eon-je-na nun-
mu-ri na(-yo)

▪ I'm afraid I won't be able to come to the funeral.

장례식에 참석할 수 없을 것 같아(요).

jang-nye-si-ge cham-seo-kal ssu eop-
sseul ggeot ga-ta(-yo)

▪ When I die, I want to be cremated.

난 죽으면, 화장하려고(요).

nan ju-geu-myeon,
hwa-jang-ha-ryeo-go(-yo)

▪ He wanted to be buried in his hometown.

그는 고향에 묻히기를 원했어(요).

geu-neun go-hyang-e mu-chi-gi-reul
won-hae-sseo(-yo)

Condolences

▪ My condolences to you.

조의를 표합니다.

jo-i-reul pyo-ham-ni-da

▪ My sympathies to you.

얼마나 상심이 크세요.

eol-ma-na sang-si-mi keu-se-yo

▪ We lament her health.

우리는 그녀의 죽음을 애도합니다.

u-ri-neun geu-nyeo-e ju-geu-meul
ae-do-ham-ni-da

▪ I don't know how to convey a message of condolence.

어떻게 위로해야 할지 모르겠네요.

eo-ddeo-ke wi-ro-hae-ya hal-jji
mo-reu-gen-ne-yo

▪ It was a privilege to know her/ him.

고인을 알게 되어 영광이었습니다.

go-i-neul al-ge doe-eo
yeong-gwang-i-eot-sseum-ni-da

▪ Thank you for coming and offering your condolences.

조문하러 와 주셔서 감사합니다.

jo-mun-ha-reo wa ju-syeo-seo
gam-sa-ham-ni-da

Chapter 12

Convenient Devices

Computers 컴퓨터 keom-pyu-teo

n. computer 컴퓨터 [컴퓨터] keom-pyu-teo 	n. laptop computer 노트북 [노트북] no-teu-buk 	n. monitor 모니터 [모니터] mo-ni-teo
	n. keyboard 키보드 [키보드] ki-bo-deu 	v. tap 치다 [치다] chi-da
	n. mouse 마우스 [마우스] ma-u-seu 	n. click 클릭 [클릭] keul-rik
	n. file 파일 [파일] pa-il 	n. folder 폴더 [폴더] pol-deo
	n. save 저장 [저:장] jeo-jang 	n. deletion 삭제 [삭쩨] sak-jje
	n. security 보안 [보:안] bo-an 	n. blog 블로그 [블로그] beul-ro-geu

Computers 1

- How much do you know about computers?

  컴퓨터를 얼마나 알아(요)?

  keom-pyu-teo-reul eol-ma-na a-ra(-yo)?

- I don't know much about computers.

  컴퓨터에 대해 많이 몰라(요).

  keom-pyu-teo-e dae-hae ma-ni mol-ra(-yo)

- She's very confident with computers.

  그녀는 컴퓨터를 잘 다뤄(요).

  geu-nyeo-neun keom-pyu-teo-reul jal da-rwo(-yo)

- Even my grandmother can use a computer.

  우리 할머니도 컴퓨터를 하실 줄 알아(요).

  u-ri hal-meo-ni-do keom-pyu-teo-reul ha-sil jjul a-ra(-yo)

- I'm computer-illiterate.

  컴맹이에요.

  keom-maeng-i-e-yo

- Can I use your computer for two minutes?

  네 컴퓨터를 잠깐 써도 될까(요)?

  ne keom-pyu-teo-reul jam-ggan sseo-do doel-gga(-yo)?

Computers 2

- My computer crashed.

  컴퓨터가 고장 났어(요).

  keom-pyu-teo-ga go-jang na-sseo(-yo)

- My computer is extemely slow and won't open any files.

  컴퓨터가 느려서 파일이 안 열려(요).

  keom-pyu-teo-ga neu-ryeo-seo pa-i-ri an yeol-ryeo(-yo)

- Sang-mi's computer is down.

  상미의 컴퓨터는 다운됐어(요).

  sang-mi-e keom-pyu-teo-neun da-un-dwae-sseo(-yo)

- What happened to your laptop?

  네 노트북 (컴퓨터) 어떻게 된 거야?

  ne no-teu-buk (keom-pyu-teo) eo-ddeo-ke doen geo-ya?

  Tip: 노트북 [no-teu-buk] **means laptop and has become the most common word to refer to one's computer.**

- Would you be able to come over this weekend and help me set up my new computer?

  이번 주말에 와서 새 컴퓨터 설치하는 것 좀 도와줄 수 있어(요)?

  i-beon ju-ma-re wa-seo sae keom-pyu-teo seol-chi-ha-neun geot jom do-wa-jul ssu i-sseo(-yo)?

Monitors

■ What happened to your monitor?

컴퓨터 모니터가 어떻게 된 거예요?

keom-pyu-teo mo-ni-teo-ga eo-ddeo-ke doen geo-ye-yo?

■ The computer monitor wasn't turned on.

컴퓨터 모니터가 켜지지 않았어(요).

keom-pyu-teo mo-ni-teo-ga kyeo-ji-ji a-na-sseo(-yo)

■ My screen died.

모니터 화면이 나갔어(요).

mo-ni-teo hwa-myeo-ni na-ga-sseo(-yo)

■ The screen froze up and I couldn't continue my work.

모니터가 먹통이 되는 바람에 작업을 계속할 수 없었어(요).

mo-ni-teo-ga meok-tong-i doe-neun ba-ra-me ja-geo-beul gye-so-kal ssu eop-sseo-sseo(-yo)

■ The monitor is fuzzy.

모니터 화면이 흔들려(요).

mo-ni-teo hwa-myeo-ni heun-deul-ryeo(-yo)

Keyboard & Mouse

■ He's typing on a keyboard.

그는 키보드로 입력하고 있어(요).

geu-neun ki-bo-deu-ro im-nyeo-ka-go i-sseo(-yo)

■ Some of the keys are sticking.

키 몇 개가 안 되는데(요).

ki myeot gae-ga an doe-neun-de(-yo)

■ I'd like a wireless mouse.

무선 마우스가 있으면 좋겠는데(요).

mu-seon ma-u-seu-ga i-sseu-myeon jo-ken-neun-de(-yo)

■ Right-click anywhere on the screen.

화면 아무데나 마우스 오른쪽을 클릭해라.

hwa-myeon a-mu-de-na ma-u-seu o-reun-jjo-geul keul-ri-kae-ra

■ Try picking up your mouse and moving it to another location.

마우스를 들어 다른 곳으로 옮겨 보세요.

ma-u-seu-reul deu-reo da-reun go-seu-ro om-gyeo bo-se-yo

Printers

- A test page is now being sent to the printer.

  프린터로 테스트 페이지를 이미 보냈는데(요).

  peu-rin-teo-ro te-seu-teu pe-i-ji-reul i-mi bo-naen-neun-de(-yo)

- The printer is out of toner.

  프린터기의 토너가 떨어졌어(요).

  peu-rin-teo-gi-e to-neo-ga ddeo-reo-jeo-sseo(-yo)

- How much do these printer cartridges cost?

  이 프린터기의 새 카트리지는 얼마예요?

  i peu-rin-teo-gi-e sae ka-teu-ri-ji-neun eol-ma-ye-yo?

- The printer is jammed.

  프린터기에 종이가 걸렸어(요).

  peu-rin-teo-gi-e jong-i-ga geol-ryeo-sseo(-yo)

- The printer is out of paper.

  프린터기에 종이가 없어(요).

  peu-rin-teo-gi-e jong-i-ga eop-sseo(-yo)

  프린터 용지가 다 떨어졌어(요).

  peu-rin-teo yong-ji-ga da ddeo-reo-jeo-sseo(-yo)

SIM Cards & Phone Plans

Staying connected in Korea isn't hard. It's Korea after all, land of the wired. From coffee houses to subways, Wi-Fi hotspots are everywhere. The problem is during those in-between moments.

One option is to purchase a prepaid SIM card, either online before your flight (to be picked up at your arrival airport or another location, on production of your passport) or in Korea itself. There are many choices. Convenience stores such as 7-Eleven, CU and GS25 will fix you up as will Korean mobile outlets KT, SKT or LG U+. Be prepared for some registration business though, and here too you'll need to show your passport. And then there's the "egg," a pocket-sized modem that locks in your Wi-Fi connection. Pre-book or inquire at your arrival airport for daily rental.

Copiers

- **Can you show me how to use the copier?**

  복사기를 어떻게 사용하는지 알려 줄 수 있어(요)?

  bok-ssa-gi-reul eo-ddeo-ke sa-yong-ha-neun-ji al-ryeo jul ssu i-sseo(-yo)?

- **The copy machine is jammed. Can you give me a hand?**

  복사기에 종이가 걸렸어(요). 도와줄 수 있어(요)?

  bok-ssa-gi-e jong-i-ga geol-ryeo-sseo(-yo). do-wa-jul ssu i-sseo(-yo)?

- **How can I make double-sided copies?**

  양면 복사는 어떻게 해(요)?

  yang-myeon bok-ssa-neun eo-ddeo-ke hae(-yo)?

- **Can you copy this for me?**

  이거 복사 좀 해 줄 수 있어(요)?

  i-geo bok-ssa jom hae jul ssu i-sseo(-yo)?

- **Please make an enlarged copy of this document.**

  이 문서를 확대 복사해 주세요.

  i mun-seo-reul hwak-ddae bok-ssa-hae ju-se-yo

Documents 1

- **I only know how to use a word processor.**

  워드프로세서만 사용할 줄 알아(요).

  wo-deu-peu-ro-se-seo-man sa-yong-hal jjul a-ra(-yo)

- **Are you good at Excel?**

  엑셀 잘해(요)?

  ek-ssel jal-hae(-yo)?

- **Click the "open" button.**

  열기 버튼을 클릭하세요.

  yeol-gi beo-teu-neul keul-ri-ka-se-yo

- **Change the font to Gothic.**

  서체를 고딕으로 바꿔(요).

  seo-che-reul go-di-geu-ro ba-ggwo(-yo)

- **How about enlarging the font size?**

  글자 크기를 좀 크게 하면 어때(요)?

  geul-jja keu-gi-reul jom keu-ge ha-myeon eo-ddae(-yo)?

- **You can also change the size and color of the font.**

  글꼴의 색상과 크기를 변경할 수 있어(요).

  geul-ggo-re saek-ssang-gwa keu-gi-reul byeon-gyeong-hal ssu i-sseo(-yo)

Documents 2

- **How about making the title bold?**

  제목을 더 굵게 하면 어때(요)?

  je-mo-geul deo gul-gge ha-myeon
  eo-ddae(-yo)?

- **Copy the paragraph and paste it into your document.**

  이 단락을 복사해서 문서에
  붙이세요.

  i dal-ra-geul bok-ssa-hae-seo
  mun-seo-e bu-chi-se-yo

- **Do you want to include tables or graphs?**

  표나 그래프가 포함되게
  할까(요)?

  pyo-na geu-rae-peu-ga po-ham-doe-ge
  hal-gga(-yo)?

- **Please insert page numbers into the document.**

  문서에 페이지 번호를 넣어
  주세요.

  mun-seo-e pe-i-ji beon-ho-reul neo-eo
  ju-se-yo

- **Please mark the quotations in blue.**

  인용문은 파란색으로 표시해
  주세요.

  i-nyong-mu-neun pa-ran-sae-geu-ro
  pyo-si-hae ju-se-yo

Itaewon & COEX

At the northern border of the Hangang River (한강) is one of Seoul's most unique neighborhoods, an international gathering place named **Itaewon** (이태원). The area has had a mixed reputation over the years, for various reasons, but seems more equipped than ever to cater to its multi-ethnic crowds. Imported clothing, antique furniture and custom-made suits are some of the wares sold along this busy strip, but no summary is complete without plugging the restaurants—Indian, Greek, French, Thai and many more. If there's a more diverse collection of world cuisines in Korea, we'd like to know.

If you still have money to spend, the **COEX** (코엑스) is waiting. Or you can go there just to admire its immensity. This mall is Asia's largest underground shopping complex with more stores than you can shake a shopping cart at. But it's something of an attraction too, with concerts, food and drink expos and festivals year round. There's also an aquarium and a kimchi (김치) museum . . . there's honestly no end to its attractions. The COEX can be found in the business district of Gangnam (강남), southern Seoul.

Saving Files 1

- **I accidentally deleted the file.**

  실수로 문서를 지웠어(요).

  sil-ssu-ro mun-seo-reul ji-wo-sseo(-yo)

- **Do you have the original file?**

  원본 파일 갖고 있어(요)?

  won-bon pa-il gat-ggo i-sseo(-yo)?

- **It's important to save the file before you close the program.**

  프로그램을 닫기 전에 문서를 저장하는 것은 중요해(요).

  peu-ro-geu-rae-meul dat-ggi jeo-ne mun-seo-reul jeo-jang-ha-neun geo-seun jung-yo-hae(-yo)

- **Which folder did you save it in?**

  어떤 폴더에 저장했어(요)?

  eo-ddeon pol-deo-e jeo-jang-hae-sseo(-yo)?

- **Please choose a new name to save the file.**

  문서를 저장할 때 새 이름으로 하세요.

  mun-seo-reul jeo-jang-hal ddae sae i-reu-meu-ro ha-se-yo

- **Oh, I overwrote the file!**

  아, 파일을 덮어 써 버렸네(요)!

  a, pa-i-reul deo-peo sseo beo-ryeon-ne(-yo)!

Saving Files 2

- **I set a password for this file.**

  이 파일에 비밀번호를 설정했어(요).

  i pa-i-re bi-mil-beon-ho-reul seol-jjeong-hae-sseo(-yo)

- **I backed up the data on my portable hard drive.**

  자료를 외장하드에 백업했어(요).

  ja-ryo-reul oe-jang-ha-deu-e bae-geo-paet-sseo(-yo)

- **Could you restore the damaged file?**

  손상된 파일을 복구할 수 있어(요)?

  son-sang-doen pa-i-reul bok-ggu-hal ssu i-sseo(-yo)?

- **Don't forget to check for viruses on a regular basis.**

  정기적으로 바이러스 체크하는 거 잊지 마(세요).

  jeong-gi-jeo-geu-ro ba-i-reo-seu che-keu-ha-neun geo it-jji ma(se-yo)

- **It's on my USB.**

  내 USB에 있어(요).

  nae yu-e-seu-bi-e i-sseo(-yo)

The Internet 인터넷 in-teo-net

n. Internet 인터넷 [인터넫] in-teo-net	**n.** Wi-Fi 와이파이 [와이파이] wa-i-pa-i	**n.** search 검색 [검:색] geom-saek
	n. connection 접속 [접쏙] jeop-ssok	**n.** e-mail 이메일 [이메일] i-me-il = 전자우편 [전자우편] jeon-ja-u-pyeon
	n. online shopping 온라인 쇼핑 [올라인 쇼핑] ol-ra-in syo-ping	**n.** online gaming 온라인 게임 [올라인 게임] ol-ra-in ge-im

Internet 1

■ **I surf the Internet to kill time.**

인터넷 웹 서핑 하면서 시간을
때워(요).

in-teo-net wep seo-ping ha-myeon-seo
si-ga-neul ddae-wo(-yo)

■ **Put the keyword "Korea" in the search box.**

검색창에 "한국"이라는
키워드를 치세요.

geom-saek-chang-e "han-gu"-gi-ra-
neun ki-wo-deu-reul chi-se-yo

■ **These days a lot of people use Google Chrome**

요즘은 구글 크롬을 많이
쓰지(요).

yo-jeu-meun gu-geul keu-ro-meul ma-ni
sseu-ji(-yo)

■ **I sometimes shop on the Internet.**

종종 인터넷에서 쇼핑을 해(요).

jong-jong in-teo-ne-se-seo syo-ping-eul
hae(-yo)

■ **Today, there is nothing we can't do through the Internet.**

오늘날, 우리는 인터넷에서
못 하는 게 없어(요).

o-neul-nal, u-ri-neun in-teo-ne-se-seo
mot ha-neun ge eop-sseo(-yo)

Internet 2

■ **I'm thinking of studying Korean on the Internet.**

인터넷으로 한국어를
공부하려고 해(요).

in-teo-ne-seu-ro han-gu-geo-reul
gong-bu-ha-ryeo-go hae(-yo)

■ **Check out our homepage.**

저희 홈페이지를 확인하세요.

jeo-hi hom-pe-i-ji-reul hwa-gin-ha-se-yo

■ **Please add our website to your favorites.**

저희 웹 사이트를 즐겨찾기에
추가해 주세요.

jeo-hi wep ssa-i-teu-reul
jeul-gyeo-chat-ggi-e chu-ga-hae ju-se-yo

■ **I paid my electricity bill through Internet banking.**

인터넷 뱅킹으로 전기 요금을
납부했어(요).

in-teo-net baeng-king-eu-ro jeon-gi
yo-geu-meul nap-bbu-hae-sseo(-yo)

■ **In your browser, paste or type the URL in the address bar.**

브라우저의 주소창에 URL을
붙여 넣거나 입력하세요.

beu-ra-u-jeo-e ju-so-chang-e yu-a-re-reul
bu-cheo neo-keo-na im-nyeo-ka-se-yo

E-mail 1

- **E-mail me.**

  이메일을 보내 주세요.

  i-me-i-reul bo-nae ju-se-yo

- **Could I get your e-mail address?**

  이메일 주소가 뭐예요?

  i-me-il ju-so-ga mwo-ye-yo?

- **Do you have another e-mail address?**

  다른 이메일 주소 있어요?

  da-reun i-me-il ju-so i-sseo-yo?

- **Please send a reply to my e-mail.**

  제 이메일에 답장 주세요.

  je i-me-i-re dap-jjang ju-se-yo

- **The e-mail that I had sent you was returned.**

  네게 보낸 이메일이 반송되었어(요).

  ne-ge bo-naen i-me-i-ri ban-song-doe-eo-sseo(-yo)

- **Is it possible for me to get more detailed information through e-mail?**

  이메일로 더 자세한 정보를 받을 수 있을까(요)?

  i-me-il-ro deo ja-se-han jeong-bo-reul ba-deul ssu i-sseul-gga(-yo)?

E-mail 2

- **There is no attachment in your e-mail.**

  네가 보낸 이메일에 첨부 파일이 없는데(요).

  ne-ga bo-naen i-me-i-re cheom-bu pa-i-ri eom-neun-de(-yo)

- **I can't open the attachment.**

  첨부 파일이 열리지 않아(요).

  cheom-bu pa-i-ri yeol-ri-ji a-na(-yo)

- **I'll forward Min-jeong's e-mail to you.**

  민정이의 이메일을 너한테 전달할게(요).

  min-jeong-i-e i-me-i-reul neo-han-te jeon-dal-hal-gge(-yo)

- **When you send him an e-mail, cc me.**

  그에게 이메일을 보낼 때 저도 참조로 넣어 주세요.

  geu-e-ge i-me-i-reul bo-nael ddae jeo-do cham-jo-ro neo-eo ju-se-yo

Blogging

▪ **Do you blog?**
블로그 있어(요)?
beul-ro-geu i-sseo(-yo)?

▪ **Tell me about your blog.**
네 블로그를 소개해 줘(요).
ne beul-ro-geu-reul so-gae-hae jwo(-yo)

▪ **I uploaded those pictures to my blog.**
그 사진들을 블로그에 업로드 했어(요).
geu sa-jin-deu-reul beul-ro-geu-e eom-ro-deu hae-sseo(-yo)

▪ **There is nothing special in his blog.**
그의 블로그가 썰렁해(요).
geu-e beul-ro-geu-ga sseol-reong-hae(-yo)

▪ **How many followers do you have?**
팔로워가 얼마나 돼(요)?
pal-ro-wo-ga eol-ma-na dwae(-yo)?

▪ **I know who she is after seeing her blog.**
그녀의 블로그로 어떤 사람인지 알 수 있어(요).
geu-nyeo-e beul-ro-geu-ro eo-ddeon sa-ra-min-ji al ssu i-sseo(-yo)

Social Media

▪ **Do you use Twitter or Facebook?**
트위터나 페이스북 해(요)?
teu-wi-teo-na pe-i-seu-buk hae(-yo)?

▪ **I check Facebook multiple times a day.**
하루에도 여러 번 페이스북을 확인해(요).
ha-ru-e-do yeo-reo beon pe-i-seu-bu-geul hwa-gin-hae(-yo)

▪ **Did you post your photos on Instagram yet?**
인스타그램에 사진 올렸어(요)?
in-seu-ta-geu-rae-me sa-jin ol-ryeo-sseo(-yo)?

▪ **Have you ever seen his music video on YouTube?**
유튜브에서 그의 뮤직 비디오를 본 적 있어(요)?
yu-tyu-beu-e-seo geu-e myu-jik bi-di-o-reul bon jeok i-sseo(-yo)?

▪ **Most Koreans use KakaoTalk.**
한국인 대부분은 카카오톡을 써(요).
han-gu-gin dae-bu-bu-neun ka-ka-o-to-geul sseo(-yo)

🎧 Phones 전화 jeon-hwa

n. telephone, phone 전화 [전:화] jeon-hwa 	n. cellular phone, cell phone, mobile phone 휴대폰 [휴대폰] hyu-dae-pon = 핸드폰 [핸드폰] haen-deu-pon = 휴대전화 [휴대전화] hyu-dae-jeon-hwa 	n. phone number 전화번호 [전:화번호] jeon-hwa-beon-ho
v. call 전화하다 [전:화하다] jeon-hwa-ha-da = 걸다 [걸:다] geol-da 	v. answer/take (the phone), receive (a message) 받다 [받따] bat-dda	v. hang up 끊다 [끈타] ggeun-ta
n. battery 배터리 [배터리] bae-teo-ri	n. charge 충전 [충전] chung-jeon 	n. SMS, text message 문자메시지 [문짜메시지] mun-jja-me-si-ji

Phones 1	Phones 2

Phones 1

■ Can I get your phone number?

휴대폰 번호 좀 알려 줘(요).

hyu-dae-pon beon-ho jom al-ryeo
jwo(-yo)

■ Save my phone number in your phone.

내 번호를 휴대폰에 저장해
둬(요).

nae beon-ho-reul hyu-dae-po-ne
jeo-jang-hae dwo(-yo)

■ I've changed my phone number.

휴대폰 번호가 바뀌었어(요).

hyu-dae-pon beon-ho-ga
ba-ggwi-eo-sseo(-yo)

■ I set an alarm for 6 a.m. on my cell.

휴대폰에 아침 6시 알람을
맞춰 놨어(요).

hyu-dae-po-ne a-chim yeo-seot-ssi
al-ra-meul mat-chwo nwa-sseo(-yo)

■ Don't use your phone while driving.

운전 중에 휴대폰을 쓰지
마(세요).

un-jeon jung-e hyu-dae-po-neul sseu-ji
ma(-se-yo)

Phones 2

■ I missed two calls.

부재중 전화가 두 통 있네(요).

bu-jae-jung jeon-hwa-ga du tong in-
ne(-yo)

■ Look how cool my new smartphone is!

내 새 스마트폰 정말 멋지지(요)!

nae sae seu-ma-teu-pon jeong-mal
meot-jji-ji(-yo)!

■ Don't use a smartphone too much.

스마트폰을 너무 많이 쓰지
마(세요).

seu-ma-teu-po-neul neo-mu ma-ni sseu-
ji ma(-se-yo)

■ Did you charge your phone?

휴대폰 충전했어(요)?

hyu-dae-pon chung-jeon-hae-sseo(-yo)?

■ Did you bring a phone charger?

휴대폰 충전기 가져왔어(요)?

hyu-dae-pon chung-jeon-gi
ga-jeo-wa-sseo(-yo)?

■ Almost everyone in my class has a phone.

우리 반 애들 거의 다 휴대폰을
가지고 있어(요).

u-ri ban ae-deul jeo-i da hyu-dae-po-
neul ga-ji-go i-sseo(-yo)

Problems

■ My phone battery is low.

휴대폰 배터리가 얼마 없는데(요).

hyu-dae-pon bae-teo-ri-ga eol-ma
eom-neun-de(-yo)

■ The connection is bad.

휴대폰이 잘 안 터져(요).

hyu-dae-po-ni jal an teo-jeo(-yo)

■ I dropped the phone in the
toilet.

휴대폰을 변기에 빠뜨렸어(요).

hyu-dae-po-neul byeon-gi-e
bba-ddeu-ryeo-sseo(-yo)

■ The LCD is cracked because
I dropped my phone.

휴대폰을 떨어뜨려서 액정이
깨졌어(요).

hyu-dae-po-neul ddeo-reo-ddeu-ryeo-
seo aek-jjeong-i ggae-jeo-sseo(-yo)

■ I used up all the data on my
phone.

휴대폰 데이터를 다 썼어(요).

hyu-dae-pon de-i-teo-reul da sseo-
sseo(-yo)

Functions 1

■ Doesn't your phone have a
calculator?

휴대폰으로 계산하면 안 돼(요)?

hyu-dae-po-neu-ro gye-san-ha-myeon
an dwae(-yo)?

■ I have the newest games on
my phone.

내 휴대폰에 최신 게임이
있어(요).

nae hyu-dae-po-ne choe-sin ge-i-mi
i-sseo(-yo)

■ With a smartphone, you can
send an e-mail whenever
you want.

스마트폰이 있으면, 언제든
이메일을 보낼 수 있어(요).

seu-ma-teu-po-ni i-sseu-myeon,
eon-je-deun i-me-i-reul bo-nael ssu
i-sseo(-yo)

■ I often pay with my phone.

휴대폰으로 자주 결제해(요).

hyu-dae-po-neu-ro ja-ju
gyeol-jje-hae(-yo)

Functions 2

■ I have video calls with my girlfriend.

여자 친구와 영상통화를 해(요).

yeo-ja chin-gu-wa
yeong-sang-tong-hwa-reul hae(-yo)

■ I locked my phone.

휴대폰에 비밀번호를
걸어놨어(요).

hyu-dae-po-ne bi-mil-beon-ho-reul
geo-reo-nwa-sseo(-yo)

■ Have you tried this app?

이 앱 써 봤어(요)?

i aep sseo bwa-sseo(-yo)?

■ Launch the camera app, then take a photo.

카메라 어플로 사진을 찍어(요).

ka-me-ra eo-peul-ro sa-ji-neul jji-geo(-yo)

Tip: 앱 [ep] and 어플 [eo-peul], both meaning "app," are short for 애플리케이션 [e-peul-ri-ke-i-syeon] "application."

■ She likes to take pictures with her phone.

그녀는 휴대폰으로 사진 찍기를
좋아해(요).

geu-nyeo-neun hyu-dae-po-neu-ro sa-jin jjik-ggi-reul jo-a-hae(-yo)

Texting

■ Text me.

문자메시지 보내라.

mun-jja-me-si-ji bo-nae-ra

■ Could you send me a text message?

나한테 문자메시지
보내 줄래(요)?

na-han-te mun-jja-me-si-ji
bo-nae jul-rae(-yo)?

■ Text me your phone number.

네 전화번호를 문자메시지로
알려 줘(요).

ne jeon-hwa-beon-ho-reul
mun-jja-me-si-ji-ro al-ryeo jwo(-yo)

■ I haven't received your text message.

네 문자메시지를 못
받았는데(요).

ne mun-jja-me-si-ji-reul mot
ba-dan-neun-de(-yo)

■ I got a voice mail.

음성메시지를 받았어(요).

eum-seong-me-si-ji-reul ba-da-sseo(-yo)

■ I'm sick of phone spam mail.

휴대폰 스팸 문자는 지겨워(요).

hyu-dae-pon seu-paem mun-jja-neun
ji-gyeo-wo(-yo)

Ringtones

■ It's a good ringtone.

벨소리 괜찮은데(요).

bel-so-ri gwaen-cha-neun-de(-yo)

■ Put your phone on manner mode.

휴대폰을 매너모드로 하세요.

hyu-dae-po-neul mae-neo-mo-deu-ro ha-se-yo

■ Turn your phone to vibrate mode, please.

진동모드로 바꿔 주세요.

jin-dong-mo-deu-ro ba-ggwo ju-se-yo

■ Put your phone on vibrate before the meeting.

회의 전에 휴대폰을 진동모드로 바꿨는지 확인해 주세요.

hoe-i jeo-ne hyu-dae-po-neul jin-dong-mo-deu-ro ba-ggwon-neun-ji hwa-gin-hae ju-se-yo

■ Turn your ringtone off when we watch the movie.

영화 볼 때 휴대폰을 무음으로 바꿔 주세요.

yeong-hwa bol ddae hyu-dae-po-neul mu-eu-meu-ro ba-ggwo ju-se-yo

Camera Basics 1

■ Don't turn on the flash.

플래시를 켜지 마(세요).

peul-rae-si-reul kyeo-ji ma(-se-yo)

■ How do you zoom in?

줌을 하려면 어떻게 해(요)?

ju-meul ha-ryeo-myeon eo-ddeo-ke hae(-yo)?

■ How many pixels does it have?

카메라는 몇 화소예요?

ka-me-ra-neun myeot hwa-so-ye-yo?

■ This digital camera takes good pictures.

이 디지털 카메라는 사진이 잘 나와(요).

i di-ji-teol ka-me-ra-neun sa-ji-ni jal na-wa(-yo)

■ I forgot to charge the battery.

배터리 충전하는 걸 깜박했어(요).

bae-teo-ri chung-jeon-ha-neun geol ggam-ba-kae-sseo(-yo)

■ This camera has an image stabilizer.

이 카메라는 손떨림 방지가 돼(요).

i ka-me-ra-neun son-ddeol-rim bang-ji-ga dwae(-yo)

Camera Basics 2

■ How do you like your new digital camera?

새로 산 디카는 마음에 들어(요)?

sae-ro san di-ka-neun ma-eu-me deu-reo(-yo)?

Tip: 디카 [di-ka] is short for 디지털 카메라 [di-ji-teol ka-me-ra], **"digital camera."**

■ You can store a lot of pictures on a memory card.

메모리 카드에 사진을 많이 저장할 수 있어(요).

me-mo-ri ka-deu-e sa-ji-neul ma-ni jeo-jang-hal ssu i-sseo(-yo)

■ I can't take any more pictures. The memory card is full.

메모리 카드가 꽉 차서 더 이상 찍을 수 없어(요).

me-mo-ri ka-deu-ga ggwak cha-seo deo i-sang jji-geul ssu eop-sseo(-yo)

■ Be careful. Shooting video chews up a lot of memory.

주의해(요). 동영상 촬영은 메모리를 많이 차지해(요).

ju-i-hae(-yo). dong-yeong-sang chwa-ryeong-eun me-mo-ri-reul ma-ni cha-ji-hae(-yo)

■ It is easy to hold.

이건 그립감이 좋은데(요).

i-geon geu-rip-gga-mi jo-eun-de(-yo)

Taking Pictures

■ Just press this button, please.

이 버튼을 눌러 주세요.

i beo-teu-neul nul-reo ju-se-yo

■ How about taking a picture together?

같이 사진 찍을래(요)?

ga-chi sa-jin jji-geul-rae(-yo)?

■ Everyone smile and say "kimchi."

모두 웃으면서, "김치"라고 해(요).

mo-du u-seu-myeon-seo, "gim-chi"-ra-go hae(-yo)

Tip: When most Koreans take pictures, they say "kimchi" because the mouth forms a smile.

■ Excuse me. Would you mind taking a picture of us?

실례합니다. 사진 좀 찍어 주실래요?

sil-rye-ham-ni-da. sa-jin jom jji-geo ju-sil-rae-yo?

■ The pictures are backlit.

사진이 역광이에요.

sa-ji-ni yeok-ggwang-i-e-yo

■ That picture is out of focus.

그 사진은 초점이 안 맞아(요).

geu sa-ji-neun cho-jjeo-mi an ma-ja(-yo)